Software Engineering Perspectives in Computer Game Development

Software Engineering Perspectives in Computer Game Development

Edited by
Kendra M. L. Cooper

CRC Press
Taylor & Francis Group
Boca Raton London New York

CRC Press is an imprint of the
Taylor & Francis Group, an **informa** business
A CHAPMAN & HALL BOOK

First Edition published 2021
by CRC Press
6000 Broken Sound Parkway NW, Suite 300, Boca Raton, FL 33487-2742

and by CRC Press
2 Park Square, Milton Park, Abingdon, Oxon, OX14 4RN

CRC Press is an imprint of Taylor & Francis Group, LLC

Library of Congress Cataloging-in-Publication Data
Names: Cooper, Kendra M. L., editor.
Title: Software engineering perspectives in computer game development / edited by Kendra M. L. Cooper.
Description: First edition. | Boca Raton : CRC Press, 2021. | Includes bibliographical references and index.
Identifiers: LCCN 2020057801 | ISBN 9781138503786 (hbk) | ISBN 9781315145549 (ebk)
Subjects: LCSH: Computer games--Programming. | Software engineering.
Classification: LCC QA76.76.C672 S647 2021 | DDC 794.8/1525--dc23
LC record available at https://lccn.loc.gov/2020057801

ISBN: 978-1-138-50378-6 (hbk)
ISBN: 978-1-032-01164-6 (pbk)
ISBN: 978-1-315-14554-9 (ebk)

Typeset in Times
by SPi Global, India

Contents

SECTION I   Emerging Research on Serious Games for Software Engineering Education

SECTION II   Emerging Research on Software Engineering Methods for Game Development

Preface

The tremendous success of today's large-scale, complex computer games relies on an extensive history of advances in research and development that spans numerous disciplines. The earliest computer games emerged over seven decades ago as creations from research-oriented environments that possessed rare and expensive computing systems. In the 1950s, game developers were individuals who had access to mainframe computers and possessed the skills to write assembly code using punch tape. This small community was located in isolated research environments where they developed and played relatively simple games like tic-tac-toe to explore research topics or support public demonstrations. From these early beginnings, computer games have become ubiquitous. Their transition into popular cultures began in the late 1960s with on-going introductions of home console, arcade, personal computer, portable console, mobile phone, virtual reality/augmented reality, and multiplatform streaming games. The community continues to grow and embraces stakeholders with broad interests spanning entertainment games, serious games, gamification, and related research topics. Game development has emerged as a distinct research field with its own specialized journals (e.g., ACM *Computers in Entertainment* and IEEE *Transactions on Games*), conferences (e.g., Foundations of Digital Games and Game Developers Conference), and online communities (e.g., Games and Software Engineering Research). Universities worldwide offer Bachelor, Master, and Doctorate degrees in game development.

In practice, today's large-scale entertainment games are increasingly complex and can take years to develop. They have demanding traditional quality of service requirements: availability, backward compatibility, multiple platform deployment, performance, reliability, scalability, security, usability, and so on. In addition, they have distinct user experience requirements to provide the player with a game that is engaging and fun. In order to produce compelling user experiences, a wide variety of game elements and genres are used. Game elements include avatars, challenges, economies, flow, haptic and audiovisual interactions, progression (e.g., levels), rewards (e.g., points, badges, and leaderboards), and enabling social interactions among players. Genres include action, adventure, massively multiplayer online, role-playing, simulation, sports, and strategy. Game development relies on teams of specialists including game designers, artists, software developers (e.g., computer scientists and software engineers), and managers. The team composition in practice reflects the interdisciplinary foundations of game development, which include the arts and humanities; behavioral sciences; business; engineering; and physical sciences and mathematics.

The increasing complexity of game development continues to drive innovative research. This book focuses on emerging results that focus on game development issues from software engineering perspectives. It is an excellent reference for software engineers, developers, educators, and researchers. To capture a current snapshot, this collection includes contributions prepared by 21 authors from nine countries; these have been provided by leaders in the community. Overall, the results are organized into two broad categories: serious games for software engineering education and software engineering methods for game development. The nine core chapters of the collection include five chapters on topics in serious games for software engineering education and four chapters on architecture and design methods for game development. In the first and final chapters, the interdisciplinary nature of games, a brief history of game development, and a summary of the recent peer-reviewed literature (i.e., 2015–2020) on game development from software engineering perspectives are presented. The literature summary includes 18 articles on games for software engineering education and 65 articles on software engineering methods for game development. The articles are at multiple levels of maturity and appear in workshops, conferences, and journals. Based on the contributions in the book, possible future research opportunities are identified for consideration in terms of high-level questions. The wide breadth of the discipline provides researchers with ample opportunities to identify and pursue topics of interest.

et ludos incipere!
Kendra M. L. Cooper

Editor

Kendra M. L. Cooper is an independent Scholar and Editor. Her research interests are in software and systems engineering (requirements engineering, architecture) and engineering education; these topics are explored within the context of game engineering. Dr. Cooper has an extensive publication, teaching, and service record. Current research topics include the modelling, analyses, and automated transformations of complex game systems using graph-based methods; the ontological foundations of serious educational games are also under investigation. She has co-edited the book *Computer Games and Software Engineering* published by CRC Press. Dr. Cooper has co-organized/organized ICSE Workshops on Games and Software Engineering (GAS 2012, GAS 2013, GAS 2015, and GAS 2016) and the CSEE&T Workshop on Essence in Education and Training (2020). She has served as a co-editor of three *JSPE* Special Issues on Software Engineering in Practice (2018, 2019, 2020). She received a PhD in Electrical and Computer Engineering from The University of British Columbia, Canada.

Contributors

Steve Benford
University of Nottingham
Nottingham, UK
steve.benford@nottingham.ac.uk

Adriano Ferreti Borgatto
Federal University of Santa Catarina
Florianópolis, Brazil
adriano.borgatto@ufsc.br

Brian Chau
University of Washington Bothell
Bothell, Washington
chautime@msn.com

Micah M. Hrehovcsik
HKU University of the Arts Utrecht
Utrecht, Netherlands
micah.hrehovcsik@hku.nl

Katherine Isbister
University of California, Santa Cruz
Santa Cruz, California
kisbiste@ucsc.edu

Rahul Kumar
University of Auckland
Auckland, New Zealand
rahulkumar28@outlook.co.nz

Edward F. Melcer
University of California, Santa Cruz
Santa Cruz, California
eddie.melcer@ucsc.edu

Rob Nash
University of Washington Bothell
Bothell, Washington
rundaemon@gmail.com

Njål Nordmark
Norwegian University of Science and
    Technology
Trondheim, Norway
njaal.nordmark@sonat.no

Jason Pace
University of Washington Bothell
Bothell, Washington
jasonpa@uw.edu

Giani Petri
Federal University of Santa Maria
Santa Maria, Brazil
giani.petri@ufsm.br

Jöran Pieper
Hochschule Stralsund—University of
    Applied Sciences, IACS
Stralsund, Germany
joeran.pieper@hochschulestralsund.de

Paul Ralph
Dalhousie University
Halifax, Canada
paulralph@dal.ca

Tom Rodden
University of Nottingham
Nottingham, UK
tom.rodden@nottingham.ac.uk

Walt Scacchi
University of California, Irvine
Irvine, California
wscacchi@ics.uci.edu

Kelvin Sung
University of Washington Bothell
Bothell, Washington
ksung@uw.edu

Jak Tan
University of Auckland
Auckland, New Zealand
jtan325@aucklanduni.ac.nz

Christiane Gresse von Wangenheim
Federal University of Santa Catarina
Florianópolis, Brazil
c.wangenheim@ufsc.br

Alf Inge Wang
Norwegian University of Science and
    Technology
Trondheim, Norway
alfw@idi.ntnu.no

Richard Wetzel
Lucerne University of Applied Sciences
    and Arts
Lucerne, Switzerland
richard.wetzel@hslu.ch

1 Introduction to Software Engineering Perspectives in Computer Game Development

Kendra M. L. Cooper

Independent Scholar, Canada

CONTENTS

1.1 THE INTERDISCIPLINARY NATURE OF COMPUTER GAMES

Today's success of large-scale, complex computer games relies on an extensive history of advances in research and development spanning numerous disciplines. The earliest computer games emerged over 70 years ago as creations from research-oriented environments that possessed rare and expensive computing systems. In the 1950s, game developers were individuals who had access to mainframe computers and possessed the skills to write assembly code using punch tape. This small community was located in isolated academic or industrial research environments where they developed relatively simple games like tic-tac-toe to explore research topics or support public demonstrations. They were the original code hackers [62]. In this era, the software and hardware development infrastructure we take for granted today did not exist. For example, development methodologies, high-level programming languages, integrated development environments, specialized libraries (e.g., artificial intelligence, graphics, and physics), large-scale components (e.g., database management systems, cloud services, and game engines), multiuser operating systems, data communication networks, code repositories (e.g., GitHub), and inexpensive consumer hardware were not available.

From these early beginnings, computer games have become ubiquitous. The community continues to grow and embraces stakeholders with broad interests spanning entertainment games, serious games, gamification, and related research topics. Game development has emerged as a distinct research field with its own specialized journals (e.g., *ACM Computers in Entertainment* and *IEEE Transactions on Games*), conferences (e.g., *Foundations of Digital Games* and *Game Developers Conference*), and on-line communities (e.g., The LinkedIn *Games and Software Engineering Research Group https://www.linkedin.com/groups/13944027*). Universities worldwide offer Bachelor, Master, and Doctorate degrees in game development. There are games for entertainment, games with a purpose (serious games), and gamified business applications. Entertainment games are a thriving industry with over two billion players around the world with 120 billion in revenues; higher numbers for both are anticipated in the future. In 2020, a long list of releases by major studios has been announced including the much anticipated sequels to *Doom*, *Half-life*, *Halo*, *The Last of Us*, and *Wasteland* franchises; new Marvel games include the *Avengers*, *Iron Man VR*, and *Spider-man 2*. Remakes to *Final Fantasy VII*, *Resident Evil 3*, and *System Shock* have also been announced as well as updated versions of *Spongebob square pants* and the 13th version of Microsoft's *Flight Simulator*. The recent release of two ninth-generation consoles (Sony's PlayStation 5 and Microsoft's Xbox Series X) continues to drive game development. The AAA launch title for Microsoft's new console is *Halo Infinite*; Sony's launch event for their new console includes announcements for *Spider-Man: Miles Morales*, *Horizon: Zero Dawn*, and *Resident Evil 7* sequels.

Beyond entertainment games, serious games are available for education and training purposes; games are also used as example applications in non-gaming research. Young players can learn fundamental skills in reading and mathematics with simpler games. Business students play games to learn about finance and risk management topics. Computer science and engineering students can learn programming and software engineering skills (e.g., architecture, design, requirements engineering, project management, and testing). Medical students can learn anatomy with virtual reality (VR) applications that utilize Microsoft's HoloLens. Serious games are available for training individuals in numerous domains such as fire safety, infrastructure inspection, manufacturing, and healthcare. Serious healthcare-related games on exercise, healthy lifestyles, mental health, patient care, and physiotherapy abound. More recently, gamified applications that integrate game elements (e.g., points, badges, and leaderboards) have emerged. In business environments, gamification efforts centre on improving the productivity and satisfaction of their employees by providing more engaging applications. In educational environments, learning management systems are gamified to improve the students' learning outcomes and satisfaction. Games are also utilized to validate non-gaming research as well as for student projects in capstone design courses in computer science and software engineering degree programs.

In practice, today's large-scale entertainment games are complex and can take years to develop. They have demanding traditional quality of service requirements: availability, backward compatibility (e.g., earlier platforms), multiple platform deployment, performance, reliability, scalability, security, usability, and so on. In addition, they have distinct user experience requirements to provide the player with a game that is engaging and fun. In order to produce compelling user experiences, a wide variety of game elements and genres are used. Game elements include avatars, challenges, economies, flow, haptic and audiovisual interactions, progression (e.g., levels), rewards (e.g., points, badges, and leaderboards), and enabling social interactions among players. Game genres include action, adventure, massively multiplayer online (MMO), role-playing, simulation, sports, and strategy. Game development relies on teams of specialists including game designers, artists, software developers (e.g., computer scientists and software engineers), and managers. The team composition in practice reflects the interdisciplinary foundations of game development (Figure 1.1): arts and humanities; behavioural sciences; business; engineering; and physical sciences and mathematics.

The more creative aspects of game development rely heavily on the arts, humanities, and behavioural sciences. From the arts, games utilize digital media (e.g., 2D/3D modelling), performing arts (e.g., music composition), visual arts (e.g., scene composition), and literature (e.g., storytelling via characters, narrative, plot, and setting). From the humanities, games invoke ethical questions addressed in philosophy, such as issues around game addiction. From the behavioural sciences, games rely on contributions in the disciplines of anthropology, sociology, and psychology. Anthropology supports game development in terms of considering the social and cultural norms of their target audiences. Sociology supports multiplayer game development in terms of the interactions of players in communities, both in real life and virtual. Psychology addresses topics around the gameplay experience: motivation, engagement, retention, and reward systems. For serious educational games, psychology encompasses learning theory which provides the core pedagogical foundation for these games.

Game development also draws heavily from the physical sciences, mathematics, and engineering disciplines. Within the physical sciences, game research and development utilize results from numerous specialized subfields in computer science that began to emerge in the 1960s, including artificial intelligence, distributed/embedded/information/real-time systems, human computer interactions, graphics, networking, operating systems, and programming languages. Today, these are well-established fields that remain active research areas; game developers continue to rely on these communities for innovative solutions. For example, advances in cloud computing research and development were embodied in an early cloud gaming streaming service technology, G-cluster; this service was demonstrated at the Electronic

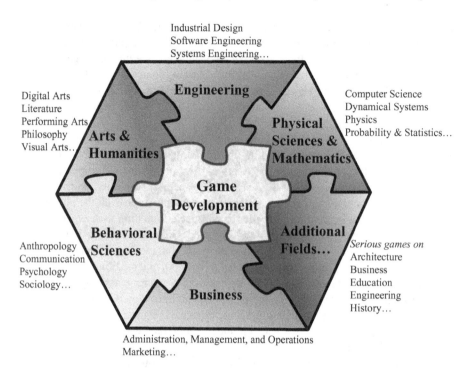

Industrial Design
Software Engineering
Systems Engineering…

Digital Arts
Literature
Performing Arts
Philosophy
Visual Arts…

Engineering

Computer Science
Dynamical Systems
Physics
Probability & Statistics…

Arts & Humanities

Physical Sciences & Mathematics

Game Development

Anthropology
Communication
Psychology
Sociology…

Behavioral Sciences

Additional Fields…

Serious games on
Architecture
Business
Education
Engineering
History…

Business

Administration, Management, and Operations
Marketing…

FIGURE 1.1   The interdisciplinary nature of game development.

Entertainment Expo in 2000. These services continued to evolve; games such as *Homefront were released just over a decade later on OnLive's streaming service.* Game streaming services were subsequently introduced by established organizations (e.g., Google, Microsoft, Nvidia, and Sony) and start-ups; Amazon announced the release of their game streaming service, Luna, for 2021.

From the engineering disciplines, game developers relied on innovations provided by the software engineering research and development communities. The software engineering discipline emerged in the late 1960s to address the challenges of developing large-scale complex applications. The declaration of the software crisis in 1968 was a pivotal moment: the cost of developing software systems had exceeded the cost of developing hardware [80]. The new field evolved into specialized subfields including lifecycle processes (e.g., Waterfall, Agile, and DevOps), engineering activities (e.g., requirements engineering, multiple levels of design, construction, and testing), umbrella activities (configuration management, project management, traceability), reuse (components, patterns, product lines), formal methods, modelling, automation (code, testing), and so on. In recognition of the 50th anniversary of the field of software engineering, articles summarizing its history from different perspectives were reported (e.g., [20, 21, 42]). Research at the intersection of games and software engineering emerged as a new discipline over the last decade (e.g., [16, 29, 30, 31, 91, 92, 109]); it spans the majority of subfields within software engineering (refer to Section 1.2).

Although other established engineering disciplines such as systems engineering and industrial design have the potential to offer valuable contributions for game development, they have received little attention. Systems engineering emerged in the late 1940s by the US Department of Defense to develop large-scale, complex projects such as missile-defence systems. Today, established resources are available that address the issues in developing systems (e.g., [53, 55]). They provide guidance for specifying, designing, constructing, and validating/verifying systems (or systems of systems) that involve comprehensive technology stacks (e.g., communication networks, data storage, hardware, operating systems, and software). Many of these development issues are encountered in today's large-scale games: they include distributed, real-time, multiplayer, multiplatform game systems that dynamically collect and analyse game play data. However, systems engineering contributions receive little attention in the game development community. Established industrial design methodologies are also available that explicitly address users' emotional or affective responses to products. For example, Kansei engineering, originally introduced in 1974, relates customers' emotional responses (i.e., physical and psychological) to the properties and characteristics of products or services [78]. In other words, they are designed to intentionally induce specific feelings. Kansei engineering continues to receive attention in a variety of communities (e.g., [54, 73]), but not in game development.

1.2 A BRIEF HISTORY OF COMPUTER GAMES

Over time, the research and development of games has driven and leveraged numerous generations of computing devices and technology infrastructures. Games have evolved from specialized, limited use software applications to the ubiquitous products we see today. The history of games has been presented from a number of perspectives (e.g., [38, 46, 47, 110]). Here, games are organized into two main categories to provide a brief overview. The first reflects the early history of game development in research environments. The second category considers the shift of games into popular cultures; it is organized into groups including home console, arcade, personal computer, portable console, mobile phone, virtual and augmented reality (VR/AR), and multiplatform streaming games (refer to Figure 1.2).

1.2.1 EARLY RESEARCH ENVIRONMENT GAMES

Researchers created a series of early games in the 1950s–1960s that generally simulated real-world board games. These games were rare, and the earliest of them were created when the specialized fields of computer science and software engineering did not yet exist. It was years before lower cost computing devices were available; the cost and complexity of developing software had not yet risen to the point where it was identified as a crisis. Games were developed as research projects to entertain the public or explore research problems in programming, human computer interactions, and computer algorithms. For example, a custom-built computer arcade game called *Bertie the Brain was created at the University of Toronto. It was installed at the* Canadian National Exhibition *in 1950, where a player competed against the*

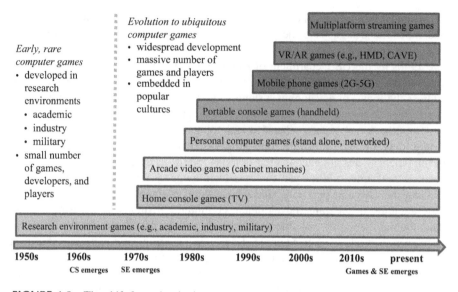

FIGURE 1.2 The shift from developing rare computer games in research environments to ubiquitous games in popular cultures began in the late 1960s with home consoles and arcade video games.

computer in a demonstration game of tic-tac-toe. Another computer called Nimrod was custom built by the company Ferranti; a player competed with the computer in a *Nim* demonstration game at the Festival of Britain in 1951. A single player version of tic-tac-toe called *OXO* was a game developed at the University of Cambridge in 1952. It ran on a computer called the Electronic Delay Storage Automatic Calculator (EDSAC). One of these machines was built by the university to serve their computing needs. The game program, based on a set of 14 available opcodes, was input using a punch tape and stored; hardware buttons, an analog telephone dial, and a green cathode ray tube (CRT) display provided the user interface devices for the game. The *OXO* game was developed as a research vehicle for investigating computer human interactions. A two-player game was developed called *Tennis for Two* in 1958. It was a demonstration game running on a commercial Donner Model 30 computer for the Brookhaven National Laboratory's annual public exhibition. *Spacewar!* was another two-player, pioneering game. It was created for entertainment purposes and had a significant influence on the gaming community: it inspired many subsequent games. It was developed in 1962 at the Massachusetts Institute of Technology and ran on a commercial Digital Equipment Corporation PDP-11 minicomputer. The *Spacewar!* program, implemented using a set of 32 available opcodes, was input using a punch tape and stored in the minicomputer. The user interface devices consisted of a CRT display and a control box; the box had two knobs and a button.

As lower cost hardware was introduced, the machines were adopted into more environments and eventually networked in research projects. These projects included the Programmed Logic for Automatic Teaching Operations (PLATO) in 1960,

ARPANet in 1969, CYCLADES in 1971, NSFNet in 1979, BITNET in 1981, and the Internet in 1989. The first version of the PLATO system was pioneered at the University of Illinois at Urbana-Champaign; this research and development project was focused on supporting high quality online education [19]. This system evolved over four versions (i.e., PLATO I, II, III, and IV). PLATO I operated on an ILLIAC computer. It used a television set for the display and a special keyboard for one user to navigate the system's function menus. PLATO II was available the following year, and it supported two users. The system was redesigned for PLATO III in 1964. This version operated on a Control Data Corporation 1604 computer and supported 20 terminals. The only remote PLATO III terminal was located near the state capitol in Springfield, Illinois, at Springfield High School. It was connected to the PLATO III system by a video connection and a separate dedicated line for keyboard data. The final version, PLATO IV, was introduced in 1972. It expanded into an internationally networked system of 10 sites that supported thousands of users and remained in service until 2006. A core contribution of the PLATO project was its role in developing an online community of users, which included game developers and players. The system was used to develop and share thousands of games in numerous genres including dungeon, space combat, simulations (e.g., flight and tank), maze, and card games. For example, networked games for 32 players developed for PLATO IV were *Empire* and *Spasim*. *Empire* began as a course project in 1973; it was a shooter-style game. *Spasim* was a space flight simulation and a first-person space shooter game that was released in 1974.

1.2.2 GAMES IN THE POPULAR CULTURE

1.2.2.1 Home Console Games

The first home game console was the *Brown Box* prototype, which was released in 1967. It had six built-in games (*chase-games*, *handball*, *light-gun*, *ping-pong*, *tennis*, and *volleyball*). Magnavox licensed the prototype, and the first console appeared on the market in 1972 called the Odyssey; it had 28 games. Rather than having to go to an arcade, people could now play the popular arcade game *PONG* at home using a television as the display, albeit without sound. The initial console offerings were quickly expanded by Magnavox, Coleco, Atari, and Nintendo; these consoles played built-in, relatively simple games such as *PONG*, *Hockey!*, and *Smash*. In the late 1970s, numerous programmable ROM cartridge-based consoles emerged as the second generation. They allowed players to add new games developed for the proprietary consoles. Among these cartridge-based consoles was the Fairchild Channel F, which offered superior graphics, and the Atari 2600; both used eight-bit microprocessors. The Atari 2600 console dominated the market with the blockbuster game *Space Invaders*. To improve their development efforts for the console, Atari encapsulated reusable functionality to access the console's display; this module was called the kernal. The commercial success of the consoles created opportunities for new studios to develop competing games that were less expensive, of variable quality, and widely available. In this changing business environment, Atari released two much anticipated titles: *E.T. The Extra Terrestrial* and *PAC-Man*. They were unsuccessful, which contributed to *The Crash* of the video game market. As part of the major consolidation that followed, it took Atari 4 years to recover in North America. In the meantime, the popularity of consoles in Japan remained high. Within 1 month in 1983, three new home consoles were released in Japan: Microsoft Japan's MSX hybrid computer-console system, Nintendo Entertainment System (Famicom), and Sega's SG-1000. These consoles were popular in Japan; within a year, Ninetendo's console dominated the market. Over the next decade, the intense competition in game consoles, known as the *Console Wars* [47], occurred involving Nintendo, Sega (USA and Japan), and later Sony. Nintendo offered Mario Brothers games and a reserved version of *Mortal Kombat* with a traditional marketing campaign. These were challenged by Sega's irreverent Sonic the Hedgehog and an uncensored version of *Mortal Kombat* (complete with red-coloured blood and the option to make the game even bloodier) and an aggressive marketing campaign. After unsuccessfully negotiating a collaboration with Sega, Sony launched its own PlayStation console in 1994. Numerous generations of consoles have been offered by Microsoft, Nintendo, Sega, and Sony; the currently available consoles are considered the eighth generation. As an example, a brief summary of Nintendo's home console product evolution is presented in Table 1.1. The table summarizes characteristics including the product name, generation, year, and technologies used.

TABLE 1.1
Evolution of Nintendo's Home Consoles

Colour TV-Game.
First-generation console, released in 1977.
Only released in Japan (five versions).
Each of the consoles contained a small number of built-in games and a controller.
No microprocessor chips were used.

Nintendo did not release a second-generation home console. Second-generation consoles deployed games in cartridges, used of microprocessor chips, provided single screen graphics (i.e., flip-screen).

Nintendo Entertainment System
Third-generation console, released in 1983.
Embraced third party game development.
Provided scrolling graphics.
Customized chips: 8-bit Ricoh 6502 CPU, 8-bit Ricoh 2A03 GPU.
Games deployed on ROM cartridges.

Super Nintendo Entertainment System
Fourth-generation console, released in 1990.
Supported game play with the Interactor haptic feedback vest (1994). Customized chips: 16-bit Ricoh 5A22 CPU, 16-bit Ricoh PPU.
Games deployed on ROM cartridges.

Virtual Boy
Fifth-generation console, released in 1995.
First VR console with stereoscopic 3D graphics. The player uses the console like an HMD.
Customized chip: 32-bit NEC V810 CPU.
Games deployed on ROM cartridges.
This product was quickly discontinued.

(Continued)

TABLE 1.1 (Continued)
Evolution of Nintendo's Home Consoles

Nintendo 64
Fifth-generation console, released in 1996.
3D graphics.
Chips: 64-bit NEC VR4300 CPU, 64-bit Reality GPU.
Connect up to four controllers (cables).
Games deployed on ROM cartridges.

Game cube
Sixth-generation console, released in 2001.
Chips: 32-bit IBM Gekko CPU, ATI Fliper GPU.
External Ethernet IEEE 802.3 LAN and dial-up modem adapters offered.
Games deployed on Game Cube Optical Discs (proprietary).

Wii
Seventh-generation console, released in 2006.
Chips: 32-bit IBM Broadway CPU, ATI Hollywood GPU.
Wii remote and Nanchuck devices, wireless Bluetooth, and infrared signals.
Wi-Fi IEEE 802.11b/g for online gameplay at the Nintendo Wi-Fi Connection site.
External Ethernet 802.2 LAN adapter available.
Games deployed on Wii Optical Discs (proprietary).

Wi U
Eighth-generation console, released in 2012.
Direct successor to the Wii console.
Chips: 32-bit IBM Espresso CPU (quad core), AMD Radeon GPU (HD graphics)
External Ethernet IEEE 802.2 LAN adapter available.
Wii remote and Nanchuck devices, wireless Bluetooth and infrared signals.
Wi-fi IEEE 802.11b/g/n for online gameplay on the Nintendo Network site.
Games deployed on Wii U Optical Discs (proprietary).

Nintendo Switch.
Eighth-generation console, released in 2017.
Convertible (home console/hand held).
Customized SoC: NVIDIA Tegra X1 (64-bit, four ARM Cortex A57 CPU cores, 256 CUDA GPU cores).
External Ethernet IEEE 802.2 LAN adapter available.
Wi-fi IEEE 802.11b/g/n/ac for online gameplay at the Nintendo Switch site.
Games and software are available on ROM cartridges and digital distribution.

Nintendo Switch Pro.
Ninth generation, announced for 2021.
Successor to the Nintendo Switch.

1.2.2.2 Arcade Video Games

The first two coin-operated arcade video games emerged in 1971: *Galaxy Game* and *Computer Space*. *Galaxy Game* was a prototype built at Stanford University using a PDP-11 minicomputer. The *Computer Space* game was a version of the pioneering game *Spacewar!* It was released by SyZyGy Engineering, the precursor of Atari, Inc. Soon after, the commercially successful arcade game *PONG* was released by Atari in 1972. This was followed by games that utilized innovative technologies and attracted a growing community of players. Game arcades flourished: they provided places for people to meet, play games, and have fun with friends. Popular games were released in 1974–1977 including *Taito's Speed Race*, which used scrolling sprites and a driving wheel; Midway MFG's *Gun Fight*, the first arcade to use a microprocessor – the Intel 8080; Sega's *Moto-Cross*, which provided haptic feedback; and Cinematronics' *Space Wars*, the first arcade game that used vector graphics. The first blockbuster arcade game was Taito's *Space Invaders* in 1978. In the next 3 years, iconic games including Atari's *Asteroids*, Namco's *PAC-MAN/Ms.PAC-MAN*, Nintendo's *Donkey Kong*, and Williams Electronics' *Defender* appeared. By 1982, there were 13,000 arcades in the USA, and each of the most popular machines brought in approximately $400.00 a week in quarters [94]. The trend turned abruptly a year later in North America, when the revenue of the game industry as a whole dropped drastically. This event, known as *The Crash*, impacted arcade games; however, they persisted. Some of the most popular arcade games of all time were released in the decade to follow, including *Street Fighter/Street Fighter II/Street Fighter Champion Edition* (Capcom, 1987, 1991, 1992), *Mortal Kombat/Mortal Kombat II* (Midway, 1992, 1993), and *NBA Jam* (Midway, 1993). Video arcades are rare today, but a nostalgic appeal for the games remains. Arcade games for the home market continue to emerge as either ¾ or full-sized cabinets. For example, full sized cabinet games were revealed at the Electronic Entertainment Expo 2019 event, including Arcade1UP's Konami's *Teenage Mutant Ninja Turtles Home Arcade Game*, Capcom's Marvel *Super Heroes Home Arcade Game*, and an *Atari Star Wars* machine.

1.2.2.3   Personal Computer Games

The growing popularity of personal computers in the late 1970s was embraced by the gaming community. The early offerings included the Commodore PET (1977), Tandy TRS-80 Model I (1977), Apple II (1977), and Atari 400/800 (1979) systems. IBM entered the personal computer market in 1981 with the 5150 model; a game friendlier home computer (graphics, sound, and price) called the PCjr was introduced in 1983. Although primarily for business applications and education, games occupied a prominent position in the software libraries of Apple, Atari, Commodore, IBM, Radio Shack, Texas Instruments, and other manufacturers. The game genres were diverse. Players purchased adventure, card, puzzle, simulation, and role playing games. For example, the first release of Microsoft's *Flight Simulator* was offered in 1982 (the latest offering, version 13, was released in 2020). The first editions of very successful franchises were also released in the early 1980s. Origin Systems' role playing game *Ultima I The First Age of Darkness* (1981) was released for the Apple II. This extremely popular game went on to offer nine sequels, game collections, and spin offs over the next three decades for multiple platforms. Sierra On-Line Systems' adventure game *King's Quest* (1983) was originally developed for the PCjr. Over the next 15 years, eight additional games in this franchise, as well as collections, were released for multiple platforms. In 1984, the game *Tetris* was created [3]. Originally programmed as a test program for the Electronika 60, it was ported and released for the IBM personal computer in 1986. Since then, *Tetris* and its variations were released on almost every platform; it's been ranked as the best video game of all times [43]. Game development for personal computers expanded rapidly in the 1990s; new genres emerged including real-time strategy adventure (e.g., *Dune*), puzzle (e.g., *SimCity*), and first-person shooter (e.g., *Doom*) games. An early game engine to support the rapid, cost effective development of 2D games was available in 1993, IDs *Doom* engine. Game engines provided collections of reusable components (e.g., animation, artificial intelligence, collision detection, graphical user interfaces, inputs, loading, and physics). Rather than creating games from scratch, developers were able to focus on the unique assets and rules for their games. Today, game engines are widely available (e.g., Amazon Lumberyard, Blender, CryEngine, Unity, and Unreal Engine) and support multiplatform development.

Beyond playing games on standalone personal computers, early advances in proprietary networking technologies provided new online gameplay opportunities. The Hayes 80-103a modem board was introduced in 1977, which utilized the S-100 personal computer bus architecture. An Apple II modem was introduced by Hayes the following year. These modems supported remote dial-up access via phone lines (i.e., using circuit connections) to bulletin board systems and online services. An early computer bulletin board system was called CBBS; it was a local bulletin board system available in 1978. Bulletin board systems flourished. The early systems were established and administered by hobbyists. They attracted computing enthusiasts primarily within their local telephone area codes. Users made free local calls via dial-up modems, as opposed to calling systems farther away that incurred long-distance phone charges. The bulletin board systems hosted Door games [40]. These games reflected the two steps players used to access games. Firstly, players connected to a bulletin board system. Secondly, they accessed a game hosted on the system. As an example, the Door game *Trade War* available in 1984 was a multiplayer, asynchronous turn play game on the Nochange bulletin board system. These bulletin board systems and Door games were very popular from the early 1980s to the mid-1990s. During this timeframe, proprietary online services were also launched to meet consumer demand (e.g., CompuServe, America on Line, and Genie). For example, CompuServe offered online services to the public in 1979. It went on to great success in the 1980s and remained a major influencer through the mid-1990s. CompuServe offered a catalogue of online games across adventure, dungeon, war, and board game genres. The catalogue included the very popular *Island of Kesmai* (1982) and *Megawars III* (1984). Users paid to play the games at hourly rates. Beyond playing the games, the community members were able to interact and discuss the games. The online services provided a space for gamers, game journalists, and game developers to share information.

Recognizing the need to move from proprietary networks to open standard-based solutions, organizations were established for the Internet and subsequently for the World Wide Web (WWW). The earliest organization was the Internet Configuration Control Board; it was created by the ARPANet program in 1979. This board was reorganized and renamed over time. It is now called the Internet Architecture Board. The board first captured the state of standardization in 1988 for the Internet protocols in RFC 1083 [52]. At that time, the standards included the foundational RFCs for IP, ICMP, UDP, TCP, DNS, TELNET, FTP, and so on. Today, the board includes the Internet Engineering Task Force (IETF) that continues to oversee the development of Internet standards. An example of gameplay shifting from proprietary to open standard-based networks is the online game *Legends of Future Past*. It was initially released in 1992 on the Digital Dream Networks proprietary service; players accessed the game via a dial-up connection. The game was subsequently ported from the proprietary network to the Internet.

Building on the Internet standards and technology, the WWW was created at the European Organization for Nuclear Research (CERN) in 1989 to support automated information sharing between scientists at universities and institutes. The first WWW server and browser emerged the following year. The World Wide Web Consortium (W3C), established in 1994, was created to develop and maintain open standards for the WWW. MMO games took advantage of the new technology based on open standards. The real-time strategy game *Earth: 2025* was an MMO browser game released in 1996; the MMO first-person shooter game *Quake* was released the same year. The real-time strategy games *Age of Empires* and *StarCraft* were released in 1997 and 1998, respectively.

Advances in local area network (LAN) technology also provided new gameplay opportunities. For example, the AppleTalk LAN was available in 1985; network versions of games (e.g., *Strategic Conquest* in 1986 and *Spectre* in 1991) were released for the Macintosh. Proprietary LAN technology evolved into products based on open standards. The IEEE Ethernet LAN standard [51] enabled the low cost, mass production of network interface cards for IBM compatible personal computers; and wireless standards followed providing players with untethered gameplay experiences (e.g., [50]). Multiplayer, networked games such as *Pathway to Darkness* and *DOOM* launched in 1993; they initiated the *LAN Party* phenomenon. Game enthusiasts collected their personal computer equipment (desktop machines, monitors, and cables), gathered together, and set up a LAN to play their favourite games. These private LAN parties, very popular from the mid-1990s–2000s, have evolved. Today, players also gather virtually via social media platforms and large-scale commercially sponsored parties are organized. For example, the international DreamHack festival events draw several hundred thousands of participants including bring your own computer LAN parties.

1.2.2.4   Portable Console Games

Handheld portable game consoles emerged in the mid-1970s that allowed players to enjoy their games on the go. These provided an alternative to playing games at home (console, personal computer) or in an arcade. In 1976, Mattel designed a game console the size of a calculator, using innovative displays based on light-emitting diode technology; the console played the game *Auto Race*. The next year, the *Football* game console was released. These electronic handheld games were very successful and attracted developers including Atari, Coleco, Parker Brothers, Milton Bradley, Entex, and Bandai. The first offering with interchangeable game cartridges was Milton Bradley's Microvision in 1979. However, this console was short lived due to its fragile, small liquid-crystal display and limited selection of 12 games. Nintendo's *Game & Watch* series of handheld consoles began its successful run in 1980, which lasted over a decade. A collection of 60 games was developed over a series of 11 consoles. The games included the iconic Donkey Kong (e.g., *Donkey Kong, Donkey Kong Jr.*, and *Donkey Kong II*) and Mario franchises (e.g., *Mario Bros., Mario's Bombs Away*, and *Super Mario*). Some of these games were later ported to the Game Boy, Game Boy Color, and Game Boy Advance consoles.

In 1989, Nintendo popularized handheld gaming with the release of its 8-bit Game Boy video game device. For the North American launch, the titles included *Super Mario Land, Alleyway, Baseball, Tetris*, and *Tennis*. Over the next 25 years, handheld consoles were released by many organizations including NEC, Sega, Sony, and Nintendo for this growing community. Nintendo dominated the field and released a number of successful successors to the Game Boy, including the 8-bit Game Boy

Color (1998) and the 32-bit Game Boy Advance series (Advanced 2001, SP 2003, Micro 2005). A collection of over 500 games was ultimately developed for the Game Boy Advance consoles. Nintendo's next handheld consoles were in the 32-bit DS series (DS 2004, DS Lite 2006, DSi 2008, DSi XLs 2009, 3DS 2011, 2DS 2013); the Nintendo Switch/Switch Lite (2017) provided the option to operate either as a handheld or a traditional console. The backward compatibility of the new consoles in the DS series was a critical design constraint. Players who purchased a new console had access to an extensive game library; there are over 2000 games available today. The current handheld consoles are the eighth generation.

1.2.2.5   Mobile Phone Games

The first games appeared on mobile cellular phones in 1994. They were preloaded, single player puzzle games on phones that utilized 2G cellular networks. *Tetris* was provided on the Hagenuk MT-2000 handset; *Scramble* was on the IBM Simon Personal Communicator smart phone. Three years later, the game *Snake* was provided on the Nokia 6110 mobile phone. The shift from playing only preloaded, single player games to being able to load new games for multiple players was a significant change. This advance relied on the Wireless Application Protocol (WAP) introduced in 1999 [108]. The protocol supported Internet access from mobile phones; WAP browsers emerged shortly after. Early on-line game sites included Starduck Central in 2001 (the predecessor to Impulse) and Valve Steam in 2003. The first Apple iPhone (IoS) was released in 2007 for 2G networks and the App Store followed the next year. This was the first on-line store dedicated to mobile apps. The game Texas Hold'em was the first game sold on the App Store in 2008. This mobile game supported up to nine players communicating via Wi-Fi. The HTC Dream phone (Android) for 3G networks and the on-line store Market were also available in 2008. The first commercially successful mobile game was *Angry Birds*, which was released in 2009. Over time, the technology and infrastructure for mobile phones continued to advance (e.g., 4G and 5G networks) and mobile games proliferated. This year, for example, the App Store's most popular category was games. There were almost one million game apps available; these represent over 20% of the apps on their site.

1.2.2.6   Virtual and Augmented Reality Games

1.2.2.6.1   *Virtual Reality Games*

The introduction of consumer VR devices began in the late 1980s. The devices for interactive gameplay expanded from traditional controllers, driving wheels, and joysticks to include devices spanning VR and AR environments that supported immersive gameplay [71]. Early devices for consoles and personal computers included a data glove, a wearable vest, and head-mounted displays (HMDs). The Mattel Power Glove was released in 1989; it was utilized in the e-sport *Super Glove Ball VR* game a year later for the Nintendo Entertainment System. Aura System's Interactor Vest, a force feedback wearable device, was released and utilized in the fighter game *Mortal Combat II* for the Super Nintendo Console (SNES) and the SEGA Genesis versions in 1994. The Forte VFX-1 HMD was released and utilized in the first-person shooter game *Descent* in 1995 for personal computers running MS-DOS. The VFX-1 had stereo headphones, stereoscopic displays, and three-axis head-tracking. This technology was acquired by Vuzix; it subsequently released two consumer HMDs: the VXF3D in 2000 and the iWear AV310 in 2009. More recently, Vuzix has focused on HMDs for commercial environments. Sony was another pioneer in consumer HMDs. It launched Glasstron in 1996, which was compatible with DOS personal computers and used in the game *MechWarrior 2*. Over a decade later, Sony launched a series of HMDs: HMZ-T1 in 2011 for the PlayStation 3; HMZ-T2 in 2012 for the Xbox 360 and PlayStation 3; and HMZ-T3W in 2013 with HDMI connectivity to consoles, mobile devices, and personal computers (wireless feature is optional). Sony also released the PlayStation VR in 2016 for the PlayStation 4 console; this product remained compatible with the PlayStation 5 console. Companies that joined the consumer HMD marketplace later include Oculus VR (a division of Facebook) and DreamWorld. Oculus VR released the Oculus Rift and Oculus Quest product lines. Their first product was the Rift CV1 consumer headset that was released in 2016; an upgraded version was available 3 years later. DreamWorld introduced the Dream Glass 4K in 2019. It provided state-of-the-art features including a 90° field of vision, 4K resolution, extensive play time, and compatibility with phones and consoles at an affordable price for home use.

Beyond consoles and personal computers, VR was utilized in arcade games and virtual world environments. The Virtuality Group created VR arcade machines in 1991 that boasted short response time and provided gamers with stereoscopic vision devices, game controllers, and the ability to cooperate in multiplayer games. Nine games were developed for the machines, and the most popular one was the first-person shooter *Dactyl Nightmare*. Cave Automatic Virtual Environments (CAVEs) emerged to support VR applications. The game *CAVE Quake II* was used to demonstrate the VisBox CAVE in 2001. CAVEs are immersive VR environments that utilize fixed projectors for three to six walls of a room-sized cube. They have a number of advantages for users: reducing the burden of carrying or wearing devices (e.g., HMDs), providing a shared experience for multiple people, and reducing the isolation of people from the real world. Currently, however, the CAVEs remain expensive to install which limits their adoption by consumers.

1.2.2.6.2 *Augmented Reality Games*

Augmented reality (AR) games, providing a mix of a virtual world and elements from the real world, initially emerged for consoles. The game *EyeToy* was released in 2003 for the PlayStation 2 console. It used a TV screen for the display and a USB camera. For the first time, players were able to see themselves on-screen interacting with virtual objects in real time. The game *Eye of Judgment* was released in 2007 for the PlayStation 3 console. This console provided enhanced image processing capabilities using motion and colour detection in the PlayStation eye system. The game allowed two players to compete in online matches with a hybrid of paper and electronic collectible cards.

AR games for handheld consoles soon followed. The game *Ghostwire: Link to the Paranormal* was an AR game first developed for the Nintendo DSi; this game was released in 2010. The game made use of the DSi's camera and microphone so the player hunted for ghosts in their actual, physical environment. Once the ghosts were detected, the player tracked down objects and used them to appease the ghosts. The Nintendo 3DS handheld console was released in 2011 with a collection of six cards (five classic characters and a question mark) and two pre-installed AR games: Archery and Star Pics. The cards were used by placing them on a table and focusing the 3DS' camera on them. The Nintendo Switch, a convertible console, was released in 2017. AR games were announced including the game *Mario Kart Live: Home Circuit*. This game uses a camera located on a remote control car and the Nintendo Switch console's screen; its expected release date is in 2021.

For mobile phones, early AR games included *ARCade* that allowed players to chase and consume virtual yellow dots like the *Pac-Man* game. It was developed as a tailored Layer browser in 2010 to celebrate the 30th anniversary of Pac-Man. The mobile AR game *Pokémon GO* became a global cultural phenomenon in 2016. At its peak, it attracted 28.5 million daily users. Players encountered, caught, and trained Pokémon creatures in real-world settings; it utilized the global position systems provided in the mobile devices.

1.2.2.7 Multiplatform Streaming Games

Multiplatform game streaming services were offered over the last two decades that allowed players to run computationally intensive games (developed for specific platforms) on a variety of personal computers, consoles, and mobile devices. For example, rather than purchasing a dedicated home console or an expensive high-end gaming computer, games were accessible via modestly priced devices. Much of the processing in these services was allocated to server clusters to maintain the quality of the graphics and gameplay. Thin clients were used on the devices to access the services. The services evolved steadily in several directions: providing fundamental technology, providing subscription services for playing games users own, providing subscription services to provide access to games they don't own.

Here, examples of game streaming services available over time are briefly presented. A pioneering service was OnLive, which focused on providing subscriptions to game players. It was launched in 2003 and allowed subscribers to rent games without installing them on their own device. Games were delivered to OnLive's client software as a streaming video that was rendered by the service's servers. Gameplay was enabled through thin clients for personal computers, mobile devices, as well as smart TVs and a dedicated video game console-styled device called the OnLive Game System. Sony Interactive Entertainment acquired the patents for the OnLive technology in 2015, and the service was discontinued. G-cluster initially focused on providing streaming services to telecommunication companies. Their first release was in 2005 for the Cyprus Telecom Authority. Over the next decade, additional roll-outs with major telecommunication companies and content acquisition deal with studios (e.g., Electronic Arts, Gameloft, Sega, and Ubisoft) made the G-cluster technology a top provider. Gaikai focused on developing cloud-based game streaming technology; it was launched in 2011. A year later, the company was acquired by Sony Interactive Entertainment. The technology was adopted in the PlayStation Now game streaming service, which was released in 2014. The Sony service provided players access to over 300 games via their personal computer

(Windows). Shadow by Blade focused on providing players with remote access to a powerful personal computer (Windows) to play games they own. This service was released in 2016. Players accessed the services from a variety of devices including personal computers (Windows, macOS) and Android devices (smartphones, tablets) for a lag-free gaming experience. Players installed their games, preferences, and account information on a dedicated Windows 10 machine; everything is retained between sessions just like a local machine. Three game streaming services were launched in 2020: Nvidia Geforce, Google Stadia, and Microsoft Project xCloud. Nvidia GeForce focused on users playing games from their Steam library on personal computers (Windows, macOS), Android devices, or an Nvidia Shield TV. Google Stadia focused on providing access to console and personal computer games they don't own via phones, Chrome browser tabs, or TVs. Microsoft Project xCloud focused on users accessing games they host; it provided 150 games at the launch. Players can currently use Android smartphones and tablets to play games; in the future the xBox one console streaming is planned.

1.3   RECENT ADVANCES IN GAMES AND SOFTWARE ENGINEERING RESEARCH

Today's large scale, complex games present distinct development challenges. Like many software projects in other domains, games frequently miss their originally announced release dates or are cancelled. For example, *Doom Eternal*, the fifth main game in the series, has recently been released for personal computers (Windows), consoles (PlayStation 4, Xbox One), and streaming (Stadia) platforms; the Nintendo Switch console port is forthcoming. This release was 4 months late and did not meet all of its requirements. The multiplayer invasion mode is not included in the release, which lets a player join another player's game disguised as a demon.

To address the challenges of developing large-scale complex games, new and customized approaches have been proposed in the literature. Table 1.2 presents a high-level overview of recent results that span software engineering and game development research topics. Since 2015, five groups of topics have received considerable attention in the peer-reviewed literature: analytics and metrics, automation, models, reuse, and user experience. The work has appeared in computer science, education, software engineering, and game development publications. In addition, games for software engineering education and training have also recently been proposed. These include games on requirements engineering, architecture and design, modelling languages, code quality (testing, refactoring), lifecycle processes, and project management. The table is intended to identify the recent results in the games and software engineering research communities. It may provide a useful foundation for a comprehensive literature survey on games and software engineering in the future.

1.4   THE CHAPTER COLLECTION

1.4.1   GAMES AND SOFTWARE ENGINEERING EDUCATION

An exploration of organizational features that characterize game competitions and related game development environments is presented by Walt Scacchi in Chapter 2,

TABLE 1.2

Examples of Recent Results: Spanning Games and Software Engineering Research Topics

Software Engineering for Games

Analytics and Metrics
  Game metrics [18, 27, 56, 83, 101]
  Game analytics [32, 57, 66, 77, 99]
Automation
  PCG algorithms [2, 12, 24, 26, 65, 90, 95, 100]
  Testing [48, 49, 60, 82, 93, 98, 104, 112]
Development Models and Methodologies
  Lifecycle process model [5, 6, 59, 61]
  Methodologies [13]
  Model-based development [37, 67, 113]
  Modelling languages [1, 9, 34, 91, 111]
Reuse
  Frameworks [81, 105, 106, 107]
  Patterns [7, 41, 58, 63]
  Product lines [4, 35, 70, 96]
  Reference architectures [68, 74, 84, 97]
User Experience
  Assessment and testing [17, 86, 88]
  Design [25, 79, 85]
  Requirements engineering [23, 33, 103]

Serious Games for Software Engineering

Engineering Activities
  Requirements [36, 44]
  Architecture and design [14, 76]
  Modelling languages (formal specification) [87]
  Code quality [11, 28, 39, 45, 72]
(e.g., debugging, refactoring, and testing)
Umbrella activities
  Lifecycle processes [8, 10, 15, 69]
  Project Management [22, 64, 75, 102]

followed by a qualitative analysis of five events the University of California, Irvine has been involved with. The organizational features focus on the setting of the event, which include academic settings (intra-mural, inter-mural, capstone projects), workshops, festivals, and additional variations; these events involve teams that typically work in parallel to make games. Intra-mural competitions involve teams from one school, whereas inter-mural teams involve teams from two or more schools. Capstone project courses utilize games as engaging problems that present teams with significant software engineering challenges. Game workshops provide a forum that offers a more structured event, including a curriculum and schedule of activities, to explore specific topics. The organizers involve subject matter experts to organize and present material on specific topics and lead interactive activities for the participants. Game showcase festivals provide a product-centric environment, where participants vie for recognition and awards for the creative games they have developed. These festivals are like well-known film festivals (e.g., Sundance), in which the films are shown and critiqued, but little attention is paid to their production process.

The five locally held events selected and analysed include two intra-mural game jams, a regional inter-mural game showcase, an intra-mural game capstone project course, and an international multiteam game development workshop focused on producing game modules for incorporation within a common game software architecture. Each event is described and comparatively analysed to present observations, lessons learned, and opportunities for how to organize and design game jams. The lessons learned and opportunities identified are summarized for the reader as nine items; they span topics of interest to researchers and educators. Recognizing the potential to utilize these competitions in empirical studies, there are fundamental questions around establishing rigorous, reusable methodologies that support the execution of repeated studies. The competitions offer a number of opportunities to explore additional possible organizations, in particular with respect to their suitability for investigating questions of interest to local, regional, national, or international populations. The numerous characteristics and trade-offs to consider for a project in a game development competition are also a rich source of research and education opportunities. For example, decisions on a game project competition span the purpose, duration, team formation, supervision, rewards, tools, and specific development skills to focus on. Such skills can include the development of large-scale courses (e.g., MOOCs), collaboration in distributed development, and use of game publishing platforms. While often focusing on programming aspects, development artefacts beyond the code can also be addressed including engineering (e.g., requirements, design, and testing) and project management.

The characterization of the organizational features for game development events, as well as the lessons learned from the analysis of five events the University of California Irvine has been involved with, can facilitate playful learning and showcase opportunities in the future. Beyond the valuable educational opportunities, these events can also be organized to support the empirical evaluation of game software engineering research proposals.

Digital-based learning games for software engineering education are the focus of the results presented by Jöran Pieper in Chapter 3. The need for students to develop transferrable, flexible software engineering competencies remains a challenging problem. These competencies are clusters of related knowledge, skills, and attitudes that can be applied to accomplish tasks in different contexts. The contexts span academic (e.g., course on software engineering, capstone project), and industry (e.g., internships, positions after graduation) environments. The use of serious games in software engineering education continues to receive the attention of researchers. The author explores the simulation games for software engineering that have been proposed in the literature; a survey is presented that includes 11 games evaluated using nine characteristics. The characteristics include gameplay (e.g., single-player or multiplayer) and subject domain (e.g., support for different SE processes/methods) specific criteria. The survey identifies an important gap in the literature: the games focus one well-established software process, rather than facilitating a perspective on the use of flexible SE practices; alternative processes are not embodied in the games. As a result, the currently available games do not focus on the development of transferrable, flexible competencies.

To focus on a game that establishes flexible and transferrable SE competencies, the author selects the SEMAT Essence Kernel as a core element of the SE learning objectives. SEMAT Essence is an emerging OMG standard that provides a language for the unified description of SE practices and methods and a compact kernel. This kernel captures the essentials of SE endeavours in a process- and practice independent way; these essential elements can be selected and composed (i.e., flexible) to provide tailored SE methods that address the needs of a particular project (i.e., transferrable).

The author develops two separate and complementary learning games, the Essence Kernel Puzzler and the Essence Simulation Game; in addition, a recommendation tool is also presented called the Essence Navigator. By separating the two games, their learning outcomes and game genres have been identified and set independently, rather than attempting to create a single game with a broad scope. In addition, they can be adopted as needed by instructors to support a course curriculum and schedule. The games are both established on social constructivist learning theory to provide a rigorous pedagogical foundation and the Revised Bloom's taxonomy is used to characterize the learning objectives. The Essence Kernel Puzzler game addresses the introduction of concepts and vocabulary at lower competency levels, remember and understand in the knowledge dimension. Two genres are selected for this game: drill and practice; and puzzle games. This game prepares the student to play the second game, the Essence Simulation Game, which addresses more advanced learning objectives at higher competency levels, remember, understand, and apply in the knowledge dimension. It utilizes the features and characteristics of adventure and simulation games to impart the desired procedural knowledge and skills. The learning content is an integral part of the gameplay and is tightly linked to the SE domain. The design couples the mastery of the learning content with achieving success in the game; a high degree of reflection is embodied in this simulation game to provide the time needed to think and rethink decisions. These two games are complemented by the Essence Navigator, a supporting tool, connecting game experiences and real-world course project work of students. This tool has been integrated into the Essence Simulation Game to help monitor the progress of a virtual team's project; it provides basic recommendations to the player on the next step to take. The navigation tool can also be used separately, for example, in a capstone project course, to assist teams.

The proposed game-based learning approach, which includes two games and a navigation tool, is validated with a case study conducted with students. A questionnaire is used to collect data on the utility of the approach. The analysis of the data collected indicates the approach is promising; however, additional research is needed to assess the value of game mechanics including "time travel" (to provide opportunities to reflect upon earlier decisions, make alternative choices), rankings, and leaderboards.

A collection of serious educational games targeting introductory programming concepts is under development by Brian Chau et al. in Chapter 4. The games within the collection are small, independent, and fun. Each game focusses on one or two specific programming concepts (e.g., conditionals and arrays), which allows instructors to flexibly choose an ensemble of games to meet their needs. Each game is designed, built, and extensively play tested almost entirely by undergraduate students, ensuring they are fun and engaging for the target audience. For each game, an API is extracted which allows instructors and students to modify the game. Faculty can construct small and fun games to demonstrate concepts; students can exercise their own understanding and creativity by customizing the game and making it their own. The games are variations of popular casual genres; two completed games are Space Smasher (a variant of Super Breakout-style games) and Corrupted (a variant of Bubble Shooter games). The Smasher gameplay involves players removing blocks on the screen by bouncing a ball with a moveable paddle. Space Smasher introduces more interesting gameplay by adding *customizable* blocks that are capable of triggering events such as swapping blocks or enabling/disabling unbreakable blocks. Also included are more premium sets of graphics tiles and sounds than are typically found in this genre. The ball-block-paddle collision tests, the special event logic, and the iteration through all blocks present an excellent structured sandbox for teaching and playing with conditionals and loops. The Corrupted gameplay involves players launching a coloured tile into a larger group of tiles and attempting to make matches of three until all tiles are removed or until the tiles advance to meet the player at the opposite end of the screen. Bubble shooters also tend to be simple match-and-remove games with minimalist graphics. Corrupted recasts the game with an active automated opponent employing a variety of tricks to increase the challenge and intrigue, and the game itself has been given a distinct artistic style. The visual, spatial, and multidimensional aspects of the colour tiles present a rich domain of concepts for use in teaching 1D and 2D arrays.

The research adopts four design goals for the API development. Firstly, the usability and simplicity of the APIS facilitate the creation of effective CS1/2 materials by users with no background in graphics or gaming. Secondly, users must be able to build simple applications quickly with minimum familiarity of the APIs; over time the users can gradually explore more the advanced functionality at their own pace. Thirdly, the APIs primarily support building effective teaching materials as vehicles for educational content delivery. Lastly, the APIs encapsulate the graphics and gaming functionality while selectively exposing concepts for educational purposes. Based on two completed games and their associated teaching materials, feedback from novice student programmers indicates that the games are engaging and the associated APIs are straightforward to use. The games are currently being field tested in CS1/2 classrooms.

A new version of a model for systematically evaluating the quality of games for software engineering education is presented by Giani Petri et al. in Chapter 5. An existing model for the evaluation of educational games (MEEGA) has already been proposed in the literature; it has been widely adopted. MEEGA can be applied to evaluate educational games (digital and non-digital ones) in terms of motivation, user experience, and learning; it utilizes a standardized questionnaire to measure the reaction of students after playing the game. A thorough analysis of MEEGA is reported in this chapter, which reveals opportunities for its improvement related to the presence of overlapping theoretical concepts (motivation and user experience), in addition to some ambiguous phrasing in the questionnaire. The authors then propose an enhanced model to address these concerns called MEEGA+; it improves the reliability and validity of the model. This chapter reports on the design and evaluation of MEEGA+. The design consists of four steps. Firstly, the factors to be measured are defined to provide the foundation for the measurement instrument (questionnaire). This is achieved using the established Goal/Question/Metric approach, in which the high-level evaluation objective is defined and is systematically decomposed into specific factors for measurement. Secondly, the measurement of these factors is operationalized by decomposing them into measurement instrument items (i.e., questions). The specific learning objectives of a game are included in these items. In order to standardize the selected items, all of the items are transformed into positive statements. Thirdly, the response format for the items of the measurement instrument is defined (i.e., 5-point Likert scale). Lastly, an expert panel composed of four senior researchers with backgrounds in computing/SE and/or statistics is convened to analyse the clarity, relevance, consistency, and completeness of the measurement instrument items. Feedback from this panel has been used in the design of MEEGA+.

The evaluation of the model focusses on three analysis questions related to evidence for internal consistency, how underlying factors influence the responses, and evidence for the convergent and discriminant validity of the measurement instrument. An extensive case study evaluation is reported on the evaluation of MEEGA+. It consists of 29 case studies, spanning 13 games (four digital, nine non-digital), responses from 589 students, and six different educational institutions. The results indicate the reliability of the MEEGA+ model as satisfactory; two quality factors have a significant role (player experience and usability). Thus, MEEGA+ provides a valuable contribution in the systematic development, improvement, and adoption of serious educational games for SE.

An assemblage of applied game design methods for educators is presented by Micah Hrehovcsik in Chapter 6 to help address the current lack of a comprehensive design theory, best practices, and didactic approaches. Applied games are those that go beyond entertainment, for example, serious games or games with a purpose. The proposed collection relies on the Vitruvius principles. These principles are the foundation for ancient Roman architecture, which forms the triad of *utilitas*, *firmitas*, and *venustas*. Repurposed for applied game design, the principles encourage critical design awareness and offer a perspective on balancing a serious game's *utilitas* (purpose), *firmitas* (sustainability), and *venustas* (gameplay experience). *Utilitas*, or purpose, is when a game fulfills its tactical purpose. *Firmitas*, or sustainability, is when the game is properly embedded in the context, available to players, has a syllabus designed around it, and aims to create a perceivable impact in the chosen domain. *Venustas*, or gameplay experience, is when the game provides a meaningful holistic experience (e.g., gameplay, graphics, and sound) for the player.

The assemblage has been used to educate game designers at the HKU University of the Arts Utrecht about the design of applied games. It addresses three instructional goals: provide students with a means to critique serious games, provide a means to categorize games according to their design, rather than their domain or genre, and provide a tool which guides design choices, spurs design research, and supports the rationale for design choices. The assemblage consists of four components. The first component is a classification scheme for serious games, which has a collection of tactical forms: transmissive, aggregative, adaptive, and collaborative. The transmissive form, for example, is designed to attract and engage players to 'transmit' skills, knowledge, rhetoric, therapy, etc., in serious games. The second component is a scope model, which supports the analysis of the content, context, and knowledge transfer by asking the classic who, what, where, when, why, and how questions. Once these questions have been answered the game designer has a quick-scan, or summary, that is used for subsequent steps in the design of the applied game in question. The third component is the use of epistemic cards as a tool for structuring the dissemination of design decision or understanding how design decisions are being made. There are six kinds of cards that define this epistemic framework including context, content, and transfer analysis; stakeholders; design; artefact; process; and project. These kinds of cards represent a collection of skills, identities, interests, understanding, and knowledge. Lastly, the game jam format provides an intensive practice-based learning experience concerning applied game design theories, co-design, best practices, and studio operations related to development. The format values putting students under time and peer pressure, while having them work autonomously in multidisciplinary teams.

1.4.2 SOFTWARE ENGINEERING GAME DESIGN

A novel design framework for embodiment is presented by Edward Melcer and Katherine Isbiter in Chapter 7. Embodiment is an important concept which recognizes cognition as emergent and multifaceted, involving the mind, physical interactions, and social interactions in the environment. It has significant potential to enhance the design of educational games and simulations and has been investigated by diverse communities, including games. These investigations have resulted in the use of terms (e.g., embodiment, embodied cognition, and embodied interaction) with distinct definitions and operationalization, making the concept difficult to apply in practice. The authors propose a new framework to synthesize these results that supports the design for digital and non-digital systems. It is based on a careful selection and analysis of 90 articles that focus on embodiment and design descriptions, spanning 66 distinct games and simulations. The analysis results are used to establish the design framework taxonomy. The taxonomy is intended to make designers aware of design choices, rather than prescribing strict mappings of design choices into values, like sorting bins. It is organized into three levels: groups, dimensions, and possible values (i.e., design choices). At the highest level there are three groups: physical interactions, social interactions, and the world. The physical interactions group describes how learning is physically embodied in a system. This group has four dimensions, which are physicality, transformity, mapping, and correspondence. Within the physicality dimension, for example, one value is the augmented option, which refers to the use of an AR system as a design decision. The social interactions group describes how individuals socially interact, play, and coordinate within a system. This group has two dimensions: mode of play and coordination. For example, the mode of play dimension has three design options which are individual, collaborative, and competitive. The world group describes the context of the embodied learning and has a single dimension, the environment. This dimension has three values: physical, mixed, and virtual.

The proposed taxonomy is evaluated using three example studies. The first study examines the ability to describe and categorize embodied games and simulations using the framework. The second and third studies apply the framework to identify problematic design spaces and design gaps, respectively. These studies indicate that the framework elucidates design decisions by providing a unifying foundation for the categorization and analyses of designs for existing games. The potential impact of the framework for designing new games and simulations is promising.

The design of mixed reality games including pervasive games, location-based games, and AR games is explored by Richard Wetzel et al. in Chapter 8. These mixed reality games enrich the physical world with technology to create new and exciting possibilities for games. For example, a player's location can be tracked with a GPS service in real time; arriving at a physical location can trigger changes in the game play. The new approach proposed by the authors is based on ideation cards, which are an established design technique. The physical cards are the size of traditional playing cards; each one focuses on a specific concept. The cards often provide a brief description of the concept and an indicative image. They may also provide a more detailed explanation or an example of its use. The mixed reality game card desk consists of Opportunity Cards, Question Cards, Challenge Cards, and Theme Cards. Opportunity Cards highlight game elements that may be adopted, such as tracking sensors. Question Cards probe a deeper exploration of design decisions, such as defining a design concept, or alternative scenarios. Challenge Cards present designers with issues that arise in mixed reality games, such as safety, adverse weather conditions, or congestion at a particular location. Theme Cards are not specific to mixed reality or games; their purpose is to provide additional inspiration for designers. The Theme Cards are realized using a collection of existing cards with images of abstract paintings. The final deck of the Mixed Reality Game Cards contains 93 unique cards (51 Opportunity Cards, 18 Question Cards, and 24 Challenge Cards). The cards are organized into nine categories to both make them more appealing and distinguishable. These categories are audio, gameplay, locations, management, physical, players, sensors, technology, and time.

A lightweight design process is also introduced that consists of two activities. The first activity is idea generation, in which the goal is to use the cards to rapidly generate numerous ideas over several iterations. In each of the iterations, three Opportunity Cards and one Theme Card are randomly drawn to initiate discussions. Ultimately, one idea is selected to pursue. The second activity has four phases. The first is the idea development in which ideas are explored with Opportunity Cards. Secondly, the ideas are refined with Question Cards. Thirdly, the ideas are grounded with Challenge Cards. Lastly, the ideas are finalized by spatially organizing the cards and removing irrelevant ones. The authors report their experiences using the process and the card deck to develop a game for a non-profit organization.

A novel design for an exergame is presented in Chapter 9 by Rahul Kumjar et al. The purpose of exergames is to motivate players to participate in physical exercise by providing enjoyable, immersive environments. The current designs of many exergames present some limitations as effectively combining immersive environments and intense activities at the same time is challenging; intense activity is considered by some as the most beneficial kind of exercise. For example, playing a game and cycling on roadways at the same time can present safety concerns. Consequently, the design of an exergame that promotes exercise outside of play sessions is investigated by the authors. To accomplish this, a popular role playing game "The Elder Scrolls V: Skyrim" is redesigned as an exergame. The original game is multilevel, which is central to the players' progression in the game. The player character has three attributes: health, stamina, and magicka. Health is how much damage a character can take before dying; stamina is the energy system used for running and performing special physical attacks; and magicka is the energy system for performing magic. It is a popular game available on multiple platforms, and it has an extensive community of users and collections of content (over 300 hours). A modification kit is built into the game, which is called the Creation Kit. This kit provides a graphical interface and allows players to readily create new quests, non-player characters, texture-packs, armour models, and so on. The kit uses a proprietary language, Papyrus, to support the modifications. In addition, the modding community for the game has produced resources and documentation for the kit and made them widely available on forums and Internet relay chat channels.

In the modified game called the Skyrim Exergaming Mode, the player character levels up based on their real-world physical activity, rather than their in-game activity. The exergame design model weaves together physical exercise, quests, points, and a levelling system. Overall, there are four main steps in the exergame. In the first step, the player accepts a quest while playing the game. Later, the player engages in physical activities outside the game (e.g., fitness classes, stretching, and sport). In the second step, they log their activity using the exercise logging platform called Exercise. In the third step, the player opens the game; the game acquires the exercise data from Exercise to update the player's points and levelling status. The player is notified of their updated levelling status and resumes playing the game in the fourth step. The design maps alternative types of physical activity as points into the character's attributes. For example, weight training increases maximum health, cardio increases maximum stamina, and everything else (sports, stretching, and so on) increases the maximum magicka. The inherent progression of the game difficulty in the levelling design creates an incentive for players to continue exercising to make progress in the game.

Chapter 10 by Alf Inge Wang and Njål Nordmark design, run, and analyse a two-part survey that explores a variety of perspectives on software engineering and game development. The research goals are to delve into how game developers think about and use software architecture in the development of games, how creative development processes are managed and supported, and the use of game technology. The authors define four research questions (refer to Table 1.3). In the first part of the study, a questionnaire consisting of 20 statements is prepared which are derived from the research questions. The respondents provide their responses using the Likert's scale. In addition, the questionnaire provides a free text comment area for every statement. There are 13 subjects for the study; these are a mix of attendees at the Nordic booth at the Game Developer Conference in San Francisco and game developers contacted by email. The questionnaire has been answered both on paper and using web-forms created using SurveyMonkey. The results show that software architectures play a central role in game development; the main focus is on achieving software with good performance and high modifiability. The creative processes are supported using a wide variety of tools such as game engines, middleware, scripting languages, and dynamically loading assets. Feature-based teams have shifted over the last several years to using more game-specific engines, tools, and middleware in their development; these teams consist of both creative and technical professionals.

TABLE 1.3
Questionnaire Summary

Question No.	Questionnaire Statement
RQ1: What role does software architecture play in game development?	
1	Design of software architecture is an important part of our game development process.
2	The main goal of our software architecture is performance.
3	Our game concept heavily influences the software architecture.
4	The creative team is included in the design of the software architecture.
5	Our existing software suite provides features aimed at helping the creative team do their job.
6	Our existing software architecture dictates the future game concepts we can develop.
RQ2: How do game developers manage changes to the software architecture?	
7	The creative team has to adopt their ideas to the existing game engine.
8	During development, the creative team can demand changes to the software architecture.
9	Who decides if change-requests from the creative team are implemented?
10	The technical team implements all features requested by the creative team.
11	It is easy to add new gameplay elements after the core of our game engine has been completed.
12	During development, the creative team has to use the tools and features already available.
RQ3: How are the creative processes managed and supported in game development?	
13	Our game engine supports dynamic loading of new content.
14	Our game engine has a scripting system the creative team can use to try out and implement new ideas.
15	The creative team is included in our development feedback loop (e.g., scrum meetings).
16	Our game engine allows rapid prototyping of new levels, scenarios, and NPCs/behaviour.
RQ4: How has game development evolved in the last couple of years?	
17	Today our company uses more 3rd party modules than 3 years ago.
18	It is easier to develop games today than it was 5 years ago.
19	Middleware is more important to our company today than 3 years ago.
20	Game development is more like ordinary software development today than 5 years ago.

After receiving the questionnaire responses from part one, a follow-up survey with eight open-ended questions is sent to six subjects; these individuals had participated in the first questionnaire and indicated they would provide more detailed answers. This part of the study has been conducted on the web only using SurveyMonkey. Summaries of the results are reported by the authors and are organized around three areas: the future of game engines; how the creative team affects the software architecture; and how companies are reasoning and making decisions on implementing changes. The respondents describe the future of game engines with four key quality attributes: multiplatform, quality of the features provided, simplicity of use, and completeness with respect to its integration into a diverse tool suite. The creative team indirectly affects the software architecture through requests made to the technical team; the main areas affected are related to how tools interact with the game. The respondents strongly favour the use of integrated feature-based teams and rapid prototyping to enable the interactions among the technical and creative team members. With respect to managing changes, a two-step process involving the assessment of the change in terms of the gameplay experience and the cost is revealed as a common pattern. In addition, the responses indicate the management, technical, and creative teams all providing input to the decision-making process for making changes; ultimately the management team makes the decision.

1.5   SUMMARY

This chapter introduces a collection of recent research papers that provide on software engineering perspectives on computer game development. It begins with a bird's eye view of game development as an interdisciplinary problem. It draws upon the arts and humanities, behavioural sciences, business, engineering, physical sciences, and mathematics. In addition, serious games can be developed for any domain. A brief history of computer games is presented, which is organized into two main categories: early research environment games and games for popular cultures. This followed by a snapshot of recent peer-reviewed publications focused on interdisciplinary work in games and software engineering. The nature of game development incurs significant complexity, which may, at least in part, be addressed by software engineering techniques. The following chapters present the core of this book, which is followed by a brief outlook on the future of research in computer games and software engineering.

REFERENCES

[1] Abbadi, M. et al. (2015) *Casanova: A Simple, High-Performance Language for Game Development.* Vol. 9090. [Online]. Cham: Springer International Publishing.

[2] Abuzuraiq, A. M. et al. (2019) '*Taksim: A Constrained Graph Partitioning Framework for Procedural Content Generation*'. In *2019 IEEE Conference on Games (CoG)*. [Online]. August 2019 IEEE. pp. 1–8.

[3] Ackerman, D. 2016 *The Tetris Effect: The Game that Hypnotized the World*, PublicAffairs.

[4] Åkesson, J., Nilsson, S., Krüger, J., & Berger, T. (2019). *Migrating the Android Apo-Games into an Annotation-Based Software Product Line.* In *Proceedings of the 23rd International Systems and Software Product Line Conference - Volume A (SPLC '19).* New York, NY, USA: Association for Computing Machinery, 103–107. doi: 10.1145/3336294.3342362

[5] Aleem, S., Capretz, L. F., & Ahmed, F. (2016). Critical success factors to improve the game development process from a developer's perspective. *Journal of Computer Science and Technology, 31*(5), 925–950.

[6] Aleem, S., Capretz, L. F., & Ahmed, F. (2016). Game development software engineering process life cycle: A systematic review. *Journal of Software Engineering Research and Development, 4*(1), 6.

[7] Allison, F., Carter, M., Gibbs, M., & Smith, W. (2018). *Design patterns for voice interaction in games.* In *Proceedings of the 2018 Annual Symposium on Computer-Human Interaction in Play (CHI PLAY 18).* Association for Computing Machinery, New York, NY, USA, 5–17. DOI:10.1145/3242671.3242712

[8] Ammons, B., & Bansal, S. K. (2017). Scrumify: A software game to introduce Agile Software development methods. *Journal of Engineering Education Transformations.* doi: 10.16920/jeet/2017/v0i0/111752

[9] Arias J., Marczak R., & Desainte-Catherine M. (2019) Timed automata for video games and interaction. In: Lee N. (eds) *Encyclopedia of Computer Graphics and Games.* Springer, Cham. doi: 10.1007/978-3-319-08234-9_298-1

[10] Aydan, U., Yilmaz, M., Clarke, P. M., & O'Connor, R. V. (2017). Teaching ISO/IEC 12207 software lifecycle processes: A serious game approach. *Computer Standards & Interfaces, 54*, 129–138.

[11] Baars, S., & Meester, S. (2019, May). *CodeArena: Inspecting and improving code quality metrics using minecraft.* In *2019 IEEE/ACM International Conference on Technical Debt (TechDebt)* (pp. 68–70). IEEE.

[12] Baldwin, A., Dahlskog, S., Font, J.M., & Holmberg, J. (2017). Towards pattern-based mixed-initiative dungeon generation. In *Proceedings of the 12th International Conference on the Foundations of Digital Games (FDG'17).* New York, NY, USA: Association for Computing Machinery, Article 74, 1–10. doi: 10.1145/3102071.3110572

[13] Barnard, J., Huisman, M., & Drevin, G. R. (2018). The development of a systems development methodology for location-based games *Computers in Entertainments, 16* (3), Article 1 (September 2018), 47. doi:10.1145/3236492

[14] Bartel, A. & Hagel, G. (2016, April). *Gamifying the learning of design patterns in software engineering education.* In *2016 IEEE Global Engineering Education Conference (EDUCON)* (pp. 74–79). IEEE.

[15] Baumann, A. (2020). *Teaching software engineering methods with agile games.* In *Proceedings of the 2020 IEEE Global Engineering Education Conference (EDUCON),* Porto, Portugal, pp. 1550–1553, doi: 10.1109/EDUCON45650.2020.9125129.

[16] Bell, J., Cooper, K., Kaiser, G., & Sheth, S. 2012. *Proceedings of the Second International Workshop on Games and Software Engineering: Realizing User Engagement with Game Engineering Techniques, GAS,* Zurich, Switzerland, June 9, 2012. IEEE/ACM 2012, ISBN 978-1-4673-1768-9

[17] Bernhaupt, R. (2015). User experience evaluation methods in the games development life cycle. In *Game User Experience Evaluation* (pp. 1–8). Cham: Springer.

[18] Birk, M. V., Lürig, C., & Mandryk, R. L. (2015). *A metric for automatically flagging problem levels in games from prototype walkthrough data ACADEMICMINDTREK 2015 - Proceedings of the 19th International Academic Mindtrek Conference,* pp. 33–40.

[19] Bitzer, D., Braunfeld, P., & Lichtenberger, W. (1961). PLATO: An automatic teaching device. *IRE Transactions on Education, 4*(4), 157–161.

[20] Booch, G., "The history of software engineering." In *IEEE Software,* vol. 35, no. 5, pp. 108–114, September/October 2018, doi: 10.1109/MS.2018.3571234.

[21] Broy, M. "Yesterday, today, and tomorrow: 50 years of software engineering." In *IEEE Software,* vol. 35, no. 5, pp. 38–43, September/October 2018, doi: 10.1109/MS.2018.290111138.

[22] Calderón, A., Ruiz, M., & O'Connor, R. V. (2017, September). *ProDecAdmin: A game scenario design tool for software project management training*. In *European Conference on Software Process Improvement*, Cham. pp. 241–248. Springer.

[23] Callele, D., Dueck, P., Wnuk, K., & Hynninen, P. (2015). *Experience requirements in video games definition and testability*. In *IEEE 23rd International Requirements Engineering Conference (RE)*, Ottawa, ON, 2015, pp. 324–333, doi: 10.1109/RE.2015.7320449.

[24] Campos, J. & Rieder, R. (2019). *Procedural Content Generation using Artificial Intelligence for Unique Virtual Reality Game Experiences*. In *2019 21st Symposium on Virtual and Augmented Reality (SVR)*, Rio de Janeiro, Brazil. pp. 147–151.

[25] Canossa, A., Badler, J. B., El-Nasr, M. S., & Anderson, E. (2016). Eliciting emotions in design of games-a theory driven approach. In *EMPIRE@ RecSys*. Boston, MA, USA. pp. 34–42.

[26] Capasso-Ballesteros, I. & De la Rosa-Rosero, F. (2020). Semi-automatic Construction of Video Game Design Prototypes with MaruGen. *Revista Facultad de Ingeniería Universidad de Antioquia*. (99), 9–20.

[27] Charleer, S., Verbert, K., Gutiérrez, F., & Gerling, K. (2018). *Towards an open standard for gameplay metrics CHI PLAY 2018 - Proceedings of the 2018 Annual Symposium on Computer-Human Interaction in Play Companion Extended Abstracts*, New York, NY, USA. pp. 399–406.

[28] Clegg, B. S., Rojas, J. M., &Fraser, G. (2017, May). *Teaching software testing concepts using a mutation testing game*. In *2017 IEEE/ACM 39th International Conference on Software Engineering: Software Engineering Education and Training Track (ICSE-SEET)*, Buenos Aires, Argentina. pp. 33–36.

[29] Cooper, K. (2016). *Proceedings of the 5th International Workshop on Games and Software Engineering, GAS*, Austin, Texas, USA, May 16, 2016. ACM, ISBN 978-1-4503-4160-8

[30] Cooper, K., Scacchi, W., & Wang, A.-I. 2013. *Proceedings of the 3rd International Workshop on Games and Software Engineering: Engineering Computer Games to Enable Positive, Progressive Change, GAS*, May 18, 2013. IEEE Computer Society, San Francisco, CA, USA, ISBN 978-1-4673-6263-4

[31] Cooper, K. & Scacchi, W. (Eds.) 2015. *Computer Games and Software Engineering*, CRC Press, Taylor & Francis Group, Boca Raton, Florida.

[32] Dalpiaz, F. & Cooper, K. (2020). Games for requirements engineers: Analysis and directions. In *IEEE Software*, vol. 37, no. 1, pp. 50–59, Jan.-Feb. 2020, doi: 10.1109/MS.2018.227105450.

[33] Daneva, M. (2017) Striving for balance: A look at gameplay requirements of massively multiplayer online role-playing games. *The Journal of Systems and Software*, 134. 54–75.

[34] De Lope, R. P., & Medina-Medina, N. (2016). *Using UML to model educational games*. In *2016 8th International Conference on Games and Virtual Worlds for Serious Applications (VS-GAMES)*, Barcelona, Spain. pp. 1–4.

[35] Debbiche, J., Lignell, O., Krüger, J., & Berger, T. (2019). *Migrating Java-based apogames into a composition-based software product line*. In *Proceedings of the 23rd International Systems and Software Product Line Conference - Volume A (SPLC'19)*. *Association for Computing Machinery*, New York, NY, USA, 98–102. doi: 10.1145/3336294.3342361

[36] Delen, M., Dalpiaz, F., & Cooper, K. (2019, September). *BakeRE: A Serious Educational Game on the Specification and Analysis of User Stories*. In *2019 IEEE 27th International Requirements Engineering Conference (RE)*, Jeju, Korea (South). pp. 369–374.

[37] do Prado, E. & Lucredio, D. (2015), *A Flexible Model-Driven Game Development Approach, 2015 IX Brazilian Symposium on Components, Architectures and Reuse Software*, Belo Horizonte, pp. 130–139, doi: 10.1109/SBCARS.2015.24.

[38] Donovan, T. 2010. *Replay: The History of Video Games*, Lewes, Great Britain: Yellow Ant.

[39] dos Santos, H. M., Durelli, V. H., Souza, M., Figueiredo, E., da Silva, L. T., & Durelli, R. S. (2019). *CleanGame: Gamifying the identification of code smells.* In *Proceedings of the XXXIII Brazilian Symposium on Software Engineering.* pp. 437–446.

[40] Edwards, B. (2016), The forgotten world of BBS door games. *PC Magazine*, January 14, 2016, https://www.pcmag.com/news/the-forgotten-world-of-bbs-door-games

[41] Emmerich, K. & Masuch, M. (2017). *The impact of game patterns on player experience and social interaction in Co-located multiplayer games.* In *Proceedings of the Annual Symposium on Computer-Human Interaction in Play (CHI PLAY'17). Association for Computing Machinery,* New York, NY, USA, pp. 411–422. doi: 10.1145/3116595.3116606

[42] Erdogmus, H., Medvidović, N., & Paulisch, F. (2018). 50 years of software engineering. In *IEEE Software*, vol. 35, no. 5, pp. 20–24, September/October 2018, doi: 10.1109/MS.2018.3571240.

[43] Fitzpatrick, A., Pullen, J., Raab, J., Grossman, L., Eadicicco, L., Peckham, M., & Vella, M. (2016), The best 50 video games of all time, *Time Magazine, 2016*, https://time.com/4458554/best-video-games-all-time/

[44] García, I., Pacheco, C., León, A., & Calvo-Manzano, J. A. (2020). A serious game for teaching the fundamentals of ISO/IEC/IEEE 29148 systems and software engineering–Lifecycle processes–Requirements engineering at undergraduate level. *Computer Standards & Interfaces, 67*, 103377.

[45] Haendler, T., & Neumann, G. (2019). *Serious refactoring games.* In *Proceedings of the 52nd Hawaii International Conference on System Sciences.*

[46] Hansen, D. 2016. *Game On!: Video Game History from Pong and Pac-Man to Mario, Minecraft, and More*, New York, New York: Macmillan Publishing Group.

[47] Harris, B. 2014. *Console Wars: Sega, Nintendo, and the Battle that Defined a Generation*, New York, NY: HarperCollins Publishing.

[48] Hernández Bécares, J. et al. (2017) An approach to automated videogame beta testing. *Entertainment Computing, 18*, 79–92.

[49] Iftikhar, S. et al. (2015) '*An automated model based testing approach for platform games.*' In *2015 ACM/IEEE 18th International Conference on Model Driven Engineering Languages and Systems (MODELS)*, Ottawa, Ontario, Canada. September 2015 IEEE. pp. 426–435.

[50] LAN MAN Standards Committee of the IEEE Computer Society Approved: 26 June 1997 IEEE Standards Board. (1997) IEEE Standard for Wireless LAN Medium Access Control (MAC) and Physical Layer (PHY) specifications. *IEEE Std 802.11-1997*, 1–445. doi: 10.1109/IEEESTD.1997.85951.

[51] IEEE Standards for Local Area Networks: Carrier Sense Multiple Access With Collision Detection (CSMA/CD). (1985). Access method and physical layer specifications. In *ANSI/IEEE Std 802.3-1985*, doi: 10.1109/IEEESTD.1985.82837.

[52] Internet Activities Board. (1988). *RFC 1083 Official Protocol Standards.* Available at: https://tools.ietf.org/html/rfc1083

[53] INCOSE Systems Engineering Handbook A Guide for System Life Cycle Processes and Activities (2015), 4th Edition, Hoboken, New Jersey: John Wiley & Sons.

[54] Ismail, N. & Lokman, A. (2020). *Kansei engineering implementation in web-based systems: A review study.* In Shoji, H. et al. (eds) *Proceedings of the 8th International Conference on Kansei Engineering and Emotion Research. KEER 2020*, Singapore: Springer. pp. 66–76.

[55] ISO/IEC/IEEE International Standard. 2015. Systems and software engineering: System life cycle processes. In *ISO/IEC/IEEE* 15288 1st edition, 1–118, 15 May 2015, doi: 10.1109/IEEESTD.2015.7106435.

[56] Junaidi, J., Anwar, N., Safrizal, W.H.L.H.S., & Hashimoto, K. (2018). Perfecting a video game with game metrics. *Telkomnika (Telecommunication Computing Electronics and Control)*, *16*(3), 1324–1331.

[57] Kang, S. J., & Kim, S. K. (2015). Automated spatio-temporal analysis techniques for game environment. *Multimedia Tools and Applications*, *74*(16), 6323–6329.

[58] Karavolos, D., Liapis, A., & Yannakakis, G. (2017). *Learning the patterns of balance in a multi-player shooter game.* In *Proceedings of the 12th International Conference on the Foundations of Digital Games (FDG'17). Association for Computing Machinery*, New York, NY, USA, Article 70, pp. 1–10. DOI:10.1145/3102071.3110568

[59] Kasurinen, J., Palacin-Silva, M., & Vanhala, E. (2017). *What concerns game developers? a study on game development processes, sustainability and metrics.* In *Proceedings of the 8th Workshop on Emerging Trends in Software Metrics (WETSoM'17). IEEE Press, pp. 15–21.

[60] Kim, W. H. (2016) Efficient acceptance testing framework for interactive computer game applications. *International Journal of Applied Engineering*, *11*(3), pp. 1815–1819.

[61] Kristiadi, D. P., Sudarto, F., Sugiarto, D., Sambera, R., Warnars, H. L. H. S., & Hashimoto, K. (2019). *Game Development with Scrum methodology.* In *2019 International Congress on Applied Information Technology (AIT).* pp. 1–6.

[62] Levey, S. 2010. *Hackers: Heroes of the Computer Revolution - 25th Anniversary Edition*, O'Reilly Media.

[63] Liszio, S., & Masuch, M. (2016). Lost in *Open Worlds: Design Patterns for Player Navigation in Virtual Reality Games.* In *Proceedings of the 13th International Conference on Advances in Computer Entertainment Technology (ACE'16). Association for Computing Machinery*, New York, NY, USA, Article 7, pp. 1–7. DOI:10.1145/3001773.3001794.

[64] Lui, R. W. C. , Geng, S., & Law, K. M. Y. (2017). *Project management SPOC with animation.* In *Proceedings on 2017 IEEE 6th International Conference on Teaching, Assessment, and Learning for Engineering (TALE)*, Hong Kong, pp. 29–34, doi: 10.1109/TALE.2017.8252299.

[65] Liu, S. et al. (2019) '*Automatic generation of tower defense levels using PCG*'. In *Proceedings of the 14th International Conference on the Foundations of Digital Games.* [Online]. 2019 ACM. pp. 1–9.

[66] Loh, C. S., Li, I.-H., & Sheng, Y. (2016). Comparison of similarity measures to differentiate players' actions and decision-making profiles in serious games analytics. *Computers in Human Behavior*, *64*, 562–574.

[67] Matallaoui, A., Herzig, P., & Zarnekow, R. (2015, January). *Model-driven serious game development integration of the gamification modeling language gaml with unity.* In *2015 48th Hawaii International Conference on System Sciences* pp. 643–651.

[68] Marin, C., Chover, M., & Sotoca, J. M. (2019). *Prototyping a game engine architecture as a multi-agent system.* In *2019 International Conference in Central Europe on Computer Graphics, Visualization and Computer Vision*, pp. 27–34.

[69] Maxim, B. R., Kaur, R., Apzynski, C., Edwards, D., & Evans, E. (2016, October). *An agile software engineering process improvement game.* In *2016 IEEE Frontiers in education Conference (FIE).* pp. 1–4.

[70] Meftah, C. et al. (2019) Mobile serious game design using user experience: Modeling of software product line variability. *International Journal of Emerging Technologies in Learning*. [Online] 14(23), pp. 55–66.

[71] Milgram, P., Takemura, H., Utsumi, A., & Kishino, F. (1994). *"Augmented Reality: A class of displays on the reality-virtuality continuum."* In *Proceedings of Telemanipulator and Telepresence Technologies*. pp. 2351–2354.

[72] Miljanovic, M. A., & Bradbury, J. S. (2017 August). *Robobug: A serious game for learning debugging techniques*. In *Proceedings of the 2017 ACM Conference on International Computing Education Research*. pp. 93–100.

[73] Mimura, Y., Tsuchiya, T., Moriyama, K., Murata, K., & Takasuka, S. (2020, July). *UX design for mobile application of E-commerce site by using Kansei interface*. In *International Conference on Applied Human Factors and Ergonomics*. pp. 641–647.

[74] Mizutani, W. & Kon, F. (2020). *'Unlimited rulebook: A reference architecture for economy mechanics in digital games.'* In *2020 IEEE International Conference on Software Architecture (ICSA)*. [Online]. March 2020 IEEE. pp. 58–68.

[75] Molléri, J. S., Gonzalez-Huerta, J., & Henningsson, K. (2018). *A legacy game for project management in software engineering courses*. In *Proceedings of the 3rd European Conference of Software Engineering Education*. pp. 72–76.

[76] Montenegro, C. H., Astudillo, H., &Álvarez, M. C. G. (2017, September). *ATAM-RPG: A role-playing game to teach architecture trade-off analysis method (ATAM)*. In *2017 XLIII Latin American Computer Conference (CLEI)*. pp. 1–9.

[77] Morisaki, S., Kasai, N., Kanamori, K., & Yamamoto, S. (2019) *Detecting source code hotspot in games software using call flow analysis*. In *20th IEEE/ACIS International Conference on Software Engineering, Artificial Intelligence, Networking and Parallel/ Distributed Computing (SNPD)*, Toyama, Japan, 2019, pp. 484–489, doi: 10.1109/ SNPD.2019.8935822.

[78] Nagamachi, M. (Editor) 2017 *Kansei/Affective Engineering*, Boca Raton, Florida: CRC Press.

[79] Nalepa, G. J., Gizycka, B., Kutt, K., & Argasinski, J. K. (2017). *Affective Design Patterns in Computer Games: Scrollrunner Case Study*. In *FedCSIS (Communication Papers)*. pp. 345–352.

[80] Naur, P. & Randell, B. Highlights (1968) *Software Engineering: Report on A Conference Sponsored by the NATO Science Committee*, Garmisch, Germany, 7th to 11th October 1968, NATOs http://homepages.cs.ncl.ac.uk/brian.randell/NATO/index.html.

[81] O'Shea, Z. & Freeman, J. (2019). *Game design frameworks: Where do we start?* In *Proceedings of the 14th International Conference on the Foundations of Digital Games (FDG '19). Association for Computing Machinery*, New York, NY, USA, Article 25, pp. 1–10. doi:10.1145/3337722.3337753

[82] Paduraru, C. and Paduraru, M. (2019). *'Automatic difficulty management and testing in games using a framework based on behavior trees and genetic algorithms.'*. In *24th International Conference on Engineering of Complex Computer Systems (ICECCS)*. pp. 170–179.

[83] Paschali, E., Ampatzoglou, A., Escourrou, R., Chatzigeorgiou, A., & Stamelos, I. (2020). *A metric suite for evaluating interactive scenarios in video games: An empirical validation*. In *Proceedings of the 35th Annual ACM Symposium on Applied Computing (SAC'20). Association for Computing Machinery*, New York, NY, USA, pp. 1614–1623. DOI:10.1145/3341105.3373985

[84] Perez-Medina, J.-L. et al. (2019) ePHoRt: Towards a reference architecture for tele-rehabilitation systems. *IEEE Access: Practical Innovations, Open Solutions*. pp. 797159–797176.

[85] Peters, D., Calvo, R. A., & Ryan, R. M. (2018). Designing for motivation, engagement and wellbeing in digital experience. *Frontiers in Psychology, 9*, 797.

[86] Politowski, C., Petrillo, F., & Guéhéneuc, Y. G. (2020, June). *Improving engagement assessment in gameplay testing sessions using IoT sensors.* In *Proceedings of the IEEE/ACM 42nd International Conference on Software Engineering Workshops.* pp. 655–659.

[87] Prasetya, W., et al. (2019, May). *Having fun in learning formal specifications.* In *2019 IEEE/ACM 41st International Conference on Software Engineering: Software Engineering Education and Training (ICSE-SEET).* pp. 192–196.

[88] Pyae, A., & Potter, L. E. (2016). *A player engagement model for an augmented reality game: A case of Pokémon go.* In *Proceedings of the 28th Australian Conference on Computer-Human Interaction.* pp. 11–15.

[89] Quinones, J. & Fernandez-Leiva, A. (2020) XML-based video game description language. *IEEE Access: Practical Innovations, Open Solutions.* pp. 84679–84692.

[90] Sandhu, A. & McCoy, J. (2019). *A framework for integrating architectural design patterns into PCG.* In *Proceedings of the 14th International Conference on the Foundations of Digital Games (FDG'19). Association for Computing Machinery,* New York, NY, USA, Article 49, pp. 1–5. DOI:10.1145/3337722.3341839

[91] Scacchi, W. & Whitehead, J. (2015) In *Proceedings of the 4th IEEE/ACM International Workshop on Games and Software Engineering, GAS 2015,* Florence, Italy, May 18, 2015. IEEE Computer Society 2015, ISBN 978-1-4673-7046-2

[92] Scacchi, W. & Cooper, K. (2015). *Research Challenges at the Intersection of Computer Games and Software Engineering.* In *Proceedings of the 10th International Conference on the Foundations of Digital Games, FDG 2015,* Pacific Grove, CA, USA, June 22–25, 2015. https://dblp.org/rec/bib/conf/fdg/ScacchiC15

[93] Schatten, M. et al. (2017). *Towards an agent-based automated testing environment for massively multi-player role playing games.* In *2017 40th International Convention on Information and Communication Technology, Electronics and Microelectronics (MIPRO).* pp. 1149–1154.

[94] Time Magazine cover article (1982). http://content.time.com/time/covers/0,16641, 19820118,00.html January 18, 1982, Vol. 119, No. 3.

[95] Shi, W., Kaneko, K., Ma, C., & Okada, Y. (2019). A framework for automatically generating quiz-type serious games based on linked data. *International Journal of Information and Education Technology, 9*(4), pp. 250–256.

[96] Sierra, M., Pabón, M., Rincón, L., Navarro-Newball, A., & Linares, D. (2019). *A Comparative Analysis of Game Engines to Develop Core Assets for a Software Product Line of Mini-Games.* In *International Conference on Software and Systems Reuse.* pp. 64–74.

[97] Söbke, H. & Streicher, A. (2016) Serious games architectures and engines. In Dörner R., Göbel S., Kickmeier-Rust M., Masuch M., Zweig K. (eds.) *Entertainment Computing and Serious Games.* Lecture Notes in Computer Science, vol 9970. Cham: Springer. doi: 10.1007/978-3-319-46152-6_7

[98] Stahlke, S. et al. (2019) '*Artificial playfulness*'. In *Extended Abstracts of the 2019 CHI Conference on Human Factors in Computing Systems.* pp. 6984–6986.

[99] Su, Y. Game Analytics Research: Status and Trends (2020) *Lecture Notes on Data Engineering and Communications Technologies*, vol. 41, pp. 572–589.

[100] Summerville, A., Snodgrass, S., Guzdial, M., Holmgård, C., Hoover, A. K., Isaksen, A., & Togelius, J. (2018). Procedural content generation via machine learning (PCGML). *IEEE Transactions on Games, 10*(3), pp. 257–270.

[101] Taborda, J., Arango-López, J., Collazos, C., Vela, F., & Moreira, F. (2019) Effectiveness and fun metrics in a pervasive game experience: A systematic literature review. *Advances in Intelligent Systems and Computing*, 932, pp. 184–194.

[102] Vakaliuk, T., Kontsedailo, V. V., Antoniuk, D. S., Korotun, O. V., Mintii, I. S., & Pikilnyak, A. V. (2019). *Using game simulator Software Inc in the Software Engineering education*. In *Proceedings of the 2nd International Workshop on Augmented Reality in Education*, Kryvyi Rih, Ukraine, March 22, 2019, No. 2547, pp. 66–80.

[103] Valente, L. et al. (2017) Mapping quality requirements for pervasive mobile games. *Requirements Engineering*, 22 (1), pp. 137–165.

[104] Varvaressos, S. et al. (2017) Automated bug finding in video games. *Computers in Entertainment: CIE*, 15 (1), pp. 1–28.

[105] Vegt, W., Bahreini, K., Nyamsuren, E., & Westera, W. (2019). Toward reusable game technologies: Assessing the usability of the RAGE component-based architecture framework. *EAI Endorsed Transactions on Serious Games*, 5(17). doi: 10.4108/eai.11-7-2019.159527

[106] Walk, W., Görlich, D., & Barrett, M. (2017). Design, dynamics, experience (DDE): An advancement of the MDA framework for game design. In *Game Dynamics*. pp. 27–45.

[107] Wang, Y., Ijaz, K., Yuan, D., & Calvo, R. (2020). VR-Rides: An object-oriented application framework for immersive virtual reality exergames, *Software: Practice and Experience*, 50 (7), pp. 1305–1324.

[108] WAP Forum. June 1999. *Wireless Application Protocol*, WAP White Paper, Mountain View, California.

[109] Whitehead, J. & Lewis, C. (2011) *Workshop on games and software engineering (GAS 2011)*. In *Proceedings of the 33rd International Conference on Software Engineering (ICSE '11). Association for Computing Machinery*, New York, NY, USA, 1194–1195. doi:10.1145/1985793.1986042

[110] Wolf, M. 2007. *The Video Game Explosion*. Greenwood, Westport, CT.

[111] Zahari, A. S., Ab Rahim, L., Nurhadi, N. A., & Aslam, M. A. (2020) Domain-specific modelling language for adventure educational games and flow theory. *International Journal onn Advanced Science Engineering Information Technology*, *10*(3), pp. 999–1007.

[112] Zheng, Y. et al. (2019) '*Wuji: Automatic online combat game testing using evolutionary deep reinforcement learning.*' In *2019 34th IEEE/ACM International Conference on Automated Software Engineering (ASE)*. [Online]. November 2019 IEEE. pp. 772–784.

[113] Zhu, M., Wang, A. I., & Trætteberg, H. (2016, November). *Engine-Cooperative Game Modeling (ECGM) Bridge Model-Driven Game Development and Game Engine Toolchains*. In *Proceedings of the 13th International Conference on Advances in Computer Entertainment Technology*. pp. 1–10.

Section I

Emerging Research on Serious Games for Software Engineering Education

2 Case Studies and Practices in Local Game Jam Software Development Organization
A Software Engineering Perspective

Walt Scacchi
University of California, Irvine

CONTENTS

2.1   INTRODUCTION

Many students and independent game developers participate in computer game development competitions, hackathons [41], or game jams [12, 17, 22, 23, 29, 34, 42]. These team-based game making efforts typically focus on clean-sheet production of a playable game usually in a limited time frame, like 24–96 hours though shorter and longer competitions have been engaged. Sometimes these jams have external for-profit or non-profit sponsors, who in turn may offer financial or technology product rewards to motivate participants to excel. Other times, jams offer no tangible rewards, but instead focus on going "for the win," résumé building, demonstrating game development competency, and earning local geek status and shared learning experience as the desired outcome. In any case, game jams offer the potential to serve as innovation factories that can rapidly prototype many games in a short period of time [17, 21].

Game jams vary in geographic scope, from *global* game jams to regional or venue-specific (hereafter, *local*) game making events. This paper focuses attention on local game jams and game creation efforts, with an eye on examining organizational practices and possibilities in such game development activities. Local game jams, game development competitions, and game making events are those where game developers commonly know one another across teams, and celebrate the *sturm und drang* of their mutual game development successes and problems together. As such, such locality more readily embraces convivial as well as competitive game development.

An interesting set of research potentials arise associated with game jams, perhaps most relevant to empirical studies of alternative computer game software engineering (CGSE) processes, practices, methods, or tools used. For example, within local intramural game jams, it may be possible to structure and balance the game development teams by team size, game developer roles, and SE skill level from students at hand. Students can indicate their skill level and developer role preferences, then have participants randomly assigned to teams in ways that balance team size, role, and skill level. This can mitigate against pre-formed teams with established collaborators, high skill distribution, and relatively mature game development capabilities. How might such teamwork structures affect how games are made, or the quality of the game products that are produced? Such questions require empirical study, and game jams may provide the venues for such studies to be conducted.

Short-duration jams mitigate against the consequences of team failure or participant drop out, and instead make these events more of a CGSE learning experience. In this way, in addition to focusing on game production, the overall game jam can serve as a "field site" where selected CG design, SE processes, and technologies [e.g., 16, 17, 20, 29, 30, 31] can be comparatively investigated, following empirical SE approaches introduced more than 25 years ago [2, 3]. Such field sites can allow for informal or systematic empirical study of teams using a new game software development kit (SDK) for indie game development [9, 30], or development process/ technique (e.g., SCRUM, agile development [42], or game modding [27, 28]) versus those who do not; or those who produce traditional SE documents (requirements specifications, architectural designs, test plans) and follow SE processes for their game [42] versus those who just focus on game design [32] or "minimum viable product" (MVP) methods. Intramural game jams so structured may therefore be well-suited for longer durations (e.g., from days to weeks), though ultimately this is a game jam design choice.

Game making competitions may stress short duration and co-location, along with targeted game production on a topic that is announced at the beginning of the competition. Inter-mural game jams, those open to teams from different schools, may not be so readily structured or balanced at little cost, but instead may address other CGSE questions that better match their natural field organization, geographic distribution, and project heterogeneity. However, there is no inherent requirement that game development competitions must be of short duration, as it is possible to create or find examples of those extending for years.

More generally, game jams offer the opportunity to organize, design, and conduct empirical studies in CGSE that can inform both new game design practices or processes, as well as new SE practices and technologies [7, 42]. Some game SDK vendors have sponsored game jams that focus on participating team's usage of specific proprietary products or platforms (e.g., Epic Games' *Make Something Unreal* and Microsoft's *Imagine Cup: Game Design*). These competitions can be used to address CGSE research questions in ways underutilized in SE research, and thus highlight similarities and differences between traditional approaches to computer game design [32] and software engineering [16, 31]. Ultimately, this can mean that game jam-focused SE can be viewed as a competitive team-based sport activity that can be fun for students, as well as structured to support careful empirical study [14, 29, 31], rather than SE being a business endeavor to produce application systems hosted on back-end infrastructures accompanied by voluminous documents that few will ever read.

Finally, it is also possible to recognize new, under-explored ways and means for organizing game jams for further empirical study. For example, local computer game jams may be organized and designed as a kind of *meta-game*—a game about (making) games. Such game making events can be organized as a game, whose form resembles a game-based course, where student participants earn points and rewards while leveling up to a higher level of academic proficiency [33]. Such jams may take organizational forms whose goal is to structure the outcomes (i.e., the games produced) to embody certain functional features or the CGSE production processes to reward accumulative levels of progress achieved or skills mastered by different teams ("leveling up"), rather than just leading to winning and losing teams. Alternatively, game jams may be both experimentally modeled and studied as teamwork structured, CGSE role-playing games [18]. Last, game jams may focus on exploring cross-cultural or global CGSE development processes, whereby teams involve participants who collaborate across time, space, or cultural distance, via global CGSE processes and practices [1].

With these alternative forms for organizing game making events, it is now appropriate to identify and briefly describe different kinds of local game jams that we have been able to put into practice and study.

2.2   ORGANIZATIONAL FORMS FOR LOCAL GAME JAMS AND RELATED GAME CREATION EVENTS

Local game jams may be located in academic settings of different kinds. This may be especially important to academic scholars in game design or game studies, who seek innovative ways and means for conducting some form of empirical or experimental approaches to game development. Much like team sports in schools, game development competitions can be organized as *intramural* (within school) and *inter-mural* (across schools). These team-based game development efforts can be undertaken in ways that complement formal CGSE (or just SE) educational principles and practices [5, 6, 29, 34, 40]. Sub-types of intramural and inter-mural game jams can be identified, for example, when external sponsors are involved and tangible rewards are offered as incentives to motivate game jam participants, in contrast to jams where there are no external sponsors or tangible rewards so that game developers focus on symbolic rewards and convivial learning experiences as their motivation to participate. Such variations allow for examination of whether and how external versus internal motivations affect the resulting games, local game development practices, teamwork, and the satisfaction of overall participant experience [22, 23].

Capstone project courses are growing in popularity in computer game design, software engineering, or computer science degree programs. These projects are organized and managed by faculty who determine constraints on matters like team composition, choice of game SDK, or game deployment platform (e.g., games for Android smartphones, web browsers, or PCs). Alternatively, faculty may allow their students to make some/all of these choices. The faculty often serve as coaches that mediate and motivate student teams to be creative and collaborative, yet assure their need to develop and deliver a complete project, along with required documentation, demonstration, and final presentation. Sometimes these project courses benefit from external or non-academic project sponsors who see capstone project courses as a low-cost means for prototyping new game concepts, utilizing emerging technologies, or making serious games targeted to some appropriate application problem domain.

Another variation of the capstone project can be seen in tracing back the roots of jams to earlier exemplars in (non-game) domains like "Anijams" introduced and popularized for years within the film animation production community (not to be confused with *Ani-Jams* which are more recent community events for anime fans). Legendary film animator Marv Newland and his International Rocketship Ltd. production company created a collaborative animated film making project where 22 animators in different locations each created a short-animated film segment, given only the first and last key frame (graphic image) that they would then create the in-between frame sequences that would be included in the final composite film [19]. This collaborative development project effectively employed a common baseline visual outline that served as an animation storytelling architecture via the sequence of key frames. The project was envisioned to accommodate the independent, parallel creation of in-between animation sequences. A game-oriented repurposing of this approach might take the form of a multi-team game development project where the game segments conform to a common software architecture design and run-time platform environment [39]. These semi-autonomous games could then be treated as modular architectural plug-ins, can interoperate to exchange gameplay data/content assets across game modules.

Game development workshops are another kind of game making event that can explore or structure the development of game products and artifacts. Workshops can also experiment with and determine the practical efficacy of different tool/SDK selections, as well as the enactment of CGSE processes, project team forms, and work practices. Again, these workshops may be intramural or inter-mural, though it is easier to see them as open in some way to participants who are not specifically seeking academic coursework credit, but more of an advanced or focused game development experience. Furthermore, such workshops may be externally sponsored and may invite international participants, perhaps in ways that resemble the once-popular NATO Summer School Workshops that attract graduate or post-doctoral students in local, scientific, or policy problem-solving programs.

Intensive workshops rely on the organizers to provide intellectual leadership and technical guidance for the participants. In practical terms, a game development workshop may differ from an intramural game jam or capstone project through administrative and management choices. For example, a game development workshop may involve the engagement and direction of multiple project leaders or subject-matter experts who serve to formulate, plan, and guide those activities engaged by workshop participants. Workshops may have an explicit curriculum and process plans that articulate a schedule of activities that correspond to the delivery and engagement of participants with specific topics. A CGSE workshop may therefore have faculty or industry experts who lecture (perhaps using a "flipped class" format) on a topic like a selected game software architecture and run-time environment that is conceived to demonstrate and embody SE concepts like mini-games as architectural plug-ins; extension mechanisms that support multiple target platforms and modding via the use of multiple databases; and use of specified interfaces (APIs) to online banking/commerce services for encrypted user-specific transactions. Addressing such issues is commonly beyond what can be done in short-duration game jams, or game making events where participant teams are open and ad hoc, such that game makers determine the design of everything in the game.

Game development showcase festivals may be organized as either intramural, inter-mural, or open to independent game developers (whether or not affiliated with a university, school, or game studio). Game showcase festivals are organized in ways similar to film festivals (e.g., Sundance, Tribeca, and Berlin), where game development processes, tools used, team structures, artifacts produced, budget, schedules, etc., are all non-issues in the festival, which instead focuses near-exclusive attention to the games as products (or online services). With a product-centered focus, game developers focus attention to winning awards or recognition, as well as possible publication, distribution, or investment deals from third parties (now including crowd-sourced funders). So game showcase festivals can marginalize the significance of game development practices, other than to telegraph that winning teams must somehow be creative and technically competent in game development, but with little/no knowledge of anything learned or experienced by the game developers or of game development.

2.2.1 OTHER VARIATIONS

Beyond the game jam types just identified, it is also possible to classify other recurring models of multi-game production competitions as game jam variations. For instance, game modding communities and portals routinely host contributed games/mods developed by teams, which are then played, reviewed, and ranked by other online game players. Examples of mod development competitions include the *Thief Modding Contest*, *Make Arma Not War*, and *Star Citizen Modding Competition*. Next, there are multiple, independent yet coordinated team research projects funded by external sponsors or government agencies, like the DARPA Crowdsourced Formal Verification initiative called *Verigames* [38] in which a number of research-grade university teams undertook sustained, multi-year efforts to produce, deploy, and assess games that embody different approaches to crowdsourced gameplay for verifying large software systems (e.g., the Linux Kernel). Last, there are also competitions that focus on game materiality, such as costumes and wearables as game controllers [35], and case modding. Examples of the latter include Nvidia's *Mod24*, a full day long case modding competition, and *Cooler Master* case modding competition. So there is no shortage of formats, platforms, and venues that address different configurations of game development competitions.

Any or all of the above categories can be classified as collective, participatory teams working in parallel to make games or game technologies. Most often, attention is directed to the products of game development efforts, principally the games produced. However, game jams can also focus attention to the comparative study of *game development practices*, collaborative game software *development teamwork processes*, evaluation of game development *artifacts* (game design versus run-time implementation versus game post-mortem), efficacy of *game development tools/SDKs employed*, or some combination of these socio-technical elements. Game competitions can also be extended to support other CGSE challenges like team-based game play-testing jams, or be aligned with game playing competitions, depending of the participants sought, and the audiences (or external sponsors) to be embraced.

With these different organizational forms for game making events, we now turn to describe a set of five field studies where we have observed multi-team game making events.

2.3   LOCAL GAME JAM AND GAME PRODUCTION FIELD STUDIES

Game development competitions can arise in diverse settings with different constraints and game development affordances. Five different kinds of game making efforts have been systematically observed as field studies in multi-team game development. These include (a) local intramural game jams hosted by a student-run game development club, just for the fun of the experience; (b) local intramural serious game jams with external sponsor and post-jam development contract to the overall winning team; (c) a regional inter-mural game showcase with teams from different schools, along with multi-school teams; (d) intramural game capstone project course for academic credit; and (e) an international multi-team game development workshop focused on producing game modules for incorporation within a common game software architecture. Each is described in turn, then comparatively analyzed to identify observations, lessons, and opportunities for how to organize and design game jams. Such results may facilitate playful game making learning experiences and potentially innovative games, as well as do so in ways that generate new, empirically substantiated game software engineering research findings.

2.3.1 INTRAMURAL GAME JAMS AT UCI VDGC

Video game developer clubs (VGDCs) are up and running at many colleges and universities. As a student-run venture, they can elect to host game jams as extracurricular activities that are non-academic (no faculty mentors, no course credit) and open to all students who voluntarily attend. The UCI VGDC has students from many academic majors, including those not directly connected to computer games (e.g., biological sciences), as well as students from off-campus groups (e.g., nearby high schools and technical schools).

Since 2009, the VGDC has organized and run game jams, commonly three times per year. As the VGDC annual membership fluctuates between 60–100+ students per year, the game jams also serve as a recurring, core social event for the club that focuses on student teams building games on short schedules (weekend or week long) on a single topic or theme (e.g., electricity, health, and friction) that is randomly selected at the beginning of the game jam. See Figure 2.1 for an example. Dozens of games have been developed and demonstrated across the jams, with 5–12 games presented at the end of each jam. The resulting games, as suggested by Figure 2.2, are demonstrated live before a public audience and panel of faculty judges. The live demo presentation includes a brief post-mortem, that highlights team-specific lessons learned. As Grossman [10] reports, compiled post-mortems reiterate common problems with team projects, such as running out of time, need to continually reduce

FIGURE 2.1 Online photo documentation from intramural game jam held at UCI in 2011.

FIGURE 2.2   Online video documentation that demonstrates the operation of a game produced in an intramural game jam at UCI.

game design scope [cf. 32], and a small number of team members underperforming or failing to perform as promised. The volunteer faculty judges evaluate the games on subjective criteria jointly identified with the VGDC (e.g., game graphic design, interesting use of sound/music, user experience, and efficacy of the post-mortem confessional). The judges are asked to provide overall rankings, as well as brief written feedback for the teams. The winning team receives hardy applause from the audience, and pats on the back, along with symbolic pride points and improved local reputation. The success and frequent recurrence of these local game jams as a fun but challenging way to rapidly prototype new games even caught the attention of local news media [11].

Over time, and in concert with student-voiced demands, the jam organization has evolved to forms where team members are chosen at random by role preference (programmers, artists, musicians, modelers, producers, writers) and balanced. This means teams have roughly the same number of team members and skill sets and do not necessarily have prior game development teamwork relationships. This helps to ameliorate that chance for established collaborators teaming up time and again as an uneven competitive advantage, since VGDC students prefer "friendly competitions" that stress challenges that are bounded and learning-oriented, rather than cutthroat, winner-take-all competitions. This is a recognition that most competitions produce few/one winner, but mostly produce "losers," which goes against the spirit of a learning environment, where gentle (and sometimes frequent) failure leads to improvement.

Student teams are free to choose the game development tools and techniques they want to use. So, teams may choose complex game SDKs like *Unity* or *Unreal Development Kit*, or something very generic like open source Java game development libraries or now deprecated *Microsoft XNA* libraries (which seem to reinforce development of 2D platformer games), as well as popular cloud-based software tools/services like Slack, Discord, GitHub, Steam, and others. In general, students have chosen not to utilize other popular game SDKs [30] like *Aurora* for Never Winter Nights, *GameMaker*, *Construct 2*, extensible virtual worlds like *Second Life*, or open-source game software approaches [25, 28], out of a lack of prior experience, lack of interest, or belief that these are not "professional" game development environments. Tool choice is generally decided by team programmers based on their prior experience, current preferences, or trust in declarations by reputable game developers communicated via online social media.

Teams also decide which game/software development artifacts to produce. Most common are game design documents, but also shared are persistent chat transcripts, online/in-game user tutorials, and game jam demo presentation slide decks. Finally, some teams find sufficient self-interest and enthusiastic play-testing responses from users that they elect to continue to develop the game after the jam, with the goal of publishing the result in an online game store like *Microsoft Xbox Live*. In contrast, student teams do not produce CGSE documents like explicit functional or non-functional requirements, nor systematic test and integration plan specifications [4]. Thus, it is unclear if this is a missed opportunity or just something the students find irrelevant to their game jam development efforts [31].

Last, VGDC students have stated their interest to prefer to participate in these local intramural game jams where they can know the other students developing games and participate in a local game making scene. This is in contrast to their seeking the same level of participation in events like the Global Game Jam. In previous years, VGDC students indicated they felt the GGJ was too remote and weakly engaged, and open to teams with independent game development "ringers" who may unbalance the game jam playing field competition, thus focused more attention to prize winning (and thus to producing mostly losing teams and games that are lost in large under-differentiated game submission repositories). Similarly, the UCI VGDC students have multiple game jams to elect to participate in, including those described below. Nonetheless, in 2015, the VGDC mobilized participation and game submissions for the GGJ, due in large part to the leadership and encouragement of a new UCI faculty member focused on computer games. More recent VGDC efforts at UCI are found on their online sites hosted by Google Sites, Facebook, LinkedIn, GitHub, and Itch.io, along with their Twitter and Discord channels. Beyond this, may other collegiate clubs that participate in local or regional game jams can be found via the Student Game Developer Alliance website.

2.3.2   VGDC Intramural Serious Game Jams

As the VGDC developed a reputation for engaging undergraduate students in independent game development outside of their coursework, outside industry, academic, and government partners have sought to sponsor game jams aligned with their institutional interests. In this regard, these outside groups want to sponsor a jam that produces serious games that address their interests. Often at times, these jams are envisioned to allow the external sponsor to reach out to students as way to encourage student innovators/entrepreneurs or as a form of job recruitment. These arrangements may bypass the engagement of the host school, their faculty, external grants

FIGURE 2.3   Screenshots from the *HeartRace* game initially produced for a UCI serious game jam to encourage healthy heart lifestyle choices. Support for this game's ongoing development was provided by the American Heart Association, Orange County Chapter.

development offices, and student placement services, but in general no major administrative problems or resistant academic politics seem to surface.

As an example, the local chapter of the American Heart Association approached the VGDC to sponsor a game jam whose game efforts would focus on the topic of "healthy hearts" and related healthy lifestyle choices. Six teams completed and presented their games after a week-long jam for review and evaluation by panel of judges from the AHA, local game industry, and UCI faculty. The winning team then received a cash prize, along with a 6-month contract to further develop the game for possible deployment and release under AHA sponsorship. See Figure 2.3 for example screenshots from this game.

2.3.3   INTER-MURAL GAME DEVELOPMENT SHOWCASE

Based on part from the successes and experiences of the intramural game jams at UCI, and the growing participation of students from other nearby trade schools, colleges, and universities, an effort was mounted to elevate these regional game jams into an inter-mural form. As a number of faculty, both local to UCI and nearby, were also active in the local chapter of the IEEE Computer Society (as well as the Independent Game Developers Association) that hosted a special interest group in Games (SIGG), and the local IEEE advocates were searching for new ways to enlist students into their profession (mostly populated by mature engineers), then a relationship with SIGG

FIGURE 2.4 Online website banner for the 2013 edition of IEEE GameSIG Intercollegiate Game Showcase held at UCI.

emerged to establish and host such an inter-mural event. See Figure 2.4 for example. However, as different schools have different levels of student interest and coursework in computer games (e.g., UCI has 4-year CS degree program with a dozen game focused courses, while other schools may offer only 1–2 courses in game design), the SIGG people decided to organize the game jam in a manner more like a game show-case (similar to IndieCade or film festivals) where development time or team size is not constrained, rather than as is common in a time-limited game jam. This means student teams would be unbalanced, could take as long as they wanted to make their game, engage whatever tools and techniques they found appropriate, and even be able to submit games that were projects in a capstone project course, or those submitted from other game jams unrelated to this competition and its sponsors.

The showcase requires that game software and content assets must also be pack-aged and posted on servers, for download and installation. Also, teams had to submit a 5-minute or less video of the game team and design pitch (present the game con-cept) and recordings of live play sessions, as seen in Figure 2.5. Numerous example game demo videos can be found on *YouTube* via a search for "IEEE gamesig" and "IEEE game sig." Game teams compete for recognition from game industry veterans, who select the best games and game demo/presentations, to determine the winners in different categories (e.g., best mobile game and best game overall), as suggested in Figure 2.6. The industry judges include executives and lead designers from large multimillion-dollar game studios, long-term independent game developers, or lead-ing game artists/musicians, all of whom are familiar and experienced with publishing successful, moneymaking games. The judges' final decisions then determine prize winners. Noteworthy here is that some of the overall game showcase winning game

FIGURE 2.5   Sample of game demo video deliverables associated with the 2018 edition of the IEEE GameSIG Intercollegiate Game Showcase.

FIGURE 2.6   Photo documentation from a 2015 inter-mural game showcase highlighting live game demos (upper left), a winning team (upper right), game project presentation, and local game industry participants from Blizzard Entertainment (lower left and right).

teams have gone on to receive external investment from either angel investors who attend the showcase and observe audience reactions/interest, or from crowdfunding sites (*Kickstarter, Indiegogo, Patreon*, and others). Such investments thus help to evolve and transform a student team game jam result or game project into a new venture. Again, the boundaries and outcomes of such inter-mural games showcase competitions merit further consideration and study.

As this form of game development competition is an inter-mural activity that engages students teams from multiple university or colleges, then it may be natural to ask if the competition can be formalized into something approaching an intercollegiate sport—in effect, treating game development as a team sport [29]. While scholars like Taylor [36] and others have examined the socio-technical, material, and creative dynamics of esport events that focus on competitive game play, it is probably too early to expect that inter-mural game jams may get elevated to full-fledged collegiate sport. But maybe our expectations are too low or misdirected. Alternatively, inter-mural game jams can grow to incorporate teams that span multiple schools that are geographically dispersed, thus affording participants firsthand experience in distributed, multi-site project work that relies on shared online information, social media, and related information repositories, all of which are key to the future of SE work in the Internet age [1].

2.3.4 Capstone Game Development Project Course

Faculty and students are increasingly familiar with capstone project courses whose goal is to unify and demonstrate what students have learned through their prior coursework. Such project courses can span common academic periods like 10-week quarter or 15-week semester, or longer (UCI's game capstone project courses for majors are now for 20 weeks). These project courses are not explicitly organized as formal competitions with winners and losers, but more like long-duration intramural game jams, where sustained focus, hard work, collaborative development, and self-satisfaction are all desirable elements of open, multi-team software development project work [26, 27].

Capstone projects have been employed in SE education (SEE) programs for decades. SE project courses first appeared in the 1970s (cf. "Programming in the Large" c. 1975) and began to flourish in the 1980s, along with the establishment of the Software Engineering Institute at Carnegie-Mellon University in the mid-1980s. Part of the early charter of the SEI was to encourage and advance SEE as a national priority. Different project organizations and SE processes were thus encouraged and celebrated in research papers addressing SEE. Some educators further specialized in operationalizing their SE project courses as research test beds where experiments or other empirical studies of SE could be performed, analyzed, compared, and published [2, 3]. Among the SE practices that were subject to empirical study were the use of rapid prototyping versus conventional approaches to software development [3, 21], and utilization of balanced student teams developing common formal and informal software development artifacts, with/without reusable exemplars, on a short schedule [2]. Other SEE projects employed either a common software architecture

[39], or one with plug-in modules for each team to develop [40], or else a common software development infrastructure of tools/services [24].

As game capstone project courses are still emerging, as is the community of practice focusing on CGSE, then it is still common to find such courses organized as independent student teams each pursuing their personal interests in their game development efforts. Again, this also reflects popular practices that are used in independent game festivals and inter-mural game showcases. At UCI, the first capstone project course featured three student teams, while the most recent effort featured nine teams, reflecting the growth of this local program.

2.3.5 International Game Development Workshop for Global Game Software Engineering Education

In Fall 2014, the author and other faculty at UCI were approached by a group of companies and universities from South Korea and China. They were interested in us developing and offering a 6-to-8-week long computer game development workshop for international students from these nations. The resulting Workshop was planned for 2016, so the description that follows is for the effort as designed, rather than an historical record describing what it was. But like some software development projects, and many game development projects, the project was cancelled early on due to schedule volatility, recurring delays, and multiple budgetary reductions [10]. Thus, this is a case for the speculative design [8] of an international game development workshop, rather than of accomplished design outcome for such.

The Workshop was conceived and organized as a multi-week summer school, in the spirit of the NATO Summer Schools organized about new scientific research topics. The 30 or so participating students are grouped in near-balanced teams (to accommodate the uncertainties in student experience and game development capabilities), with six or so teams anticipated. There are five academic faculty who are co-organizing and co-teaching the Workshop, which is to be run as a large game development studio with all teams working on a common game architecture and target deployment platforms (e.g., online Web and mobile devices). The faculty have also recruited more than a dozen game industry veterans to serve as guest lecturers on specific topics, or who may participate in student project reviews. A common software architecture has been designed, along with a common game development infrastructure of tools to be used, and game development artifacts to be produced for faculty and peer review. The game software architecture is structured around plug-in game modules, where each module provides, at minimum, a complete mini-game experience, as well as exchange and interoperation of game play assets (in-game resources and play scores that can move across modules, accumulate, and persist). The game development infrastructure assumes multiple loosely coupled repositories for sharing game software files (versioned, as done using GitHub), in-game content/assets, models, and textures (versioned); user play data (in-game character customizations, resource holdings, and scores); and anticipated online store repositories for game distribution.

So, what kind of a game making event is this Workshop? Is it a game jam? First and overall, the Workshop is inspired by the alternative game jam organizational forms described above, with elements drawn from intramural jams (all local teams, working collocated and in parallel on same schedule, producing common deliverable types), inter-mural jams (students are from different schools in their home countries, though student teams are expected to be pre-formed at the home institution before the Workshop), and capstone project following the SE project forms that utilize balanced teams working on recurring short (bursty) schedules to produce targeted game artifacts (design documents, character designs, etc.). In addition, this Workshop enables one form of global software engineering education (SEE), specifically global game software engineering, where cross-cultural game developers and project managers must rapidly learn how to productively work together [1], rather than not engaging in cross-cultural game development challenges, as is often the practice in global game jams.

Second, competition in the form of comparative assessment of each participating team's effort, along with team pride, can be utilized as a constructive motivation [12, 22, 23]. Also, as the teams are expected to produce games (or game modules) that will be part of a commercial release, then the short product development cycle tends more toward a game jam, where severe time limitations help to encourage (or force) timely decision-making on creative or technical choices.

Last, whether this style of game jam is the one that relies on practices such as gamified coursework [33]; advanced CGSE education [5, 6, 15, 16, 40]; rapid prototyping [3, 17, 21]; or software development work forms that resemble industrial "playbour" [13, 38] rather than hard work and fun that is mutually beneficial and exploitative for both game studios/sponsors and game modders/hobbyists [27]; etc. is an open question for further study. Suffice to say that other large software development projects have followed such development organizational forms, that the effort merits investigation as yet another viable method for a game jam, in this case, one that focuses all teams to contribute to the development of a single overall game experience, but one that is factored into plug-in functional modules that can share and exchange common game play resources and assets.

2.4   OBSERVATIONS, LESSONS LEARNED AND LEARNABLE LESSONS FOR GAME JAM ORGANIZATIONAL FORMS

Based on a comparative review of the five field studies presented above, a number of observations follow from these five field studies of local game jams.

First, local game jams are a promising venue for empirical studies of game development and software engineering. Many different kinds of configurations for organizing such jams have been identified. More potential configurations and reconfigurations therefore seem likely. Similarly, there is more potential opportunity to look for ways and means for structuring such software development competitions, or for analytically framing such competitions as a team sport [29], and thus also suitable for further gamification.

Second, most game jams, whether local or global, have primary emphasis on the product of the development effort—*the game produced*—while discounting or ignoring attending to the affordances and capabilities that are rendered in *game development artifacts* (e.g., game design documents; persistent online game developer chat transcripts to codify the knowledge and team logic underlying a game's development; choices made regarding use of game development tools or SDKs as a mediating factor in game production; and whether development teams are balanced by role and team size versus ad hoc and open). Game development competitions also represent a relatively unexplored domain for empirical studies of collaborative software development teamwork [15, 25], particularly those that rely on online artifacts (e.g., game design documents, persistent chat transcripts, game screen layout and artwork mockups, and game mods) moving within/across shared repositories and social media [26], which may therefore represent a promising approach to renovate traditional non-game software development projects.

Third, local game jams accommodate organizational design variables that may be more readily structured and (experimentally) controlled compared to open global game jams. This is not to say that local is better than global, but instead to draw attention to what variables can be addressed in different or comparative studies of game development competitions. Global game jams are well-suited to studies of cross-cultural game development practices, and perhaps readily extended to also investigate global SE or global CGSE issues. Much remains to be investigated, observed, analyzed, and compared here. So spatial, temporal, and cultural distances within or across GGJ teams, or within international game development workshops, seems like another opportunity to explore or put into practice.

Fourth, game development competitions are yet (?) to embrace participation in large-scale game development (e.g., MMOG) whereby teams compete based on their contribution to an overall established game software and asset/content architecture as the common focus for all participating teams. Game jams (rather than singular game development teams) could also be designed to focus on development of new "features" for established free-to-play games that are taking over the world of online, mobile games. Game jams with such foci may be of great interest to the game studios, old and new, as ways to demonstrate whether/how such game jams can create MMOGs/F2P features with plausible economic value as well as enabling (student) participants experience in game development practices that are not as well addressed by traditional game design approaches. As before, whether such competitions are seen as providing asymmetric benefit to the game studios (thus denoting a playbour dynamic [13, 37]), or are also mutually beneficial to participating students/indie game developers [27, 31]), remains an open question.

Fifth, as game jams vary in the duration, product/artifact submission requirements, team size, and role composition, then there are conceptual challenges for how to articulate both plausible and reusable research methods for field studies or systematic artifact studies. Similarly, how might a game jam be designed to focus the efforts of participating teams on maximizing product quality and development productivity, within limited duration jams? Such a question addresses a classic challenge in identifying how best to engineer a new software system within time and budget constraints.

Sixth, the five field studies and different forms of game development competitions help reveal that such events vary by the amount of technical and creative leadership versus free choices provided by local game jam organizers. The more short-term and informal, the less guidance and commitment required, while longer-term and more structured, the greater guidance, commitment, and quality assurance oversight required. This is of course a lesson learned long ago within the SE community, and thus one that is shared and relearned by game jam organizers and focused game development project leaders. The competitive element of game making on a common time box schedule, and on reliance of project leaders to mentor, plan, and guide development teams, helps better prepare participants for understanding what is required for making games that must go beyond being recognized as "weekend wonders." Accordingly, whether software engineering educators will choose to embrace longer-term challenges that can arise from repeated SE-focused game jams, or game-focused SE capstone project courses remain an open question, except for those who recognize the academic research opportunities such innovation factories can provide [1, 17, 24].

Seventh, the five field studies also demonstrate the potential to engage in experimental SEE projects and practices. Many students (and probably most software engineering educators) can benefit from first engaging in comparative game analysis studies that employ analytical rubrics/templates for classifying and assessing the features and capabilities of different games appropriate for student engagement [24]. Such analysis can yield insights about the relative ease/difficulty of reusing or repurposing the functional capabilities observed in games open for analysis. Insights also come from actually playing the games being analyzed—again, this might be an uncertain challenge for established software engineering educators, rather than for students. Furthermore, insights also come from classroom and homework efforts that focus attention to designing and playtesting of analog games—games that do not involve computers or programming—that help produce a better sense of how game mechanics might make a new game fun and playful, Finally, from more of an academic research perspective, the time box limited schedules of intramural game jams and capstone project coursework allows for both natural and controlled experiments when involving enough students that can be formed into comparable team groups [2, 3]. Similarly, the comparative analysis of games conforming to a theoretical sample or game genre of interest, affords the opportunity to engage in domain analysis that in turn can give rise to reusable game software patterns that can shape future game research, development, and education [31].

Eighth, game jams traditionally ignore or marginalize topics that are important to commercial game software success. These include: (a) how to support secure cheating-free game play, as well as utilize secure in-game (or in-app) content purchase interfaces; (b) how to develop games that resist efforts of players to cheat, or create grief for unsuspecting players; (c) how to embrace the rise of game architectures for free-to-play games that are centered about periodic addition of modular "features" (new in-game play objects or character adornments rather than expansion packs) that support game play update experiences and micro-transactions for purchasing in-game (or across game) resources/assets; (d) game jams that encourage user-directed extension or repurposing other existing games that are open to such evolutionary adaptation [27, 30, 31]; (e) how to make serious game jams more open to participants with domain-specific expertise who may not be skilled in game design, programming, or artwork creation, but who can help specify valuable domain topics for players to learn or master; (f) games produced with built-in libraries and architectural middleware providing scalable support for multiple players; and (g) how best to rapidly produce games within a jam style competition that embrace software sustainability issues that do arise (e.g., software designed for reuse as a sustainability technique), or do not arise (games that are not envisioned as products, but instead as demonstrations of mastery or development skill potential) in game development competitions.

Last, the emergence and pervasiveness of mobile games is also transforming the landscape for game production and dissemination. Games have become the most popular kind of software app found in online mobile app stores like *Apple App Store* and *Google Play*, or via online game publishing networks like *Steam* for desktop computer games. Thus, there is also opportunity for structuring game jams around the utilization of commercial game publishing platform services such as these, as games so published are games that student developers can highlight as career milestone products. Developing games for these platforms can entail from simple to complex integration of platform libraries accessed through application programming interfaces (APIs) that can provide statistics on downloads and usage patterns, elicit remote user feedback and review ratings, accommodate game sales for confident game developers, and more.

2.5 CONCLUSIONS

Game software development competitions are fun, hard work, low-cost, of varying duration, and intensive. Most are neither motivated nor rewarded academically (i.e., no transcript grades or formal examinations given). However, they can be intra-mural or inter-mural, and can stipulate balanced or ad hoc team configurations. Capstone game projects can also be organized as intramural competitions that may or may not have external game project sponsors. In such capstone project courses, emphasis is generally focused on learning how to practice and demonstrate competency in game software development, but in the future may also focus on CGSE. Game competitions can also be open-ended or closed-ended. But their organizations often at times impose constraints that may unnecessarily inhibit the competitors, limit their skill development or learning, impose game development frameworks that limit rather than facilitate creativity and rapid development.

Multi-team game development competitions vary by the amount of leadership, commitment, and guidance provided to participants by the competition organizers. Lower effort requires more independent choice by game makers, greater risk of making common/known mistakes, and good luck, while higher effort reduces choices, requires more resources and project management, may produce more sophisticated and accomplished results, yet does not guarantee a winning product. Such are the lessons so far seen within CGSE as a lens focusing on game jams and related game making competitions.

Game software development competitions can serve as a test bed for exploring, observing, or evaluating new SE tools, techniques, and concepts. Such events can therefore also serve as field sites for careful empirically grounded field studies of game making processes and practices. Equalized and balanced competitions represent time-compressed ways and means for conducting empirical SE studies. Competitions can precede or follow SEE coursework, as follows: jams conducted before SEE coursework draw attention to raw talent, while jams after SEE coursework emphasize demonstration of learned SE skills that is more accomplished and better balanced, if the SEE was successful. This may help students and others in industry understand the value of presenting SE experiences in ways that entail tough technical, time-constrained team collaboration challenges that are ultimately perceived as a fun thing to do.

ACKNOWLEDGMENTS

Preparation of this article was supported by grant #1256593 from the National Science Foundation. No review, approval, or endorsement is implied.

REFERENCES

[1] S. Beecham, T. Clear, D. Damien, J. Barr, J. Noll and W. Scacchi (2017). How Best to Teach Global Software Engineering, *IEEE Software*, 35(1), 16–19.

[2] S. Bendifallah and W. Scacchi. (1989). *Work Structures and Shifts: An Empirical Analysis of Software Specification Teamwork, Proc. 11th. Intern. Conf. Software Engineering*, Pittsburgh, PA, ACM Press, 260–270.

[3] B. Boehm, T. Gray, and T. Seewaldt. (1984). Prototyping Versus Specifying: A Multiproject Experiment. *IEEE Trans. Software Engineering*, 10(3): 290–303.

[4] D. Callele, E. Neufeld, and K. Schneider. (2005). *Requirements Engineering and the Creative Process in the Video Game Industry, Proc. 13th Intern. Conf. Requirements Engineering, (RE'05)*, Paris, France. 240–250.

[5] K. Claypool and M. Claypool. (2005). *Teaching Software Engineering through Game Design*, in *Proc. 10th SIGCSE Conf. Innovation and Technology in Computer Science Education (ITiCSE '05)*, Portugal. pp. 123–127.

[6] K.M. Cooper. and C. Longstreet. (2015) Model-Driven Engineering of Serious Games: Integrating Learning Objectives for Subject Specific Topics and Transferable Skills, in K.M. Cooper. and W. Scacchi. (Eds.), *Computer Games and Software Engineering*, CRC Press, Taylor & Francis Group, Boca Raton, FL, 59–90.

[7] A. Dorling and F. McCaffery. (2012). *The Gamification of SPICE*, in *Software Process Improvement and Capability Determination, Communications in Computer and Information Science*, Berlin, Germany, Volume 290, Springer, pp. 295–301.

[8] A. Dunne and F. Raby (2013). *Speculative Everything: Design Fiction and Social Dreaming*, MIT Press, Cambridge, MA.

[9] T. Francis (2012). The Indies Guide to Game Making, *PC Gamer UK*, 246. November.

[10] A. A. Grossman. (2003). *Postmortems from Game Developer: Insights from the Developers of Unreal Tournament, Black and White, Age of Empires, and Other Top-Selling Games*. Focal Press, San Francisco, USA.

[11] I. Hamilton. (2011). *UCI Students Build Games in a Week, OC Register*, http://ocunwired.ocregister.com/2011/04/13/uci-students-build-games-in-a-week/7131/ Accessed 15 April 2015.

[12] C. Kaitila. (2012). *The Game Jam Survival Guide*, Packt Publishing, Birmingham, UK.

[13] J. Kücklich. (2005). Precarious Playbour: Modders and the digital games industry. *Fiberculture Journal*, 3. http://www.journal.fibreculture.org/issue5/kucklich.html.

[14] M. Lampolski and W. Scacchi (2016). *Learning Game Design and Software Engineering through a Game Prototyping Experience: A Case Study*, in *Proc. 5th Games and Software Engineering Workshop (GAS 2016), 38th Intern. Conf. Software Engineering, ACM*, Austin, TX.

[15] I. Mistrík, J. Grundy, A. van der Hoek, and J. Whitehead. (2010), *Collaborative Software Engineering*, Springer, New York.

[16] E. Murphy-Hill, T. Zimmerman, and N. Nagappan. (2014). *Cowboys, Ankle Sprains, and Keepers of Quality: How is Video Game Development Different from Software Development?*, in *Proc. 36th Intern. Conf. Software Engineering (ICSE 2014), ACM*, Hyderabad, India, 1–11, June.

[17] J. Musil, A. Schweda, D. Winkler, and S. Biffl. (2010). *Synthesized Essence: What Game Jams Teach about Prototyping of New Software Products*, in *Proc. 32nd Intern. Conf. Software Engineering (ICSE'10), ACM*, Cape Town, SA, 183–186.

[18] E. Navarro and A. van der Hoek. (2004). Software Process Modeling for an Educational Software Engineering Simulation Game, *Software Process Improvement and Practice*, 10 (3), 311–325.

[19] M. Newland. (1984) *Marv Newland's Anijam*, International Rocketship Limited, https://www.youtube.com/watch?v=4DMopYl8eR4, Accessed 28 April 2018.

[20] O.A. O'Hagan, G. Coleman, R.V. O'Connor. (2014) Software Development Processes for Games: A Systematic Literature Review. In B. Barafort, R.V. O'Connor, A. Poth, R. Messnarz (eds.) *Systems, Software and Services Process Improvement*. EuroSPI 2014. Communications in Computer and Information Science, vol 425. Springer, Berlin, Heidelberg.

[21] J. Pirker, A. Kultima, and C. Gütl. (2016). *The Value of Game Prototyping Projects for Students and Industry. Proc. Intern. Conf. Game Jams, Hackathons, and Game Creation Events (GJH&GC '16). ACM*, New York, NY, USA, 54–57. DOI: https://doi.org/10.1145/2897167.2897180

[22] J.A. Preston, J. Chastine, C. O'Donnell, T. Tseng, and B. MacIntyre. (2012). Game Jams: Community, motivations, and learning among jammers. *Intern. J. Game-Based Learning*, 2(3), 51–70.

[23] L. Reng, H. Schoenau-Fog, and L.B. Kofoed. (2013). *The Motivational Power of Game Communities - Engaged through Game Jamming, Proc. Foundations of Digital Games 2013 Workshop on the Global Game Jam*, Chania, Crete, Greece, 2013.

[24] W. Scacchi. (1991). The Software Infrastructure for a Distributed System Factory, *Software Engineering Journal*, 6(5), 355–369, September.

[25] W. Scacchi. (2004). Free/Open Source Software Development Practices in the Game Community, *IEEE Software*, 21(1), 59–67, January/February.

[26] W. Scacchi. (2010). *Collaboration Practices and Affordances in Free/Open Source Software Development*, in I. Mistrík, J. Grundy, A. van der Hoek, and J. Whitehead, (Eds.), *Collaborative Software Engineering*, Springer, New York, 307–328.

[27] W. Scacchi. (2010). Computer Game Mods, Modders, Modding, and the Mod Scene, *First Monday*, 15(5), May.

[28] W. Scacchi. (2011). Modding as an Open Source Software Approach to Extending Computer Game Systems, *Intern. J. Open Source Software and Processes*, 3(3), 36–47, July-September 2011.

[29] W. Scacchi. (2012). *Competitive Game Development: Software Engineering as a Team Sport. Keynote Address*, 2nd Intern. Workshop on Games and Software Engineering (GAS2012), Intern. Conf. Software Engineering, Zurich, CH, May 2012.

[30] W. Scacchi. (2017). Practices and Technologies for Computer Game Software Engineering, *IEEE Software*, 35(1), 110–116, January-February 2017.

[31] W. Scacchi. and K.M. Cooper. (2015). Emerging Research Challenges in Computer Games and Software Engineering, in K.M. Cooper. and W. Scacchi. (Eds.), *Computer Games and Software Engineering*, CRC Press, Taylor & Francis Group, Boca Raton, FL, 261–283.

[32] J. Schell (2014). *The Art of Game Design: A book of Lenses,* 2nd Edition, AK Peters/ CRC Press, Burlington, MA.

[33] L. Sheldon. (2011). *The Multiplayer Classroom: Designing Coursework as a Game,* Cengage Learning PTR, Independence, KY.

[34] K. Shin, K. Kaneko, M. Matsui, et al. (2012). Localizing *Global Game Jam*: Designing Game Development for Collaborative Learning in the Social Context, in A. Nijholt, T. Romano, and D. Reidsma. (Eds). *Advances in Computer Entertainment, Lecture Notes in Computer Science,* Vol. 7624, Springer, Berlin, 117–132.

[35] J. Tanenbaum, K. Tanenbaum, K. Ibestier, K. Abe, A. Sullivan, and L. Anzivino (2015). *Costumes & Wearables as Game Controllers, TEI '15 Proc. Ninth International Conference on Tangible, Embedded, and Embodied Interaction,* Stanford, CA. 477–480.

[36] T.L. Taylor. (2013). *E-Sports and the Professionalization of Computer Gaming,* MIT Press, Cambridge, MA.

[37] T.L. Taylor, K. Bergstrom, J. Jenson, and S. de Castell. (2015). Alienated Playbour: Relations of Production in EVE Online, *Games and Culture,* doi:10.1177/1555412014565507

[38] V. Verigames (2015). http://www.verigames.com/, Accessed April 2018.

[39] A.I. Wang. (2011). Extensive Evaluation of Using a Game Project in a Software Architecture Course, *ACM Transactions on Computing Education,* 11(1), 1–28.

[40] A.I. Wang. (2015). The Use of Game Development in Computer Science and Software Engineering Education, in K.M. Cooper. and W. Scacchi. (Eds.), *Computer Games and Software Engineering,* CRC Press, Taylor & Francis Group, Boca Raton, FL, 31–58.

[41] Wikipedia (2018), *Hackathon,* http://en.wikipedia.org/wiki/Hackathon. Accessed 15 May 2018.

[42] A. Zook, and M.O. Riedl. (2013). *Game Conceptualization and Development Processes in the Global Game Jam, Proc. Foundations of Digital Games Workshop on the Global Game Jam,* Crete, GR.Received May 2018.

3 Developing Essential Software Engineering Competencies Supported by Digital Game-Based Learning

Jöran Pieper

Hochschule Stralsund – University Of Applied Sciences, IACS, Germany

CONTENTS

3.1   INTRODUCTION

Software Engineering (SE) education is challenged in many ways. Educators and curriculum designers must take enormous diversity into account and offer a well-rounded range of knowledge to enable tomorrow's software engineers. Conditioned by limited time, all contents provided are just a selection out of a vast, diverse spectrum. While depth and breadth of selected contents vary in detail, it is of consent, that beside all technical aspects and tools a profound knowledge of SE methods, which describe approaches to the production and evolution of software, are crucial for successful SE practice. Emerging agile and lean approaches propagate the renouncement of ballast—the disuse of practices or tools, which form the foundation of more traditional development processes. Lacking experience in developing complex software systems, the consequences of (not) using practices and tools can be judged hardly.

While some of the SE knowledge areas are well suited to be learned by lectures and associated laboratory tutorials, others are less eligible. Those include SE methods[1]. "These are critical topics for industrial practice, yet it is a particular challenge to motivate students to feel passionate in these areas, and hence learn what they need to know." [2] Without experience building more complex software systems the need for such disciplined approaches may not be as apparent as desired. A perception that (trivial) projects in the past were manageable without "restricting rules" is widely spread. Discussion, deeper analysis, or comparison of SE practices and methods in the form of a dialog, which would be beneficial to learning, is complicated by the fact that students often cannot draw on any own experiences. So, they would have to take it for granted—or not. In course or capstone projects, commonly required by curriculum guidelines, students losing a holistic view due to remarkable cognitive load can be observed. Just delivering artifacts under time pressure, requested by a preselected software process, can hardly provide the deep impression that practices, methods, and tools were supporting students' work.

In the course or capstone projects the following observations can be made:

- Students struggle to orientate inside a given SE method.
- They have got difficulties answering the question(s) *by who*m, *how*, *when*, and in particular *why* specific activities should be accomplished.
- The reasonable division of responsibilities and a rigid fixation on technological and functional details make them lose the holistic view on the development process as a whole—with all its relevant dimensions.
- Takeaways from such projects are too specific and hardly transferable to other contexts and future challenges.

In his review of SE in the 20th and 21st century, Boehm concludes that SE education is required to "Keeping courses […] up-to-date; Anticipating future trends and preparing students to deal with them; Monitoring current principles and practices and separating timeless principles from out-of-date practices; Packaging smaller-scale educational experiences in ways that apply to large-scale projects; [… and] Helping students learn how to learn, through […] future-oriented educational games and exercises […]." [3]

The binding of current approaches to single software processes, both in conducting course projects as well as in game-based approaches, limits their transferability to new contexts that require a different set of SE practices. Sommerville emphasized that "engineering is all about selecting the most appropriate method for a set of circumstances." [4] To enable conscious decisions of tomorrow's software engineers, they have to know their options and be able to take multiple aspects and perspectives into account.

Preceding research showed that simulation and games were able to foster empathy with the necessity of employing software processes to accomplish more complex software projects to a certain level. However, evaluation of these approaches showed that they were not able to impart new knowledge too. [5]

At this point, SE education has to provide concepts for retaining a holistic view of the whole SE endeavor while working focused on the required details at the same time. SE education must provide competencies—clusters of related *knowledge*, *skills*, and *attitudes* enabling persons to accomplish all the tasks in a given context. Moreover, these competencies must also be transferable to different contexts to meet students' upcoming challenges.

In the field of software processes, a trend toward flexible practices and composed of SE methods, tailored to the needs of a team, instead of monolithic software processes is noticeable. The proponents deliver strong arguments to do so. SE education is asked to utilize these advantages to achieve its educational objectives.

3.1.1 RESEARCH OBJECTIVES

This research aims at overcoming the described challenges. It is in search for a DGBL approach that provides students with a familiar environment already appreciated at the start of the course or capstone projects, lowering the overall cognitive load, and increasing the transferability of the knowledge gained. Instead of offering a somewhat isolated game-based learning activity, this research aims at delivering an approach to provide transferable skills preparing students for their real project, work to enable experiences that support the development of desired SE attitudes. All in all, students should be empowered to apply a systematic, disciplined, and quantifiable approach to the development of their software—and appreciate the guidance given by SE concepts and methods.

"Each meaning, which I realize by myself, each rule, I establish according to my own lights, convinces me more and motivates me higher than any extrinsic meaning that I hardly comprehend." [6] This guideline of constructivist didactics describes an ideal result of learning and deep understanding. To foster such learning, this research targets an active constructivist learning experience utilizing DGBL that is encouraging intrinsic motivation and social interaction through articulation, reflection, collaboration, and—where applicable—competition.

3.1.2 RESEARCH DESIGN

Based on a broad literature review about required SE competencies, learning theories, and existing game-based approaches in the field of SE methods, requirements were defined for a DGBL approach that allows students to acquire essential and highly transferable SE competencies. Based on a comparison of existing meta-models for standardized software process description concerning their suitability in the context of SE education, SEMAT Essence was chosen as the foundation of a game-based approach. An *intrinsic* and *reflective* game, *tightly linked*[2] to the underlying domain and addressing higher competency levels, as well as a supporting game and an integrating tool to be utilized in that approach had to be designed, implemented, and integrated to provide a learning experience that got evaluated in a case study.

3.1.3 OUTLINE

This chapter is structured as follows: Section 2 provides some background about SEMAT Essence, the OMG standard providing the foundation of games developed to achieve the objectives described. Section 3 summarizes results from a literature review that provided findings on state of the art in game-based learning in SE education and helped to develop suitable design strategies for the games that got developed. These games and underlying concepts are described in detail in Section 4. The evaluation of concepts and approaches taken was conducted with a case study that gets described in Section 5. This chapter closes with a discussion of results in Section 6 and delivers an outlook of future work and proposed research directions in Section 7.

3.2   KERNEL AND LANGUAGE FOR SOFTWARE ENGINEERING METHODS (ESSENCE)

SEMAT[3] Essence, an emerging OMG standard [9], provides a language for the unified description of SE practices and methods as well as a compact kernel, capturing the essentials of any SE endeavor in a process- and practice-independent way. The kernel provides the foundation to create practices, which eventually get picked and composed to complete SE methods, tailored to the needs of SE teams in their respective contexts. Designed primarily for software professionals' daily practical and intuitive use, it delivers a significant paradigm shift compared to other attempts of unified process definition, for example, SPEM or ISO24744, which are primarily targeting process engineers. Instead of just describing an SE method, the *actionable* kernel provides support to use a method dynamically while working on an SE endeavor. This section describes some of the characteristics that make Essence a good foundation for this research, both, regarding the support of objectives of SE education as well as providing a foundation for educational games.

3.2.1   THE ESSENCE KERNEL

The Essence Kernel "is a stripped-down, light-weight set of definitions that captures the essence of effective, scalable software engineering in a practice independent way." [9] It was designed to be as small and universal as possible to represent the inherent essence of each SE endeavor. The Essence authors separated the common ground, a stable kernel, from the varying details, depending on the respective context represented in SE practices. With that common foundation, practices can be defined, exchanged, and applied independently. They can be cherry-picked, mixed, and matched by project teams, organizations, and communities based on their unique needs. By combining the kernel and a set of chosen best (fitting to the context) practices, teams are empowered to form their own methods. This method composition is illustrated in Figure 3.1.

Providing a common ground, an anchor and thinking framework, this kernel facilitates learning of new SE practices and methods—making it easier to notice similarities and differences between those newly introduced practices and those already known by a person or organization.

To provide the essential elements of *any* SE endeavor, the Essence Kernel uses the concepts of *Alphas, Activity Spaces,* and *Competencies.* To facilitate orientation inside of the kernel, it is structured into three discrete *areas of concern,* each focusing on specific aspects of SE. Table 3.1 summarizes the elements of the kernel.

Interrelationships between the seven provided Alphas and between Alphas, their states, and Activity Spaces are defined. The kernel omits the inclusion of other elements, like *work products* and *activities,* to preserve its independence from any practice. These elements are reserved for practices, which link their elements to the kernel's respective elements.

The Essence Kernel is made tangible by providing a card metaphor. SEMAT provides a set of printable cards containing Alphas' definitions and Alpha States'

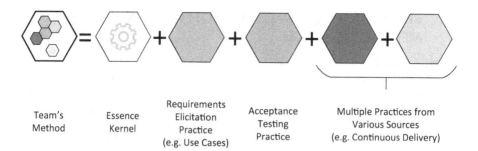

Team's Method | Essence Kernel | Requirements Elicitation Practice (e.g. Use Cases) | Acceptance Testing Practice | Multiple Practices from Various Sources (e.g. Continuous Delivery)

FIGURE 3.1   SEMAT Essence Method Composition by Combining a Kernel and Chosen Practices.

TABLE 3.1
Essence Kernel Elements

Area of Concern	Alphas	Activity Spaces	Competencies
Customer	Stakeholders, Opportunity	Explore Possibilities, Understand Stakeholder Needs, Ensure Stakeholder Satisfaction	Stakeholder Representation
Solution	Requirements, Software System	Understand the Requirements, Shape the System, Implement the System, Test the System, Deploy the System, Operate the System	Analysis, Development, Testing
Endeavor	Team, Work, Way-of-Working	Prepare to do the Work, Coordinate Activity, Support the Team, Track Progress, Stop the Work	Leadership, Management

checklists. Such a set of cards is easy to carry around and supports agile team sessions. By summarizing the most important concepts, cards facilitate learning by doing without the need for rote memorization before starting to use Essence. Figure 3.2 shows an example of both, an Alpha card and an Alpha State card.

3.2.2 ALPHAS, ALPHA STATES, AND THEIR CHECKLISTS

Alphas represent the essential elements of an SE endeavor that are relevant to a continual assessment of the progress and health of an endeavor. [9] Each Alpha is provided with a set of Alpha States. Each Alpha State owns a checklist supporting its assessment (cf. Figure 3.2). An SE endeavor is progressed by progressing the states of all Alphas and retaining their health. The checklist provided to assess each of the Alpha States provides immediately available expert knowledge enabling even less experienced teams to think holistically about the endeavor and to recognize aspects that otherwise, based solely on team members' experiences, might be forgotten.

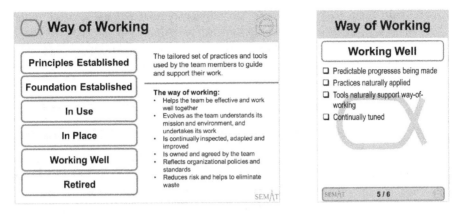

FIGURE 3.2   Examples of an Alpha Card and an Alpha State Card for the Alpha "Way-of-Working" [10].

3.2.3   ACTIVITY SPACES—THE THINGS TO DO

A team must perform an activity addressing the next target state to progress an Alpha. The Essence Kernel does not provide concrete activities since they would prescribe a specific way to perform a set of tasks and bind the kernel to a particular practice. Instead, the Essence Kernel provides a set of Activity Spaces serving as abstract placeholders. These Activity Spaces are the things to do in every SE endeavor. Activity Spaces are provided with entry and completion criteria represented by Alpha States. While Activity Spaces provide the *What* and (concerning the Alpha States) *When* to do, practices deliver concrete activities—the *How* to do. Activities provided by an Essence practice are grouped and classified by an Activity Space.

3.2.4   UTILIZING ESSENCE TO DRIVE AN SE ENDEAVOR

Essence and its kernel support a structured, quantifiable, and goal-oriented approach to progress an SE endeavor. A typical proceeding follows a *Plan-Do-Check-Adapt (PDCA)* cycle[4] [12]:

1) *Plan*: A team starts with assessing the current state of the endeavor. Alphas and their Alpha States ensure that all relevant dimensions are considered. Checkpoints support the assessment of each of the Alpha States. *Walkthroughs* or *Assessment Poker* sessions are suitable to assess an endeavor in a team session. [12] The Activity Spaces addressing next targeted Alpha States provide support by identifying next activities. Checkpoints of next planned Alpha States help to identify necessary tasks.
2) *Do*: The team works on accomplishing the identified tasks. Emerging obstacles are removed as they occur.
3) *Check*: By continuously tracking progress toward defined objectives and tasks, the team ensures to keep focused and following its chosen way of working.

4) *Adapt*: Team's way of working is continuously reviewed and assessed in the same way as all other essential dimensions (Alphas) of the endeavor. As a team recognizes impediments, caused by their way of working, better (suiting) ways of getting things done get identified and used. Plans are adapted accordingly.

3.2.5 ESSENCE AND TRADITIONAL METHODS AND IMPROVEMENT FRAMEWORKS

While the Essence language can be used to implement existing SE methods, it "is not in competition with any existing practice or method. It is agnostic to your chosen approach and can be implemented by your team today without changing what you are currently doing. It is more about helping you do what you are already doing so you can keep doing it even better in the future." [13] By adding a common ground, or a *reference model*, that all teams can use, regardless of their chosen (agile or not) method, Essence adds to the ability to continually measure health and progress of endeavors and to improve teams' way of working. [14, 15]

3.2.6 CONCLUSIONS

Essence provides a shift toward flexible and composable SE practices instead of monolithic software processes prevalent in past and presence. With the Essence Kernel, this standard provides a compact, practical, actionable, and extensible set of elements inherent in all SE endeavors. As such this kernel serves as a thinking framework as well as a foundation to define practices and compose them to tailored methods. Since the kernel is actionable, it enables a team to continually and holistically monitor progress and health of all essential dimensions efficiently. With utilizing a PDCA cycle to steer the SE endeavor, the kernel provides the foundation for continuous improvement throughout an SE endeavor. A mapping of Essence's characteristics with competencies demanded by SE curriculum guidelines manifests its suitability in SE education. As Ng and Huang, experimenting with Essence concepts in a workshop with professors and Ph.D. students, concluded "Universities cannot teach everything that industry requires. But university can provide students with a firm grasp of the fundamentals and give them the tools to learn and understand the diversity of software engineering later in their career." [16]

Therefore, SEMAT Essence was chosen as the foundation of the approaches taken in this research.

3.3 EXPLORING THE FIELD OF GAME-BASED LEARNING IN SE METHODS EDUCATION

To consider the findings of relevant preceding research, the field of game-based learning approaches in SE education was explored.

3.3.1   REVIEW DESIGN

Several rigorous and comprehensive meta-studies [5, 17–19] provided a good starting point to investigate the field of game-based learning activities in SE education. The focus of those studies varied but delivered an excellent foundation for data extraction of aspects of interest for this research. An own SLR to catch up with most recent developments was conducted. The research design of that SLR widely follows the procedures of [5] but includes the years 2014–2016. Additionally, doctoral theses related to the field and a paper [20], which became known to the author at a national conference and was therefore not covered by the search criteria, were considered too. [21]

3.3.2   RESULTS AND CONCLUSIONS

Table 3.2 summarizes characteristics of the Systematic Literature Reviews (SLRs). These results of the literature reviews naturally overlap to some extent.

The timeline of DGBL approaches in SE education proves an ongoing interest and research activity in this field. [21] Recurring entries of simulation games indicate the effort affiliated with the development and evaluation of approaches—it may take several years from initial concept descriptions till the implementation and evaluation of approaches.

Some implemented games or environments, i.e., *SimSE*, *SESAM*, and *AMEISE*, show an impressive body of work of several researchers covering long periods, both for refinement of initial versions as well as the evaluation of taken approaches.

Besides the utilization of DGBL, pure non-game-based rather industrial simulation models were used in training and education sessions. Several attempts to utilize DGBL in SE education have been made. Several games were focused on specific, somewhat isolated, SE knowledge areas. Table 3.3 summarizes such games that are addressing the area of SE methods that are of particular interest for this research.

TABLE 3.2
Systematic Literature Reviews of Simulation and DGBL in SE Education

	[6]	[52]	[37]	[17]	This Research[19]
Period	1996-2006	1990-2008	1999-2009	open-2013	2014-2016
Simulation games	Y	Y	Y	Y	Y
Only computer-based	Y	N	Y	Y	N
Non-Game simulations	N	Y	N	Y	N
Number of papers	21	16	16	42	17
Number of simulators and games	12	12	8	15	13

TABLE 3.3

Existing Simulation Games in SE Methods and Management Education and Training

	SimSE [31, 32]	SimjavaSP [46]	SESAM [9, 10, 24], AMEISE[26]	90 Incredible Manager [2]	90 OSS [45]	90 MO-SEProcess [53]	90 SimVBSE [16]	90 Simsoft [5]	90 Nassal's PMG [28–30]	90 SPIAL [38]	90 PMG-2D [23]
Single-player (S) or multi-player (M) game	S	S	S	S	S	M	S	M	S	S	S
Collaboration and/or competition of players	-	-	-	-	-	-	-	+[a]	-	-	-
Team, course and lecturer dashboards	-	-	o[b]	-	-	-	-	-	-	-	-
Player in the role of a project manager	+	+	+	+	o	o	+	+	+	+	+
Player(s) with different roles or tasks	-	-	-	-	+	+	-	-	-	o	-
Enabled for different SE processes/methods	+	-	+	-	-	-	-	-	+	+	-
Number of available predefined SE process/method models	6	1	3[c]	1	1	1	1	1[d]	1	1	1[e]
Integrating industry standards for software process description	-	-	-	-	-	-	-	-	-	o[f]	o[g]
Utilizing real world tools, used in SE contexts	-	-	-	-	-	-	-	-	+	-	-

"+" = yes/included, "-" = no/not included, and "o" = partially included

[a] Players are collaborating in teams. No competition.

[b] Only for administrative purposes.

[c] Two models are provided by the AMEISE project.

[d] "Work-to-do, review, rework, work-completed cycle."

[e] "Life cycle of the project management process according to PMBOK."

[f] With extracted rules from CMMI.

[g] Based on and linked with PMBOK.

The educational approaches taken within these games vary considerably. *Simsoft* is explicitly oriented toward *Problem-Based Learning*. All approaches represent more or less constructivist learning approaches by providing kinds of *experiential learning*, *active learning*, *learning by doing*, *situated learning*, and *discovery learning*. The amount of scaffolding provided differs considerably. *SimjavaSP* explicitly does *"not guiding"* the learner, which represents kind of *minimally guided instruction* [38] (tending toward unguided instruction). Considering Vygotsky's *Zone of Proximal Development* [39], Sweller's *Cognitive Load Theory* [40], and Reigeluth's *Elaboration Theory* [41], this might not contribute to ideal learning experiences. Concepts of *Social Constructivism* seem clearly to be underemployed in existing approaches.

Players of *Simsoft* appreciated to work in teams, to share opinions, and learn from more experienced teammates. The extent to what learners collaborated in *MO-SEProcess* is not explicitly described. All other approaches are provided as pure single-player games. In these games, collaboration and motivating competition between isolated participants are not promoted.

The architectures of the game environments, except those of the *AMEISE* project, do not enable a lecturer to get a quick summary of the performance of all players in a course. Such an overview could facilitate quick, supportive individual or group interactions in the case of occurring misconceptions as well as support debriefing activities.

The usage of real-world tools, as implemented in Nassal's *Project Management Game*, enables the beneficial development of skills in the knowledge domain and at using the utilized tool. On the other hand, it makes the approach depending on the tool. If the chosen tool does not represent the acknowledged mindset or essential principles of a given SE method, the approach may be rejected for just that reason. For instance, it might be less acceptable to play a *Scrum*-based or a *Kanban*-based method based on *Microsoft Project*, since these agile and lean methods do not advocate elaborated long-term planning and are based on pull-mechanisms. Almost all authors recognize that their games alone are not sufficient learning vehicles and hence have to be complemented by other educational approaches. Game-based learning activities must be integrated into the context as a whole in order to address intended learning objectives [5].

Most approaches offer only one fixed model of a software process or similar concepts. Model customization capabilities seem crucial in today's software engineering education taken the real diversity of software processes into account.

To transfer knowledge gained in one specific SE method to new upcoming challenges requiring different practices is an exercise left to students. None of the existing approaches facilitate a perspective on the use of flexible SE practices instead of software processes that provide common ground as a thinking framework yet.

Most simulation-based approaches lack integrated documentation of the process or method to follow. Without such descriptions, players are strongly dependent on prior knowledge to accomplish the game—given that the same vocab with same semantics is used. By assigning activities, represented by just a word or short word group, concepts and semantics may keep unclear. Most simulation-based games, enabling the learning of whole SE methods, promote a focus on workload optimization of team members with specific skills. Given the increasing recognition of agile and lean methods based on pull-approaches, where team members choose appropriate work packages depending on their abilities, this seems not to be an essential task in all SE contexts anymore. Unfortunately, it occupies a lot of learner's attention—that could be focused on other essential problem-solving issues.

While all of the introduced approaches provide an opportunity to familiarize with the field of SE methods and their management, each with different focus and approach, they were not explicitly built to directly support students in the course or capstone project work that is demanded by curriculum guidelines. If SE students should acquire an SE mindset, genuinely appreciating the guidance and support of utilized methods and practices, they should be provided with experiences facilitating such perceptions.

3.4 DEVELOPING GAMES AND TOOLS WITHIN CONTEXT AND UNDER CONSTRAINTS

Two games, the Essence Kernel Puzzler and the Essence Simulation Game, as well as an integrating tool, the Essence Kernel Navigator, were developed. Both games and the Navigator get introduced in the following section. At designing and developing these games, clear learning objectives guided the process.

The objective to support a holistic application of a systematic, disciplined, and quantifiable approach to the development of their software in course projects demands for higher learning objectives—to *apply conceptual* and *procedural* knowledge. This requires prior mastery of *remembering* and *understanding* of *factual* and, to some extent, *conceptual* knowledge[5]. It may seem tempting to build the one game that solves all problems at once. However, this can quickly lead to an overloaded gaming experience and require a more expensive game development. With limited resources, it seems more advisable to keep a clear focus and scope, for example, to provide learning experiences at intended competency levels. Within this research work, two games were developed. The first game addressing lower competency levels was developed to prepare a student for the second one, addressing higher competency levels and learning objectives.

By separating these two games, it was possible to pick the recommended game genres to benefit from their inherent features. This is important since not all game types support all learning outcomes equally well [43, 44]. Following a methodological approach to select proper game genres [45], the genres *drill and practice* as well as *puzzle games* were selected to support the first game, the *Essence Kernel Puzzler*. The second game, the *Simulation Game*, utilizes features and characteristics of *simulation* and *adventure* games to impart the desired procedural knowledge and skills. To enable the desired learning outcomes, this was designed to be *intrinsic*, making the learning content an integral part of the gameplay, *tightly linked* to the domain, making the mastery of the learning content vital to succeed in the game, and *reflective*, allowing a high degree of reflection by providing as much time as needed to (re-) think about decisions.[6]

This separation also allowed for focused game design and resulting game experiences. To combine both games, they are arranged and glued by other activities in an overall learning arrangement.

It is not necessary to compete with multi-million-dollar productions concerning game visuals. As Prensky states "[...] creating engagement is not about those fancy, expensive graphics but rather about ideas. Sure, today's video games have the best graphics ever, but kids' long-term engagement in a game depends much less on what they see than on what they do and learn. In gamer terms, 'gameplay' trumps 'eye candy' any day of the week." [23]

Learning theories provided guidance toward desired learning experiences. The games introduced in this chapter were designed with a focus on (social) constructivist approaches but without neglecting insights of cognitive learning theories arguing against minimally guided instruction.

Games and simulations, which are based on models, may lead to misconceptions in learning due to reductions and "simulation shortcuts." [16] At this point, the careful embedding of the serious game into the whole learning scenario and environment including debriefing actions is of enormous importance. "If the educators are aware of these 'flaws', they can use these as links to address questions that are posed or left open by and in these games. They serve as an ideal anchor for complementing educational activities." [9]

The Simulation Game introduced in this section is focused on essentials and built on top of a simplified simulation model that intentionally ignores details represented in other games. Questions that may arise from this are a welcome trigger for discussion and social interaction in a recommended debriefing session [40].

No game engine was utilized to implement the games with the desired characteristics. Instead, a technology stack common to current web development was utilized.

3.4.1 ESSENCE KERNEL PUZZLER

The *Essence Kernel Puzzler*, from now on short *Puzzler*, was designed as a markedly low-threshold offer to get familiar with Essence Kernel's vocab and some of its concepts. With just choosing a nickname everyone can use the Puzzler online[7].

It was designed to make people entering the Essence world familiar with definitions of terms used in the Essence Kernel vocab and to delve into the relationships of these elements in a more accessible and enjoyable way. The Puzzler focuses on Alphas and their associations. It introduces Activity Spaces as well as the Competencies defined by the Essence Kernel.

After mastering the Puzzler, students should be able to name elements, to assign definitions correctly, and to establish connections between them. Mapping the learning objectives to the cognitive process and knowledge dimensions of the *Revised Bloom's Taxonomy* [46], it targets lower cognitive levels, esp. the first levels *factual* and *conceptual* of the cognitive process dimension as well as *remember* and *understand* of the knowledge dimension. As such, mastering the Puzzler is a good starting point before beginning to strive for higher learning goals.

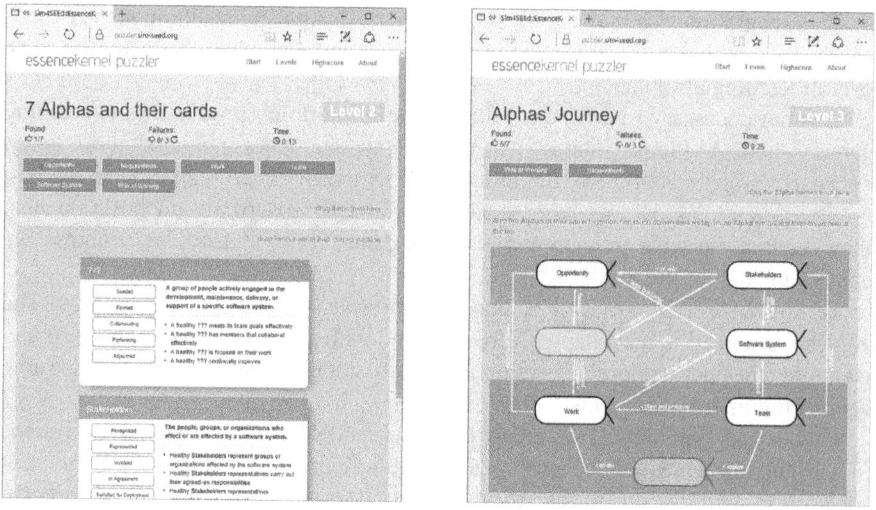

FIGURE 3.3 Two Screenshots of the Essence Kernel Puzzler Presenting Alpha Cards and Alpha Relationships.

The Puzzler is provided with a simple user interface. Each of the eight levels gets introduced with some basic information about the topic to master. Each level presents a task to handle via dragging and dropping elements to their correct position, for example, a name of an Alpha to its corresponding card. The time needed to master the level is measured and motivates to solve the puzzle faster once repeated. Feedback about the progress is provided by counting the number of correctly assigned elements and the number of failed attempts. Unconscious trial-and-error-acting gets not rewarded. If a player fails too often, the progress of the current level gets lost, and the level starts again. The player gets an overview of achieved results in her high score list. Figure 3.3 presents two screenshots of the UI, each showing one of the eight Puzzler levels.

3.4.2 Essence Kernel Navigator

The Essence Navigator represents an elementary execution environment for the SEMAT Essence Kernel as defined by the operational semantics of the Essence specification [9]. It provides the functionality to track the overall state of the SE endeavor, to determine the current overall state of the endeavor, and to give elementary advice about next steps to do. The Navigator provides its unique features in the same way to the player in a Simulation Game as it does to the teams assessing and controlling their individual course projects.

The Screenshot in Figure 3.4 illustrates the Alpha overview provided to individual players and project teams by the Navigator. Each Alpha is easily recognizable with its currently assessed state. The balance indicator at the right side of the figure gives a hint if all Alphas are progressed in a balanced way. The more this indicator forms a harmonic circle, the more balanced is the progress achieved—or better assessed—so

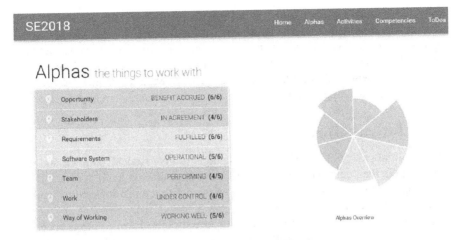

FIGURE 3.4 Screenshot of the Essence Kernel Navigator: Alphas Overview.

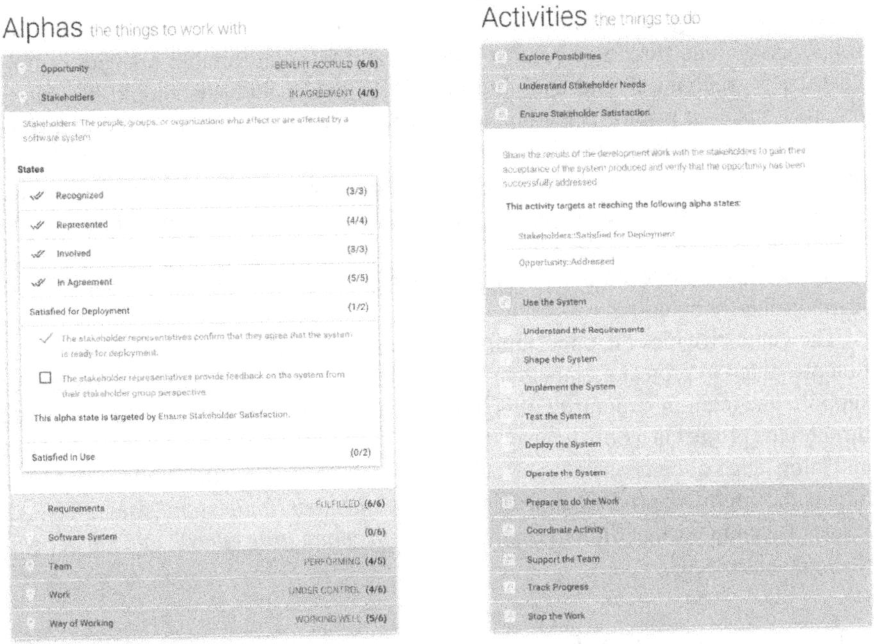

FIGURE 3.5 Screenshots of the Essence Kernel Navigator.

far in the project. Figure 3.5 (left) illustrates Navigator's support at assessing the current state of an Alpha. All Alpha States are provided with their respective checklists. In the example given, the Activity Space *Ensure Stakeholder Satisfaction* has to be performed to achieve the state *Satisfied for Deployment* of the Alpha *Stakeholders*. The Navigator integrates Activity Spaces in the learning experience and establishes bidirectional links between Alpha States and the Activity Spaces leading to their achievement. Figure 3.5 (right) illustrates the detail view of the Activity Space *Ensure Stakeholder Satisfaction*. A short description and links to all the Alpha States that can be achieved by performing this Activity Space are provided. Based on the current assessment of all the Alphas, the Navigator provides elementary recommendations for next activities guiding a student through a virtual or a real project.

3.4.3 Essence Simulation Game

The design objective of the Simulation Game is to give students a quick and profound start in their course project activities, to provide already familiar concepts and tool support—hence raise conscious goal-oriented attitude and lower the cognitive load students face in such projects.

The Simulation Game addresses students already introduced to the goals of the SEMAT Essence Kernel and familiar with basic concepts like Alphas, Alpha States, their checkpoints as well as Activity Spaces. Playing the Simulation Game based on the Essence Kernel should not take longer than a standard course unit of 90 minutes and be supplemented by debriefing activities.

After mastering the game, students should be able to apply acquired concepts in a simplified defined simulated context. They should feel comfortable with performing Essence's "mechanics" and applying the PDCA-cycle. Students should be able to orientate inside a given SE method/kernel and to consider all essential dimensions (Alphas) of the SE endeavor. They should be able to assess the progress and health of their endeavor in a structured and continuous way (at least at the presented abstracted level). It would not be realistic to assume that students would know all the Alpha States and their checklists in detail after playing for about 90 minutes. However, this is not even necessary, since Essence, as described, provides cards to learn on-the-fly by doing.

The game provides the opportunity to explore the multitude of different information presented to project members in an SE endeavor and to experience how Essence supports the team in structuring this information—how Essence is guiding the team through the project in a holistic way. Mapping the learning objectives to the cognitive and knowledge dimensions of the Revised Bloom's Taxonomy, the Simulation Game targets the cognitive process dimension levels *remember*, *understand*, and *apply*. All levels of the knowledge dimension (*factual*, *conceptual*, *procedural*, and *metacognitive*) get addressed.

3.4.4 Focusing on the Essentials and Supporting Knowledge Transfer

Since the game is designed to support students at their subsequent real project work, not to steal time from this task, the time allocated to playing the game is limited by intention. That is why the game does not impart all known phenomena and effects that might appear at driving an SE endeavor. The SEMAT Essence Kernel encloses the essential aspects common to all SE endeavors but not every detail and aspect that might be of interest only under certain circumstances. By integrating the kernel, the Simulation Game follows that approach. It is as concrete as the kernel itself. No distractions were added in order to keep players focused. Topics and aspects omitted or just broached might be deepened and discussed in debriefing activities or at the following course project itself.

By choosing the Essence Kernel as the foundation of the Simulation Game, students get familiar with a compact thinking framework which is not bound to any practice or software process and supports driving any SE endeavor. By integrating the fundamental mechanisms of endeavor assessment, the definition of next goals, choosing the next appropriate activities to accomplish these goals, and monitoring the progress and health of all essential dimensions directly into the gameplay, students acquire highly transferable knowledge and skills.

3.4.5   Facilitating Interaction and Discussion in the Real World

The game provides occasions for discussion to facilitate thoughtful analysis and social interaction. It delivers feedback indicating how well a player's decisions were, compared to the decisions of other team members—and how well the whole team performed, compared to other teams in the course. The game collects results of all players and their teams to support debriefing activities.

3.4.6   Supporting the Acquisition of New Knowledge

In a meta-study, the authors stressed that "[…] game-based learning appears to have more impact on lower cognitive levels, reinforcing knowledge learned earlier. It seems inadequate for teaching new knowledge." [43] While the Puzzler was designed to learn and reinforce concepts and vocab, overall addressing lower cognitive levels, it is the objective of this game to let players actively apply concepts, to analyze and reflect on their application in a PDCA-cycle.

3.4.7   Gameplay

Players slip into the role of a coach directing a virtual team of three developers through an SE endeavor having a fixed budget and a fixed cost rate per day. By assigning activities to their virtual team, the endeavor gets progressed as far as all preconditions for performing the assigned activity are satisfied. Before a player may assign an activity to her virtual team, she must explore that activity first. For that, a player makes use of the Navigator integrated into the game. Inside a game environment, it provides the opportunity to explore and collect Activities. When an activity is assigned to the virtual team, it depends on the fact, if all the prerequisites to successfully perform the activity are met. If this is the case, the virtual team delivers feedback about their current tasks via messages. The list of messages grows while the game progresses and serves as an activity log, enabling the analysis of decisions taken by just scrolling down the list of messages.

The analysis of a message from the virtual team might trigger a new assessment of an Alpha State. The player should utilize the provided Navigator to get support at this point. The player must find the Checkpoint corresponding to the incoming message and decide if it should be checked. The Navigator acts inside the game as it would in a real SE endeavor. It does not define the state of the virtual endeavor but gives support to assess it. To a player consciously processing all incoming information, the Navigator perfectly provides the current state of his virtual endeavor—just like the Navigator would in an ideal situation in a real SE endeavor. If a player does not process the incoming information correctly, he runs into danger to make wrong decisions at assigning activities based on a misconceived impression of endeavors' current state—just like in a real SE endeavor.

When all Checkpoints of an Alpha State got fulfilled, a new Alpha State is reached. In that case, the player has to decide if a new activity should be assigned to the virtual team. The Navigator supports at this point by linking all the Activities addressing the next targeted Alpha State and by providing an elementary to-do list. Should the player assign an activity with open preconditions on its addressed Alpha States or Checkpoints, a tutor message gets sent to the player. If the player assigns only activities that cannot be progressed a tutor message gets sent, stating that no progress was made for several days. Because the cost rate per working day is fixed, a player would have spent money without achieving any progress on the endeavor and might regret decisions made.

To enable learning from failure the game provides a *time travel* feature enabling the player to travel back in time and make decisions once again—now with increased knowledge. To avoid abuse of the time travel feature and not to promote unconscious try-error-time-travel cycles, this feature is burdened with cost, making it more attractive to try finding good decisions and to use the time travel feature only in case of need.

The virtual team of a player starts with low performance to reflect the assumption that a new team starting an endeavor does not start with full performance [47]. To unfold the team's full potential, it has to organize itself and its work, find its ideal way of working, has to get support, and track its progress. In SEMAT Essence, all these issues are implemented by the Alphas of the Endeavor area of concern. To raise the performance of the virtual team, the Alphas of this area of concern must be progressed.

Figure 3.6 shows the user interface of the Simulation Game. The game provides a simple non-distracting user interface oriented toward instant messengers, requiring no further introduction. At the left side, we see the Essence Navigator, deeply integrated into the gameplay. By designing and providing a lean interface with scaffolding where needed, the extrinsic cognitive load is kept low allowing learners to focus on the essential learning content.

3.4.8 TEAMWORK—COLLABORATION AND COMPETITION

Experts in the field of game-based learning demand a "wider use of social interactive learning." [48] The game adds the idea of teams to the individual gameplay of every participant. In this setting, each player is exploring the whole game and the integrated learning content on her own but is a member of a team at the same time. Measuring the performance of the whole team as a primary success indicator of the game fosters collaboration and discussion inside the teams trying to perform better than other teams. This opens new opportunities for interaction. Utilizing provided leaderboards of team rankings as well as the ranking of individual players gives

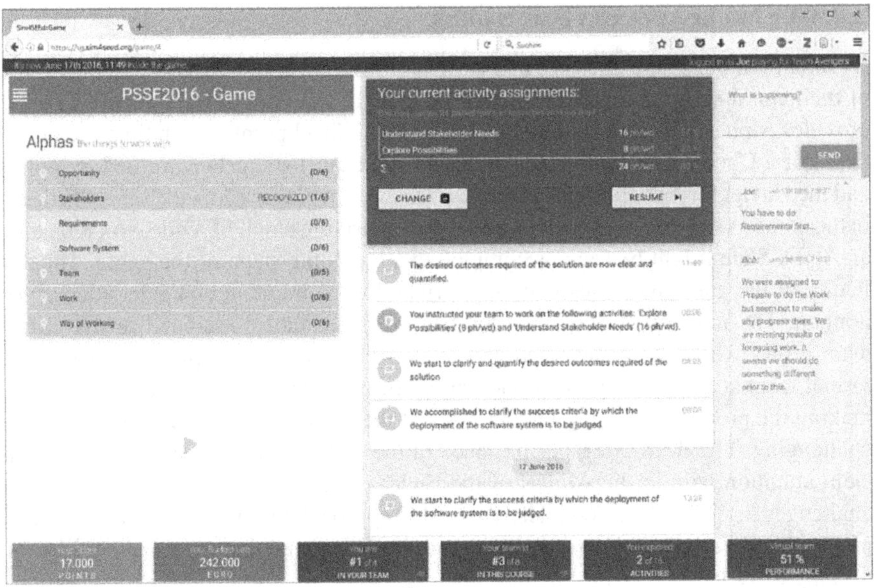

FIGURE 3.6 Screenshot of the Essence Simulation Game.

orientation how optimized chosen paths are in relation to other one's results. This orientation gives immediate feedback and is the starting point for further interactions inside a team. Since all players try to master the same challenges, a team member performing better at a given time may support other members of the team—having their common goal in mind. This approach combines collaboration aspects of social interaction inside teams with the competition aspect between teams. The game provides an elementary team chat.

3.4.9 Rewarding Good SE Practice at Scoring and Ranking

As SE is defined as "the application of a systematic, disciplined, quantifiable approach to the development, operation, and maintenance of software [...]" [4], the game rewards good SE practices and penalizes bad ones, assuring that the chance to get points by accident is minor. The point system integrated into the game reflects Essence's usage in the real world and rewards conscious decisions. Essence reflects the progress of an endeavor in the Checkpoints fulfilled, and the Alpha States reached. Representing that, the game rewards fulfilled checkpoints in the underlying simulation model driven by players' decisions. To reward conscious practice, the assessment of a Checkpoint itself gets rewarded, if that one gets checked after such an assessment is indicated by the game's state. To facilitate players' reflective thinking about decisions made so far, the game provides rankings and leaderboards of players inside a team, as well as a ranking of the team inside the whole course. Rankings are presented in the status bar and are always visible to the player. A click at one of the ranking stats reveals corresponding leaderboards. All players get presented with the leaderboards corresponding to their individual progressed virtual time inside the game.

3.4.10 No Levels and Game Badges

By intention, this game does not make use of levels and badges. Instead, it makes use of the natural structure and "rewarding system" of the underlying domain. Essence provides Alphas with their Alpha States and their Checkpoints. Each time the player ticks off a Checkpoint (and that action was indicated) she gets rewarded by points and the Navigator visualizes the progress. This way, a player earns the same "badges" in the game as she does as a software engineer at driving a real SE endeavor. Reaching an Alpha State might be seen as completing a level-like stage of the game. The difficulty of the game increases naturally, driven by the inherent characteristics of the domain. The number of activities that can be (reasonably) assigned to the virtual team grows while the game is progressing. By assigning multiple activities to the virtual team at once, the number and variety of information flowing in are growing, making the proper processing and analysis of the current state of the endeavor more challenging. The decreasing performance of the virtual team, caused by the insufficient attention paid to the Alphas of the Endeavor area of concern, might add new challenges too. With these characteristics, this approach provides an *intrinsic*, *tightly integrated*, *reflected*, and *asynchronous* (turn-based) game that is utilizing a *blended paradigm* [7, 49].

3.5 EVALUATING STUDY

This section describes the evaluation of concepts and approaches described in this chapter. A case study was conducted to evaluate concepts and games developed. Details follow in the next subsection. Also, in order to establish the consideration of all relevant dimensions, the characteristics of the approaches and the learning games provided were mapped to quality criteria of learning games proposed by Dondi and Moretti [45]. This mapping ensures that all relevant dimensions of learning games were considered, and the demanded quality criteria are provided. Two additional mappings to heuristics were conducted to compare the approaches taken with recommendations based on the synthesis of a comprehensive SLR by Jiang et al. [18] as well as with SE education requirements based on conclusions of Boehm [3] reviewing SE in the 20th and 21st century. Further was ensured that the described approaches represent the characteristics of constructivist learning environments, which are widely accepted to be facilitating learning, collected by Jonassen [21, 50].

3.5.1 Study Design

This section describes the setup of the case study used to evaluate the chosen approaches. Two groups of participants took part in the case study. Both consisted of students of the Hochschule Stralsund—University of Applied Sciences, Germany.

3.5.2 Characteristics of Participating Groups

Both groups were employed in the summer semester of 2016. They provided the observations and results reported. The first group (Group 1) consisted of 12 students

(11 male, one female) taking the course "SMIB4500—Project Seminar Software Engineering" embedded in the 4th semester of the undergraduate curriculum of "SMIB—Applied Computer Science, Software Development and Media Informatics." Within the scope of the course, students got introduced to SEMAT Essence for the first time. Traditionally in the course, students exercise a software project from start to end, following a given software process based on the OpenUP [41] and AgileUP [49] and heavily customized to the organizational needs of the course. This software process should not be utilized in a real SE endeavor customized that way. Students got introduced to SEMAT Essence and in particular the Essence Kernel to get provided with transferable concepts and a thinking framework being of use in any future SE endeavor.

The second group (Group 2) consisted of seven volunteers, visiting the 6th semester of the undergraduate program "SMIB—Applied Computer Science, Software Development and Media Informatics" and interested in learning something about SE in general and Essence in particular. This group differs to some extent from Group 1.

One year before, they got shortly introduced to SEMAT Essence. Generally, students of SMIB in sixth semester already had their practical semester where they gain experience in real software industry. In their 6th semester, they are processing a bigger software project within the scope of a course. Within that course, they got in touch with Essence again. So, they were already working with Essence Kernel Cards to some extent. Students of both groups are enjoying digital games. 53% (n = 10) play regularly and further 37% (n = 7) to a lesser extent. 47.3% of the participants play more than 5 hours per week. 68% of the participants connect learning with games. None of the participants disagreed with the statement that "games provide learning." 42% (n = 5) of Group 1 and 86% (n = 6) of Group 2 stated to have collected practical experience in software projects outside of the curriculum.

3.5.3 THE PROCEDURE OF GROUP 1

Within the regular course students of Group 1 were introduced into SEMAT Essence by an educational case study [8], presenting a small team of software developers at kickstart of a software project. SEMAT provides this case study. Students were invited to play the Essence Kernel Puzzler in preparation of the Simulation Game. At the next course meeting, a few days later, two course units of 90 minutes were used for playing the Simulation Game and a debriefing session. The students were already organized into four teams for their project work. These project teams were used for the game too. The author provided an introduction into the gameplay, provided technical support, answered questions regarding the game, and moderated the debriefing session. Finally, students filled in the questionnaire. After this session, students used the Essence Navigator in their project work. The tool supported project team meetings and helped teams to keep on track. The Essence Navigator provided an enacted Essence Kernel. Since the process to follow was not modeled as Essence practices forming an Essence method, students had to do some mental mapping between Essence concepts, for example, Activity Spaces and activities required by the given software process to follow. In an optional exercise, the teams were asked to map explicitly the assigned activities of the given process to Activity Spaces of the

Essence Kernel and the points in time, when all the Alpha States got achieved, to phases and concrete iterations of the given software process. The Alpha States that were not part of the assigned project work had to be marked. At each mapping, the students were asked to provide a short explanation.

3.5.4   THE PROCEDURE OF GROUP 2

Students were invited by the author to take part in a Simulation Game session and (optionally) to take the Essence Kernel Puzzler in preparation of the Simulation Game. Since students already had contact with SEMAT Essence, no further preparation was provided. The group was partitioned into three teams. In one session, lasting 2 hours, the simulation game was played followed by the debriefing session. The author provided an introduction into the gameplay, provided technical support, and answered questions regarding the game. Finally, the questionnaire was filled in by the students.

3.5.5   WHY IS THERE NO COMPARATIVE EXPERIMENT?

Having only access to quite small groups of students for this case study, it was chosen to provide all of them with the chance to learn from new concepts and approaches and to collect as much feedback on the tools and concepts developed as possible. With just 19 participants a division into treatment and control groups would have made the results less informative and significant. Furthermore, SEMAT Essence is a new standard with growing—but at the time of conducting—limited learning material. With no prepared rich and ready to use learning material, rated competitive to the provided approach, any attempt to produce that material alongside with limited resources was judged to be in danger of getting exposed to a biased performance.

3.5.6   WHY ARE THERE NO PRE-TEST/POST-TESTS?

The skills and competencies striven for in this approach and facilitated by the games provided are to orientate inside an SE endeavor. This includes utilizing SE concepts and tools provided to act in an SE endeavor in a goal-oriented and structured way, for example, by holistically assessing the current state of an SE endeavor and determining next reasonable steps to take. Such skills and the corresponding attitudes are not, or only to a small extent, measurable in a test. Rote memorization is not a primary concept of Essence, which provides the foundation of the approach. Instead, it is providing rich as well as compact documentation, for example, in the form of physical cards to carry with you. There is no need to rote memorization of all states and their checkpoints. Essence promotes learning by doing and enables to learn and deepen knowledge on the fly—once basic concepts are understood. The Essence Kernel Puzzler, as well as the Simulation Game, provides embedded assessment, in-game measurements allowing drawing inferences from the gameplay about the learning progress to, some extent. This approach avoids disadvantages associated with examinations of learning progress separated from the gameplay reported by existing studies of DGBL [51].

3.5.7   Questionnaire Design and Statistical Hypotheses Testing

The questionnaire was designed to survey different aspects of the approaches taken. The answer types include dichotomic choices, 5-point Likert-type scales and other rating scales resulting in ordinal scaled data, as well as free text answers to collect remarks of participants.

To establish statistical significance answers undergone hypothesis testing where appropriate. Having only a small set of observations ($n < 20$) without any knowledge about the particular distribution of the data only a *non-parametric* statistical test, able to handle small sets of observations, is qualified for this study. The *Sign-test* fulfilling these criteria was chosen. It is a non-parametric binomial test about the median η of a population.

3.6   RESULTS

This section describes results of the evaluating case study. For the sake of brevity, no representation of the mapping of presented concepts on recognized heuristics done [21] is given here.

3.6.1   In-Game Measurements of the Essence Kernel Puzzler

At conducting the evaluating study 76 game instances and 788 attempts to master levels of the Puzzler were counted. 508 (64.5%) of these attempts were successful while 280 (35.5%) failed. Players spent in sum 22 hours trying to master the levels of the Puzzler. On average each level of the Puzzler was played 98.5 times (sd 58.6, median 88). Not all the game instances ($n = 76$) resulted in a mastered first level ($n = 69$). While remarkable a part of the players masters each level just once, others repeat to master the levels multiple times, which might be motivated by the wish to improve the time needed or to decrease failures made. Of the 280 failed attempts to master a level of the Puzzler, 83.9% ($n = 235$) were mastered afterward. Overall, the number of players mastering Puzzler's levels is decreasing from level to level. Starting with 69 players, who mastered level 1, only 21 were mastering level 8. This decrease correlates with the assumed difficulty of single levels.

3.6.2   In-Game Measurements of the Simulation Game

Teams' scores, concerning both, points for achieving Checkpoints of Alpha States in the underlying simulation model as well as points for consciously assessing these Checkpoints, indicate that the players were able to master the gameplay, the tools provided for support, and, hence, the underlying learning content. To get these points, players had to progress their virtual endeavors and assess its Alphas consciously. Players' scores prove that they were able to follow the PDCA cycle. Players had to utilize relationships between Essence Kernel's elements and to show that they are already familiar with them.

The results indicate different types of players and learners. Results show players aiming at performing without mistakes right from the start and others, which are willing to take the given opportunities to improve results iteratively. The *time travel* feature that was designed to provide the opportunity to learn from failures. Overall, the players of the case study traveled 95 times in time and covered 810 days thereby. Results show that the usage of this feature varies widely and ranges from 0% to 100% of team members utilizing this feature. One team of Group 1 and one team of Group 2 provide interesting extreme manifestations of this issue. While none of the members of the Group 1 team did use the time travel feature, all players the Group 2 team used it with the highest count of performed time travels. Both teams achieved high scores—at different efficiency.

Group 2, the more experienced students, were not able to outperform Group 1 in the setting of this case study. The mixed rankings of teams from Group 1 and Group 2 indicate that the Simulation Game provided the opportunity to learn for both the more and the less experienced student groups.

3.6.3 QUESTIONNAIRE RESULTS

77% (n = 10) of the respondents stated that the Puzzler prepared them well for the Simulation Game. 92% of responding students (n = 12) would recommend the Puzzler to a friend or fellow student. Students stated they found it to be a neat tool to learn the vocab fast and to get familiar with first relationships between elements.

The Simulation Game was considered to be fun and students attributed learning success to it. The difficulty of the Simulation Game was perceived as "just right" by 42.1% (n = 8) of the participants. 26.3% (n = 5) found it slightly easy and 31.6% (n = 6) of the players found it slightly hard. The vast majority (78.9%, n = 15) of all students assessed the duration as "just right," 3 players (15.8%) felt the duration was "too long" and only one player (5,3%) felt it was "too short."

Students (95%, n = 18) stated that they learned something about SE by playing the Simulation Game. Interestingly the more experienced students of Group 2 perceived occurred learning even stronger than those of Group 1.86% of Group 2 chose the answer item representing the highest agreement. 89.5% (n = 17) of all participants stated they would play the Simulation Game again and students would recommend the game to a friend or fellow student. Students stated they would play the game again to optimize their performance and to improve their high score. They would like to benefit from experiences of the first run and to test findings in a next one.

Students stated that learning was perceived faster and deeper as in lectures. Asked for the reasons, why they recommend the Simulation Game as a standard part of SE courses, participants stated, that they appreciated the focus on essential content, the relatively short duration of the game, the overview, and the preparation of upcoming projects provided. The students liked that relationships between elements, for example, Activities and Alphas, got visible. Students mentioned fast feedback, focus on virtually practicing steps in an endeavor and the opportunity to learn from failures as particularly advantageous. Students perceived to have improved their performance while playing the Simulation Game. This seems to be a good indicator of felt self-efficacy and fits well to the perceived learning.

The majority, 79% of the participants (n = 15), stated that they reinforced SE knowledge of previous lectures or courses. Students stated too that they perceived that they learned something new about SE by playing the Simulation Game. They stated that having to think about the next steps to take action and to have to repeat-edly process Alphas and their Checkpoints, to recurrently think about them in detail, helped to recognize relationships between elements and to internalize concepts.

All (100%, n = 19) students stated that the fun at playing the game, the necessity to make own active decisions, and the Essence Navigator helped at learning. Of these features, active decision-making, was assessed as very strongly helping by the high-est number of participants (79%, n = 15| Group 1: 75%, n = 9|Group 2: 86%, n = 6) followed by fun (74%, n = 14|Group 1: 75%, n = 9|Group 2: 71%, n = 5). These results indicate strong arguments for DGBL and inherent constructivist learning approaches. That the Essence Navigator was perceived as that helpful, confirms the assumption that digital learning games should embed learning content about the pro-cess, method, or kernel in this case. This was an aspect identified as lacking by most of the existing DGBL approaches so far.

Students stated that debriefing activities (89%, n = 17), as well as team communi-cation (84%, n = 16), provided learning. Out of them, almost one-third of the stu-dents indicated these two aspects as very strongly supporting learning, and two-thirds considered them as helpful.

The author observed that the game provided triggers and initiated social interac-tions. Active and direct face-to-face communication was preferred over utilizing the elementary chat provided by the game. As one student stated: "We did not need the team chat because we were sitting next to each other." These results indicate strong arguments for social constructivist learning approaches.

Individual team results strongly indicate that providing the opportunity to play as a team may work well, but does not guarantee such desired cooperation. Depending on the initial situation of teams' members, the short period allocated to playing the game in the case study may not have provided enough opportunity to get to that state.

The *time travel* feature could not prove its support of learning with statistical sig-nificance (Sign-test, $\alpha = 0.05$) It seems that not all students recognized this feature as supportive as anticipated. 63% (n = 12) of participating students stated that this fea-ture was helpful at learning. One-half of them perceived this feature as very strongly helping. This assertion is supported by the free text answers stating several times that students appreciated the "opportunity to learn from mistakes." Results show that only 63% of all players used this feature. This value of 63% matches the ratio of players appreciating the time travel feature as supportive of learning. Since the answers to the questionnaire were collected anonymously, no clear correlation can be deter-mined, but the results may indicate that players using this feature appreciate it as supportive at learning.

Other features built into the Simulation Game that were not able to show statisti-cally significant support (Sign-test, $\alpha = 0.05$) to learning are *rankings* and *leader-boards*. Only 42% (n = 8) of participating students stated that rankings and leaderboards provided support at learning, 58% of the students (n = 11) did not. As students' agreement to helping *team communication* indicates, the game provided triggers for interaction. Why *rankings* and *leaderboards* were not perceived support-ive by the majority of players might have several reasons and be caused by the dynam-ics of the gameplay of the teams. Once team communication got started and had been ongoing, not all team members had to look at the leaderboards provided. Results may have been compared as part of verbal team communication too. Such assumption is supported by the observation that ten out of the eleven players not valuing rankings and leaderboards assessed team communication as supportive to learning.

Responding students stated that they think SEMAT Essence and the Essence Kernel will be of help in their future projects. None of the students reported that they believe it would not provide support. Students stated that they want to deploy SEMAT Essence in their future projects. While none of the students stated not to want to use Essence in future projects, a third (n = 6) of all participating students chose the neutral item at answering this question.

3.6.4 Course Project Work

Students of Group 1 utilized the Essence Navigator, provided in addition to a given SE process, to drive their course project work. As part of regular mandatory team meetings, hold two times a week, the Alpha States and their Checkpoints were assessed. To assess the Alpha States in real project required to think about the project's progress and health. Different from the Simulation Game, teams now had to provide feedback on their own–triggered by Checkpoints of the Alpha States, which guided group discussions. Students were able to utilize the already familiar Essence Navigator mostly right from the start of the project work and without further support by the lecturer. This indicates that concepts were understood, and students were able to apply them. At some points and depending on individual working style, some teams had slightly more a tendency to quickly answer questions and assess the Checkpoints in a rather superficial way than others. Based on limited experience developing more complex software systems, this comes as no real surprise and may reflect the approach of any novice acting in SE projects. By asking to explain the reasoning behind the assessment of the Checkpoints and the Alpha States, those teams were motivated to think further about specific issues.

Altogether it can be summarized that the working style of the teams in the case study was much more oriented toward a holistic perspective of the SE endeavor than the working style of teams in the years before, where the same course was held. Teams discussed much more about essential aspects that got ignored in the past where only the SE process was given to the teams. Thereby the teams did not lose the focus on operative SE tasks to do in the process but were additionally able to give reasons for doing those tasks.

Three out of four teams performed the optional mapping exercise and delivered reasonable results. As students perceived the activities to do, besides designing and implementing source code, as very comprehensive, they were surprised their assigned project work did not cover some essential aspects of an SE endeavor for organizational reasons of the course. Those aspects got clearly visible by the non-addressed Alpha States and put the project work done into perspective.

3.7 DISCUSSION AND CONCLUSIONS

Corresponding to the findings of other deployments of the Essence Kernel [52], some ambiguous formulations and single terms used in the descriptions of checkpoints provided reasons for requesting and discussions. Péraire and Sedano reported that these ambiguities were leading to situations "where the team discusses the meaning of a checklist item instead of having a conversation about the project" [24]. In the context of the described course project, aiming at introducing students into SE practices and methods, such discussions were not judged as impeding but welcome since they provided occasions to reflect on approaches prescribed by the process provided and to think about alternatives.

Since students of Group 1 mainly had no chance to develop more complex software systems in the past, they were not able to draw on any existing experiences utilizing SE practices covering the essential aspects of an SE endeavor. That is why they were provided with an SE process tailored to the need of the course. Since the given SE process was not implemented using the Essence language, some concepts had to be mapped and discussed. For instance, the given SE process made use of Use Cases to structure requirements. The Essence Kernel on its own does not provide substructures of requirements since different practices handle this in various ways.

This challenging aspect was reported by Péraire and Sedano [52] too. Differing from their study students in this case study did not already have considerable average work experience in industrial practice.

The observation that students were able to utilize the Essence Navigator, as well as the provided enacted Essence Kernel, right from the start of their course project work indicates that the Simulation Game contributed to lowering the cognitive load that students faced in their project work. Following the *Cognitive Load Theory (CLT)*, any knowledge already learned, in terms of CLT stored in long-term memory, frees room in the rather limited working memory and facilitates learning of related new knowledge. [53] This indicates too that the Simulation Game provided a valuable anchor that students were able to refer to in their thinking and discussions with teammates.

Introducing additional concepts like Essence takes time. Alpha assessment sessions as part of regular team meetings need time too. Without time added to a course, the time available for remaining tasks is inevitably reduced. Students of Group 1 in the case study were able to deliver their projects with at least the same quality as teams on the same course in years before. Some of the less prioritized features of the required software project outcome had to be omitted in the course project in favor of a more holistic and conscious working style.

By utilizing the generalist approach of the SEMAT Essence Kernel, students were provided with a highly transferable thinking framework acting as an anchor and providing support, orientation, and guidance in any future SE endeavor. All in all, students applied a systematic, disciplined and quantifiable approach to the development of their software—and appreciated the guidance given by that approach. Hence, they acted as software engineers-to-be.

The results indicate that the decision to develop games with a focus on the intended learning objectives as well as the design decisions introduced in Section 4 vitally contributed to the performance of the approaches taken.

The case study, conducted to evaluate the developed games, provided first insights and encouraging results. Since the number of participants was rather small, results cannot be considered to be conclusive. A wider utilization of the proposed approaches is needed to compare the results with those of the case study and to collect a broader base for evaluation.

3.8   FUTURE WORK AND RESEARCH DIRECTIONS

Since the conduction of the case study described in this chapter, much activity inside the SEMAT community and their global SEMAT Education Project created valuable learning material, including a textbook and accompanying material like exercises and quizzes.

The games introduced in this chapter will get integrated into the efforts to make SEMAT Essence easily accessible to the broad community in education and training. To accomplish that, the Simulation Game needs to be adapted to learning scenarios different than the in-class and face-to-face courses that it was designed for initially.

Team dynamics while playing the Simulation Game provide an exciting field of research for future work. The game elements, which were not able to show statistically significant support at learning, provide interesting fields of observation and research for future studies of the game. It would be interesting to prove or disprove the hypothesis that players, assessing *time travels* as well as *rankings* and *leaderboards* as not supportive to learning, draw primarily from team's experience and team communication—and may be trying to avoid failures already made by others. To support such findings, the results of the game and the questionnaires would need some mapping—something that was not implemented in this first study.

The broad inclusion of Essence in SE education worldwide opens opportunities for replicated studies to evaluate the effectiveness and efficiency of the approach further. The learning material that is now available allows for experimental study designs including comparison groups.

ACKNOWLEDGMENTS

Most findings presented in this chapter are the results of the author's Ph.D. research, which would not have been possible without the support of the author's university and faculty. In particular, the author would like to thank the supervisors and reviewers of his dissertation for stimulating discussions. Special thanks go to the IACS for the opportunities of exchanging ideas and supporting the presentation of author's ideas and results at colloquia, workshops, and conferences. Essential impulses for author's work resulted from these events.

NOTES

1   In this chapter, the term *SE method* is preferred to the term *software process*. Both are used in literature and community partly synonymously, but also in parts with different semantics. SWEBOK states "[...] methods provide an organized and systematic approach to developing software [...]." *Computer Society* [1] Depending on the context, a *software process* or *SE method* may represent a complete life cycle (*SDLC* or *SPLC*), but it does not have to necessarily.

2   following the categorization of Prensky [7].

3   *Software Engineering Method and Theory*, an initiative that "drives a process to re-found software engineering based on a solid theory, proven principles and best practices." [8], http://semat.org

4   The PDCA cycle represents an adapted Demen or Shewart cycle [11], well known in the field of modern quality control and continuous improvement and, as such, part of lean thinking principles.

5 This work uses the widely accepted *Revised Bloom's Taxonomy* [42] to characterize learning objectives.
6 This characterization utilizes those proposed by Prensky [7].
7 https://puzzler.sim4seed.org

REFERENCES

[1] IEEE Computer Society. 2014. *Guide to the Software Engineering Body of Knowledge (SWEBOK(R)): Version 3.0* (3rd ed.). IEEE Computer Society Press, Los Alamitos, CA, USA.

[2] T. C. Lethbridge, J. Diaz-Herrera, R. J. LeBlanc, and J. Barrie Thompson. 2007. *Improving Software Practice Through Education: Challenges and Future Trends*. In *2007 Future of Software Engineering (FOSE'07)*. IEEE Computer Society, Washington, DC, USA, 12–28. doi: 10.1109/FOSE.2007.13

[3] B. Boehm. 2006. *A View of 20th and 21st Century Software Engineering*. In *Proceedings of the 28th International Conference on Software Engineering (ICSE'06)*. ACM, New York, NY, USA, 12–29. doi: 10.1145/1134285.1134288

[4] I. Sommerville. 2010. *Software Engineering* (9th revised ed.). Addison-Wesley Longman, Amsterdam.

[5] C. G. von Wangenheim and F. Shull. 2009. To Game or Not to Game? *IEEE Software* 26, 2, 92–94.

[6] K. Reich. 2012. *Konstruktivistische Didaktik: Das Lehr- und Studienbuch mit Online-Methodenpool* (5. erweiterte auflage ed.). Beltz.

[7] M. Prensky. 2007. *Digital Game-Based Learning*. Paragon House.

[8] SEMAT Community. 2018. *What is SEMAT?* http://semat.org/what-is-semat-

[9] Object Management Group (OMG). 2015. *Essence - Kernel and Language for Software Engineering Methods, Version 1.1*. http://www.omg.org/spec/Essence/1.1/

[10] The SEMAT Community. 2016. *SEMAT - Alpha State Cards*. http://semat.org/de/alpha-state-cards-with-abbrev-checklists

[11] R. Moen and C. Norman. 2006. *Evolution of the PDCA cycle*. http://pkpinc.com/files/NA01_Moen_Norman_fullpaper.pdf

[12] I. Jacobson, P.-W. Ng, P. E. McMahon, I. Spence, and S. Lidman. 2013. *The Essence of Software Engineering: Applying the SEMAT Kernel* (1st ed.). Addison-Wesley Professional, Upper Saddle River, NJ.

[13] P. E. McMahon. 2013. *Essence: Why do we need it?* http://sematblog.wordpress.com/2013/11/16/essence-why-do-we-need-it/

[14] I. Jacobson, P.-W. Ng, I. Spence, and P. E. McMahon. 2014. Major-league SEMAT: Why should an executive care? *Commun. ACM* 57, 4, 44–50. http://dl.acm.org/citation.cfm?id=2580712

[15] I. Jacobson, I. Spence, and P.-W. Ng. 2013. Agile and SEMAT - Perfect Partners. *Queue* 11, 9, 30:30–30:41. doi: 10.1145/2538031.2541674

[16] P.-W. Ng and S. Huang. 2013. Essence: A framework to help bridge the gap between software engineering education and industry needs. *IEEE*, 304–308. doi: 10.1109/CSEET.2013.6595266

[17] M. Thomas Connolly, E. A. Boyle, E. MacArthur, T. Hainey, and J. M. Boyle. 2012. A systematic literature review of empirical evidence on computer games and serious games. *Computers & Education* 59, 2 (Sept. 2012), 661–686. doi: 10.1016/j.compedu.2012.03.004

[18] S. Jiang, H. Zhang, C. Gao, D. Shao, and G. Rong. 2015. *Process Simulation for Software Engineering Education*. In *Proceedings of the 2015 International Conference on Software and System Process (ICSSP 2015)*. ACM, New York, NY, USA, 147–156. doi: 10.1145/2785592.2785606

[19] D. C. C. Peixoto, R. M. Possa, R. F. Resende, and C. I. P. S. Pádua. 2011. *An Overview of the Main Design Characteristics of Simulation Games in Software Engineering Education.* In *2011 24th IEEE-CS Conference on Software Engineering Education and Training (CSEE T).* 101–110. https://doi.org/10.1109/CSEET.2011.5876076

[20] A. Nassal. 2015. *Projektmanagement Spielend Lernen.* In *Software Engineering im Unterricht der Hochschulen (SEUH).* 53–64.

[21] J. Pieper. 2017. Simulation and Digital Game-based Learning in Software Engineering Education: An Integrated Approach to Learn Software Engineering Methods. Ph.D. Dissertation. Universität Rostock, Rostock.

[22] E. Navarro. 2006. SimSE: A Software Engineering Simulation Environment for Software Process Education. Ph.D. Dissertation. University of California, Irvine, CA. http://www.ics.uci.edu/~emilyo/papers/Dissertation.pdf

[23] E. O. Navarro and A. van der Hoek. 2004. *SIMSE: An Interactive Simulation Game for Software Engineering Education.* In *Proceedings of the 7th IASTED International Conference on Computers and Advanced Technology in Education (CATE).* Kauai, Hawaii, 12–17.

[24] K. Shaw and J. Dermoudy. 2005. *Engendering an Empathy for Software Engineering.* In *Proceedings of the 7th Australasian conference on Computing education - Volume 42 (ACE '05).* Australian Computer Society, Inc., Darlinghurst, Australia, 135–144. http://dl.acm.org/citation.cfm?id=1082424.1082441

[25] A Drappa and J. Ludewig. 1999. Quantitative modeling for the interactive simulation of software projects. *Journal of Systems and Software* 46, 2–3, 113–122. doi: 10.1016/S0164-1212(99)00005-9

[26] A. Drappa and J. Ludewig. 2000. *Simulation in software engineering training.* In *Proceedings of the 22nd International Conference on Software Engineering (ICSE'00).* ACM, New York, NY, USA, 199–208. doi: 10.1145/337180.337203

[27] P. Mandl-Striegnitz. 2001. *How to Successfully Use Software Project Simulation for Educating Software Project Managers.* In *Frontiers in Education Conference, 2001. 31st Annual,* Vol. 1. IEEE, T2D–19. http://ieeexplore.ieee.org/xpls/abs_all.jsp?arnumber=963884

[28] R. T. Mittermeir, E. Hochmüller, A. Bollin, S. Jäger, and M. Nusser. 2003. *AMEISE – A Media Education Initiative for Software Engineering Concepts, the Environment and Initial Experiences.* In *Proceedings of the Interactive Computer aided Learning (ICL) 2003 International Workshop.* Villach, Austria.

[29] M. O. Barros, A. R. Dantas, G. O. Veronese, and C. M. L. Werner. 2006. Model-driven game development: Experience and model enhancements in software project management education. *Software Process: Improvement and Practice* 11, 4, 411–421.

[30] H. Sharp and P. Hall. 2000. *An Interactive Multimedia Software House Simulation for Postgraduate Software Engineers.* In *Software Engineering, International Conference on.* IEEE Computer Society, Los Alamitos, CA, USA, 688. doi: 10.1109/ICSE.2000.10053

[31] E. Ye, C. Liu, and J. A. Polack-Wahl. 2007. *Enhancing Software Engineering Education Using Teaching Aids In 3-D Online Virtual Worlds.* In *2007 37th Annual Frontiers In Education Conference-Global Engineering: Knowledge Without Borders, Opportunities Without Passports.* IEEE, T1E–8. http://ieeexplore.ieee.org/xpls/abs_all.jsp?arnumber=4417884

[32] A. Jain and B. Boehm. 2006. *SimVBSE: Developing a game for value-based software engineering.* In *Proceedings of the 19th Conference on Software Engineering Education and Training.* 103–114.

[33] C. Caulfield. 2011. Shall We Play a Game? Ph.D. Dissertation. Edith Cowan University, Joondalup, Australia. http://ro.ecu.edu.au/theses/447/

[34] A. Nassal. 2014. *A General Framework For Software Project Management Simulation Games.* In *2014 9th Iberian Conference on Information Systems and Technologies (CISTI).* 1–5. doi: 10.1109/CISTI.2014.6877074

[35] A. Nassal and M. Tichy. 2016. *Modeling Human Behavior for Software Engineering Simulation Games.* In *Proceedings of the 5th International Workshop on Games and Software Engineering (GAS '16). ACM,* New York, NY, USA, 8–14. doi: 10.1145/2896958.2896961

[36] D. C. C. Peixoto, R. M. Possa, R. F. Resende, and C. I. P. S. Pádua. 2012. *Challenges and Issues in the Development of a Software Engineering Simulation Game.* In *2012 Frontiers in Education Conference Proceedings.* 1–6. doi: 10.1109/FIE.2012.6462318

[37] J. E. N. Lino, M. A. Paludo, F. V. Binder, S. Reinehr, and A. Malucelli. 2015. *Project Management Game 2d (Pmg-2d): A Serious Game To Assist Software Project Managers Training.* In *IEEE Frontiers in Education Conference (FIE), 2015.32614 2015.*1–8. doi: 10.1109/FIE.2015.7344168

[38] P. A. Kirschner, J. Sweller, and R. E. Clark. 2006. Why minimal guidance during instruction does not work: An analysis of the failure of constructivist, discovery, problem-based, experiential, and inquiry-based teaching. *Educational Psychologist* 41, 2, 75–86.

[39] L. Harasim. 2011. *Learning Theory and Online Technologies.* Routledge, New York, NY.

[40] Fred Paas and John Sweller. 2014. Implications of Cognitive Load Theory for Multimedia Learning. In R. Mayer (Ed.), *The Cambridge Handbook of Multimedia Learning,* Cambridge University Press, Cambridge, UK (Cambridge Handbooks in Psychology, pp. 27–42).

[41] C. M. Reigeluth. 1999. *The Elaboration Theory: Guidance for Scope and Sequence Decisions.* In *Instructional Design Theories and Models: A New Paradigm of Instructional Theory.* Vol. 2. Lawrence Erlbaum Associates, Mahwah, NJ, 425–453. https://books.google.de/books?hl=de&lr=&id=FW9BA3c_VRkC&oi=fnd&pg=PT438&dq=The+elaboration+theory:+Guidance+for+Scope+and+Sequences+Decisions&ots=hq8AVzgEQQ&sig=CKlb4oNo3GK9G7NbLIKw9GecpDU

[42] L. W. Anderson and D. Krathwohl. 2001. *A Taxonomy for Learning, Teaching, and Assessing: A Revision of Bloom's Taxonomy of Educational Objectives.* Addison Wesley, Longman, New York.

[43] J. S. Breuer and G. Bente. 2010. Why so serious? On the relation of serious games and learning. *Eludamos. Journal for Computer Game Culture* 4, 1, 7–24.

[44] R. Van Eck. 2006. Digital game-based learning: It's not just the digital natives who are restless. *Educause Review* 41, 2, 16–30.

[45] C. Dondi and M. Moretti. 2007. A methodological proposal for learning games selection and quality assessment. *British Journal of Educational Technology* 38, 3, 502–512. doi: 10.1111/j.1467-8535.2007.00713.x

[46] D. R. Krathwohl. 2002. A revision of Bloom's taxonomy: An overview. *Theory into Practice* 41, 4, 212–218. http://www.tandfonline.com/doi/pdf/10.1207/s15430421tip4104_2

[47] B. W. Tuckman and M. A. C. Jensen. 1977. Stages of small-group development revisited. *Group & Organization Management* 2, 4, 419–427. http://gom.sagepub.com/content/2/4/419.short

[48] S. de Freitas and F. Liarokapis. 2011. *Serious Games: A New Paradigm for Education?* In *Serious Games and Edutainment Applications.* Springer, 9–23. http://link.springer.com/chapter/10.1007/978-1-4471-2161-9_2

[49] U. Ritterfeld and R. Weber. 2006. Video games for entertainment and education. In *Playing Video Games: Motives, Responses, and Consequences*, P. Vorderer and J. Bryant (Eds.). Lawrence Erlbaum Associates, Mahwah, NJ, 399–413. http://ocw.metu.edu.tr/pluginfile.php/2382/mod_resource/content/0/ceit706/week7/Ritterfeld_Weber.PDF

[50] D. H. Jonassen. 1994. Thinking Technology: Toward a Constructivist Design Model. *Educational Technology* 34, 4, 34–37.

[51] V. J. Shute, M. Ventura, M. Bauer, and D. Zapata-Rivera. 2009. Melding the power of serious games and embedded assessment to monitor and foster learning. *Serious Games: Mechanisms and Effects* 2 (2009), 295–321. https://books.google.de/books?hl=de&lr=&id=eGORAgAAQBAJ&oi=fnd&pg=PA295&dq=Melding+the+Power+of+Serious+Games+and+Embedded+Assessment+to+Monitor+and+Foster+Learning:+Flow+and+Grow.&ots=1u8qv2LcRv&sig=geOS7ZfG-DA-rpWbzod0uQCbwJQ

[52] C. Péraire and T. Sedano. 2014. *State-Based Monitoring and Goal-Driven Project Steering: Field Study of the Semat Essence Framework*. In *Companion Proceedings of the 36th International Conference on Software Engineering (ICSE Companion 2014)*. ACM, New York, NY, USA, 325–334. doi: 10.1145/2591062.2591155

[53] J. J. G. van Merriënboer and J. Sweller. 2005. Cognitive Load Theory and Complex Learning: Recent Developments and Future Directions. *Educational Psychology Review* 17, 2, 147–177. doi: 10.1007/s10648-005-3951-0

4 Building Casual Games and APIs for Teaching Introductory Programming Concepts

Brian Chau, Rob Nash, and Kelvin Sung
Comp. & Software Sys., University of Washington Bothell

Jason Pace
Digital Future Lab, University of Washington Bothell

CONTENTS

4.1   INTRODUCTION

When properly integrated into coursework, using videogames to teach computer science (CS) accomplishes desired student learning outcomes, builds excitement and enthusiasm for the discipline, and attracts a bright new generation of students early in their academic careers [1, 2]. As a relatively new approach, interested faculty require assistance in the form of elementary sample materials and tutorials to support their exploration and experimentation [3].

The Game-Themed Computer Science (GTCS) project and the associated library [3] are designed specifically for this purpose with elaborate sets of sample teaching materials that hide the graphics and gaming details [4]. The self-contained nature of the materials allows faculty to adopt and use each without significant modification to their existing classes. Results from adopting GTCS materials have demonstrated effectiveness in engaging students and achieving the desired learning outcomes [5–7]. In addition, results from the many workshops (e.g., [8]) showed that although interested faculty members with no background in graphics or gaming found the GTCS materials to be non-trivial, they were able to comprehend and begin developing game applications based on the GTCS library within a matter of hours [3].

Student feedback on GTCS materials indicated that though they find the materials motivating, they were also frustrated by the simplicity, for example, the absence of fundamental gaming features like power-ups or win conditions. On the other hand, faculty workshop participants pointed out that the most demanding efforts in building game-specific teaching materials are often unrelated to the educational goals which include the time-intensive processes of locating or generating art and audio assets, or implementing the annoying details of various object interaction rules.

To address this seemingly contradictory feedback while preserving the important characteristics of simplicity and usability for a targeted curriculum, the GTCS project group is building a series of causal games and corresponding APIs. These stand-alone games each showcase one or two programming concepts, allowing faculty to pick and choose for selective adoption. The games have gone through elaborate play-testing to ensure an engaging and complete gameplay experience. Each API is methodically extracted from the finished game and refined based on usability and support for the presentation of targeted programming concepts so that faculty can build their own aesthetically engaging materials while focusing on the pedagogy rather than irrelevant details such as asset management.

Currently, there are five games under development in various stages of completion. Two of the games in particular—Space Smasher and Corrupted—include finalized APIs, and the sample teaching materials for Space Smasher are currently being field tested in CS1/2 classrooms. This paper uses these two games and their respective APIs as examples to discuss our game development and API refinement processes and results.

In the rest of this paper, Section 2 briefly surveys previous work; section 3 reviews existing API studies and articulates a design guideline for our game APIs; section 4 discusses our game and API development processes; section 5 presents our APIs from Space Smasher and Corrupted; and section 6 concludes the paper.

4.2   GAMES AND CS1/2 CLASSES

Existing work on presenting CS1/2 concepts in the context of computer games can be broadly categorized into three approaches [4]: little or no game programming (e.g., [9]) where students learn by *playing* custom games; per-assignment game development (e.g., [10]) where individual assignments are games designed around technical topics being studied; and extensive game development where faculty and students work with custom game engines (e.g., [11]) or specialized environments (e.g., [12]).

As pointed out by Levy and Ben-Ari [13] and Ni [14], issues that faculty consider when examining new and innovative teaching materials for adoption include (among others) preparation time, material contents, and topic coverage. Yet, most of the existing results from integrating games in CS1/2 classes are typically from faculty members with expertise in graphics or games and are *"student-centric,"* where the main goals are student engagement and various learning outcomes—preparation time for adoption and flexibility of the materials for topic coverage are usually not primary concerns. Indeed, it can be challenging to take advantage of these results for the general faculty teaching CS1/2, since many have little to no background in computer graphics or games.

As discussed in the previous section, while effective in addressing the issues of faculty background and curricula modularity, the feedback from previous GTCS materials identified the seemingly contradictory student desire for complexity and faculty need for simplicity [3]. This paper presents the recent GTCS project group efforts in addressing this interesting dichotomy—building complete casual games that offer meaningful gameplay experiences for the students while designing APIs that ensure simple and straightforward curriculum development for the faculty.

4.3   API DESIGN GUIDELINES

An API can be described as a well-defined interface that exposes the external services of a singular component to clients who will consume these services as elemental software building blocks [15]. In our case of designing an interface for developing casual games, our APIs are a collection of functions intended to be reused by other programmers to perform common tasks that may be difficult, cumbersome, or tedious [16].

Well-defined APIs foster productivity, code reuse, encapsulation of complex systems, and consistent behaviors for their users [17]. A sound API should be easy to use and hard to misuse [18]. In the design of our API, some of the fundamental goals overlap (e.g., productivity and code reuse) while others oppose one another, offering interesting challenges. For example, while achieving tight encapsulation is desirable, our APIs must purposefully expose details relating to the concepts that they are designed to teach, for example, exposing the details of underlying 2D arrays that represent the grid system of Corrupted for student manipulation. To add to this, our end users are on the two ends of the spectrum of programming expertise—faculty and students of CS1/2 classes.

To address our requirements, the following considerations are articulated to guide the design of our APIs.

Usability and Structured Simplicity: usability and simplicity facilitate the creation of effective CS1/2 materials accessible to students and faculty with no background in graphics or gaming

Discoverability and Learnability: our end users must be able to build simple applications quickly with minimum familiarity of the APIs but also have the opportunity to gradually explore advanced functionality at their own pace

Expressiveness and Productivity: while the final products built by the students may resemble casual games, the APIs primarily support the building of effective teaching materials as vehicles for educational content delivery

Encapsulation and Modularity: as previously discussed, the goals are to tightly encapsulate the complex graphics and gaming functionality while strategically exposing selected concepts for teaching purposes.

Though important, performance is only a referencing factor in our API design—as long as an acceptable frame rate and memory footprint are maintained.

4.4 THE DEVELOPMENT PROCESSES

The ideal game design and implementation for our purposes must be simple enough so that neither students nor faculty become mired in graphics or game complexity, and yet the gameplay must be genuinely fun so that students can connect their work to a final experience that stands on its own merits. Fortunately, simple and fun are not mutually exclusive when it comes to game design.

4.4.1 THE TWO GAMES

Space Smasher is a variant of Super Breakout-style games, where players remove blocks on the screen by bouncing a ball with a moveable paddle. The popularity of this type of game spans generations, and the numerous variants tend to be largely identical and feature basic color block graphics. Space Smasher introduces more interesting gameplay by adding *customizable* blocks that are capable of triggering events such as swapping blocks or enabling/disabling unbreakable blocks. Also included are more premium sets of graphics tiles and sounds than are typically found in this genre. The ball-block-paddle collision tests, the special event logic, and the iteration through all blocks present an excellent structured sandbox for teaching and playing with conditionals and loops conceptually.

Corrupted is a variation on the Bubble Shooter genre, where players launch a colored tile into a larger group of tiles and attempt to make matches of three until all tiles are removed or until the tiles advance to meet the player at the opposite end of the screen [19]. Bubble shooters also tend to be simple match-and-remove games with minimalist graphics. Corrupted recasts the game with an active automated opponent employing a variety of tricks to increase the challenge and intrigue, and the game itself has been given a distinct artistic style. The visual, spatial, and multi-dimensional aspects of the color tiles present a rich domain of concepts for use in teaching 1D and 2D arrays.

Note that it is relatively straightforward to design custom levels and additional gameplay elements to both Space Smasher and Corrupted. The game mechanics for either do not require extensive balancing or tuning to make levels enjoyable. Even novice designers can quickly create fun and challenging custom levels. In this way, after a basic process of discovery and familiarization with the concepts and APIs, students can implement their own unique levels as practice exercises.

4.4.2   THE TEAMS

We knew from the outset that creating casual games designed both to teach fundamental programming concepts and to engage players would require teams with varying expertise: making fun games is an interdisciplinary undertaking and requires a wide variety of skills. Thus, we established a partnership that includes frontline CS1/2 faculty members and the Digital Future Lab (DFL)[1] of the University of Washington Bothell (UWB) campus—an interactive media R&D studio developing original interactive works supporting education, entertainment, and social justice.

The DFL emphasizes students' dual role as creators and learners, while working with students across disciplines and backgrounds to ensure that each core component of the game is well designed. The games are developed almost entirely by undergraduate students, including CS and non-CS majors. Roles include level design, visual and user-interface design, sound and music composition, game development, testing, and project management.

4.4.3   GAME DEVELOPMENT PROCESS

Our design approach begins with a unique brainstorming process where game designers generate ideas using familiar game mechanics to facilitate learning while practicing a specific programming concept, and also to gauge the fun factor of the prescribed activities. Faculty contributors help guide the design toward modular and feasible outcomes by providing simple and clearly defined coding requirements.

The photo in Figure 4.1 exemplifies our unique approach with the initial whiteboard sketches for the Space Smasher game. Notice that the left side of the board charts the "if" control structure that the game is being designed to teach, the center shows a gameplay screen mockup, and basic game rules are listed on the right. The conditional programming construct (on the left) provides the underlying impulse guiding the design process from its initial stages.

As an initial idea gains momentum, the DFL designers examine and refine fundamental gaming mechanics to maximize overall entertainment value, while CS1/2 faculty evaluate implementation, simplicity, and the level of exposure to the intended programming concept. Simultaneously, student developers create simple digital prototypes so designers can experiment interactively with their ideas and make

FIGURE 4.1   Initial whiteboard sketches for Space Smasher.

improvements to the core gaming experience. Playable versions of the game then undergo rigorous hands-on testing to refine each design choice or mechanic.

4.4.4 API Definition and Refinement Process

The final game and corresponding API development overlap significantly through a three-step process: (1) finalize the game prototype, (2) define and refine the API while completing the game implementation, and (3) build tutorials and teaching materials based on the API. In our process, the API refinement spans from the stabilization of the prototype game until the team finishes tutorials and teaching materials. This allows for verification of initial usability of the APIs [20].

Once these pieces are in place, the team fine-tunes gameplay while integrating production–quality graphic and audio assets. The result is a game that has the look-and-feel of a studio-quality production, while containing library and game features that will challenge new CS students to program individual game variations as part of a larger learning process.

4.5 RESULTS

The APIs are defined based on our previous experience from the GTCS foundations game engine [6] where the user code subclasses from an API-defined superclass and overrides two protected methods: *initialize()* and *update()*. The API calls the *initialize()* method exactly once before the game begins and the *update()* method continuously at a real-time rate until the game ends.

The underlying philosophy of the API is to provide all the functionality such that user code can focus on implementing just the game logic that targets the selected CS1/2 concepts. This adds responsibilities to the API as it must anticipate and provide a slew of resources to accomplish such as exercises, including pre-defined win and lose menu screens, access to all art and audio assets (user code can override these if desired), and anything related to the gameplay environment (e.g., window size and UI layout). In addition, the APIs provide access to each in-game object (e.g., balls, paddles, or tiles) and their behaviors (e.g., move, speed, and remove) plus all potential object-to-object interactions (e.g., ball-and-block collisions and reflections). All created objects are drawn automatically unless explicitly removed or set to invisible. To ensure user testability, mouse and keyboard input are both supported and special debugging modes are built into each API (e.g., stopping and allowing the player to control the ball movement in Space Smasher or key binding to create specific-colored tiles in Corrupted).

In the following we present actual sample teaching materials for Space Smasher and Corrupted to further illustrate each API.

4.5.1 The Space Smasher API

The screen shots (left: full game, right: teaching example) and code listing in Figure 4.2 show an example for teaching conditionals and loops. Note that the *MySpaceSmasherGame* class is a subclass of the API defined *SpaceSmasher*

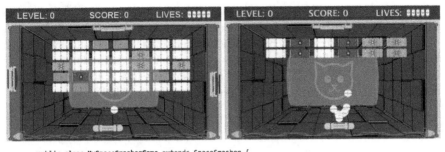

```
public class MySpaceSmasherGame extends SpaceSmasher {
    // init the game, called once by the API
    protected void initialize() {
        lifeSet.add(5);                    //create 5 lives: show in top-left
        paddleSet.add(1);                  //create 1 paddle
        blockSet.setBlocksPerRow(6);       //num of blocks per row
        for (int i = 0; i < 2; i++) {      //create two rows of blocks
            blockSet.addNormalBlock(1);        //normal block (light gray)
            blockSet.addFireBlock(1);          //fire block (red)
            blockSet.addNormalBlock(1);        //normal block (light gray)
            blockSet.addFireBlock(1);          //fire block (red)
            blockSet.addFreezingBlock(1);      //ice block (blue)
            blockSet.addFreezingBlock(1);      //ice block (blue)
        }
    }

    //update is called continuously >40 times per second
    protected void update() {
        //control the paddle left/right movement
        Paddle paddle = paddleSet.get(0);              //get the paddle
        if (keyboard.isButtonDown(KeyEvent.VK_LEFT))
            paddle.moveLeft();                         //move paddle left
        if (keyboard.isButtonDown(KeyEvent.VK_RIGHT))
            paddle.moveRight();                        //move paddle right

        //conditionally spawning balls with loops
        if (keyboard.isButtonDown(KeyEvent.VK_1)) {
            Ball foo = new Ball();                 //make a new ball
            ballSet.add(foo);                      //add to set of balls
            foo.spawn(paddle);                     //put it on screen  above the paddle
        } else if (keyboard.isButtonDown(KeyEvent.VK_2)) {
            for (int i=0; i<2; i++) {              //do the logic in loop twice
                Ball foo = new Ball();                 //make a new ball
                ballSet.add(foo);                      //add to set of balls
                foo.spawn(paddle);                     //put it on screen above the paddle
            }
        } else if (keyboard.isButtonDown(KeyEvent.VK_3)) {
            for (int i=0; i<3; i++) {              //do the logic in loop thrice
                Ball foo = new Ball();                 //make a new ball
                ballSet.add(foo);                      //add to set of balls
                foo.spawn(paddle);                     //put it on screen above the paddle
            }
        }
    }
}
```

FIGURE 4.2   Space Smasher and Conditional/Loop Example.

superclass. The entire game is then defined by the two protected overridden methods: *ininitialize()* and *update()*. Note that game object sets (e.g., lifeSet and paddleSet) are pre-defined with intuitive and convenient behaviors (e.g., add, get, moveLeft, and moveRight).

In this example, the *initialize()* method creates five lives, a paddle, and uses a "for" loop to generate the two rows of various blocks. The *update()* method showcases the simple and chained conditional statements to parse user input and the corresponding responses with the simple "for" loops. The right screen shot at the top of Figure 4.2 captures the program after the player types in a series of 1, 2, and 3's.

In this case, since the student's code did not define the gaming logic necessary to support multiple balls with collision detection, all the spawned balls will travel through the blocks and window bounds and disappear. After leading students through initial interaction with this example, it is an excellent opportunity to introduce the ball *collide()* and *reflect()* methods and engage students in articulating solutions to keep the balls within the game window bounds and clearing all the blocks.

4.5.2   THE CORRUPTED API

The screen shots (left: full game, right: teaching example) and code listing in Figure 4.3 show games developed based on the Corrupted API for teaching 2D arrays. In the *ColorLineBlaster* code, notice the similarity in structure to the Space Smasher example in Figure 4.2, where the subclass from the API-defined *Corrupted* class overrides the *initialize()* and *update()* methods. Once again, we require the API intuitive and convenient pre-defined behaviors (e.g., player movements and tile color access).

In this example, the *initialize()* method populates a 2D grid array with random color tiles. The *update()* method polls for keyboard input and triggers game behavior correspondingly. The up and down keys move the player's cannon, and the right key clears all tiles in a given row that match the color of the player's cannon. This

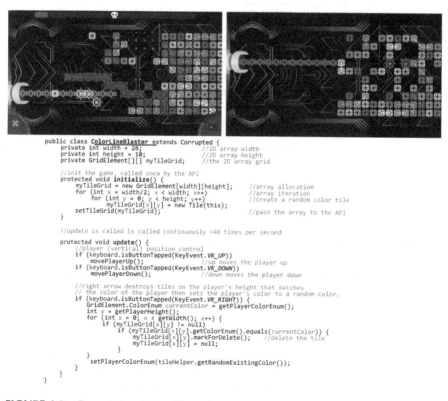

```java
public class ColorLineBlaster extends Corrupted {
    private int width = 26;                      //2D array width
    private int height = 10;                     //2D array height
    private GridElement[][] myTileGrid;          //the 2D array grid

    //init the game, called once by the API
    protected void initialize() {
        myTileGrid = new GridElement[width][height];    //array allocation
        for (int x = width/2; x < width; x++)           //array iteration
            for (int y = 0; y < height; y++)            //create a random color tile
                myTileGrid[x][y] = new Tile(this);
        setTileGrid(myTileGrid);                         //pass the array to the API
    }

    //update is called is called continuously >40 times per second

    protected void update() {
        //player (vertical) position control
        if (keyboard.isButtonTapped(KeyEvent.VK_UP))
            movePlayerUp();                             //up moves the player up
        if (keyboard.isButtonTapped(KeyEvent.VK_DOWN))
            movePlayerDown();                           //down moves the player down

        //right arrow destroys tiles on the player's height that matches
        // the color of the player then sets the player's color to a random color.
        if (keyboard.isButtonTapped(KeyEvent.VK_RIGHT)) {
            GridElement.ColorEnum currentColor = getPlayerColorEnum();
            int y = getPlayerHeight();
            for (int x = 0; x < getWidth(); x++) {
                if (myTileGrid[x][y] != null)
                    if (myTileGrid[x][y].getColorEnum().equals(currentColor)) {
                        myTileGrid[x][y].markForDelete();   //delete the tile
                        myTileGrid[x][y] = null;
                    }
            }
            setPlayerColorEnum(tileHelper.getRandomExistingColor());
        }
    }
}
```

FIGURE 4.3   Corrupted and Array Example.

example highlights linear searching by traversing an array and checking for matching colors as novel animations illustrate the results of their code graphically onscreen.

4.5.3 DISCUSSIONS

As exemplified in the case studies of Space Smasher and Corrupted, our casual games are rich yet simple platforms for prominently showcasing CS1/2 programming constructs with support to build engaging user interaction. The APIs are bridges between classic textbook teaching examples and game-themed teaching materials. This unity is achieved by exposing only the familiar programming constructs used in a typical CS 1/2 course while hiding the details that govern image rendering, sound, and animation, which may be foreign to students and faculty.

When evaluated against our own design guidelines, the structure of both APIs is based on simple subclass extensions and requires only two functions to implement. With the provided sample teaching materials, a faculty member can begin experimentation without referencing the API documentation. Each casual game and corresponding game objects (e.g., balls, paddles, or grid cells) provide an excellent digital playground for discoveries—users can experience functionality by interacting with the provided games and explore the defined objects to learn more about the API. With the game design being driven by programming concepts, as illustrated in the listings of Figures 4.2 and 4.3, it is straightforward to build examples showcasing desired educational concepts. Lastly, we have hidden all art and audio assets, as well as the implementation of game rules, allowing faculty and students to focus on the more important programming constructs at hand.

As an educational tool, the APIs provide students with a sandbox framework that allows them to build simple games and applications. By providing rich visualizations and supporting engaged interactions, students can develop creative games that capture their interest while they learn and explore concepts. A full set of short tutorials and sample materials similar to those of Figures 4.2 and 4.3 are freely available on our project website.[2]

4.6 CONCLUSION

While welcomed by both students and faculty, adopting examples of game-themed materials from the earlier GTCS efforts presented an interesting dichotomy—students requested a more complete and sophisticated gaming experience while faculty demanded less effort in composing art assets and handling game rules when building the teaching materials. The GTCS project team responded to this seemingly contradictory feedback by building causal games and then designing practical APIs to support these games. In this way, students can interact with the games first before delving into the challenging concepts and faculty can construct rich and engaging examples that showcase their selected educational concepts with only a small amount of code and time invested.

Of the five games in development, Space Smasher and Corrupted are the most complete and include refined APIs. The sample teaching materials based on Space Smasher focus on conditionals and loops, and are currently being field tested by faculty members with no background in graphics or games with encouraging preliminary feedback.

The appeal of video games typically arises from the interplay between game mechanics, audiovisual aesthetics, and user interaction metaphors (i.e., the keys, clicks, and gestures used to interact with the game environment). Our project attempts to build upon this appeal by providing engaging games interwoven with structured pedagogy to produce new and meaningful learning experiences for new programmers.

ACKNOWLEDGMENTS

This work was supported in part by the National Science Foundation grant DUE-1140410, Microsoft Research Connection, and Google under the Google CS Engagement Award. All opinions, findings, conclusions, and recommendations in this work are those of the authors and do not necessarily reflect the views of the sponsors.

NOTES

1   http://www.bothell.washington.edu/digitalfuture
2   The games, source code, and all art and audio assets are freely available at https://depts.washington.edu/cmmr/GTCS/.

REFERENCES

[1] U. Wolz, T. Barnes, I. Parberry, and M. Wick, *"Digital gaming as a vehicle for learning,"* in *SIGCSE'06: Proceedings of the 37th SIGCSE technical symposium on Computer science education*, Houston, Texas, USA, 2006, pp. 394–395.

[2] S. Leutenegger and J. Edgington, *"A games first approach to teaching introductory programming,"* in *SIGCSE'07: Proceedings of the 38th SIGCSE technical symposium on Computer science education*, Covington, Kentucky, USA, 2007, pp. 115–118.

[3] K. Sung, M. Panitz, C. Hillyard, R. Angotti, D. Goldstein, and J. Nordlinger, "Game-Themed Programming Assignment Modules: A Pathway for Gradual Integration of Gaming Context into Existing Introductory Programming Courses," *IEEE Trans. Educ.*, vol. 54, no. 3, pp. 416 –427, Aug. 2011.

[4] K. Sung, M. Panitz, S. Wallace, R. Anderson, and J. Nordlinger, *"Game-themed programming assignments: the faculty perspective,"* in *SIGCSE'08: Proceedings of the 39th SIGCSE technical symposium on Computer science education*, Portland, OR, USA, 2008, pp. 300–304.

[5] K. Sung, R. Rosenberg, M. Panitz, and R. Anderson, *"Assessing game-themed programming assignments for CS1/2 courses,"* in *GDCSE'08: Proceedings of the 3rd international conference on Game development in computer science education*, Miami, Florida, 2008, pp. 51–55.

[6] R. Angotti, C. Hillyard, M. Panitz, K. Sung, and K. Marino, *"Game-themed instructional modules: a video case study,"* in *FDG'10: Proceedings of the Fifth International Conference on the Foundations of Digital Games*, Monterey, California, 2010, pp. 9–16.

[7] C. Hillyard, R. Angotti, M. Panitz, K. Sung, J. Nordlinger, and D. Goldstein, *"Game-themed programming assignments for faculty: a case study,"* in *SIGCSE'10: Proceedings of the 41st ACM technical symposium on Computer science education*, Milwaukee, Wisconsin, USA, 2010, pp. 270–274.

[8] K. Sung, *"XNA game-themed applications for teaching introductory programming courses,"* Invit. Pre-Conf. Workshop Fourth Int. Conf. Found. Digit. Games Orlando Fla., Apr. 2009.

[9] K. Bromwich, M. Masoodian, and B. Rogers, *"Crossing the game threshold: a system for teaching basic programming constructs,"* in *Proceedings of the 13th International Conference of the NZ Chapter of the ACM's Special Interest Group on Human-Computer Interaction*, New York, NY, USA, 2012, pp. 56–63.

[10] A. Luxton-Reilly and P. Denny, *"A simple framework for interactive games in CS1,"* in *SIGCSE'09: Proceedings of the 40th ACM technical symposium on Computer science education*, Chattanooga, TN, USA, 2009, pp. 216–220.

[11] M. C. Lewis and B. Massingill, *"Graphical game development in CS2: a flexible infrastructure for a semester long project,"* in *SIGCSE'06: Proceedings of the 37th SIGCSE technical symposium on Computer science education*, Houston, Texas, USA, 2006, pp. 505–509.

[12] M. Külling and P. Henriksen, *"Game programming in introductory courses with direct state manipulation,"* in *ITiCSE'05: Proceedings of the 10th annual SIGCSE conference on Innovation and technology in computer science education*, Caparica, Portugal, 2005, pp. 59–63.

[13] R. B.-B. Levy and M. Ben-Ari, "We work so hard and they don't use it: acceptance of software tools by teachers," *SIGCSE Bull*, vol. 39, no. 3, pp. 246–250, 2007.

[14] L. Ni, *"What makes CS teachers change?: factors influencing CS teachers' adoption of curriculum innovations,"* in *SIGCSE'09: Proceedings of the 40th ACM technical symposium on Computer science education*, Chattanooga, TN, USA, 2009, pp. 544–548.

[15] C. R. B. de Souza, D. Redmiles, L.-T. Cheng, D. Millen, and J. Patterson, *"Sometimes you need to see through walls: a field study of application programming interfaces,"* in *Proceedings of the 2004 acm conference on computer supported cooperative work*, New York, NY, USA, 2004, pp. 63–71.

[16] J. Stylos and B. Myers, *"Mapping the space of API design decisions,"* in *Visual Languages and Human-Centric Computing, 2007. VL/HCC 2007. IEEE Symposium on*, 2007, pp. 50–60.

[17] J. Tuloch, *Practical API Design: Confessions of a Java Framework Architect*. A Press, 2008.

[18] B. Ellis, J. Stylos, and B. Myers, *"The factory pattern in api design: a usability evaluation,"* in *Software Engineering, 2007. ICSE 2007. 29th International Conference on, 2007*, USA. pp. 302–312.

[19] B. Chau, A. Robinson, J. Pace, R. Nash, and K. Sung, "Corrupted: A Game to Teach Programming Concepts," *Computer*, vol. 47, no. 12, pp. 100–103, Dec. 2014.

[20] J. Bloch, *"How to design a good api and why it matters,"* in *Companion to the 21st ACM SIGPLAN Symposium on Object-oriented Programming Systems, Languages, and Applications*, New York, NY, USA, 2006, pp. 506–507.

5 Evolution of a Model for the Evaluation of Games for Software Engineering Education

Giani Petri
Federal University of Santa Maria, Brazil

*Christiane Gresse von Wangenheim
and Adriano Ferreti Borgatto*
Federal University of Santa Catarina, Brazil

CONTENTS

5.1   INTRODUCTION

Software Engineering (SE) is the discipline concerned with the application of a systematic, disciplined, and quantifiable approach to the development, operation, and maintenance of software [1, 2]. In this context, it is expected that SE professionals can work successfully with both technical and non-technical issues, such as teamwork, communication, and management [2].[1] Theoretical aspects of SE are typically well covered in computing/SE undergraduate courses [2, 3]. On the other hand, one of the main challenges in SE education is to provide sufficient practical experience to students on SE methods, processes, and techniques, etc. [3, 4]. In order to cover this challenge in SE education, different active instructional strategies have been adopted by SE instructors [3–6].

Educational games have been widely used to provide more hands-on learning opportunities to SE students [3, 5, 7, 8]. Educational games are a kind of instructional strategy that, typically, involves competition among the players, being organized by rules and restrictions to achieve the educational objective(s). Besides promoting entertainment, educational games are designed to teach people certain knowledge, and/or to develop skills and/or attitudes [9–11]. Currently, there is a large number of games developed for SE education, including digital and non-digital games [8, 12, 13]. Most SE games are simulation games, covering topics of SE Management (e.g., DELIVER! [14], SimSoft [15], and SCRUMIA [16]), in which the learner assumes the role of a project manager and performs the planning, monitoring, and control of a software project [12]; the SE Process (e.g., SimSE [17], Problems, and Programmers [18]), simulating the execution of a specific kind of software development process or requirements engineering; Software Testing (e.g., Secret Ninja Testing [19] and U-Test [20]), in which the player must solve challenges by preparing unit test cases. In addition, there can also be observed a trend to quiz games in order to review SE knowledge (e.g., PMMaster [21] and KahootPMQuiz [22]).

Although educational games are widely used for SE education, it is essential to evaluate such games in order to obtain empirical evidence of the games' quality as a basis for an effective and efficient adoption. However, several literature reviews indicate that there are few empirical studies providing evidence of their effectiveness, motivation, engagement, etc. [8, 23]. This can be explained by the fact that most evaluations of educational games for SE education are performed in an ad hoc manner without a definition of the research design, measurement program, data collection instruments, and analysis methods, lacking scientific rigor [7, 8, 13, 24]. A reason for this may be the low number of approaches developed to provide systematic support for the execution of game evaluations [7, 13, 25–27].

However, a prominent model for the evaluation of educational games for SE education seems to be MEEGA (Model for the Evaluation of Educational GAmes) proposed by Savi et al. [28]. MEEGA is a model for the evaluation of educational games (digital and non-digital ones) in terms of motivation, user experience, and learning, by measuring the reaction of students after the game play through a standardized questionnaire. Currently, the MEEGA model seems to be the most widely used approach to game evaluation in practice, being used by different authors in different contexts [7, 13, 25, 29]. Yet, although demonstrating initially acceptable validity and reliability [28], a more comprehensive analysis of the MEEGA model based on a sample of 723 responses, indicated some improvement opportunities regarding its validity [30]. These improvement opportunities are related to an overlap of theoretical concepts of the factors' motivation and user experience, as well as a lack of understanding of the wording of some questionnaire items [28, 30]. Thus, research opportunities have been identified in order to improve the reliability and validity of a widely used model for the evaluation of games for SE education.

In this respect, the objective of this chapter is to present the design and evaluation of the MEEGA+ model, a systematic model for the evaluation of games used for SE education, as an evolution of the MEEGA model. The results presented allow SE researchers/instructors adopt a systematic evaluation model in order to evaluate SE games and, thus, contribute to their development and improvement and to direct effective and efficient adoption for SE education.

5.2   RESEARCH METHOD

In order to design and evaluate the MEEGA+ model, a multi-method research is adopted, as presented in Figure 5.1

Preceding the present study, we elicited the state of the art identifying existing approaches (methods, models, frameworks, and scales) for the systematic evaluation of educational games [25]. We also analyzed the state of practice, aiming at identifying how games used for computing/SE education are currently evaluated [13]. As a result, we identified the MEEGA model as a systematic and well-defined approach used for the evaluation of games for SE education that is being widely used in practice.

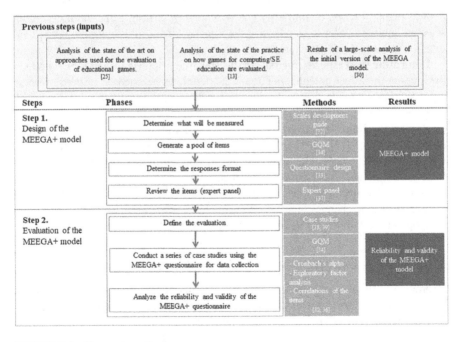

FIGURE 5.1   Research method.

Furthermore, we also conducted a large-scale study of the initial version of the MEEGA model analyzing its validity and reliability. The analysis was conducted based on data collected in 43 case studies, evaluating 20 different games for SE education, involving a population of 723 students [30]. As a result, we identified that the initial version of the MEEGA model is acceptable in terms of reliability (α=.915). However, in terms of its validity, a conceptual overlap with respect to the factors' motivation and user experience has been identified, thus, indicating a need for the redesign of the MEEGA model.

5.2.1   STEP 1. DESIGN OF THE MEEGA+ MODEL

The MEEGA+ model has been developed, as an evolution of the initial version of the MEEGA model [28], considering the results of literature reviews [13, 25] and the large-scale evaluation of the initial version of the MEEGA model [30]. The development of the MEEGA+ model is based on the process of the scales development guide proposed by DeVellis [32] and the guide for questionnaire designed by Kasunic [33].

Determine what will be measured. In this step, the factors to be measured are defined in order to support the development of the measurement instrument (questionnaire). Adopting the GQM (Goal/Question/Metric) approach [34], the evaluation objective is defined and systematically decomposed into factors to be measured. The factors are determined based on a mapping study following the procedure proposed by Budgen et al. [35].

Generate a pool of items. The measurement of these factors is operationalized by decomposing them into measurement instrument items. The definition of the items is based on related standardized questionnaires found in literature. We analyzed the pool of items in terms of similarity and redundancy, customizing, and unifying the selected items. In order to standardize the selected items, all items were refined and transformed into positive statements.

Determine the response format. In this step, the response format for the items of the measurement instrument is defined. This definition is based on response formats typically used in standardized questionnaires following the scales development guide proposed by DeVellis [32].

Review the items by experts. In this step, face validity [36] is reviewed through an expert panel [37]. The expert panel is composed of a multi-disciplinary group of four senior researchers with backgrounds in computing/SE and/or statistics. The review aims at analyzing clarity, relevance, consistency, and completeness of the measurement instrument items of the MEEGA+ model. The suggestions of the experts, including changes in the wording and text formatting, were considered in the development of the MEEGA+ measurement instrument.

5.2.2   STEP 2. EVALUATION OF THE MEEGA+ MODEL

In order to evaluate the MEEGA+ model in terms of reliability and validity of its measurement instrument (questionnaire), we perform a series of case studies [38, 39]. The studies are organized into three phases:

Define the evaluation (definition). In this phase, the evaluation objective is defined using the GQM goal template [34] and decomposed into quality aspects and analysis questions (AQs). The research design and the data collection process are defined based on the MEEGA+ model, which is adopted for the game evaluation. Therefore, the research design adopted is a case study and data collection is operationalized using the MEEGA+ measurement instrument.

Conduct a series of case studies (execution). A series of case studies applying several educational games for SE education are conducted in a one-shot post-test only design. In each case study, after the game session (treatment), the MEEGA+ measurement instrument is used for collecting data of the participants' perceptions about the game. We use a non-probability sampling technique in each case study applying the convenience sampling method [36], in which our sample is composed by computing students enrolled in SE courses.

Analyze the reliability and validity (analysis). In this phase, we pooled the data collected in a single sample for data analysis. The data collected were analyzed in order to answer our AQs. Data with respect to reliability and construct validity were analyzed following the definition of Trochim & Donnelly [36] and the scale development guide proposed by DeVellis [32]. In terms of reliability, we analyzed the internal consistency through the Cronbach's alpha coefficient [40]. Construct validity, was measured using an exploratory factor analysis and based on evidence of convergent and discriminant validity, analyzed through the degree of correlations of the items [32, 36]. The results of the statistical analysis were interpreted by researchers in the context of SE education in order to identify the reliability and validity of the MEEGA+ measurement instrument.

5.3   RELATED STUDIES

Based on a systematic literature review [25] analyzing the last two decades, we identified only seven approaches to evaluate educational games for teaching any knowledge area [28, 42–47]. Most of these approaches are frameworks rather than models or methods [42, 43, 45]. Freitas and Oliver [42] propose a four-dimensional framework that evaluates dimensions of learner's profile, the process of learning, the internal representation world, and context. Although this framework can be customized for the evaluation of any educational game, it does not provide information on how to operationalize the evaluation, neither defines explicitly a research design, data collection instrument, nor data analysis methods. And, although, the framework was partially validated through pilot studies, applying the approach to evaluate an educational game in class, it does not explicitly provide evidence of its reliability and validity. Similarly, Connolly et al. [43] proposed the Evaluation Framework for Effective Games-based Learning (GBL), which evaluates games with respect to learner performance, learner/academic motivation, learner/academic perceptions, learner/academic preferences, the GBL environment itself, and the collaboration among players. This framework was developed based on theoretical constructs, yet, again there is a lack of information on how to conduct the evaluation. Moreover, this framework was only validated through pilot studies, leaving its validity questionable. Another framework was proposed by Carvalho [45], which assesses the games' efficiency in terms of gameplay, game story, mechanisms, usability, knowledge, motivation, and satisfaction. Although this framework proposes the use of tests and interviews for data collection, no information on how the framework and its data collection instruments were developed is provided. And, its validation was performed only with pilot studies in one class. This shows that these frameworks typically define a set of dimensions that can be adapted to particular requirements in an evaluation of a game, but they fail to provide concrete support on how to perform the evaluations in practice.

Fu et al. [44] propose the EGameFlow scale that assesses user enjoyment of e-learning games in terms of immersion, social interaction, challenge, goal clarity, feedback, concentration, control, and knowledge improvement by using a questionnaire for data collection. EGameFlow was developed using a systematic methodology and validated in terms of its item analysis, reliability, and validity through four game sessions. Yet, although the EGameFlow scale presented a satisfactory validity and reliability, it seems to be discontinued by its authors.

Another scale was proposed by Ak [46]. This scale aims at measuring the quality of games before applying it in class. Game quality is measured in terms of enjoyment and learning. However, no further information on its development process, data collection, and analysis methods, nor its validation are provided, leaving its validity and reliability questionable.

Mayer [47] proposes a method for the evaluation of serious games, defining a framework, a theoretical model, and a scale. Again, the study does not report information about how this method was developed. And, although, the method seems to be partially evaluated through only one pilot study applying one game in a class, no information about its statistical validation is reported.

Only one encountered approach was developed specifically for the evaluation of SE games. The MEEGA model, as proposed by Savi et al [28], measures three factors of educational games: motivation, user experience, and learning. MEEGA was systematically developed and explicitly defines the evaluation objective and provides a standardized questionnaire to be applied in order to collect data on the learners' perception using a non-experimental research design. The model also has been statistically evaluated in terms of reliability and validity based on data collected from various case studies.

In summary, we can observe that besides existing few approaches to systematically evaluate educational games, only one approach has been specifically developed for the evaluation of SE games. In addition, we also observed that there is no consensus on which quality factors to evaluate. Furthermore, the majority of these approaches has neither been developed in an ad hoc manner nor systematically validated through larger-scale studies.

An exception seems to be the MEEGA model [28], been developed following a systematic process, using a standardized questionnaire, evaluated in terms of validity and reliability. However, the results of a systematic analysis of a large-scale evaluation of the initial version of the MEEGA model show that there are some limitations in terms of its validity [30], indicating a conceptual overlap between the factors of motivation and user experience.

Therefore, analyzing the related studies, we observe a need to evolve the existing approaches that are being used in practice in order to improve their validity and reliability to provide more valid results that can be used to as a basis for a decision of SE instructors/researchers on the adoption of such games and/or for their continuous improvement.

5.4   THE MEEGA+ MODEL

According to the improvement opportunities observed, we evolve the MEEGA model into the MEEGA+ model for the evaluation of games for SE education. Adopting the GQM goal template [34], the objective of the MEEGA+ model is to analyze educational games in order to evaluate their quality from the students' point of view in the context of SE education [48].

Following the GQM approach, this objective is systematically decomposed into factors to be measured. The initial version of the MEEGA model evaluates games in terms of motivation, user experience, and learning [28]. However, the results of its large-scale evaluation show that there is a conceptual overlap between the factors of motivation and user experience [30]. And, analyzing the results of our previous literature review [13], we identified a trend, covering a set of factors used for the games' evaluation mainly related to motivation, user experience, usability, engagement, enjoyment, and perceived learning. In this respect, most of these factors (motivation, user experience, usability, engagement, enjoyment, and perceived learning) are still fragmented in dimensions (Table 5.1) that can overlap conceptually with another factor, for example, immersion and focused attention. Thus, some dimensions of different factors are similar or related to another dimension of another factor. Therefore, we identified similar dimensions, analyzing their conceptual definitions, through a mapping study as presented in Table 5.1.

As a result of the mapping (Table 5.1), we defined a set of dimensions to be measured by the MEEGA+ model for the evaluations of digital and non-digital games for SE education. Table 5.2. presents the definition of each dimension/sub-dimension supported by its references.

In order to operationalize the evaluation of these defined factors, a research design is determined.

5.4.1   DEFINITION OF THE RESEARCH DESIGN

Evaluations of educational games are typically conducted through empirical studies [55], which aim to measure if the target audience has achieved the defined objectives [55]. These studies may range from experimental to non-experimental studies [39]. In order to define a research design for an empirical study, its practical limitations and objective(s) need to be considered. In the context of this study, related to the evaluation of SE games in an educational context, it is expected that the evaluation can be conducted quickly, in a non-intrusive way in order to not interrupt the normal

TABLE 5.1
Mapping of Evaluation Factors

Factor/ Dimension	Motivation [28, 49]	User Experience [13]	Usability [50]	Engagement [51]	Enjoyment [44]	Perceived Learning [28, 52]
Attention	X			X (Focused Attention)	X (Concentration)	
Relevance	X					
Confidence	X					
Satisfaction	X			X		
Immersion		X		X (Focused Attention)	X	
Social Interaction		X			X	
Challenge		X			X	
Fun		X		X (Satisfaction)		
Competence		X				
Control/ Operability/ Autonomy		X (Control)	X (Operability)		X (Autonomy)	
Learnability			X			
Aesthetics			X	X		
Accessibility			X			
User error protection			X			
Perceived usability				X		
Goal clarity					X	X
Feedback					X	
Knowledge Improvement					X	X

flow of a class and to not impair the participants involved in the study. Therefore, we chose a case study design, which allows an in-depth research of an individual, group, or event [38, 39]. The study is classified as a one-shot post-test only design, in which the case study begins with the application of the treatment (educational game) and then a measurement instrument (questionnaire) is answered by the students in order to collect data on their perceptions about the game. This kind of evaluation using self-assessment is supported by the science of psychometrics, applying questionnaires to capture people's perceptions in a variety of knowledge areas [56, 57].

Self-assessment, although being well accepted for measuring diverse factors, such as quality of life, motivation, or usability, it may still be questionable, if learning can also be measured trough this manner. However, recent studies are discussing the importance and the use of self-assessment in a contemporary education [62–65]. Different studies report that this process can help students stay involved and motivated and encourages self-reflection and responsibility for their learning [62, 64].

TABLE 5.2

Definition of Dimensions/Sub-Dimensions

Dimension/Sub-Dimension		Definition
Focused Attention		Evaluating the attention, focused concentration, absorption, and the temporal dissociation of the students [28, 49, 51].
Fun		Evaluating the students' feeling of pleasure, happiness, relaxation, and distraction [28, 53].
Challenge		Evaluating how much the game is sufficiently challenging with respect to the learner's competency level. The increase of difficulty should occur at an appropriate pace accompanying the learning curve. New obstacles and situations should be presented throughout the game to keep the students interested [28, 54].
Social Interaction		Evaluating, if the game promotes a feeling of a shared environment and being connected with others in activities of cooperation or competition [28, 44].
Confidence		Evaluating, if students are able to make progress in the study of educational content through their effort and ability (e.g., through tasks with increasing level of difficulty) [28, 49].
Relevance		Evaluating, if students realize that the educational proposal is consistent with their goals and that they can link content with their professional or academic future [28, 49].
Satisfaction		Evaluating, if students feel that the dedicated effort results in learning [28, 49].
	Learnability	Evaluating, if the game can be used by specified users to achieve specified goals of learning, to use the game with effectiveness, efficiency, freedom from risk, and satisfaction in a specified context of use [50].
	Operability	Evaluating, the degree to which a game has attributes that make it easy to operate and control [50].
Usability	Aesthetics	Evaluating, if the game interface enables pleasing and satisfying interaction for the user [50].
	Accessibility	Evaluating, if the game can be used by people with low/moderate visual impairment and/or color blindness [50].
	User error protection	Evaluating, if the game protects users against making errors [50]. Applied only for the evaluation of digital games.
Perceived Learning		Evaluating the perceptions of the overall effect of the game on students' learning in the course [28, 52].

And, although no consensus is reached, there is evidence that self-assessment using questionnaires provides reliable and valid information [62, 64, 65].

The conduction of case studies in this context is justified by typical restrictions applying the games in the classroom. And, while experiments adopt more rigorous research designs, they may have significant limitations when conducted in educational contexts, such as SE education [58, 59]. For example, regarding the feasibility of implementing an experiment, students may feel impaired by random allocation in control and experimental group(s) by the use of different interventions considered inferior [59, 60]. Threats can also be introduced through differences between pre-/post- tests and/or the impact of additional causal factors on the tests results. In addition, in order to obtain significant statistical results from such experiments, a considerable sample size is required [39, 59, 60]. However, this may not be feasible due to the small number of students commonly enrolled in computing courses [61]. Thus, even when undertaking this substantial amount of effort, the study may not yield significant results [59].

It, thus, becomes clear that evaluating the learning is a complex topic. The development of non-intrusive evaluation approaches using self-assessment may lead to results with low validity, if data are collected through unreliable questionnaires developed in an ad hoc manner. Therefore, a compromise may be the development of standardized questionnaires increasing the validity and reliability of the data being collected, as proposed in the MEEGA+ model.

5.4.2 Definition of the MEEGA+ Measurement Instrument

In accordance with the defined research design and based on the defined dimensions, we generate a set of items, improving the initial version of the MEEGA questionnaire, customizing and unifying existing standardized questionnaires found in the literature [28, 44, 49, 51–54, 66–72]. Table 5.3 shows the items for the MEEGA+ measurement instrument for each dimension/sub-dimension and their sources/references.

The items presented in Table 5.3 compose the MEEGA+ measurement instrument in order to evaluate both digital and non-digital games for SE education. However, the items 10, 11, and 12 are specifically used to measure the usability of digital games, referring to the games' customization and user error protection. Thus, when evaluating non-digital games, these items are to be disregarded.

In addition, items related to the learning objectives of each game are included in the measurement instrument to be customized in accordance with the specific learning objectives of each educational game. Typically, games for SE education are used to improve the knowledge on the cognitive levels of remembering, understanding, and application [2] in accordance with the revised version of Bloom's taxonomy [73]. However, the MEEGA+ model is also flexible to cover objectives on higher cognitive levels, such as analyzing, evaluating, and creating as well as other competencies, including soft skills or attitudes to be classified in accordance with corresponding taxonomies [74, 75]. Thus, for each learning objective of each evaluated game, the following statement should be customized in the MEEGA+ measurement instrument: The game contributed to <verb related to the level of the learning goal (cognitive, psychomotor, affective)> <goal/concept>. For example, in accordance with the learning objectives of SCRUMIA [16], a game to reinforce the understanding of SCRUM concepts and to practice the SCRUM process, such statement would be: "The game contributed to recall concepts related to Sprint Planning." These statements related to the learning objectives of the game compose the MEEGA+ measurement instrument that is applied after the game session in order to capture the students'

TABLE 5.3

MEEGA+ Measurement Instrument Items and Their References

Dimension/Sub-Dimension		Item No.	Description
	Aesthetics	1	The game design is attractive (interface, graphics, cards, boards, etc.).
		2	The text font and colors are well blended and consistent.
	Learnability	3	I needed to learn a few things before I could play the game.
		4	Learning to play this game was easy for me.
		5	I think that most people would learn to play this game very quickly.
	Operability	6	I think that the game is easy to play.
Usability [50]		7	The game rules are clear and easy to understand.
	Accessibility	8	The fonts (size and style) used in the game are easy to read.
		9	The colors used in the game are meaningful.
		10	The game allows customizing the appearance (font and/or color) according to my preferences.
	User error protection	11	The game prevents me from making mistakes.
		12	When I make a mistake, it is easy to recover from it quickly.
		13	When I first looked at the game, I had the impression that it would be easy for me.
Confidence [28, 49]		14	The contents and structure helped me to become confident that I would learn with this game.
		15	This game is appropriately challenging for me.
Challenge [28, 54]		16	The game provides new challenges (offers new obstacles, situations, or variations) at an appropriate pace.
		17	The game does not become monotonous as it progresses (repetitive or boring tasks).
		18	Completing the game tasks gave me a satisfying feeling of accomplishment.
		19	It is due to my personal effort that I managed to advance in the game.
Satisfaction [28, 49]		20	I feel satisfied with the things that I learned from the game.
		21	I would recommend this game to my colleagues.
		22	I was able to interact with other players during the game.
Social Interaction [28, 44]		23	The game promotes cooperation and/or competition among the players.
		24	I felt good interacting with other players during the game.

(*Continued*)

TABLE 5.3 (Continued)
MEEGA+ Measurement Instrument Items and Their References

Dimension/Sub-Dimension	Item No.	Description
	25	I had fun with the game.
Fun [28, 53]	26	Something happened during the game (game elements, competition, etc.) which made me smile.
	27	There was something interesting at the beginning of the game that captured my attention.
Focused Attention [28, 49, 51]	28	I was so involved in my gaming task that I lost track of time.
	29	I forgot about my immediate surroundings while playing this game.
	30	The game contents are relevant to my interests.
	31	It is clear to me how the contents of the game are related to the course.
Relevance [28, 49]	32	This game is an adequate teaching method for this course.
	33	I prefer learning with this game to learning through other ways (e.g., other teaching methods).
	34	The game contributed to my learning in this course.
Perceived Learning [28, 52]	35	The game allowed for efficient learning compared with other activities in the course.

perceptions about their level of agreement (or disagreement) in the achieving of the learning objectives of the game.

5.4.3 RESPONSE FORMAT

As response format, we adopt a 5-point Likert scale with response alternatives ranging from strongly disagree to strongly agree [32, 76]. The use of a Likert scale, in its original 5-point format, allows to express the opinion of the individual (student) under the object of study (educational game) with precision, allowing the individual being comfortable to express their opinion, using a neutral point and, thus, contributing to the quality of the answers [77].

The complete material of the MEEGA+ model is available under a Creative Commons License in English, Brazilian, Portuguese, and Spanish at: http://www.gqs.ufsc.br/quality-evaluation/meega-plus/.

5.5 EVALUATION OF THE MEEGA+ MODEL

In order to evaluate the reliability and validity of the MEEGA+ measurement instrument, we conduct a case study [38, 39].

5.5.1 Definition

The objective of this evaluation is to analyze the MEEGA+ measurement instrument in order to evaluate its reliability and construct validity from the viewpoint of the researchers in the context of SE education. Reliability and construct validity are important characteristics of a measurement instrument such as questionnaires [32, 36]. Reliability refers to the degree of consistency of the instrument items. Internal consistency reliability is measured in order to evaluate the consistency of results across items within a questionnaire [36], typically measured through the Cronbach's alpha coefficient [40]. Construct validity of a questionnaire is explained as its ability to measure what it purports to measure, including convergent and discriminant validity, which are measured through the degree of correlation between the instrument items [36].

Following the GQM approach, the study objective is decomposed into quality aspects and AQs to be analyzed, defined based on aspects of evaluation of measurement instruments [32, 36]:

Reliability

AQ1: Is there evidence for internal consistency of the MEEGA+ measurement instrument?

Construct Validity

AQ2: How do underlying factors influence the responses on the items of the MEEGA+ measurement instrument?

AQ3: Is there evidence of convergent and discriminant validity of the MEEGA+ measurement instrument?

5.5.2 Execution

We conducted a series of 29 case studies (from July 2016 to July 2017), evaluating 13 different educational games for SE education (four digital games and nine non-digital games) using the MEEGA+ model. The majority of the case studies (20) used non-digital games and nine studies used digital games. In total, responses from 589 students in six different educational institutions were collected as summarized in Table 5.4.

Data collected in the conducted case studies (Table 5.4) were pooled in a single sample, using them cumulatively only in order to evaluate the MEEGA+ questionnaire (and not a specific game). The pooling of data was possible due to the similarity of the case studies conducted and standardization of the data collection. The conducted case studies are similar in terms of definition (with the objective to evaluate an educational SE game), research design (case studies), and context (SE education). In addition, all conducted case studies are standardized in terms of measures (quality factors/dimensions), data collection method (MEEGA+ questionnaire), and response format (5-point Likert scale).

TABLE 5.4

Summary of the Performed Case Studies

Game	Game Type	Context	Course/Semester	Institution/ Country	Sample Size
Use cases	Non-digital	Graduate course in computing program	SE Instructional Strategies/2016–2	UFSC/Brazil	6
Comunica	Non-digital	Graduate course in computing program	SE Instructional Strategies/2016-2	UFSC/Brazil	6
EAReqGame	Digital	Undergraduate course in computing program	Software Engineering/2016-2	IFC/Brazil	6
		Undergraduate course in computing program	Software Engineering/2017-1	IFC/Brazil	41
Unified Process Game	Non-digital	Graduate course in computing program	SE Instructional Strategies/2016-2	UFSC/Brazil	6
Kahoot! PMQuiz	Digital	Undergraduate course in computing program	Project planning and management/2016-2	UFSC/Brazil	29
			Project management/2016-2	UFSC/Brazil	20
			Project management/2016-2	UFSM/ Brazil	11
			Project planning and management/2017-1	UFSC/Brazil	17
			Project management/2017-1	UFSC/Brazil	24
The Class Game	Non-digital	Graduate course in computing program	SE Instructional Strategies/2016-2	UFSC/Brazil	6
PMDome	Non-digital	Graduate course in computing program	IT Management/2016-2	IFFar/Brazil	20
		Undergraduate course in computing program	PM Workshop	IFSC/Brazil	27
PMMaster	Non-digital	Undergraduate course in computing program	Project planning and management/2016-2	UFSC/Brazil	24
			Project management/2016-2	UFSC/Brazil	21
			Project planning and management/2017-1	UFSC/Brazil	17
			Project management/2017-1	UFSC/Brazil	18

(Continued)

TABLE 5.4   (Continued)
Summary of the Performed Case Studies

Game	Game Type	Context	Course/Semester	Institution/ Country	Sample Size
Project Detective	Non-digital	Undergraduate course in computing program	Project planning and management/2016-2	UFSC/Brazil	26
			Project planning and management/2017-1	UFSC/Brazil	17
QuizGame	Digital	Undergraduate course in computing program	Project management/2017-1	UFSC/Brazil	21
Risk Management Game	Non-digital	Undergraduate course in computing program	Project management/2016-2	UFSC/Brazil	31
			Project management/2016-2	UFSC/Brazil	23
			Project management/2017-1	UFSC/Brazil	21
			Project management/2017-1	UFSC/Brazil	21
			Software Engineering/2017-01	IFSC/Brazil	36
			Software Engineering/2017-01	IFSC/Brazil	31
SCRUM'ed	Digital	Undergraduate course in computing program	Software Engineering/2016-2	ULBRA/ Brazil	18
SCRUMIA	Non-digital	Undergraduate course in computing program	Project planning and management/2016-2	UFSC/Brazil	26
			Project planning and management/2017-1	UFSC/Brazil	19
Total					589

5.5.3   ANALYSIS

We analyze the AQs as defined in the research method performing a statistical evaluation. The evaluation follows the approach for the scale development as proposed by DeVellis [32] considering the procedures for the evaluation of internal consistency and construct validity of a measurement instrument [36]. Data analysis was executed using IBM SPSS Statistics trial version 23.

5.5.3.1   Reliability

AQ1: Is there evidence for internal consistency of the MEEGA+ measurement instrument?

Evaluation of the Standardized Items

We measured the internal consistency of the MEEGA+ questionnaire through the Cronbach's alpha coefficient [32, 36]. Cronbach's alpha coefficient indicates the degree to which a set of items measure a single factor [40]. Here, we want to know whether the MEEGA+ measurement instrument measures the quality of the educational game. Typically, values of Cronbach's alpha between $0.8 > \alpha \geq 0.7$ are acceptable, between $0.9 > \alpha \geq 0.8$ are good, and $\alpha \geq 0.9$ are excellent [36].

We analyzed the Cronbach's alpha coefficient separately (Table 5.5) for the sample with data collected from the evaluations of digital games (n = 187), with data collected from non-digital games (n = 402) and both type of games (n = 589), only discarding the items specific to the evaluation of digital games in the latter two (items 10, 11, and 12).

Analyzing the 35 standardized items of the MEEGA+ measurement instrument, the value of Cronbach's alpha is excellent considering the data from digital games ($\alpha = .914$) as well as non-digital games ($\alpha = .939$). And, grouping the data from digital and non-digital games (excluding only the items to evaluate digital games), the value of Cronbach's alpha is again considered excellent ($\alpha = .929$). Therefore, we can conclude that the answers to the items are consistent and precise, indicating the reliability of the standardized items of the MEEGA+ measurement instrument.

Evaluation of the Customized Items
Analyzing the reliability of the items that are customized in accordance with the specific learning objectives of each educational game, we again, obtained an excellent Cronbach's alpha coefficient ($\alpha = .953$). This also indicates an excellent reliability of this part of the MEEGA+ measurement instrument

5.5.3.2   Construct Validity
AQ2: How do underlying factors influence the responses on the items of the MEEGA+ measurement instrument?

In order to analyze the conceptual structure in terms of the number of quality factors that represents the responses of the 35 standardized items of the MEEGA+ measurement instrument, we performed an exploratory factor analysis.

In order to analyze whether the items of the MEEGA+ measurement instrument can be submitted to the factor analysis process [78], we used the Kaiser-Meyer-Olkin (KMO) index and Bartlett's test of sphericity being the most commonly used ones [78]. These methods indicate how much the realization of the exploratory factor analysis is appropriate for a specific set of items [78]. The KMO index measures the sampling adequacy with values between 0 and 1. An index value near 1.0 supports a factor analysis and anything less than 0.5 is probably not amenable to useful factor analysis [79]. Bartlett's sphericity test also indicates whether the factor analysis is appropriate, considering acceptable values of a significance level <0.05 [79]. Analyzing the items of the MEEGA+ measurement instrument, we obtained a KMO index of .918 and a significance level of 0.000. Consequently, this indicates that factor analysis is adequate to analyze the number of factors that represents the responses of the MEEGA+ measurement instrument.

Applying the factorial analysis, the number of factors retained in the analysis is defined [78]. Here we used the Cattell's scree test [80] for this decision, as it is one of the most used strategies to determine the number of components to retain [81]. The Cattell's scree test plots the components (items) as the X-axis and the

TABLE 5.5
Cronbach's Alpha Coefficients

Dimension/ Sub-Dimension		Item No.	Description	Cronbach's Alpha, If Item was Deleted		
				Digital Games Only (n = 187)	Non-digital Games Only (n = 402)	All Games (n = 589)
Usability	Aesthetics	1	The game design is attractive (interface, graphics, cards, boards, etc.).	.910	.938	.927
		2	The text font and colors are well blended and consistent.	.913	.939	.929
	Learnability	3	I needed to learn a few things before I could play the game.	.913	.939	.929
		4	Learning to play this game was easy for me.	.913	.939	.929
		5	I think that most people would learn to play this game very quickly.	.913	.939	.929
	Operability	6	I think that the game is easy to play.	.913	.938	.928
		7	The game rules are clear and easy to understand.	.911	.937	.927
	Accessibility	8	The fonts (size and style) used in the game are easy to read.	.914	.940	.930
		9	The colors used in the game are meaningful.	.914	.940	.930
		10	The game allows customizing the appearance (font and/ or color) according to my preferences.	.913	Items specific of digital games.	
	User error protection	11	The game prevents me from making mistakes.	.913		
		12	When I make a mistake, it is easy to recover from it quickly.	.915		
Confidence		13	When I first looked at the game, I had the impression that it would be easy for me.	.914	.936	.930
		14	The contents and structure helped me to become confident that I would learn with this game.	.910	.937	.926

(Continued)

TABLE 5.5   (Continued)
Cronbach's Alpha Coefficients

Dimension/ Sub-Dimension	Item No.	Description	Cronbach's Alpha, If Item was Deleted		
			Digital Games Only (n = 187)	Non-digital Games Only (n = 402)	All Games (n = 589)
	15	This game is appropriately challenging for me.	.909	.937	.927
Challenge	16	The game provides new challenges (offers new obstacles, situations, or variations) at an appropriate pace.	.910	.937	.927
	17	The game does not become monotonous as it progresses (repetitive or boring tasks).	.911	.936	.926
	18	Completing the game tasks gave me a satisfying feeling of accomplishment.	.908	.931	.925
Satisfaction	19	It is due to my personal effort that I managed to advance in the game.	.910	.939	.928
	20	I feel satisfied with the things that I learned from the game.	.909	.936	.925
	21	I would recommend this game to my colleagues.	.907	.935	.924
	22	I was able to interact with other players during the game.	.911	.938	.928
Social Interaction	23	The game promotes cooperation and/or competition among the players.	.910	.938	.928
	24	I felt good interacting with other players during the game.	.910	.936	.926
Fun	25	I had fun with the game.	.908	.935	.924
	26	Something happened during the game (game elements, competition, etc.) which made me smile.	.910	.937	.926

(Continued)

TABLE 5.5 (Continued)
Cronbach's Alpha Coefficients

Dimension/ Sub-Dimension	Item No.	Description	Cronbach's Alpha, If Item was Deleted		
			Digital Games Only (n = 187)	Non-digital Games Only (n = 402)	All Games (n = 589)
	27	There was something interesting at the beginning of the game that captured my attention.	.909	.937	.926
Focused Attention	28	I was so involved in my gaming task that I lost track of time.	.909	.937	.926
	29	I forgot about my immediate surroundings while playing this game.	.910	.937	.927
	30	The game contents are relevant to my interests.	.909	.937	.927
	31	It is clear to me how the contents of the game are related to the course.	.913	.938	.928
Relevance	32	This game is an adequate teaching method for this course.	.901	.936	.926
	33	I prefer learning with this game to learning through other ways (e.g., other teaching methods).	.914	.937	.928
	34	The game contributed to my learning in this course.	.911	.936	.926
Perceived Learning	35	The game allowed for efficient learning compared with other activities in the course.	.912	.936	.926
	Total		**.914**	**.939**	**.929**

corresponding eigenvalues as the Y-axis. The Cattell's scree test involves plotting the eigenvalues in descending order of their magnitude against their component numbers and determining where they level off. The break between the steep slope and a leveling off (named the elbow) indicates the number of meaningful factors. Thus, the Cattell's scree test disregard all further components after the one starting the elbow [80]. Based on this definition, the scree plot (Figure 5.2) shows that the quick change of the slope of the curve (the elbow) appears in the third factor. In addition, the dotted

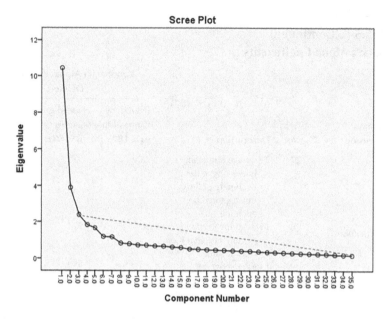

FIGURE 5.2   Scree Plot.

line (Figure 5.2) shows that the drop of the curve is less abrupt (leveling off) from the third factor. Therefore, justifying the retention of two factors in our analysis.

However, sometimes the Cattell's scree test is criticized as a researcher bias may be included due to the level of subjectivity involved in the decision on the number of factors to retain using a visual inspection device (scree test) [82]. In order to minimize this bias, we also analyzed the percent of cumulative variance of the factors as a complementary method for the decision on the number of factors retained in the analysis. In this respect, the two factors retained in our analysis explain 41.07% of the cumulative variance. This variance is considered as adequate for the decision in the retention of the factors, considering 40% of the threshold of the variance as acceptable [83]. With respect to the MEEGA+, this means that the responses of the measurement instrument are representing two underlying concepts (quality factors).

Once the number of underlying factors is identified, another issue is to analyze which items are loaded into which factor. In order to identify the factor loadings of the items, we used the Varimax with Kaiser Normalization rotation method, being the most widely used rotation method [36]. Table 5.6 shows the factor loadings of the items associated with the two retained factors. The highest factor loading of each item, indicating to which factor the item is most related, is marked in bold.

Analyzing the factor loadings of the items (Table 5.6), we can observe that the first factor (factor 1) consists of a set of 25 items (items no. 10 to 12 and 14 to 35), including items from the dimensions of focused attention, fun, challenge, social interaction, confidence, relevance, satisfaction, and perceived learning. Thus, this result seems to suggest that these items (and their original dimensions), in fact, are related to measuring the quality of educational games (as shown in the mapping

TABLE 5.6
Factor Loadings

Original Dimension/ Sub-Dimension		Item No.	Description	Factors	
				1	2
	Aesthetics	1	The game design is attractive (interface, graphics, cards, boards, etc.).	.349	**.490**
		2	The text font and colors are well blended and consistent.	.160	**.494**
	Learnability	3	I needed to learn a few things before I could play the game.	.028	**.681**
		4	Learning to play this game was easy for me.	-.001	**.793**
		5	I think that most people would learn to play this game very quickly.	.059	**.757**
	Operability	6	I think that the game is easy to play.	.080	**.794**
Usability		7	The game rules are clear and easy to understand.	.260	**.641**
	Accessibility	8	The fonts (size and style) used in the game are easy to read.	.007	**.555**
		9	The colors used in the game are meaningful.	.060	**.506**
		10	The game allows customizing the appearance (font and/or color) according to my preferences.	**.305**	-.241
	User error protection	11	The game prevents me from making mistakes.	**.240**	-.119
		12	When I make a mistake, it is easy to recover from it quickly.	**.156**	-.111
Confidence		13	When I first looked at the game, I had the impression that it would be easy for me.	.067	**.584**
		14	The contents and structure helped me to become confident that I would learn with this game.	**.544**	.361
Challenge		15	This game is appropriately challenging for me.	**.673**	.000
		16	The game provides new challenges (offers new obstacles, situations, or variations) at an appropriate pace.	**.703**	-.065
		17	The game does not become monotonous as it progresses (repetitive or boring tasks).	**.621**	.073

(Continued)

TABLE 5.6   (Continued)

Original Dimension/ Sub-Dimension	Item No.	Description	Factors	
			1	2
	18	Completing the game tasks gave me a satisfying feeling of accomplishment.	**.741**	.114
Satisfaction	19	It is due to my personal effort that I managed to advance in the game.	**.461**	.231
	20	I feel satisfied with the things that I learned from the game.	**.722**	.220
	21	I would recommend this game to my colleagues.	**.762**	.219
	22	I was able to interact with other players during the game.	**.600**	-.057
Social Interaction	23	The game promotes cooperation and/or competition among the players.	**.622**	.018
	24	I felt good interacting with other players during the game.	**.721**	.039
	25	I had fun with the game.	**.783**	.185
Fun	26	Something happened during the game (game elements, competition, etc.) which made me smile.	**.621**	.138
	27	There was something interesting at the beginning of the game that captured my attention.	**.664**	.128
Focused Attention	28	I was so involved in my gaming task that I lost track of time.	**.707**	.041
	29	I forgot about my immediate surroundings while playing this game.	**.676**	.050
	30	The game contents are relevant to my interests.	**.568**	.239
	31	It is clear to me how the contents of the game are related to the course.	.389	.335
Relevance	32	This game is an adequate teaching method for this course.	**.572**	.324
	33	I prefer learning with this game to learning through other ways (e.g., other teaching methods).	**.489**	.227
	34	The game contributed to my learning in this course.	**.635**	.250
Perceived Learning	35	The game allowed for efficient learning compared with other activities in the course.	**.597**	.246

(Table 5.1)). As this result shows that these dimensions are integrated into one factor, we defined this quality factor as the player experience. Thus, in this study, we define player experience as a quality factor that covers a deep involvement of the student in the gaming task, including its perception of learning, feelings, pleasures, and interactions with the game, environment, and other players [28, 44, 49–52, 54, 66, 68]. In addition, the first factor also includes items 10, 11, and 12, which are specific to the evaluation of digital games, in terms of the games' customization and user error protection. However, these items were analyzed only with a sample of 187 data points (sample of digital games). Thus, the results of the factor analysis in terms of these items may be influenced by the sample size, generating a different classification of these items. For this reason, these items need to be re-analyzed with a greater sample size from digital games in order to confirm this result.

With respect to the second factor (factor 2), a set of 10 items (items no. 1 to 9, and 13) is related. This result clearly suggests that factor 2 is related to the concept of usability, measuring the aesthetics, learnability, operability, and accessibility of educational games. Although item no. 13 is originally related to confidence, the result of the analysis of this item seems to indicate that this item measures the game's usability rather than the learner's confidence.

Therefore, based on the results of the factor analysis, the MEEGA+ model is decomposed into two quality factors and their dimensions, as presented in Figure 5.3.

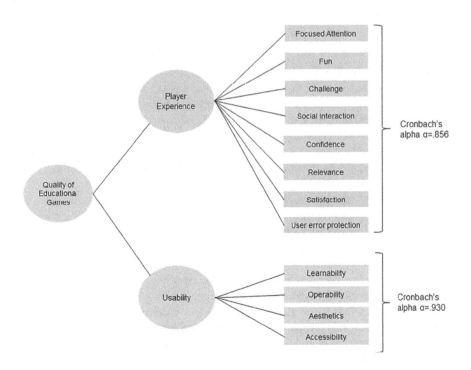

FIGURE 5.3   Structure of the MEEGA+ model as a result of the factor analysis.

TABLE 5.7

Spearman Correlation Coefficient of the Quality Factor Usability

Item/Dimension	1	2	3	4	5	6	7	8	9	13
	Aesthetics		Learnability			Operability		Accessibility		
1	1.00									
2	.58	1.00								
3	.30	.25	1.00							
4	.33	.30	.70	1.00						
5	.35	.24	.60	.72	1.00					
6	.36	.31	.56	.70	.71	1.00				
7	.38	.29	.49	.56	.56	.61	1.00			
8	.41	.54	.30	.36	.35	.40	.38	1.00		
9	.40	.64	.24	.32	.30	.38	.36	.70	1.00	
13	.26	.20	.39	.47	.45	.44	.35	.31	.26	1.00

AQ3: Is there evidence of convergent and discriminant validity of the MEEGA+ measurement instrument?

Convergent and discriminant validity are two sub-categories of construct validity [36]. Thus, in order to obtain evidence of convergent and discriminant validity of the standardized items of the MEEGA+ measurement instrument, the correlations of the items are calculated [32]. Convergent validity shows that the items that should be related are, in fact, related. On the other hand, discriminant validity shows that the items that should not be related are in fact not related [36].

Correlations of the Standardized Items

In order to obtain evidence of convergent validity, it is expected that the items of the same quality factor (e.g., items related to usability) demonstrate a large correlation [36]. On the other hand, to obtain evidence of discriminant validity it is expected that items of different quality factors demonstrate a small correlation [36]. For example, it is expected that the items of different quality factors (e.g., an item related to usability and an item related to player experience) have a small correlation, as in theory, the items are measuring different quality factors.

In order to analyze the correlations between the standardized items, we used the non-parametric Spearman correlation matrices for each quality factor (Tables 5.7 and 5.8). A complete matrix including all quality factors is presented in Appendix 5.A. The matrices show the Spearman correlation coefficient, indicating the degree of correlation between two items (item pairs). We used this correlation coefficient, as it is the most appropriate correlation analysis for Likert scales [32, 36]. The correlation coefficients between the items within of the same dimension are colored. In accordance with Cohen [84], a correlation between items is considered satisfactory, if the correlation coefficient is greater than 0.29, indicating that there is a moderate correlation, or a large correlation, if the coefficient is greater than 0.50 [84]. A coefficient of about 0.10, indicates a small correlation between the items [84]. Satisfactory correlations are marked in bold.

TABLE 5.8
Spearman Correlation Coefficient of the Quality Factor Player Experience

Item	10	11	12	14	15	16	17	18	19	20	21	22	23	24	25	26	27	28	29	30	31	32	33	34	35
	User Error Protection			Confidence	Challenge		Satisfaction					Social Interaction		Fun			Focused Attention			Relevance				Perceived Learning	
10	1.0																								
11	.54	1.0																							
12	.26	.42	1.0																						
14	.04	.11	.12	1.0																					
15	.16	.16	.11	.45	1.0																				
16	.20	.18	.18	.39	.60	1.0																			
17	.11	.11	.07	.30	.46	.50	1.0																		
18	.13	.10	.10	.40	.48	.47	.46	1.0																	
19	.03	.04	.03	.38	.36	.31	.27	.46	1.0																
20	.13	.11	.09	.49	.44	.44	.35	.57	.49	1.0															
21	.18	.20	.11	.47	.44	.43	.46	.58	.40	.71	1.0														
22	.22	.15	.12	.27	.32	.34	.34	.37	.20	.37	.40	1.0													
23	.16	.15	.04	.29	.37	.39	.37	.45	.26	.39	.42	.61	1.0												
24	.22	.18	.07	.36	.39	.40	.40	.48	.26	.45	.49	.67	.68	1.0											
25	.10	.10	.05	.42	.39	.43	.48	.58	.31	.49	.62	.50	.56	.63	1.0										
26	.10	.06	-.01	.31	.32	.30	.39	.45	.22	.38	.47	.43	.44	.55	.69	1.0									
27	.14	.14	.01	.38	.36	.38	.34	.43	.26	.40	.50	.31	.33	.42	.53	.46	1.0								
28	.17	.14	.05	.38	.36	.38	.43	.49	.25	.38	.49	.35	.40	.48	.58	.49	.58	1.0							
29	.19	.15	.09	.28	.31	.35	.38	.47	.24	.35	.48	.39	.40	.48	.53	.44	.51	.76	1.0						
30	.04	.05	.01	.39	.38	.29	.29	.45	.36	.52	.51	.27	.30	.34	.44	.29	.36	.34	.34	1.0					
31	-.05	-.02	-.03	.29	.25	.20	.20	.27	.30	.39	.34	.22	.25	.27	.34	.29	.22	.20	.18	.43	1.0				
32	-.01	.03	.01	.43	.33	.31	.27	.39	.37	.50	.48	.22	.29	.34	.45	.37	.34	.29	.30	.46	.62	1.0			
33	.01	.05	-.04	.29	.26	.24	.26	.31	.29	.38	.38	.20	.25	.30	.38	.31	.28	.26	.32	.31	.40	.62	1.0		
34	.01	.01	-.01	.46	.37	.39	.26	.43	.37	.58	.49	.26	.30	.34	.44	.33	.36	.33	.30	.53	.53	.65	.53	1.0	
35	-.03	.00	.02	.41	.34	.37	.28	.41	.36	.53	.47	.22	.26	.33	.44	.32	.34	.31	.28	.44	.43	.56	.55	.72	1.0

Analyzing the correlations between the items of the quality factor usability (Table 5.7), we can observe that most of the item pairs present a moderate or large correlation. This result indicates that, although usability is fragmented into its dimensions, the items present a satisfactory correlation in order to measure what the factor purports to measure (the usability of the educational games). With respect to item no. 13 (originally related to confidence), the results show that this item has a moderate correlation to items of the dimensions of learnability and operability. Thus, in fact, item no. 13 seems to be measuring rather the game's usability. On the other hand, few items pairs (6) presented a low correlation according to Cohen's coefficient. Even so, these item pairs have a correlation coefficient very close to the level of moderate correlation. Therefore, based on the correlation coefficients of the quality factor usability, we can establish a convergent validity.

Analyzing the quality factor of player experience (Table 5.8), we can observe again that the majority of the item pairs presents a moderate or a large correlation coefficient. This result indicates that, in fact, the player experience in educational games is measured in terms of confidence, challenge, satisfaction, social interaction, fun, focused attention, relevance, and perceived learning as suggested by the large correlation coefficients between the items. However, as shown in Table 5.8, we can also observe that the items no. 10, 11, and 12 present a small correlation to other items of this quality factor. Thus, although the result of the factor analysis indicates that these items compose the quality factor of player experience, the correlation coefficients seem to be indicating that these items are not measuring player experience, when compared to other items of this quality factor. An explanation for this result may be that the sample size of these items' analysis (n = 187) is smaller than the sample size of the other items (n = 589) and, thus, may have influenced the results. Therefore, these items should be re-analyzed with a greater sample size on digital games in order to confirm, if these items, in fact, are composing the quality factor of player experience when evaluating games for SE education. However, considering the majority of moderate and large correlation coefficients, we can observe that there is evidence of convergent validity in the quality factor of player experience.

In order to obtain evidence of discriminant validity, we analyzed the correlation coefficients of the different quality factors. In this respect, we evaluated, if the items of different quality factors demonstrate a small correlation [36]. As shown in the Spearman correlation matrix (Appendix 5.A), the majority of the items pairs of different quality factors (e.g., 3–22 and 8–28) presented a small correlation coefficient, indicating evidence of discriminant validity.

In summary, we can observe that, in general, there is a correlation between items within a quality factor. This indicates that convergent validity can be established for the two quality factors (usability and player experience). On the other hand, few item pairs (items no. 10, 11, and 12) present small or negative correlations, which indicate that these items need be revised and/or, principally, re-analyzed with a greater sample size with respect to digital games in order to confirm this result. In general, items of different quality factors presented a small correlation, thus, we also can identify evidence of discriminant validity. Based on these results, we can conclude that the MEEGA+ measurement instrument actually measures what it purports to measure (the quality of games for SE education in terms of usability and player experience).

5.6   DISCUSSION

Based on the results obtained in the statistical evaluation of the MEEGA+ measurement instrument, we can consider that there is evidence of reliability and construct validity of the MEEGA+ model, considering it an acceptable model for the evaluation of the quality of games used for SE education.

Analyzing the reliability (AQ1), our results of the analysis indicate an excellent Cronbach's alpha coefficient (α = .929), indicating the internal consistency of the MEEGA+ measurement instrument. Comparing the reliability of the MEEGA+ model to the initial version of the MEEGA model (Cronbach's alpha α = .915) [30], we obtained an increase in the reliability. This indicates that the items of the MEEGA+ measurement instrument are consistent and precise with respect to the evaluation of games' quality and that the evolution of the model, in fact, presents an improvement with respect to its reliability. Also comparing our results with the reliability of the related approaches, although most of them do not present a reliability analysis, we also obtained a greater reliability than that presented in each factor of the EGameFlow scale (Cronbach's alpha α = .80) [44].

Analyzing the construct validity of the MEEGA+ model, based on the results of the exploratory factor analysis (AQ2), we identified that the responses of the MEEGA+ measurement instrument are explained by two underlying concepts (quality factors). This result indicates that the quality of games for SE education is evaluated through two quality factors (player experience and usability). The first factor measuring the player experience consists of a set of 25 items including dimensions such as focused attention, fun, challenge, social interaction, confidence, relevance, satisfaction, and perceived learning. This factor also includes items, which are specific to the evaluation of digital games. However, as these items presented only a small correlation with other items of this factor, seem to be indicating that these items may not be measuring player experience, thus, these items need to be re-analyzed with a greater sample size. Items related to the second factor, measuring the game's usability, measure the dimensions of aesthetics, learnability, operability, and accessibility of educational games.

Comparing the present results with the factor analysis of the initial version of the MEEGA model [30], which indicated a conceptual overlap in terms of motivation and user experience, our results indicate a well-defined decomposition composed of two quality factors (player experience and usability) (Figure 5.3) in order to evaluate games used for SE education. And, compared to the related approaches, which typically use a wide variety of factors lacking a consensus and some of them overlap conceptually, our results provide evidence of a well-defined conceptual structure, in which the dimensions were defined following a trend identified in a previous literature review [13], and through a mapping study, thus, minimizing the overlap of concepts.

Analyzing the correlation coefficients between the items of the two quality factors of the MEEGA+ model, we can observe that, in general, there is a moderate and large correlation between the majority of the items within each quality factor. This indicates that a convergent validity can be established for the two quality factors (usability and player experience). In the same way, items of different quality factors present a small correlation, and, thus, provide evidence of discriminant validity. And, compared with the initial version of the MEEGA model, again, the MEEGA+ model presents an improvement. The MEEGA model demonstrated evidence of convergent validity, but did not present evidence of discriminant validity, indicating a conceptual overlap [30]. In contrast, with respect to the MEEGA+ model, we can identify evidence of convergent and discriminant validity, presenting a well-defined and correlated structure, composed of two quality factors (player experience and usability).

Regarding the development process, in which the related approaches are typically developed in an ad hoc manner [25], we, on the other hand, followed a systematic research method defining an evaluation objective, decomposing it into factors, defining measurement instrument items in order to operationalize the data collection process and their analysis and interpretation. In addition, regarding the validation of the related approaches, the majority of the approaches is partially evaluated through some case or pilot studies and, in general, not provide information about a statistical evaluation. In our study, on the other hand, we conducted 29 case studies applying the MEEGA+ model in the evaluation of SE games, grouping the data collected in a significant sample size (n = 589) and statistically analyzing the validity and reliability of the MEEGA+ model.

Therefore, based on our results, we can conclude that the MEEGA+ measurement instrument has a high reliability and measures what it purports to measure: the quality of games used for SE education in terms of usability and player experience.

5.6.1 THREATS TO VALIDITY

Considering the characteristics of this kind of research, it is subject to threats to validity. Therefore, we identified potential threats and applied mitigation strategies in order to minimize their impact on our research. Some threats are related to the design of the study. In order to mitigate this threat, we defined and documented a systematic research method. The MEEGA+ model has been defined adopting the GQM approach, systematically decomposing the evaluation objective. The measurement instrument has been developed following scale and questionnaire development methods. In addition, for the evaluation of the MEEGA+ measurement instrument, a case study has been systematically defined and documented.

Another risk refers to the quality of the data pooled into a single sample, in terms of standardization of data (response format) and adequacy of the MEEGA+ model. As our study is limited exclusively to evaluations that used the MEEGA+ model, this risk is minimized as in all studies the same data collection instrument has been used. Another issue refers to the pooled data from different contexts. To mitigate this threat all case studies have been conducted in similar contexts (SE courses in higher education).

Another issue refers to the evaluation of the learning. Adopting a non-experimental research design (case studies), only a post-test using self-assessment has been applied in order to evaluate the students' perceived learning. A pre-test has not been applied and, therefore, it was not possible to accurately evaluate the learning difference promoted by the games. Regarding the self-assessment, although there is no consensus, there is evidence that self-assessment provides reliable, valid, and useful information for this type of study [60, 64, 65], mainly when using a systematic, reliable, and valid evaluation model as MEEGA+.

In terms of external validity, a threat to the possibility to generalize the results is related to the sample size and diversity of the data used for the evaluation. In respect to sample size, our evaluation used data collected from 29 case studies evaluating 13 different educational games, involving a population of 589 students from six different educational institutions. In terms of statistical significance, this is a satisfactory sample size, allowing the generation of significant results [39, 59].

In terms of reliability, a threat refers to what extent the data and the analysis are dependent on the specific researchers. In order to mitigate this threat, we systematically documented the evaluation of the MEEGA+ model, defining clearly the study objective, the process of data collection, and the statistical methods used for data analysis. Another issue refers to the correct choice of statistical tests for data analysis. To minimize this threat, we performed a statistical evaluation following the guide for the construction of measurement scales as proposed by DeVellis [32], which is aligned with procedures for the evaluation of internal consistency and construct validity of a measurement instrument proposed by Trochim and Donnelly [36].

5.7 CONCLUSIONS

In this study, we present the design and evaluation of the MEEGA+ model in order to evaluate the quality of games used for SE education, an evolution of the MEEGA model proposed by Savi et al. [28]. Following a systematic research method, the MEEGA+ model has been designed based on the results of previous literature reviews and a large-scale analysis of the initial version of the MEEGA model. A set of dimensions has been defined and a measurement instrument has been designed to be used for the evaluation of educational games in case studies with a one-shot post-test only design. The MEEGA+ model has been statistically evaluated in terms of reliability and construct validity based on a sample of data from 589 participants in 29 case studies evaluating 13 different digital and non-digital games for SE education. The results indicate that the MEEGA+ measurement instrument has a satisfactory reliability and construct validity. With respect to reliability, a Cronbach's alpha $\alpha = .929$ indicates an excellent internal consistency, which means that the responses between the items are consistent and precise. The results of an exploratory factor analysis indicate that the quality of games for SE education is evaluated through two quality factors (player experience and usability). In addition, the results show evidence of convergent validity through a satisfactory degree of correlation found between most of the items for all quality factors. Thus, providing evidence of a well-defined and correlated conceptual structure composed of two quality factors (player experience and usability).

Based on the results of our study, we can conclude that the MEEGA+ model, in fact, presents an evolution of its initial version proposed by Savi et al. [28], clearly indicating an improvement with respect to its reliability and validity. Therefore, the MEEGA+ model can be considered a reliable and valid model for evaluating the quality of games used as an instructional strategy for SE education.

APPENDIX 5.A
Spearman Correlation Coefficients of all Quality Factors (Player Experience and Usability)

Usability — items 1–9 · Player Experience — items 13 onward

Item No.	1	2	3	4	5	6	7	8	9	10	11	12	13	14	15	16	17	18	19	20	21	22	23	24	25	26	27	28	29	30	31	32	33	34	35
1	1.0																																		
2	.58	1.0																																	
3	.30	.25	1.0																																
4	.33	.30	.70	1.0																															
5	.35	.24	.60	.72	1.0																														
6	.36	.31	.56	.70	.71	1.0																													
7	.38	.29	.49	.56	.56	.61	1.0																												
8	.41	.54	.30	.36	.35	.40	.38	1.0																											
9	.40	.64	.24	.32	.30	.38	.36	.70	1.0																										
10	-.04	-.06	-.09	-.10	-.10	-.12	.00	-.07	-.11	1.0																									
11	.04	.01	-.03	-.06	-.04	-.04	.05	-.02	.00	.54	1.0																								
12	-.04	-.02	-.01	-.05	-.02	-.05	.01	-.05	-.03	.26	.42	1.0																							
13	.26	.20	.39	.47	.45	.42	.35	.31	.26	-.07	.02	.00	1.0																						
14	.36	.25	.22	.24	.28	.29	.38	.26	.24	.04	.11	.12	.32	1.0																					
15	.23	.17	.03	.04	.10	.08	.22	.01	.09	.16	.16	.11	.09	.45	1.0																				
16	.21	.14	.00	-.06	.14	.20	.17	.03	.07	.20	.18	.11	.02	.39	.60	1.0																			
17	.29	.19	.06	.08	.16	.16	.20	.01	.13	.11	.11	.07	.09	.30	.46	.50	1.0																		
18	.26	.10	.14	.15	.17	.19	.30	.05	.14	.13	.10	.10	.11	.40	.48	.47	.46	1.0																	
19	.21	.12	.19	.22	.22	.18	.32	.14	.14	.03	.04	.03	.22	.38	.36	.31	.27	.46	1.0																
20	.26	.19	.17	.18	.22	.22	.32	.14	.14	.13	.20	.11	.17	.49	.44	.43	.34	.58	.40	1.0															
21	.34	.21	.21	.22	.23	.25	.34	.09	.13	.18	.15	.12	.21	.47	.44	.34	.39	.45	.49	.71	1.0														
22	.19	.18	.08	.08	.09	.14	.27	.10	.06	.22	.15	.07	.05	.27	.32	.34	.37	.37	.20	.37	.40	1.0													
23	.28	.15	.12	.17	.13	.21	.27	.12	.11	.16	.18	.04	.10	.29	.37	.39	.34	.45	.26	.39	.42	.61	1.0												
24	.31	.20	.15	.13	.22	.19	.25	.11	.15	.22	.18	.07	.10	.36	.39	.38	.37	.43	.24	.45	.49	.67	.68	1.0											
25	.42	.24	.13	.20	.22	.30	.34	.13	.15	.11	.10	.05	.19	.38	.36	.44	.43	.49	.36	.52	.62	.50	.56	.63	1.0										
26	.34	.19	.09	.15	.18	.22	.27	.11	.12	.10	.06	-.01	.17	.31	.31	.30	.38	.45	.36	.39	.47	.43	.44	.55	.69	1.0									
27	.33	.18	.10	.07	.16	.16	.28	.08	.27	.14	.14	.01	.22	.28	.25	.20	.34	.27	.30	.50	.50	.31	.33	.42	.53	.46	1.0								
28	.30	.12	.07	.07	.20	.15	.28	.02	.18	.17	.14	.05	.90	.38	.38	.38	.43	.49	.25	.38	.49	.35	.40	.48	.58	.49	.58	1.0								
29	.26	.13	.01	.05	.16	.13	.19	.05	.08	.04	.15	.01	.10	.24	.31	.35	.24	.47	.36	.35	.48	.39	.40	.48	.53	.44	.51	.76	1.0							
30	.18	.19	.15	.17	.19	.24	.29	.16	.18	-.05	.05	-.03	.12	.39	.38	.30	.27	.45	.30	.52	.34	.30	.30	.34	.44	.29	.36	.34	.34	1.0					
31	.20	.22	.15	.20	.16	.22	.28	.25	.21	-.01	-.02	.01	.14	.29	.25	.20	.20	.27	.37	.39	.48	.25	.25	.27	.34	.29	.22	.20	.18	.43	1.0				
32	.30	.27	.15	.18	.18	.23	.28	.26	.27	.03	.03	-.04	.21	.43	.33	.31	.27	.39	.37	.50	.38	.29	.29	.34	.45	.37	.34	.29	.30	.46	.62	1.0			
33	.25	.20	.09	.13	.13	.16	.20	.14	.17	.01	.01	-.01	.20	.29	.30	.24	.26	.31	.29	.38	.38	.20	.25	.30	.38	.31	.28	.26	.32	.31	.40	.65	1.0		
34	.23	.17	.13	.16	.17	.19	.30	.19	.18	.01	.01	.01	.46	.46	.37	.39	.26	.43	.29	.58	.49	.26	.30	.34	.44	.33	.36	.33	.30	.53	.53	.56	.55	1.0	
35	.24	.17	.12	.14	.18	.21	.26	.17	.16	-.03	.00	.02	.21	.41	.34	.37	.28	.41	.36	.53	.47	.22	.26	.33	.44	.32	.34	.31	.28	.44	.43	.56	.53	.72	1.0

As future work, we plan to expand the evaluation of the MEEGA+ model, including evaluations of different games and contexts and with a larger sample, mainly of digital games, in order to continue improving the validity and reliability of the MEEGA+ model.

ACKNOWLEDGMENTS

This work was supported by the CNPq (Conselho Nacional de Desenvolvimento Científico e Tecnológico – www.cnpq.br), an entity of the Brazilian government focused on scientific and technological development.

NOTE

REFERENCES

[1] IEEE. 2010. Systems and software engineering–vocabulary. *ISO/IEC/IEEE 24765*, vol. 2010, no. (E), 1–418.

[2] ACM. 2013. *Computer Science Curricula 2013: Curriculum Guidelines for Undergraduate Degree Programs in Computer Science, Joint Task Force on Computing Curricula, Association for Computing Machinery (ACM) and IEEE Computer Society*. ACM, New York, NY, USA.

[3] Marques, M. R., Quispe, A. and Ochoa, S. F. 2014. *A systematic mapping study on practical approaches to teaching software engineering*. In *Proc. of the IEEE Frontiers in Education Conference*. Madrid, Spain, 1–8.

[4] Sedelmaier, Y. and Landes, D. 2015. *Active and Inductive Learning in Software Engineering Education*. In *Proc. of the 37th IEEE Int. Conf. on Software Engineering*. Florence, Italy, 418–427.

[5] Gresse von Wangenheim, C. and Shull, F. 2009. To game or not to game? *IEEE Software*, vol. 26, no. 2, 92–94.

[6] Marques, M., Ochoa, S. F., Bastarrica, M. C. and Gutierrez, F. J. 2018. Enhancing the Student Learning Experience in Software Engineering Project Courses. *IEEE Transactions on Education*, vol. 61, no. 1, 63–73.

[7] Calderón, A. and Ruiz M. 2015. A systematic literature review on serious games evaluation: An application to software project management. *Computers & Education*, vol. 87, 396–422.

[8] Kosa, M., Yilmaz, M., O'Connor, R., and Clarke, P. 2016. Software engineering education and games: A systematic literature review. *Journal of Universal Computer Science*, vol. 22, no. 12, 1558–1574.

[9] Abt, C. C. 2002. *Serious Games*. University Press of America, Lanhan.

[10] Ritterfeld, U., Cody, M., and Vorderer, P. 2009. *Serious Games: Mechanisms and effects.* Routledge, New York.

[11] Djaouti, D., Alvarez, J., Jessel, J. P., and Rampnoux, O. 2011. Origins of serious games. In *Serious Games and Edutainment Applications*, Ma M., Oikonomou A., Jain L. (Eds). Springer-Verlag, London.

[12] Battistella, P. and Gresse von Wangenheim, C. 2016. Games for teaching computing in higher education: A systematic review. *IEEE Technology and Engineering Education Journal*, vol. 9, no. 1, 8–30.

[13] Petri, G. and Gresse von Wangenheim, C. 2017. How games for computing education are evaluated? A systematic literature review. *Computers & Education*, vol. 107, 68–90.

[14] Gresse von Wangenheim, C., Savi, R., and Borgatto, A. F. 2012. DELIVER! An educational game for teaching earned value management in computing courses. *Information and Software Technology*, vol. 54, no. 3, 286–298.

[15] Bavota, G., Lucia, A., Fasano, F., Oliveto, R., and Zottoli, C. 2012. *Teaching software engineering and software project management: an integrated and practical approach.* In *Proc. of the 34th Int. Conf. on Software Engineering.* Piscataway, NJ, USA, 1155–1164.

[16] Gresse von Wangenheim, C., Savi, R., and Borgatto, A. F. 2013. SCRUMIA: An educational game for teaching SCRUM in computing courses. *Journal of Systems and Software*, vol. 86, no. 10, 2675–2687.

[17] Navarro, E. O. 2006. SimSE: A Software Engineering Simulation Environment for Software Process Education. Unpublished Thesis. University of California, Irvine, CA, USA.

[18] Baker, A., Navarro, E. O., and van der Hoek, A. 2003. *Problems and Programmers: An Educational Software Engineering Card Game.* In *Proc. of the 25th Int. Conf. on Software Engineering.* Portland, OR, USA, 614–619.

[19] Bell, J., Sheth, S., and Kaiser, G. *2011. Secret ninja testing with HALO software engineering.* In *Proc. of the 4th Int. Workshop on Social software engineering.* New York, NY, USA, 43–47.

[20] Thiry, M., Zoucas, A., and Silva, A. C. 2011. *Empirical study upon software testing learning with support from educational game.* In *Proc. of the 23rd Int. Conf. on Software Engineering & Knowledge Engineering.* Miami Beach, FL, USA, 482–484.

[21] Gresse von Wangenheim, C. 2018. *PM Master.* Available at: http://www.gqs.ufsc.br/pm-master Accessed: April 20 2018.

[22] Petri, G., Battistella, P. E., Cassettari, F., Gresse von Wangenheim, C., and Hauck, J. C. R. 2016. *A Quiz Game for Knowledge Review on Project Management.* In *Proc. of the 27th Brazilian Symposium on Informatics in Education.*Uberlância/MG, Brazil (in Portuguese).

[23] Connolly, T. M., Boyle, E. A., MacArthur, E., Hainey, T., and Boyle, J. M. 2012. A systematic literature review of empirical evidence on computer games and serious games. *Computers & Education*, vol. 59, no. 2, 661–686.

[24] Boyle, E. A., Hainey, T., Connolly, T. M., Gray, G., Earp, J., Ott, M., Lim, T., Ninaus, M., Ribeiro, C., and Pereira, J. 2016. An update to the systematic literature review of empirical evidence of the impacts and outcomes of computer games and serious games. *Computers & Education*, vol. 94, 178–192.

[25] Petri, G. and Gresse von Wangenheim, C. 2016. How to evaluate educational games: A systematic literature review. *Journal of Universal Computers Science*, vol. 22, no. 7, 992–1021.

[26] Kordaki, M. and Gousiou, A. 2017. Digital card games in education: A ten year systematic review. *Computers & Education*, vol. 109, 122–161.

[27] Tahir, R. and Wangmar, A. I. 2017. *State of the art in Game Based Learning: Dimensions for Evaluating Educational Games*. In *Proc. of the European Conference on Games Based Learning*. Graz, Austria, 641–650.

[28] Savi, R., Gresse von Wangenheim, C., and Borgatto, A. F. 2011. *A model for the evaluation of educational games for teaching software engineering*. In *Proc. of the 25th Brazilian Symposium on Software Engineering*. São Paulo, Brazil, 194–203 (in Portuguese).

[29] Calderón, A., Ruiz M., and O'Connor, R. 2018. A multivocal literature review on serious games for software process standards education. *Computer Standards & Interfaces*, vol. 57, 36–48.

[30] Petri, G., Gresse von Wangenheim, C., and Borgatto, A. F. 2017. *A Large-scale Evaluation of a Model for the Evaluation of Games for Teaching Software Engineering*. In *Proc. of the IEEE/ACM 39th Int. Conf. on Software Engineering: Software Engineering Education and Training Track*. Buenos Aires, Argentina, 180–189.

[31] Kitchenham, B. 2010. Systematic literature reviews in software engineering – A tertiary study. *Information and Software Technology*, vol. 52, no. 1, 792–805.

[32] DeVellis, R. F. 2017. *Scale Development: Theory and Applications* (4th. ed.). SAGE Publications, Inc., Thousand Oaks.

[33] Kasunic, M. 2005. *Designing an effective survey. Handbook CMU/SEI-2005-HB-004*, Software Engineering Institute/Carnegie Mellon University, Pittsburgh.

[34] Basili, V. R., Caldiera, G., and Rombach, H. D. 1994. Goal, Question Metric Paradigm. In *Encyclopedia of Software Engineering*, J. J. Marciniak (Ed.). Wiley-Interscience, New York.

[35] Budgen, D., Turner, M., Brereton, P., and Kitchenham, B. 2008. *Using mapping studies in software engineering*. In *Proc. of the 20th Workshop on Psychology of Programming Interest Group*. Lancaster, UK, 195–204.

[36] Trochim, W. M., and Donnelly, J. P. 2008. *Research Methods Knowledge Base* (3rd ed.). Atomic Dog Publishing, Mason.

[37] Beecham, S., Hall, T., Britton, C., Cottee, M., and Rainer, A. 2005. Using an expert panel to validate a requirements process improvement model. *Journal of Systems and Software*, vol. 76, no. 3, 251–275.

[38] Yin, R. K. 2017. *Case Study Research: Design and Methods* (6th. ed.). SAGE Publications, Inc., Thousand Oaks.

[39] Wohlin, C., Runeson, P., Höst, M., Ohlsson, M. C., Regnell, B., and Wesslén, A. 2012. *Experimentation in Software Engineering*. Springer Science+Business Media, New York.

[40] Cronbach, L. J. 1951. Coefficient alpha and the internal structure of tests. *Psychometrika*, vol. 16, no. 3, 297–334.

[41] Abdellatif, A. J., McCollum, B., and McMullan, P. 2018. *Serious Games: Quality Characteristics Evaluation Framework and Case Study*. In *Proc. of IEEE Integrated STEM Education Conference*, Princeton, NJ, USA, 112–119.

[42] Freitas, S. D., and Oliver, M. 2006. How can exploratory learning with games and simulations within the curriculum be most effectively evaluated? *Computers & Education*, vol. 46, no.3, 249–264.

[43] Connolly, T. M., Stansfield, M. H., and Hainey, T. 2009. Towards the development of a games-based learning evaluation framework. In *Games-Based Learning Advancement for Multisensory Human Computer Interfaces: Techniques and Effective Practices*, T. M. Connolly, M. H. Stansfield, & E. Boyle (Eds.), Idea-Group Publishing, Hershey.

[44] Fu, F., Su, R., & Yu, S. 2009. EGameFlow: A scale to measure learners' enjoyment of e-learning games. *Computers & Education*, vol. 52, no. 1, 101–112.

[45] Carvalho, C. V. 2012. *Is Game-Based Learning Suitable for Engineering Education?* In *Proc. of the Global Engineering Education Conf.* Marrakech, Morocco, 1–8.

[46] Ak, O. 2012. A game scale to evaluate educational computer games. *Procedia – Social and Behavioral Sciences*, vol. 46, 2477–2481.

[47] Mayer, I. 2012. Towards a comprehensive methodology for the research and evaluation of serious games. *Procedia Computer Science*, vol. 15, 233–247.

[48] Petri, G., Gresse von Wangenheim, C., and Borgatto, A. F. 2018. MEEGA+, Systematic Model to Evaluate Educational Games. In *Encyclopedia of Computer Graphics and Games*, Newton Lee (Ed). Springer, Cham, 1–7.

[49] Keller, J. 1987. Development and use of the ARCS model of motivational design. *Journal of Instructional Development*, vol. 10, no. 3, 2–10.

[50] International Standard Organization (ISO). 2014. ISO/IEC 25010: Systems and software engineering – Systems and software Quality Requirements and Evaluation (SQuaRE) – System and software quality models, Technical Report, Switzerland.

[51] Wiebe, E. N., Lamb, A., Hardy, M., and Sharek, D. 2014. Measuring engagement in video game-based environments: Investigation of the User Engagement Scale. *Computers in Human Behavior*, vol. 32, 123–132.

[52] Sindre, G. and Moody, D. 2003. *Evaluating the Effectiveness of Learning Interventions: an Information Systems Case Study.* In *Proc. of the 11th European Conf. on Information Systems*. Naples, Italy, Paper 80.

[53] Poels, K., Kort, Y. D., and Ijsselsteijn, W. 2007. *It is always a lot of fun!: exploring dimensions of digital game experience using focus group methodology.* In *Proc. of Conf. on Future Play*. Toronto, Canada, 83–89.

[54] Sweetser, P. and Wyeth, P. 2005. GameFlow: a model for evaluating player enjoyment in games. *Computers in Entertainment*, vol. 3, no. 3, 1–24.

[55] Branch, R. M. 2010. *Instructional Design: The ADDIE Approach.* Springer Science+Business Media, New York.

[56] Seman, L. O., Hausmann, R., and Bezerra, E. A. 2018. On the students' perceptions of the knowledge formation when submitted to a Project-Based Learning environment using web applications. *Computers & Education*, vol. 117, 16–30.

[57] Ding, L., Er, E., and Orey, M. 2018. An exploratory study of student engagement in gamified online discussions. *Computers & Education*, vol. 120, 213–226.

[58] Schanzenbach, D. W. 2012. Limitations of experiments in education research. *Education Finance and Policy*, vol. 7, no. 2, 219–232.

[59] All, A., Castellar, E. P. N., and Looy, J. V. 2016. Assessing the effectiveness of digital game-based learning: Best practices. *Computers & Education*, vol. 92–93, 90–103.

[60] Sitzmann, T., Ely, K., Brown, K. G., and Bauer, K. N. 2010. Self-assessment of knowledge: A cognitive learning or affective measure? *Academy of Management Learning & Education*, vol. 9, no. 2, 169–191.

[61] Bowman, D. D. 2018. Declining talent in computer related careers. *Journal of Academic Administration in Higher Education*, vol. 14, no. 1, 1–4.

[62] Andrade, H. and Valtcheva, A. 2009. Promoting learning and achievement through self-assessment. *Theory Into Practice*, vol. 48, 12–19.

[63] Gikandi, J. W., Morrow, D., and Davis, N.D. 2011. Online formative assessment in higher education: A review of the literature. *Computers & Education*, vol. 57, no. 4, 233–235.

[64] Thomas, G., Martin, D., and Pleasants, K. 2011. Using self- and peer-assessment to enhance students' future-learning in higher education. *Journal of University Teaching & Learning Practice*, vol. 8, no. 1, 1–17.

[65] Sharma, R., Jain, A., Gupta, N., Garg, S., Batta, M., and Dhir, S. K. 2016. Impact of self-assessment by students on their learning. *International Journal of Applied and Basic Medical Research*, vol. 6, no. 3, 226–229.

[66] Tullis, T. and Albert, W. 2008. *Measuring the User Experience: Collecting, Analyzing, and Presenting Usability Metrics*. Morgan Kaufmann, Burlington.

[67] Takatalo, J., Häkkinen, J., Kaistinen, J., & Nyman, G. 2010. Presence, involvement, and flow in digital games. In *Evaluating User Experience in Games: Concepts and Methods*, Bernhaupt, R. (Ed.). Springer, London, 23–46.

[68] O'Brien, H. L. and Toms, E. G. 2010. The development and evaluation of a survey to measure user engagement. *Journal of the American Society for Information Science and Technology*, vol. 61, no.1, 50–69.

[69] Mohamed, H. and Jaafar, A. 2010. *Development and Potential Analysis of Heuristic Evaluation for Educational Computer Game (PHEG)*. In *Proc. of the 5th Int. Conf. on Computer Sciences and Convergence Information Technology*. Seoul, South Korea, 222–227.

[70] Zaibon, S. B. 2015. User testing on game usability, mobility, playability, and learning content of mobile game-based learning. *Journal Teknologi*, vol. 77, no. 29, 131–139.

[71] Brooke, J. 1996. SUS-A quick and dirty usability scale. *Usability Evaluation in Industry*, vol. 189, no. 194, 4–7.

[72] Davis, F. D. 1989. Perceived usefulness, perceived ease of use, and user acceptance of information technology. *MIS Quarterly*, vol. 13, no. 3, 319–340.

[73] Anderson, L. W., Krathwohl, D. R., & Bloom, B. S. 2011. *A Taxonomy for Learning, Teaching, and Assessing: A Revision of Bloom's Taxonomy of Educational Objectives*. Longman, New York.

[74] Simpson, E. J. 1972. *The Classification of Educational Objectives*, Psychomotor Domain. Gryphon House, Washington, DC.

[75] Krathwohl, D. R., Bloom, B. S., & Masia, B. B. 1973. *Taxonomy of Educational Objectives, the Classification of Educational Goals*, Handbook II: Affective Domain. David McKay Company, Inc. Philadelphia.

[76] Malhotra, N. K., and Birks, D. F. 2008. *Marketing Research: An Applied Approach* (3rd. ed.). Trans-Atlantic Publications, Inc., Philadelphia.

[77] Dawes, J. 2008. Do data characteristics change according to the number of scale points used? An experiment using 5-point, 7-point and 10-point scales. *International Journal of Market Research*, vol. 50, no. 1, 61–77.

[78] Brown, T. A. 2006. *Confirmatory Factor Analysis for Applied Research*. The Guilford Press, New York.

[79] Dziuban, C. D. and Shirkey, E. C. 1974. When is a correlation matrix appropriate for factor analysis? Some decision rules. *Psychological Bulletin*, vol. 81, 358–361.

[80] Cattell. R. B. 1966. The scree test for the number of factors. *Multivariate Behavioral Research*, vol. 1, no. 2, 245–276.

[81] Raiche, G., Riopel, M., and Blais, J.-G. 2006. *Nongraphical Solutions for the Cattell's Scree Test*. In *Proc. of the Annual Meeting of the Psychometric Society*. Montreal, Quebec, Canada.

[82] Garson, D. 2013. *Factor Analysis*. Statistical Associates Publishing, Raleigh.

[83] Cuesta, M. 1996. Unidimensionalidade. In *Psicometría*, J. Muñiz (Ed.). Editorial Universitas, Madrid, Spain.

[84] Cohen, J. 1998. *Statistical Power Analysis for the Behavioral Sciences*. Routledge Academic. New York.

Section II

Emerging Research on Software Engineering Methods for Game Development

6 Applied Game Design Didactics

Micah M. Hrehovcsik
HKU University of the Arts Utrecht, The Netherlands

CONTENTS

6.1 INTRODUCTION

An applied game designer is a game designer who uses his/her knowledge of game principles and practices to design games with a predefined purpose that goes beyond just entertainment. The challenge of designing applied games comes from the complexity of balancing its usefulness, game-play experience, and implementation. In the applied design process, game designers occupy a pivotal role, which places them between game design knowledge, development team, co-creators, and players. From this complex web of interaction, the designer is expected to discover games that affect its audience or impact the corresponding domain, while having the responsibility of delivering an engaging and meaningful gaming experience to players.

The results of applied game design (AGD) are known as applied games, serious games, or gamification. Applied games refer to the multitude of games designed with a real-world application, for example, training, persuasion, education, exercise, health, research, and human-computing. "Applied" refers to the tactical use and usefulness of the game activity outside the domain of the game itself [1]. Serious games are games in which education is the primary goal, rather than entertainment [2]. The definition also includes COTS (Commercial off-the-shelf) entertainment games repurposed for education and training. Gamification is the application of game elements and principles to non-game contexts to engage audiences and solve problems [3].

According to research from Harteveld et al. [4] and Keetels [5], most applied games, serious games, and gamification are developed without a unified design theory. The existing theory that does support the design and development of these games is still underdeveloped [5]. The lack of unified design theory, best practices, and didactic approach to AGD has been the core reasoning for the development of the approaches presented in this chapter.

Applied games, serious games, and gamification have a reputation for sacrificing entertainment value for applicability or applicability for entertainment value. They are also known for lower production value at a time when gamers have come to expect commercial entertainment game quality to be applied to all games. It is then easy to imagine how game design students end up with the perception that applied games are less challenging and exciting to design, and ultimately less successful. In the Netherlands, 34% of game companies only develop applied games, while another 10% develop both applied and entertainment games [6]. It is very likely that Dutch game design graduates will work in the design and development of applied games. At HKU University of the Arts Utrecht, game design and development courses have been available since 2002. At the faculty of Games and Interaction, game design students will have one or more applied game projects during their four-year education as the primary didactic method of learning about AGD. These applied game projects are all situated to connect students with real-world problems. While projects provide an excellent source of practicum, it fails to equip the student with the tools of the profession. In this chapter, the theories, practicum, and tools were devised to support the education of applied game designers.

A combination of research methods, including action-based, practice-based, and literature studies, have contributed to the formulation of the knowledge in this chapter. During the development of this knowledge, it has been taught to and used by students in a wide range of didactic formats, including workshops, lectures, events, individual mentoring, and project mentoring. Publications have been written to disseminate the theories, practicum, and tools, but until now, they have remained separate knowledge nodes. The compilation of knowledge in this chapter includes the Vitruvius Perspective and Tactical Forms theoretical frameworks, the Applied Game Design Scope Model design tool, the Applied Game Jam project method, and the Epistemic Framework design investigation method.

6.2   GAME DESIGN EDUCATION

6.2.1   EDUCATING GAME DESIGNERS

A game designer must learn to become an advocate for the player experience [7] by stimulating playful activities from his or her understanding of complex systems and their underlying relationships and rules. A designer works with formal elements (i.e., systems, rules, internal relationships, objects, boundaries, and outcomes) and through a series of design decisions eventually creating a game system that determines the player's available choices, actions, and ultimately the player's experience. A game designer is not limited by technology or genre, and capable of designing all kinds of games [8].

Education to become a game designer requires a combination of practicum, theory, and instruction from an experienced game designer [9]. Practicum must allow students a chance to gain experience through game development. Through practice, a student should learn about communication, teamwork, process, and creativity. Communication and especially listening are essential to developing into a professional. Furthermore, any additional interests and knowledge (e.g., history, psychology, public speaking, management, anthropology, and creative writing) can only add positively to the anatomy of a game designer [8]. Game design practicum can range from digital to non-digital game projects. Game projects are important because they can teach students about having real-world clients [10, 11] and finishing their games [9]. Typical game design theory comes from books like Schell's The Art of Game Design: A book of lenses [11] or Fullerton's Game Design Workshop: Designing, Prototyping, & Playtesting Games.

Before a discussion about AGD theory can begin, it is essential to cover the challenges that face teaching game design. One the primary challenges is that game design theory is often not valued as a theoretical study and often discounted as "kid's stuff" or "it is just getting a few ideas" [9]. It is not uncommon to find that there are approaches to teaching game design that allude to "game design" as something you learn through 3D modeling or programming, and game design theory is about writing pitch and design documents [9]. However, learning these video game development skills are not the same as learning about game design. Games and their design are not dependent on video game genre and computer technology, but games transcend this medium [12]. Teaching students is another challenge, as they are often impatient and want to do "something practical." Introducing theory to students at the right moment (e.g., after game development) in a game curriculum makes the theory relevant and practice related. It is necessary for game designers to have some experience in game design and development to make use of the theory. They may fail to grasp the relevance of theory otherwise [9].

6.2.2 EDUCATING APPLIED GAME DESIGNERS

New challenges arise when teaching AGD theory. One challenge is getting students to change their focus from entertainment games to applied games. The majority of students begin averse to the idea of making applied games, which the myths about applied games do no doubt contribute [2]. Students often assume that "applied games are not fun," which creates the challenge to redefine their concept of "fun" a difficult task. Students often define fun purely based on their limited experiences with video games. Novice applied game designers often make a mistake by repurposing entertainment genre paradigms to an applied purpose [13], which may result in the game being entertaining but failing to be applicable or sustainable.

Another issue with AGD is that much of the knowledge of developing these kinds of games are locked away in academic papers and studies, which make it difficult for the average game design student to distill practical design theory. Furthermore, the studies and theories are often more focused on developing knowledge for a particular domain, for example, health, education, and defense. In comparison, entertainment-oriented game design literature (e.g., *The Art of Game Design: A Book of Lenses*) and journals like *Gamasutra* provide rich sources of practical knowledge about game design.

"Quality is maximized by leaving the design of game-play up to game designers and the design of learning up to teachers," [13] describes the ideal role of the game designer in the development of an applied game. A game designer should focus on what he or she is good at—designing games, which means that the game designer cannot be expected to become a subject matter expert or didactic expert. Instead, the game designer should remain the expert on creating the game-play experience.

The didactic methods in this chapter evolved to overcome these challenges and provide a practical education in AGD. Behind the methods are the learning goals to:

- Provide a means for students to critique applied games
- Provide a way for students to categorize games according to their design and not their domains or genre
- Provide students with a design tool that supports and stimulates critical thinking
- Provides students with an intense experience that allows them to practice their AGD skills
- Provide a way for students a means for researching their design activities

6.3 TOWARD A SYLLABUS

The theory, tools, and practice method presented in this chapter were developed and used in general courses and student projects at the School of Games and Interaction at the HKU University of the Arts Utrecht. They have also been an integral part of minors given to Utrecht University and international game jam conducted at POSTECH. As a part of the curriculum, AGD is introduced to students in their second year to allow game design students to specialize in game design. Projects and courses are the two dominant means of education at the School of Games and Interaction and last half of a semester or about 8 weeks. Projects are multidisciplinary teams of students coached by mentors, including students studying game design, game development, interaction design, and game art. Courses in the second year, including lectures and workshops given by a teacher, aim to allow students to specialize in their chosen discipline (e.g., game design). AGD didactics represent knowledge that has been iterated upon, developed, and used in AGD education from 2006 to 2018 in various courses and projects, and events.

The game design tool is known as the Applied Game Design (AGD) Scope Model was first introduced in 2006 to students in projects assigned to develop an applied or entertainment game. In 2012 the design tool was introduced into regular game design courses in the form of a workshop which allowed students to apply the scope model in a pressure cooker situation. The design frameworks, the Vitruvius Approach and

Tactical Forms, were introduced into game design courses as lectures in 2012. These frameworks were used to introduce applied games and ways to think about them. The Applied Game Jam format, which includes the previously mentioned design tool and frameworks, was developed as a means to provide a short, intense AGD combined course and project. The format was first used to stimulate international exchange with POSTECH and other Korean universities. Following its success, the game jam was recreated in the Netherlands at the HKU University of the Arts Utrecht and repeated yearly both in the Netherlands, Korean and China. The Epistemic Cards investigation method became a part of game design courses in the form of a lecture in 2013. Later in 2016, the investigation method was used in design research seminars, where students were asked to use the online tool to investigate design decisions that took place in their applied game projects.

In 2016 the AGD as a separate project, course, and minor was established for half a semester. The course was given to HKU University of the Arts Utrecht and University Utrecht students. The entire course kicked-off with the Applied Game Jam which was the initial starting point for the multidisplinary project teams. During the game jam the frameworks and design tool had their initial introduction. Supporting the project was the course of lectures and workshops where students practiced to first argue the benefits of applied games and then identify domains that applied games could be useful. During the course students would be introduced to the theoretical frameworks and applied the game design tool. Finally, students had the task to take their concepts and develop them as paper-based prototypes. Students were eventually graded on their ability to connect their paper-based designs to their original goals.

The School of Games and Interaction established a stand-alone AGD course and project in 2016, which solely focused on AGD and development. Utrecht University assumed the role of the commissioner by supporting students with the design challenge and subject matter expertise. The course and project kicked-off with the Applied Game Jam format, which is the initial starting point to assemble the multidisciplinary teams. The teams formed during the game jam remained together for the duration of the project. Introducing the frameworks and design tool to students for the first time happens at the start of the game jam to support all the students (i.e., game developers, game artists, and interaction designers) with having a better understanding of applied games. Supporting the project is the AGD course where game design students deepen their understanding of AGD. The course syllabus begins with students arguing the benefits of applied games and then identifies domains that applied games could be useful. Students also take more time to deepen their understanding of the theoretical frameworks and application of the game design tool as they ideate game concepts and develop them into paper-based games. The ability of the students to connect the paper-based designs to the original design goals is the basis for evaluating their performance. The same criteria are used to evaluate the AGD aspects of the project.

It is possible to find other possible ways to incorporate the didactic elements into a game design syllabus. Any syllabus on AGD should also include the core game design activities as assignments (e.g., paper-based prototyping, brainstorming, playtesting, and documentation). The didactic elements unique here are only used to accentuate the course to fill missing aspects of AGD but do not in themselves make up the entire syllabus.

6.4 THE VITRUVIUS PERSPECTIVE

The approach to educating an applied game designer starts with the Vitruvius per-spective, which is a general theory inspired by Vitruvius's three guiding principles toward architecture. Marcus Vitruvius Pollio was an ancient Roman author, architect, and engineer and is known for his multivolume work entitled "De Architectura." Vitruvius was responsible for establishing the core principles for all ancient Roman architecture through the triadic principles of utilitas, firmitas, and venustas. The prin-ciples are repurposed for AGD, to encourage design awareness and offer a perspec-tive on balancing an applied game's utilitas (purpose), firmitas (sustainability), and venustas (game-play experience). Utilitas or purpose is the principle that a game should function for that purpose, for example, behavior change or learning. Firmitas or sustainability is the principle of embedding the game correctly in the context, where it is obtainable or available to users and players, has a service or syllabus designed around it, and aims to create a perceivable impact in the chosen domain. Venustas or game-play experience is the principle of providing a game with produc-tion value so that it becomes meaningful and a holistic experience (e.g., graphics, sound, game-play, and story) for the player (Figure 6.1).

The Vitruvius triad (utilitas, firmitas, and venustas) is a framework created to ana-lyze applied games. The analysis aims to determine the potential impact of an applied game by examining how well it balances the three principles. Because the analysis critiques the potential for impact, two applied games from different domains, game-play and purpose, become comparable. For example, two seemingly different games like Foldit and America's Army, which both have notoriety in their respective domains, can now be compared using the framework.

Foldit is an online puzzle video game developed by the University of Washington's Center for Game Science in collaboration with the UW Department of Biochemistry as part of an experimental research project. America's Army is a video game devel-oped by the United States Army and released as a global public relations initiative to help with recruitment. What do these two games have in common? Moreover, what

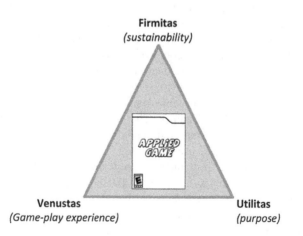

FIGURE 6.1   The Vitruvius triad for applied game design.

makes them "good" applied games? Using Vitruvius' principles, it is possible to identify the similarities. Do the games successfully fulfill their purpose? Are the games accessible to the target audience and have an active player-base? Do the games offer players a meaningful game-play experience? When asking these kinds of questions, it becomes possible to perform a critical review of the games' utilitas, firmitas, and venustas.

Using entertainment game, standards (e.g., quality of game-play, story, graphics, and sound) to judge these games would disregard the purpose of the game. While separating the games by domain would not make a comparison between these two applied games. Using validation of the content and transfer to judge the games would disregard the game-play experience and intrinsic motivation, the game provides the player.

Additionally, applied game designers can also use the three principles as a communication tool with subject matter experts (e.g., teachers) which are essential for providing input during development. Communication with subject matter experts is a known AGD challenge [1]. The Vitruvius principles facilitate communication between game designers and subject matter experts by identifying how elements combine to arrive at a balanced applied game while facilitating a dialogue about avoiding too much focus on a single principle.

6.5   CLASSIFICATIONS FOR APPLIED GAMES

The second part of educating applied game designers aims to help them identify and categorize applied games. In this approach toward categorization of applied games, we categorize the game by tactical form. "Tactical form" is used to describe the way the game is designed and deployed in a specific context. "Tactical" refers to the design considerations for deploying a game in a specific context. The "form" refers to a pattern of deployment. As frameworks, the tactical forms are used to educate game design students about identifying applied game deployment patterns and their structures. The goal is to have students rely less on domain-specific categorization.

The tactical form categories are loosely derived from Duke's [14] "game objectives" or purpose of an applied game. While current approaches categorize how a game fits a domain, Duke identified four objectives that relate to the general use of an applied game as:

1. Dialogue, the game stimulates communication about complex topics
2. Project, the game aims to inform, educate, or train
3. Extract, the game takes opinions or information from a player
4. Motivate, the game is used to motivate players, and coupled with the before-mentioned objectives

The tactical forms categorization identifies four patterns used by games for deployment of a specific context (see Figure 6.2), some of which overlap with Duke's game objectives. The anatomy of a tactical form consists of the game, the commissioner, the player, and the transfer direction. An assumption in this model is that the commissioner sets the primary purpose of the game (e.g., teaching math) and direction of

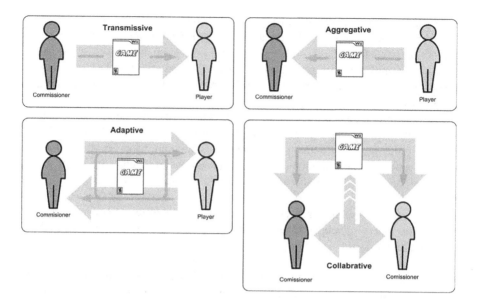

FIGURE 6.2   Four tactical forms of applied games.

arrows shows the flow of the transfer. Each tactical form includes two critical roles: the game's commissioner, who represents an organization or person who determines the primary purpose of the applied game, and the game's player(s), who represent the target audience that will "play" the game. Finally, the model includes the game, which is represented at the center of the model between commissioner and player to represent its role as facilitator. The game as a facilitator facilitates the transfer of information, instruction, rhetoric, cooperation, or creativity. Finally, modeling a tactical form creates a deployment map when all elements are brought together.

The first tactical form (see Figure 6.2 top-left) is called Transmissive. Commissioners use the game to attract and then engage players to "transmit" skills, knowledge, rhetoric, or therapy. These are games typically called serious games (e.g., America's Army, Re-Mission, abcdeSIM, Darfur is Dying, and McDonald's Video Game), and used for many purposes in many different domains.

The second tactical form (see Figure 6.2 top-right) is called Aggregative (or gathering). Commissioners use the game to attract and engage players to collect knowledge, information, user-generated content, or human-computing. These games have been labeled "games with a purpose" (e.g., Foldit, Phylo, ESP game, and Google Image Labeler) and used in the domains of science and accomplishing tasks computers cannot (a.k.a. human-computing).

The third tactical form (see Figure 6.2 bottom-left) is called Adaptive. Commissioners use this tactical form to interact with players through the game, which allows them to adapt the game to facilitate the transfer of information and collection of data to and from the player. An additional aspect of this tactical form requires a user or another kind of player (not the game's target audience) that uses the game as a tool. The new role, defined as user or user-player, manages or plays along with the intended target audience to accomplish the purpose of the game. No popular label has been coined for this kind of game using this kind of tactical form. An example of a game that employs this tactical form would be Moodbot, which is an online multiplayer game for psychiatric healthcare developed by HKU University of the Arts Utrecht, the mental healthcare organization Altrecht and back-end developer Ippo. Moodbot provides patients and healthcare workers in-game communication by allowing patients to share their mental state. Healthcare workers are then able to respond or set the course of action personalized for that patient.

The fourth tactical form (see Figure 6.2 bottom-right) is called Collaborative because the aim is to create a dialogue between participants through the design and development of a game. Examples of these games are difficult to find since their usefulness is their creation. However, some simulations create a starting point for a "game" to facilitate policy making (e.g., Climate game). Duke [14] considered this form the "prime purpose" of applied games and meant to increase dialogue about complex problems and future-oriented systems.

6.6 APPLIED GAME DESIGN SCOPE MODEL

The third part of educating an applied game designer aims to equip the student with a practical conceptual tool. The AGD (Applied Game Design) Scope Model is introduced to students as a best practice. The Scope Model is not a means to critique applied games or categorize them. It is a conceptual tool which prescribes a method for use by a game designer to "design" applied games.

The scope model is created at the beginning of a project when the game designer undergoes a process to analyze the design challenges. The results of this analysis determine the design space. The game designer then connects design decisions to this space. The analysis referred to as 2CaT (C^1ontent, C^2ontext, and Transfer) (see Figure 6.3), aims to organize the design challenges as parameters related to the content, context, or transfer. To be able to identify these three factors, the following questions need an answer: who, what, where, when, why, and how. Once these questions have been answered, the game designer has a quick-scan for the design of the applied game in question.

In the 2CaT analysis, content corresponds with the expertise of a subject matter expert, usually representing the commissioner's side. The content aspect of the analysis questions "what" the purpose of the game is. Simplified for the quick-scan, this becomes a question formulated with—what. From which a series of questions can be formulated to determine the parameters of the purpose of the game: What is the purpose of the game? What does the game need to achieve? What are the takeaways for the player? What should the game not do? Depending on how this is defined, the content may be persuasive, educational, therapeutic, or motivational, and will determine the primary aim of the game design [5, 15, 16].

The context corresponds to the player (or target audience), who determines if the game will achieve its purpose. In the 2CaT analysis, context is defined by "who" will play the game or use the game as a tool, "where" the game is played, and "when" the game is played in time. Simplified for the quick-scan, this becomes questions formulated with—who, where, and when. From which a series of questions like the

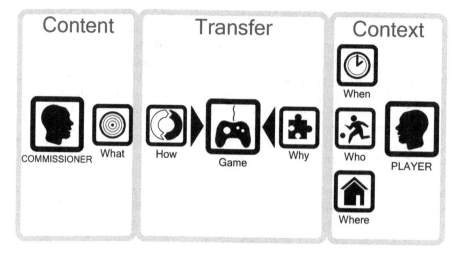

FIGURE 6.3   The 2CaT analysis.

following can be formulated to determine the parameters of the target audience: Who is the end player(s) or user(s)? What is known about their attitudes, abilities, (dis) likes, etc.? The location or environment: Where will the audience encounter the game? Is the location a logical place for a game to be played? Does the location fit with their habits? Do they have access to the game from their location? Moreover, the time: When do the players have time to play? How much time is expected from the player to dedicate to the game? How much time does the player need to play to achieve the goals of the applied game? In game design, the context pertains to the level of complexity, length of game sessions, replayability [17], and strategies that consider how the game can fit the target audience's environment [5].

The transfer corresponds to both the commissioner and player. The commissioner helps to identify the method or theory (e.g., psychology, sociology, didactic methods, political science, etc.) that structures the content for the player, while the player determines if the game-play experience is meaningful. In the 2CaT analysis, the transfer is defined by "how" the structure of the game accomplishes the purpose (content) of the game, and "why" the game will motivate the player or offer a meaningful experience. Simplified for the quick-scan, this becomes questions formulated with—how and why. From this, a series of questions like the following can be formulated to determine parameters of the transfer method: How is the goal of the project accomplished without a game and what are essential principles of this process that need incorporation into the game? Moreover, the possible game verbs: Why is the game exciting to play? What verbs or roles can (or cannot) relate to the method? What verbs are best suited to achieve the goal of the applied game? In game design, this pertains to how games reflect reality [16, 18], structure good learning [19] or offer meaningful game-play actions and roles [20].

The primary purpose of the AGD scope model is to use the 2CaT analysis to create a quick-scan of the design space. A quick-scan is generally a list or visualization (e.g., poster or diagram) of parameters that define the design space. It is not meant to be an in-depth analysis with much descriptive text. The answers to the 2CaT questions define the quick-scan, which should be no more than phrases or keywords with some allowance for some interpretation.

One aspect of AGD that the AGD Scope Model finds a crucial role in is during the concept phase when an applied game designer is ideating and developing high-level game concepts. During the process for selecting a final concept, the scope model is used to check the proposal and how well it fulfills the design space and its parameters.

Students are introduced to the AGD scope model, starting with a lecture, which explains the underlying theory of the design tool. A worksheet (see Figure 6.4) is given to students to support them during their process. The following describes the process that the worksheet supports:

1. Create a scope model by answering the 2CaT questions (see Figure 6.3)
2. If the analysis is missing answers to its questions, students use this as a signal to conduct design research to find an answer
3. Present the result of the 2CaT answers as design parameters to the commissioner for feedback and confirmation
4. Develop game concepts (e.g., brainstorming)
5. Use the design parameters from the scope model to decide if the game is suitable
6. Present the concept(s) to the commissioner using the scope model to argue their merits
7. If needed, repeat step 4 through 6 to until a suitable game concept is selected

In step 5 the students may want to include a well-known entertainment game that seems highly unlikely as being an acceptable concept (e.g., Pacman) as a control, which will help to validate the process.

Additional observations of this process include:

- The need to encourage game designers to explore alternative game solutions, while avoiding the temptation to mirror reality (i.e., simulations) immediately
- Having game design students look for game-play experience instead of "fun" based on entertainment game paradigms (e.g., genre, game mechanics, length of play, etc.)
- Helping game designers avoid information overload brought on by too much research
- Avoid content-driven design by setting design parameters and not features
- Regulate communication with the commissioner using design parameters

6.7 EPISTEMIC CARDS

The Epistemic Cards are a tool for game design students to communicate and report design decisions. The cards provide structure to design dissemination or understand the context of design decisions. Students are introduced to the tool so they can investigate design and eventually gather design knowledge. Using the tool requires the designer to think about thinking and the decision-making process. From this guided

ScoMo (Scope Model) Method

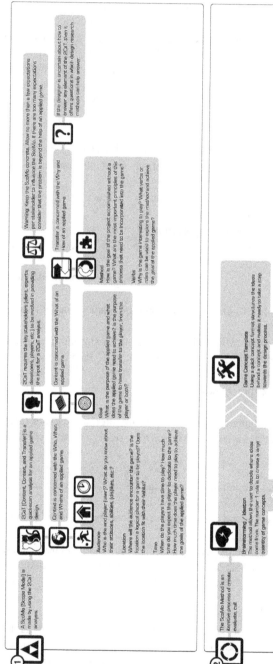

FIGURE 6.4   The AGD Scope Model worksheet.

reflection with the tool, the student is asked to disseminate the internalized design decision making hidden in their head. The goal of this form of design investigation is to make the designer's tacit knowledge "communicable, verifiable and discussable" [21].

Identifying critical design decisions is a crucial activity for students. A critical design decision pertains to the reasoning for a final decision on a game system, specification, or feature. The decision occurs after many ideas and possible choices have contended with each other. Stakeholder (e.g., clients, developers, experts, etc.) influence directly or indirectly is also considered in order to understand critical design decision making.

An epistemic framework is the skills, identities, interests, understanding, and knowledge that professionals in general use to think in innovative ways [20]. The Epistemic Cards consist of six main categories that define an epistemic framework. In theory, no two applied game designers would share the exact epistemic frame, since every designer eventually develops their own experiences, theories, and beliefs. However, some aspects of the epistemic frame are going to be similar for all applied game designers, for example, the composition of a development team, a target audience (players), and working with co-designers. The six categories that make up the epistemic framework for this approach are the following:

2CaT (Context, Content, and Transfer) Analysis: Is concerned with an analysis of the purpose, goals, and validation of the intended design. The analysis consists of gathering information about the content, context, and transfer for design parameters to be defined.

Stakeholders: Are concerned with the multidisciplinary environment that an applied game designer operates, which includes contact with co-designers and the development team.

Design: Is concerned with a theoretical model that defines game design, which is used to frame thinking about game mechanics, play mechanics, or game-play experience.

Artifact: Is concerned with the critical analysis of a game as an artifact, which takes into consideration the game-play, visual and thematic representation, sociocultural impact, usability, and technology of a game.

Process: Is concerned with the process of designing the game. Determining the progress made in design is mapped to a linear and with iterative cycles, linked to specific design tools.

Project: Is concerned with the way the design affects and is affected by business and development issues. From a designer's perspective, this accounts for factors not directly controlled or influenced by design, such as time and confidence (Figure 6.5).

Using the Epistemic Cards to investigate a critical design decision is called creating a design snapshot, which follows a process to structure how decisions are examined and communicated. The process consists of the student formulating questions that examine the origin of the current state of affairs, the action taken that changed

FIGURE 6.5 An example of the cards being arranged to report the design decision.

the design state, and the results from the changes. For example, why was a new feature added to the game? Why was the game delivered late? Why was the game not successfully received by the client or target audience? It is up to the designer to formulate the correct question to set the context of the snapshot.

Using the Epistemic Cards requires the designer to select relevant cards from the six categories. For example, the designer may begin by selecting a card from the process category to provide context for the snapshot. While adding the player card provides the designer with a topic or source of an issue, indicating relationships by grouping cards together provide the ability to speak of several elements that are integrated and cannot be separated or perhaps describe a more complex topic. Drawing lines to create connection and describe flow between topics is also a part of creating a snapshot. As the designer undergoes this process, they will question who influenced the design and where do the design problem(s) originate? The designer is then able to discover how much influence stakeholders have in critical design decisions, or understand how concepts in the design have failed to be communicated or defined correctly.

Introduce the cards in a lecture and then ask students to present in class a problem or exciting moment they experienced during a game development project. Then as an assignment, students can practice using the cards on their own. They can make their investigation by using the Epistemic Cards online tool[1] and then present the results in class. Ask students why they included specific cards and excluded others. Also, ask how they could solve or repeat the circumstances.

6.8 THE APPLIED GAME JAM FORMAT

The learning goal of the final educational method is to connect theory and methods to the complexity of practice. The Applied Game Jam Format provides the opportunity to introduce or reintroduce Vitruvius, Tactical Forms, AGD Scope Model, and the Epistemic Cards to students during an event that will test their ability to apply their knowledge. The format is designed to simulate personal experiences and perspectives from designing applied games professionally and participating in game jams. From a professional experience, the game jam aims to provide a structure of best practices. From the jammer's perspective, the game jam allows students to experience what makes a game jam not only meaningful, challenging, and fun, but also frustrating.

From the lecturer's perspective, the format aims to provide game design and development students with a meaningful learning experience where students learn about developing applied games. As an educational format, the Applied Game Jam aims to provide an intensive practice-based learning experience concerning AGD theories, co-design, best practices, and studio operations related to development. The format values putting students of AGD and development under time and peer pressure, while having them work autonomously as multidisciplinary teams.

The Applied Game Jam format consists of activities separated into four phases (see Figure 6.6.):

1. Introduction
2. Teams
3. Jam
4. Results

The challenge for students during a game jam is to develop a playable prototype under time pressure while considering the needs of the target audience (a.k.a. the players) and a client in the design of the game. At the end of the game jam, judges evaluate the team's process by challenges completed, the applied aspect of their game, and the entertainment value of their game. The game jam event runs for more than 48 hours over 3 to 4 days, where students work at a single venue. Within the space of the game jam, students make use of their game development skills (e.g., programming, game designing, visual design, audio design, project management, and even marketing) practice articulating needs of clients, ideate game concepts, and test game design assumptions.

During the Introduction Phase, students are introduced to AGD theory so that they can create mental frameworks about what makes an applied game and why applied games are different from entertainment games. The theory emphasizes how good game design equals good games, and using approaches such as the Vitruvius Perspective and Tactical Forms offers designers a way to consider the balance of game-play experience, utility, and sustainability in their games.

In the Teams Phase, students assemble their teams through a team building intervention that let students learn how to network, promote themselves, and form teams through a draft system. The intervention aims to help students understand the need to form networks and also take ownership of the roles and personalities of their teams.

Gamification drives the learning goals by valuing process and encouraging best practices. While students focus on the development of their game during the Jam Phase, "challenges" worth points are given to the teams. When completed, teams receive points which are then displayed in real-time for the duration of the game jam

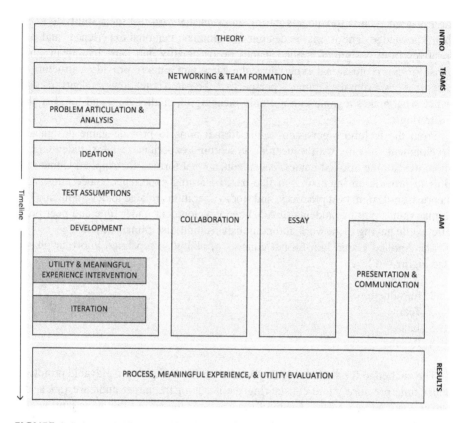

FIGURE 6.6 A schematic of the participant's activities during the four phases of the game jam.

via an online scoreboard. A lecturer designs the challenges to stimulate specific competencies and act as educational interventions. Typical challenges aim to stimulate teambuilding, design research, technology research/choices, cultural/fun activities, best practices, promotion, feedback moments, and cultural exchange. For example, participants are rewarded points for using the Applied Game Design Scope Model which helps to articulate the design space by analyzing the context, content, and transfer related to the theme and problem/question. Challenges are always optional and never mandatory. Students completing the challenges will discover that challenges are not obstacles but guides through the design and development process. Challenges aim to continuously test students' abilities to organize themselves, communicate internally and externally, cooperate as a team, use their skills wisely, and prioritize tasks.

Finally, during the Results Phase students are judged on production value, application, and process. Production value judges a game on fun and completeness factors. Application judges a game's possible impact on the domain and problem presented by the theme. Process judges the number of points collected from completing challenges during the game jam.

Current outcomes [22] have suggested that the applied game jam format is an effective way of integrating skills/competencies needed for future game designers. Additionally, it is a valid format that bridges the design methods used in the games industry and an educational setting.

6.9 CONCLUSIONS

The approaches introduced in this chapter are all directly related to educating game designers about AGD, which includes establishing a perspective, an ability to categorize, a tool that helps guides design, a reflective tool for design decisions, and a format for providing an applied game development experience.

Central to the theme of this approach is the need to minimize the complexities of AGD and maximize the creative freedom of the game designer. The goal is to create enthusiasm among students about the possibilities and challenges offered by AGD, which could result in future applied games having better game-play experiences and impact.

Currently, there is little discourse concerning AGD education. The approach presented in this paper is meant to encourage educators and researchers to share their approaches to AGD education. The quality of future applied games will depend on game designers supported by philosophies, theories, and tools. The approach to building AGD knowledge should be iterative, and change as new insights are gained. Game designers should feel free to choose their approach to designing applied games and remember that the kind of knowledge presented here can only function to support them, but could never claim to offer an infallible secret recipe. Ultimately, the intention is to open discussion about the kinds of knowledge and skills an applied game designer should have.

ACKNOWLEDGMENTS

This chapter is a compilation of previously published papers and a dissertation.

Micah Hrehovcsik and Lies Van Roessel. 2013. Using Vitruvius as a Framework for Applied Game Design. *Games for Health*, 131–152. doi: 10.1007/978-3-658-02897-8_10

Micah Hrehovcsik, Joeri Taelman, Joep Janssen, and Niels Keetels. 2014. Tactical Forms: Classification of Applied Games for Game Design. *Games for Health 2014*, 67–78. doi: 10.1007/978-3-658-07141-7_10

Micah Hrehovcsik. 2014. Teaching "Applied" Game Design: Theory and Tools. *International Journal of Multimedia and Ubiquitous Engineering*.

Micah M. Hrehovcsik. 2014. Applied Game Design: Content, Context, and Transfer. In *Proceedings of the Serious Games Conference 2014: Bridging Communities, Harnessing Technologies and Enriching Lives*. Seoul: Research Publishing.

Micah Hrehovcsik, Harald Warmelink, and Marilla Valente. 2016. The Game Jam as a Format for Formal Applied Game Design and Development Education. *Lecture Notes in Computer Science Games and Learning Alliance*, 257–267. doi: 10.1007/978-3-319-50182-6_23

Micah Hrehovcsik. 2018. *An analysis of design thinking in applied game design.* dissertation.

NOTE

1 http://gamearchitect.eu/epistemic/

REFERENCES

[1] Lies van Roessel and Jeroen van Mastrigt-Ide. 2011. *Proceedings of DiGRA 2011 Conference: Think Design Play*. Netherlands

[2] David Michael and Sande Chen. 2006. *Serious games: games that educate, train and inform*, Boston, MA: Thomson Course Technology.

[3] Gabe Zichermann and Christopher Cunningham. 2011. *Gamification by design: implementing game mechanics in web and mobile apps, O'Reilly*.

[4] Casper Harteveld, Rui Guimarães, Igor S. Mayer, and Rafael Bidarra. 2010. Balancing Play, Meaning and Reality: The Design Philosophy of Levee Patroller. *Simulation & Gaming* 41, 3 (2010), 316–340.

[5] Niels Keetels. 2012. Designing Games for Children's Rehabilitation. Thesis. Bournemouth: Bournemouth University.

[6] Olaf Koops et al. 2016. *Games Monitor 2015*, Dutch Game: Garden.

[7] Tracy Fullerton, Christopher Swain, and Steven Hoffman. 2014. *Game Design Workshop: Designing, Prototyping, and Playtesting Games*, Boca Raton, FL: CRC Press.

[8] Ernest Adams and Andrew Rollings. 2017. *Fundamentals of Futures and Options Markets*, Boston: Pearson.

[9] Padraig Nash and David Williamson Shaffer. 2012. Epistemic trajectories: Mentoring in a game design practicum. *Instructional Science* 41, 4 (2012), 745–771.

[10] Lewis Pulsipher. 2011. *Teaching Game Design: The Problems*. Retrieved June 27, 2019 from https://www.gamasutra.com/blogs/LewisPulsipher/20111201/90722/Teaching_Game_Design_The_Problems.php

[11] Christopher Totten. 2013. *DiGRA Conference*. In *DiGRA| Digital Games Research Association*. http://www.digra.org/digital-library/publications/teaching-serious-game-app-design-through-client-based-projects/

[12] Jesper Juul. 2011. *Half-Real: Video Games Between Real rules and Fictional Worlds*. Cambridge, MA: MIT Press.

[13] Richard D. Van Eck. 2006. *Digital Game-Based Learning: It's Not Just the Digital Natives Who Are Restless*. Retrieved June 27, 2019 from https://er.educause.edu/articles/2006/1/digital-gamebased-learning-its-not-just-the-digital-natives-who-are-restless

[14] Richard Duke. 1974. *Gaming: The Future's Language*, New York, NY: SAGE Publications.

[15] Brian M. Winn. 2009. *The Design, Play, and Experience Framework. Handbook of Research on Effective Electronic Gaming in Education* (2009), 1010–1024. doi: 10.4018/978-1-59904-808-6.ch058

[16] Erik D. van der Spek. 2011. Experiments in Serious Game Design: A Cognitive Approach. dissertation, Netherlands.

[17] Katrin Becker. 2008. *Video Game Pedagogy: Good Games = Good Pedagogy*. Retrieved June 27, 2019 from http://hdl.handle.net/1880/46741

[18] Casper Harteveld. 2011. *Triadic Game Design: Balancing Reality, Meaning and Play*, London: Springer.

[19] James Paul Gee. 2004. *What Video Games Have to Teach Us About Learning and Literacy*, New York: Palgrave Macmillan.

[20] David Williamson Shaffer. 2006. *How Computer Games Help Children Learn*, New York, NY: Palgrave Macmillan.

[21] Gänshirt Christian. 2007. *Tools for Ideas: An Introduction to Architectural Design*, Basel: Birkhäuser.

[22] Micah Hrehovcsik, Harald Warmelink, and Marilla Valente. 2016. The Game Jam as a Format for Formal Applied Game Design and Development Education. *Lecture Notes in Computer Science Games and Learning Alliance* (2016), 257–267. doi: 10.1007/978-3-319-50182-6_23

7 Learning with the Body
A Design Framework for Embodied Learning Games and Simulations

Edward F. Melcer and Katherine Isbister

University of California, Santa Cruz, USA

CONTENTS

7.1   INTRODUCTION

There are a number of reasons why physical interaction and embodiment—an emergent property from the interactions between brain, body, and the physical/social environment [57]—are important factors to consider in the design of educational technologies and games. From a technical perspective, the low cost, quantity, and ubiquity of sensors in recent years have made them easily accessible to incorporate into the construction of both commercial and custom hardware. For instance, modern smartphones commonly have more than half a dozen sensors built-in that allow for sensing user actions and the surrounding environment—i.e., proximity sensors for detecting distance, accelerometers and gyroscopes for detecting movement and rotation, GPS for detecting location, barometers for detecting atmospheric pressure, multiple cameras, and so forth. Additionally, the large-scale commercial success of hardware that utilizes physical sensing, such as the Wii [78], and software that employs physical interactions on such hardware, for example, Pokémon Go [64], demonstrates that there is a growing market and public interest for such products. Even commercial educational game systems utilizing augmented reality to incorporate physical interactivity, such as Osmo, have found notable success in recent years [68]. From the academic perspective, there is also a large body of work in the Human–Computer Interaction (HCI), games, and learning science disciplines demonstrating the potential benefits of incorporating physical interactions into learning, such as improved spatial recall and mental manipulation [24, 31], more intuitive interfaces and mappings [15, 84, 95, 129, 145], increased engagement [25, 37, 150], and greater positive feelings toward learning content and science in general [18, 80, 93, 139].

However, while there are a number of educational games and simulations that have incorporated physical interaction, very little is understood about what aspects of physicality actually result in beneficial learning outcomes from these designs. There is effectively a black box of design decisions that researchers and developers often employ when creating their educational systems. For instance, the physical interactions designed into a game teaching basic physics concepts could range from having players run around a room [99], slide down a large inflatable slide [87], play with tangible objects [42], move fingers on a tablet [34], or even swing limbs to enact learning concepts [7].

Looking deeper into the theoretical concepts underlying this black box reveals a commonly used set of terms: *embodiment, embodied cognition*, and *embodied interaction* to name a few. Unfortunately, embodiment and related terms are remarkably broad and fuzzy constructs—with definitions and operationalization that differs drastically depending upon the academic domain in which they are utilized [92, 94]. This large breadth of interpretation for "embodiment" is a likely cause of the seemingly ambiguous design choices underlying many educational games and simulations employing physical interactions. Furthermore, it becomes problematic when trying to understand where and how embodiment occurs in these systems, and which design elements help to facilitate embodied learning. Therefore, for designers seeking to utilize embodiment, the differences in approach to physicality, collaboration, and interaction pose a significant hurdle.

However, we posit that this fuzziness actually presents a new space of design possibility. One where, through careful exploration and synthesis of embodiment across its many domains, we can better understand the various ways physicality and embodiment can be employed in order to enhance different learning outcomes within educational technology. One particularly useful approach that can bridge conceptual differences between existing systems and domains is the creation of a design framework [38, 119]. In this chapter, we present the motivation, construction, and application of our taxonomical design framework for embodied learning games and simulations.

7.2   THE EMBODIMENT PROBLEM

As mentioned earlier, definitions and operationalization of embodiment differ drastically depending upon the academic perspectives that are utilized during the design process—resulting in a large breadth of designs employing embodiment. Notably, the extensive range of interpretations for embodiment has been well documented across multiple disciplines, for example, [142, 154], and is a likely cause for the broad and seemingly ambiguous black box of design choices underlying many educational systems employing embodiment. In order to illustrate this point, the following subsections give a brief introduction to embodiment from several disciplinary perspectives, and point to examples of various educational systems that utilized one or more of these perspectives in their design.

7.2.1   A HUMAN–COMPUTER INTERACTION PERSPECTIVE OF EMBODIMENT

In general, HCI takes a phenomenological approach to embodiment [50, 57, 89], expanding upon ideas from phenomenology that were first introduced into HCI through the work of Suchman [134] and Winograd et al. [143]. In a general sense, embodiment is centered around the notion that human reasoning and behavior is connected to, or influenced by our bodies and their physical/social experience and interaction with the world around us [114]. Some of the recent seminal work on embodiment within HCI that stems from phenomenology is by Dourish [35], where he coined the term embodied interaction to capture a number of research trends and ideas in HCI around tangible, social, and ubiquitous computing. The tangibles' community within HCI has since built upon this interpretation of embodied interaction, additionally focusing on the use of space and movement [55]. In this way, embodied interaction refers to the creation, manipulation, and sharing of meaning through engaged interaction with artifacts [110, 116], and includes material objects and environments in the process of meaning making and action formation [133]. A number of systems have employed embodied interaction utilizing physical objects and the surrounding space within HCI, including Espaistory [86], MirrorFugue [147, 148], TASC [28], Archimedes [87], Mapping Place [29], Buildasound [117], and CoCensus [118]. Notably, these games and simulations that employ embodied interaction tend to place the player in a physical space where they can physically manipulate interactive tangible tabletops, blocks, and objects.

7.2.2 A Cognitive Linguistics Perspective of Embodiment

The cognitive linguistics perspective addresses embodiment through the notion of a conceptual/embodied metaphor [75, 122]. Both in language and cognition, metaphors help us to understand or experience one concept (target domain) in terms of another (source domain) [19]. When the source domain of a metaphor involves schemata that have arisen from experience relating to the body's movements, orientation in space, or its interaction with objects [75], it becomes a conceptual or embodied metaphor [62]. Two notable types of embodied metaphors are Ontological—where an abstract concept is represented as something concrete, such as an object, substance, container, or person—and Orientational—where concepts are spatially related to each other. Some systems that have employed embodied metaphors in the design of their objects and interactions include Sound Maker [12, 13], Springboard [10, 11, 84], and MoSo Tangibles [19, 20]. These games and simulations commonly have players utilize objects and their bodies to more intuitively enact the embodied metaphor.

7.2.3 A Cognitive Science Perspective of Embodiment

The cognitive science perspective addresses embodiment through the notion of embodied cognition, focusing on how sensorimotor activity can influence human learning, knowing, and reasoning [4]. However, embodied cognition is also a divided term for education, where Wilson [142] identified six distinct views including (1) cognition is situated; (2) cognition is time-pressured; (3) we off-load cognitive work onto the environment; (4) the environment is part of the cognitive system; (5) cognition is for action; and (6) off-line cognition is body-based.

Notably, when it comes to learning, embodied cognition primarily considers how human cognition is fundamentally grounded in sensory–motor processes and in our body's internal states [60]. In this way, the body is typically the main focus of embodied cognition (rather than the environment or objects) and serves as the central framework for our understanding of and interactions with the world [128]. As a result, much of the literature applying embodied cognition has a primary focus on the amount, type, and proper integration of bodily engagement, for example, [47, 63, 122, 131, 141]. This body-centric perspective of embodied cognition has also carried over into the design of educational technology, where games and simulations tend to focus on the utilization of sensors to either (1) map full-body interaction and congruency to learning content through the use of gestures or (2) track whole-body enactment of learning material. Some notable systems that have employed embodied cognition include the Mathematical Imagery Trainer [3, 56], SpatialEase [37], Math Propulsion [96], Fingu [21], MEteor [79–81], and Embodied Poetry [52]. However, it is also important to note that recent work in cognitive science has begun to develop theories of embodied cognition that utilize broader cognitive representations, and move toward more embedded, extended, and enactive perspectives (e.g., [12, 58, 89, 140]).

7.2.4 An Artificial Intelligence and Robotics Perspective of Embodiment

The robotics and artificial intelligence (AI) perspective of embodiment is another distinct approach within HCI and human–robot interaction (HRI) that views embodiment as having a physical body where software, sensors, etc., are housed, and ultimately enables social/physical interactions [137]. Ziemke [154] has examined different approaches to embodiment within the AI and cognitive science literature, identifying six different uses of embodiment across research domains in order to identify what kind of body is required for embodied cognition and AI. The six notions identified are: (1) structural coupling between agent (AI/Robot) and environment; (2) historical embodiment where embodiment is the reflection or result of a history of agent–environment interaction, and in many cases coadaptation; (3) physical embodiment where systems/software has a physical instantiation; (4) organismoid embodiment where cognition might be limited to physical bodies that have a similar form and sensorimotor capacities to living bodies; (5) organismic embodiment where cognition is limited only to living bodies; and (6) social embodiment where states of the body—such as postures, arm movements, and facial expressions—arise during social interaction and play central roles in social information processing [22]. Notably, there has been a wide range of research utilizing and exploring the implications of embodiment within HRI in recent years, for example, [45, 72, 124, 126, 138].

7.3 EMBODIMENT IN A DESIGN FRAMEWORK FOR GAMES AND SIMULATIONS

As discussed above, embodiment and related terms such as embodied cognition and embodied interaction have many different interpretations and applications across a wide range of academic domains. For instance, HCI tends to view embodiment from a phenomenological perspective where embodiment is a physical and social phenomena that unfolds in real time and space as a part of the world in which we are situated [35]. However, learning and cognitive science views tend to be more oriented purely on the body and bodily engagement as a central focus for embodiment [63, 128, 131]. In order to capture a large corpus of embodied designs in our design framework, we take a broad, encompassing perspective of embodiment: centering it around the notion that human reasoning and behavior is connected to, or influenced by our bodies and their physical/social experience and interaction with the world [114]. This can be seen as an iterative relationship, where reasoning and behavior can shape interaction as well as the other way round, yet also complex because of the context, time, space, emotion, etc., in which interaction is situated. In this way, cognition becomes less brain-based and instead more embodied, embedded, extended, and enactive [12, 30, 58, 89, 140].

7.4   BACKGROUND AND RELATED WORK

Our goal in providing a design framework for embodied learning games and simulations is to bridge conceptual gaps and resulting design choices made from the differing uses of embodiment in various domains. In this section we present an overview of the background and related work on design frameworks, their applications, and existing embodied learning taxonomies/frameworks.

7.4.1   DESIGN FRAMEWORKS

A design framework is an important HCI tool that provides a common language for designers and researchers to discuss design knowledge, generate prototypes, formulate research questions, and conceptualize empirical studies [16]. In this way, design frameworks can help designers conceptualize nuances of particular technologies and formalize the creative process [38]. In interface design, design frameworks have been used to provide terminology to categorize ideas [111], as well as organize complex concepts into logical hierarchies [107]. Notably, there are different kinds of design frameworks. Taxonomical design frameworks, such as the one presented in this chapter, are created by treating a set of taxonomical terms as orthogonal dimensions in a design space. The resulting matrix of design choices provides structure for classification and comparison of designs [119]. The completed design framework provides a means to compare existing systems and encourage new designs by providing a unifying foundation for the description and categorization of systems. Furthermore, the methodical filling-in of this structure helps to categorize existing concepts, identify problematic design spaces, differentiate ideas, and identify unexplored terrain [38]. Some examples of taxonomic design frameworks include [38, 46, 92, 94]. However, one notable drawback of taxonomical design frameworks is that they do not elucidate the relations between concepts as other types of frameworks can.

Other important types of design frameworks include descriptive frameworks and explanatory frameworks. Descriptive frameworks provide sensitizing concepts, design considerations, and heuristics to inform design, but do not specify details about how and why certain causes create their effects [16]. Some examples of existing descriptive frameworks include [8, 36, 88, 116, 120, 127]. Conversely, explanatory frameworks not only offer concepts, relations and descriptions, but also provide explanatory accounts of framework relations [16]. They are among the more powerful types of frameworks since explanatory frameworks specifically explicate the relations between concepts, which enable them to be utilized in the development of testable hypotheses linking learning constructions, interactional behaviors, and design features. A good exemplar of explanatory design frameworks is by Antle and Wise [16].

7.4.2 Embodied Learning Taxonomies and Frameworks

Similar to the many interpretations of embodiment, embodied learning taxonomies and frameworks also have vastly different interpretations of physicality, motion, collaboration, and interaction. Johnson-Glenberg et al. [63] created an embodied learning taxonomy that specifies the strength of embodiment as a combination of the amount of motoric engagement, gestural congruency to learning content, and immersion. Black et al. [26] created the Instructional Embodiment Framework (IEF) which consists of various forms of physical embodiment (i.e., direct, surrogate, and augmented) as well as imagined embodiment (i.e., explicit and implicit) where the individual can embody action and perception through imagination. Skulmowski and Rey [131] developed a theoretical taxonomy of educational embodiment research in order to highlight the possibilities and challenges involved in translating basic embodiment research into application. Their taxonomy consists of a 2×2 grid with task integration (incidental vs. integrated) as one dimension and bodily engagement (low vs. high) as the other.

In the domain of tangibles, Fishkin [46] presented a taxonomy for the analysis of tangible interfaces which views embodiment as the distance between input and output where embodiment can be *full* (output device is input device), *nearby* (output is directly proximate to input device), *environmental* (output is "around" the user), or *distant* (output is on another screen or in another room). A related framework by Price et al. [116] for tangible learning environments focuses on different possible artifact-representation combinations and the role that they play in shaping cognition. The physical–digital links of these combinations are conceptualized into four distinct dimensions:

- *Location*—The different location couplings between physical artifacts and digital representations.
- *Dynamics*—The flow of information during interaction (e.g., is feedback immediate or delayed).
- *Correspondence*—The degree to which the physical properties of objects are closely mapped to the learning concepts.
- *Modality*—Different representation modalities in conjunction with artifact interaction.

Antle and Wise [16] also proposed an important framework to aid tangible user interface (TUI) design for learning through the lenses of theories of cognition and learning. Their Tangible Learning Design Framework provides 12 guidelines to inform the design of the five interrelated elements of TUI learning environments by drawing from five perspectives of cognition: *Information Processing, Constructivism, Embodied Cognition, Distributed Cognition*, and *Computer-Supported Collaborative Learning*.

There have also been a number of other taxonomies created to address various use cases and target populations with tangibles. Leong et al. [76] created a conceptual framework for constructive assemblies intended to facilitate systematic investigation and critical consideration of a special subset of TUIs that involve the interconnection of modular parts. Antle [8] created the CTI framework, a tool to conceptualize how the unique features of tangible and spatial interactive systems can be harnessed for children under the age of twelve. CTI consists of five themes: *Space for Action*, *Perceptual Mappings*, *Behavioral Mappings*, *Semantic Mappings*, and *Space for Friends*. Finally, focusing more on the collaborative aspects of tangibles, Tissenbaum et al. [135] developed the Divergent Collaboration Learning Mechanisms (DCLM) framework for recognizing and coding collaboration and divergent learning—i.e., where learners collaborate while seeking divergent goals, ideas, and conceptions—in tabletop learning environments.

7.5 TOWARD A DESIGN FRAMEWORK FOR EMBODIED LEARNING GAMES AND SIMULATIONS

In order to provide initial steps toward addressing the black box of design decisions for embodied learning systems, we created a taxonomical design framework for embodied learning games and simulations. A design framework is an important tool for bridging conceptual differences between diverse domains and existing systems [119], and in this instance helps to clarify various key design decisions underlying existing embodied educational games and simulations. While the taxonomical nature of this framework does not explicate the relations between concepts, by making high-level design decisions more apparent it can be employed to categorize existing embodied educational games and simulations, identify problematic design space for embodied educational systems, and identify design gaps between different dimensions to generate novel embodied educational tools.

7.5.1 SURVEYING EXISTING EMBODIED EDUCATIONAL GAMES AND SIMULATIONS

In order to create the design framework, we conducted an extensive literature review for published examples of embodied learning games and simulations in the following HCI, games, and learning science venues:

- ACM Conference on Human Factors in Computing Systems (CHI)
- International Conference on Tangible, Embedded, and Embodied Interactions (TEI)
- Foundations of Digital Games Conference (FDG)
- ACM Interaction Design and Children Conference (IDC)
- International Journal of Game-Based Learning (IJGBJ)
- *International Journal of Computer-Supported Collaborative Learning* (ijCSCL)
- *International Journal of Arts and Technology* (IJART)

- *International Journal of Child-Computer Interaction* (IJCCI)
- *British Journal of Educational Technology* (BJET)
- Computers and Education
- ACM Transactions on Computer–Human Interaction (TOCHI)

Notably, the core nature of all games is embodied to some extent, and leaving it to the authors' judgment whether a game was embodied or not could introduce significant personal bias. Therefore, for the purpose of this research, only papers that explicitly mentioned embodiment or related terms (e.g., embodied learning, embodied cognition, and embodied interaction) were collected for the literature review. We also performed a tree search of references and citations from the initial papers collected and included seminal papers concerning embodiment that were not in the aforementioned venues to increase the breadth of works collected—for example, [116, 118] were not in the initial list of surveyed papers, but identified through the tree search. In addition, we examined related frameworks and taxonomies in subdomains and communities such as TEI [8, 16, 46, 76, 104, 112, 116], cognitive and learning science [26, 63, 131], and mixed reality [38, 121] in order to identify key taxonomical terms for our design framework. The final list contained over 90 papers concerning embodiment and descriptions of designs for a total of 66 distinct embodied learning games and simulations (see Table 7.1). This list is not intended to be exhaustive, but does represent a diverse selection of designs that could be drawn upon when creating a design framework.

7.5.2 CREATING THE DESIGN FRAMEWORK

Bottom up, open coding was then performed following the process described by Ens and Hincapié-ramos [38] in order to distill a set of 25 candidate dimensions that fit concepts found in the reviewed literature and designs. Candidate dimensions were iteratively reduced and combined into a set small enough for a concise framework. Afterwards, we presented the framework to experts in HCI, game design, and learning science for feedback and additional refinements. The final design framework consists of the seven dimensions shown in Figure 7.1 (see Table 7.1 for all systems coded by their design dimensions). Dimensions were then further organized into three groups based on their overarching design themes within the construct of embodiment (i.e., physical body and interactions, social interactions, and the world where interaction is situated).

7.5.3 DESIGN SPACE DIMENSIONS OF THE FRAMEWORK

The following subsections briefly describe each dimension of the design framework, the corresponding values/design choices of the dimension, and the underlying theoretical basis with examples of existing educational games employing that design approach.

7.5.3.1 Physicality

This dimension ultimately describes how learning is physically embodied in a system. Building off of the above and other central perspectives of embodiment, we

Group	Dimension	Values				
Physical Interaction	*Physicality*	Direct Embodied	Enacted	Manipulated	Surrogate	Augmented
	Transforms	PPt		PDt		DPt
	Mapping	Discrete		Co-located		Embedded
	Correspondence	Symbolic		Indexical		Literal
Social Interaction	*Mode of Play*	Individual		Collaborative		Competitive
	Coordination	Other Player(s)		NPC(s)		None
World	*Environment*	Physical		Mixed		Virtual

FIGURE 7.1 The design framework for embodied learning games and simulations. Similar dimensions are clustered under a group based on an overarching design theme, and the different values/design choices for each dimension are shown.

have identified five key forms of physical interaction that commonly arise from employing embodiment (see Figure 7.2).

1) The ***Direct Embodied*** value refers to an embodied cognition and learning science approach where the body plays the primary constituent role in cognition [128]. This form of embodiment and resulting physical interactions focus on gestural congruency and how the body can physically represent learning concepts [63]. For instance, a full-body interaction game where players contort their bodies to match letters shown on a screen [105]

2) The ***Enacted*** value refers to Direct Embodiment from the Instructional Embodiment Framework [26], and to enactivism which focuses on knowing as physically doing [53, 77]. This form of embodiment, and resulting physical interactions, centers more on acting/enacting out knowledge through physical action of statements or sequences. For example, a gravitational physics game where payers walk along (i.e., enact) the trajectory an asteroid would travel in the vicinity of planets and their gravitational forces [80]

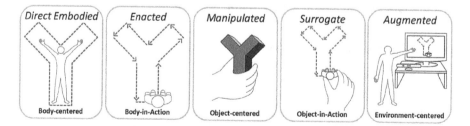

FIGURE 7.2 The five distinct values for the physicality dimension of the design framework. Consists of *Direct Embodied*, *Enacted*, *Manipulated*, *Surrogate*, and *Augmented* values.

3) The *Manipulated* value refers to the tangible embodied interactions of HCI/ TEI [90] and the use of manipulatives in learning science [110]. This form of embodiment and resulting physical interactions arise from utilization of embodied metaphors and interactions with physical objects [19], and the objects' physical embodiment of learning concepts in the material itself [61, 112]. For example, a tabletop environment where the surface shows projections illustrating light reflection, absorption, transmission, and refraction of colored blocks using a light source that can be moved around [113]

4) The *Surrogate* value refers to the Instructional Embodiment Framework concept of Surrogate Embodiment, where learners manipulate a physical agent or "surrogate" representative of themselves to enact learning concepts [26]. This form of embodiment and resulting physical interactions are often used in systems with an interactive physical environment that is directly tied to a real-time virtual simulation [44, 71]. For instance, a game where children use stuffed animals to enact and better understand animal foraging behaviors [48]

5) The *Augmented* value refers to the Instructional Embodiment Framework notion of Augmented Embodiment, where combined use of a representational system (e.g., avatar) and augmented feedback system (e.g., Microsoft Kinect and TV screen) embed the learner within an augmented reality system. This form of embodiment and resulting physical interactions are most commonly found in systems where learners' physical actions are mapped as input to control digital avatars in virtual environments [100]. For example, a game where children control a polar bear's movement in the virtual environment by rotating their accelerometer-equipped gloves in a "swimming" motion [82, 83]

7.5.3.2 Transforms

This dimension conceptualizes a space, describing the relationships between physical or digital actions and the resulting physical or digital effects in the environment. We utilize the transform types of Physical action => Physical effect (*PPt*), Physical action => Digital effect (*PDt*), and Digital action => Physical effect (*DPt*) from Rogers et al. [121] to describe the many forms of existing systems. Notably, Digital action => Digital effect (*DDt*) was excluded since these are the standard forms of interacting with a system (e.g., clicking digital buttons to move a digital avatar) and do not support embodied interactions.

7.5.3.3 Mapping

This dimension borrows from the notion of Embodiment from the taxonomy for tangible interfaces by [46] and Location from the tangible learning environment framework by Price et al. [116] which both describe the different spatial locations of output in relation to the object or action triggering the effect (i.e., how input is spatially mapped to output). Mappings can be *Discrete*—input and output are located separately (e.g., an action triggers output on a nearby screen); *Co-located*—input and output are contiguous (e.g., an action triggers output that is directly adjacent or overlaid on the physical space); and *Embedded*—input and output are embedded in the same object.

7.5.3.4   Correspondence

This dimension builds upon the notion of Physical Correspondence from the tangible learning environment framework by Price et al. [116] which refers to the degree to which the physical properties of objects are closely mapped to the learning concepts. We expand this concept to also include physical actions (e.g., congruency of gestures or physical manipulations to learning concepts [63, 131]). Correspondence can be *Symbolic*—objects and actions act as common but abstract signifiers to the learning concepts (e.g., arranging programming blocks to learn coding [145]); *Indexical*—physical properties and actions only correlate with or imply the learning concept (e.g., throwing a ball and watching it fall to learn about gravity [6]); or *Literal*—physical properties and actions are closely mapped to the learning concepts and metaphor of the domain (e.g., playing an augmented physical guitar to learn finger positioning [66]).

7.5.3.5   Mode of Play

This dimension specifies how individuals socially interact and play within a system. The system can facilitate *Individual*, *Collaborative*, or *Competitive* play for learner(s). Plass et al. [109] found differing learning benefits for each mode of play, suggesting it is also an important dimension to consider for learning outcomes.

7.5.3.6   Coordination

This dimension highlights how individuals in a system may have to socially coordinate their actions [1] in order to successfully complete learning objectives. Social coordination can occur with *Other Player(s)* and/or in a socio-collaborative experience with digital media typically in the form of *NPC(s)* [136]. Conversely, social coordination can also be of limited focus in a design and not occur or even be supported—i.e., None.

7.5.3.7   Environment

This dimension refers to the learning environment in which the educational content is situated. Environments can be either *Physical*, *Mixed*, or *Virtual* [121]. While transforms conceptualise a space through the description of actions and effects, the environment dimension focuses on the actual space where learning occurs. For instance, a PDt transform can occur in drastically different learning environments (Figure 7.3). In some systems, a player's physical actions are tracked but only used as input to control a virtual character in a virtual environment [82, 83]. In other systems, the player's physical actions are tracked and mapped to control digital effects overlaid on an augmented physical space or mixed reality environment [80]. Others still have players situated in a completely physical environment where their physical actions are tracked primarily to keep score or digitally maintain information related to learning content that is displayed during the interaction [48].

7.6   APPLYING THE DESIGN FRAMEWORK

In order to demonstrate the potential application of this design framework, we present three use cases in the following subsections. Specifically, we highlight the

FIGURE 7.3 Three systems illustrating PDt transforms in different learning environments. Left—physical actions are mapped as input into a virtual environment [83]. Middle—physical actions are mapped as input into a mixed reality environment that is overlaid on physical space [80]. Right—physical actions occur in a physical learning environment and are only tracked to digitally maintain and display information related to the physical interaction [48].

framework's ability to (1) categorize existing embodied educational games and simulations, (2) identify problematic design spaces for embodied educational systems, and (3) identify design gaps between different dimensions to generate novel embodied educational designs.

EXAMPLE 7.1 CATEGORIZING EXISTING EMBODIED GAMES AND SIMULATIONS

One fundamental feature of any framework is its descriptive capability. To exemplify how designs of existing embodied learning games and simulations can be described using the framework, we applied it to the 66 systems surveyed. For each design, we assigned dimensional values and cataloged the results (see Table 7.1). This methodical approach provided a means to systematically compare and contrast the different designs [38]. One important point to note is that the framework does not perfectly partition every design into dimensional values. There were some cases where multiple values within a dimension would match a single design or the design description would leave a chosen value open to interpretation. However, these minor discrepancies are acceptable since the intentions of a design framework are to make the designer aware of important design choices and help them weigh the potential benefits of these choices, rather than provide a set of arbitrary sorting bins [38].

During the analysis and cataloging process, varieties of similar designs emerged and were reasonably described by nine distinct categories (see Figures 7.4 and 7.5). We found the majority of reviewed designs (58 of 66) to be very good fit for one of the categories, despite all nine categories only representing a small portion of the full design space expressed by the framework. Similar to the assignment of dimensional values, categories are not absolute. Therefore, we include designs with minor variations in a category so long as they fit closely to the overall characteristics of that group.

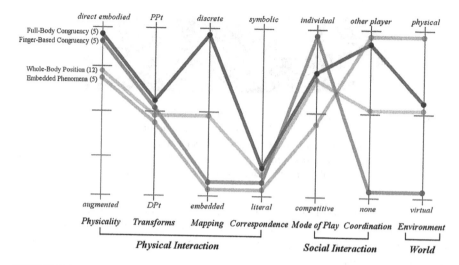

FIGURE 7.4 A parallel coordinates graph showing the categories and corresponding design choices found during analysis of existing systems that utilize *Direct Embodied* and *Enacted* physicality.

7.6.1 DIRECT EMBODIED PHYSICALITY CATEGORIES

7.6.1.1 Full-Body Congruency

This category describes designs that employ full-body interactions with all or a portion of the body being utilized as input into a mixed reality environment (Figure 7.4). The mapping of input to output is discrete and sensor-based (e.g., utilizing some form of IR or computer vision tracking), where players see augmented video feedback of themselves moving to match virtual objects or actions depicted on a screen. The educational focus of these systems is on mirroring a learning concept through bodily or gestural congruency, and instances include using the body to match shapes of alphabet letters [37, 105, 152] and geometric shapes [96].

7.6.1.2 Finger-Based Congruency

This category is conceptually similar to full-body congruency in that the educational focus of designs is on mirroring a learning concept through physical or gestural congruency. However, the interaction focus is instead on usage of fingers to achieve this congruency. This results in an embedded mapping of input to output on a physical device (e.g., tablet) where gameplay is situated in a virtual environment. Examples of this design category include usage of fingers to represent the numbers in a part–whole relation [21] and the velocity of a moving object [34].

7.6.2 ENACTED PHYSICALITY CATEGORIES

7.6.2.1 Whole-Body Position

This category is one of the largest set of systems categorized (12 designs)—focusing on tracking simple aspects of a player's body, such as their location in physical space, to enact learning concepts in a mixed reality environment (Figure 7.4). These systems typically rely on augmenting the physical space with a co-located mapping of input through motion tracking and output through top to down projections [67, 80, 81] or through different modalities such as sound [13].

7.6.2.2   Embedded Phenomena

This category is a class of simulations that embed imaginary dynamic phenomena—scientific or otherwise—into the physical space of classrooms [97]. As a result of this design approach, interaction revolves around enacting techniques performed by real world professionals in order to measure the phenomena through usage of devices embedded into the physical classroom environment that provide augmented feedback about a specific phenomenon or scientific activity. Examples of this design category include simulations of earthquake trilateration [97] and subterranean water flow [103].

7.6.3   MANIPULATED PHYSICALITY CATEGORIES

7.6.3.1   Tangible Blocks

This category describes designs that utilize notions of tangibility and embodied interaction from HCI and TEI communities combined with concepts of modularity from Computer Science (Figure 7.5). Players physically manipulate/program a set of tangible blocks with embedded sensing capabilities and feedback systems. These blocks interact within the physical environment and are usually symbolically representative of computing concepts [125, 145, 146].

7.6.3.2   Tangible Tabletops

This category describes designs that similarly utilize notions of tangibility and embodied interaction as Tangible Blocks, but instead focus on the usage of symbolic

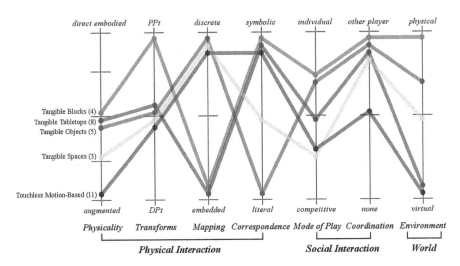

FIGURE 7.5   A parallel coordinates graph showing the categories and corresponding design choices found during analysis of existing systems that utilize *Manipulated*, *Surrogate*, and *Augmented* physicality.

tangibles or gestures in conjunction with a virtual world displayed on an interactive tabletop. The setups are commonly found in public spaces such as museums and typically facilitate large-scale social interactions. Tangible tabletop designs have been employed to teach educational concepts around energy consumption [40], sustainability [9], nanoscale [99], and African concepts for mapping history [29].

7.6.3.3 Tangible Objects

This category describes designs that utilize various tangible objects and embodied interaction as input into virtual learning environments. Physical manipulation of the tangible object results in a discrete and intuitive mapping to a virtual representation of learning content. Tangible object designs have been utilized to teach a variety of concepts such as urban planning [129] and heart anatomy [130].

7.6.4 SURROGATE PHYSICALITY CATEGORIES

7.6.4.1 Tangible Spaces

This category builds upon a space-centered view of tangible embodied interaction where interactive spaces rely on combining physical space and tangible objects with digital displays (Figure 7.5) [55]. The design focus is on creating a tangible physical environment for the player to actively manipulate—complete with a physical surrogate avatar that the player controls—and discretely mapping physical changes in that space to a virtual world that either mirrors or augments the physical one. Tangible spaces have been used to teach programming [44], animal foraging behavior [48], and diurnal motion of the sun [71].

7.6.5 AUGMENTED PHYSICALITY CATEGORIES

7.6.5.1 "Touchless" Motion-Based

Another large set of categorized designs (11 systems), designs in this category employ a discrete mapping of players' physical actions as input into a virtual world (Figure 7.5). The use of a "touchless" interaction paradigm exploits sensing devices which capture, track, and decipher body movements and gestures so that players do not need to wear additional aides [23]. Unlike full-body congruency, the focus is not on mirroring a learning concept through the body, but instead a player's physical actions are mapped to control a digital avatar in the virtual world. As a result, rather than seeing a video of themselves, players will see silhouettes, digital avatars, or a first-person perspective. These systems have been utilized to teach concepts around geometric shapes [73], climate change [83], and peer-directed social behaviors [25].

EXAMPLE 7.2 IDENTIFYING PROBLEMATIC DESIGN SPACES

Another benefit of the design framework is that it allows for systematic examination of design elements within existing systems, identifying potential problematic design spaces. As an example of this usage, we examine the Tangible Earth system (see Figure 7.6) where the authors had to create and use an assessment framework to identify and understand problems the system encountered [71]. Tangible Earth is designed to support learning of the sun's diurnal motion and Earth's rotation. It consists of a doll-like avatar, a globe, and a rotating table to represent the Earth and its rotation, an electrical light representing the Sun, and a laptop running VR universe simulator. Learners would physically manipulate the rotation of the earth and position/rotation of the avatar to observe simulated changes in Sun's position from the avatar's perspective.

One of the more significant problems identified by Kuzuoka et al. [71] for Tangible Earth was that learners spent very little time looking at the tangibles themselves (e.g., globe, lamp, and avatar), instead focusing primarily on the VR simulation in the laptop. This proved to be especially problematic for manipulation of the avatar, where users would frequently forget the position of its body and orientation of its head. This often caused the Sun to appear or disappear unexpectedly in the simulation, confusing learners and learning concepts. By analyzing this issue with the design framework, we identified a potential problematic design space (see Figure 7.7).That is, learners had difficulty remembering the position of a physical agent representative of themselves (**surrogate embodiment**) because all of their physical actions were mapped to digital effects (**PDt transform**) in a simulated world (**virtual environment**) that directly mirrored the physical one (**literal correspondence**). This difficulty makes sense considering remembering the physical position/orientation of a surrogate avatar in *both* the real world and the virtual world simultaneously would introduce a significant amount of extraneous cognitive load [108]. As a result, the design framework suggests that the intersection of surrogate embodiment, PDt transforms, literal correspondence, and virtual environments is a problematic design space that should be carefully considered when designing future embodied learning systems.

FIGURE 7.6   The Tangible Earth embodied learning system by Kuzuoka et al. [71].

Group	Dimension	Values				
Physical Interaction	Physicality	*Direct Embodied*	*Enacted*	*Manipulated*	*Surrogate*	*Augmented*
	Transforms	*PPt*		*PDt*		*DPt*
	Mapping	*Discrete*		*Co-located*		*Embedded*
	Correspondence	*Symbolic*		*Indexical*		*Literal*
Social Interaction	Mode of Play	*Individual*		*Collaborative*		*Competitive*
	Coordination	*Other Player(s)*		*NPC(s)*		*None*
World	Environment	*Physical*		*Mixed*		*Virtual*

FIGURE 7.7   A problematic design space identified in Tangible Earth [71].

EXAMPLE 7.3   IDENTIFYING DESIGN GAPS

Perhaps the most important benefit of the design framework is that it allows for methodically plugging existing systems back into the different dimensions to identify gaps and unexplored terrain [38]. As an illustration of this usage, we fill in an example pairing between the two dimensions of Physicality and Transforms (see Figure 7.8). This provides examples of relevant combinations between these two dimensions in the embodied learning systems literature that was surveyed.

Examining Figure 7.8, there are a number of design gaps for existing embodied learning games and simulations. Notably, most of these gaps highlight either unexplored or undervalued research directions within the literature base they were drawn from. Some of the more potentially useful pairings in the identified design gaps are Embodied + PPt, Manipulated + DPt, Surrogate + PPt, and Surrogate + DPt, where interesting future system designs could evolve from utilizing one of these pairings. For instance, using a Surrogate + PPt pairing could lead to the design and research of physically embodied educational board games. Additionally, a Surrogate + DPt pairing could lead to an asymmetric computational thinking game where one player controls and interacts with a physical avatar while another player digitally designs the physical courses and obstacles for the first player to complete.

7.7   CONCLUSION

Embodiment is a concept that has gained widespread usage within communities such as HCI, games, and learning science in recent years. However, the broad number of

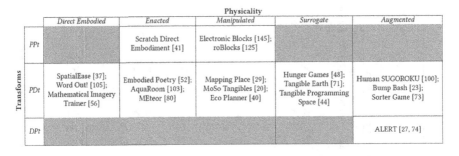

		Physicality				
		Direct Embodied	Enacted	Manipulated	Surrogate	Augmented
Transforms	PPt		Scratch Direct Embodiment [41]	Electronic Blocks [145]; roBlocks [125]		
	PDt	SpatialEase [37]; Word Out! [105]; Mathematical Imagery Trainer [56]	Embodied Poetry [52]; AquaRoom [103]; MEteor [80]	Mapping Place [29]; MoSo Tangibles [20]; Eco Planner [40]	Hunger Games [48]; Tangible Earth [71]; Tangible Programming Space [44]	Human SUGOROKU [100]; Bump Bash [23]; Sorter Game [73]
	DPt					ALERT [27, 74]

FIGURE 7.8 Example Pairings between the Physicality and Transform Dimensions for a Random Subset of 20 Surveyed Systems

academic domains that define and operationalize embodiment has often resulted in a black box of design decisions. This inconsistent application of embodiment is a substantial drawback when trying to design embodied technology to support particular use cases such as learning, where understanding the "why" of outcomes is essential. Our design framework for embodied learning games and simulations is an important tool that begins to open the black box of design decisions for embodied learning technologies—mapping out a more precise understanding of how to incorporate embodiment into the design of educational games and simulations. Ultimately, such a framework helps to explicate high-level design decisions by providing a unifying foundation for the description and categorization of embodied learning systems, and encourages new designs by identifying problematic design spaces and unexplored research/design terrain [38].

In this chapter, we created a design framework by collecting 66 exemplars of embodied learning games and simulations, followed by the application of a bottom up, open coding method to distill seven core design dimensions. We then demonstrated the design framework's importance for a variety of use cases. First, we categorized existing embodied educational games and simulations, identifying nine distinct categories that encompassed the majority of existing designs. Then, we employed the framework to identify a problematic design space for an existing embodied educational system, Tangible Earth [71], that was found to be ineffective for learners. Finally, we concluded by utilizing the framework to identify design gaps between the Physicality and Transforms dimensions—highlighting some of the particularly interesting gaps that are yet to be explored within the literature base surveyed (e.g., embodied educational board games).

LIST OF CATEGORIZED EMBODIED LEARNING GAMES AND SIMULATIONS

All 66 embodied learning game designs identified through the literature survey, coded for each of the design framework dimensions, and organized into categories of common design patterns are shown in Table 7.1. Values/design choices that do not cleanly fit into defined categories are highlighted.

TABLE 7.1
List Of Categorized Embodied Learning Games and Simulations.

			Full-Body Congruency						Finger-Based Congruency			
Design			Word Out! [105, 152]	Mathematical Imagery Trainer [3, 56]	Math Propulsion [96]	Hand Velocity [7]	Spatial Ease [37]	Finger Velocity [34]	Mirror Fugue [147, 148]	Andante [148]	Fingu [21]	AR Guitar [66]
	Physicality	Direct Embodied	X	X	X	X	X	X	X	X	X	X
		Enacted					X	X	X	X		X
		Manipulated										X
		Surrogate										
		Augmented										
		PPt										
Physical Interaction	*Transforms*	PDt	X	X	X	X	X	X	X	X	X	X
		DPt										
	Mapping	Discrete	X	X	X	X						
		Co-located					X					
		Embedded										
		Symbolic						X	X	X	X	X
	Correspondence	Indexical										
		Literal	X	X	X	X	X	X	X	X	X	X
Social Interaction	*Mode of Play*	Individual		X		X	X	X		X	X	X
		Collaborative										
		Competitive			X				X			
		Other Player	X		X				X			
		NPC										
	Coordination	None		X		X	X	X			X	
		Physical								X		X
World	*Environment*	Mixed	X		X	X	X		X	X		X
		Virtual		X				X			X	

(Continued)

TABLE 7.1 (Continued)
List Of Categorized Embodied Learning Games and Simulations.

Design			Whole-Body Position											
			Archimedes [87]	Sound Maker [12, 13]	Wobble Board Game [73]	MEteor [79–81]	Springboard [10, 11, 84]	CoCensus [118]	Music Paint Machine [101, 102]	Embodied Poetry [52, 67]	Lands of Fog [98]	Learning Physics through Play Project [39]	Social Robot [136]	Der Schwarm [51]
	Physicality	Direct		X	X		X							
		Embodied												
		Enacted	X	X	X	X	X	X	X	X		X	X	X
		Manipulated												
		Surrogate												
		Augmented									X			
Physical Interaction	*Transforms*	PPt	X	X		X		X	X	X	X	X	X	X
		PDt										X		
		DPt												
		Discrete			X		X	X	X					
	Mapping	Co-located	X	X		X				X	X			X
		Embedded												
		Symbolic						X			X		X	
	Correspondence	Indexical					X							
		Literal	X	X	X	X	X			X		X	X	X
	Mode of Play	Individual				X			X			X		X
		Collaborative	X	X	X			X	X	X	X		X	
		Competitive												
Social Interaction	*Coordination*	Other Player	X	X	X			X		X	X			
		NPC	X			X	X		X			X		
		None											X	
World	*Environment*	Physical												
		Mixed	X	X	X	X		X	X	X	X	X	X	X
		Virtual					X						X	X

(Continued)

TABLE 7.1 (Continued)
List Of Categorized Embodied Learning Games and Simulations.

			Embedded Phenomena					Tangible Blocks			
			Roomquake [97]	Espaistory [86]	AquaRoom [103]	Astronaut Challenge [65]	WallCology [65]	Note Code [70]	Electronic Blocks [145, 146]	roBlocks [125]	Buildasound [117]
Design	*Physicality*	Direct	X								
		Embodied									
		Enacted		X	X	X	X				
		Manipulated			X	X	X	X	X	X	X
		Surrogate									
		Augmented									
Physical Interaction	*Transforms*	PPt	X		X	X	X	X	X	X	X
		PDt		X							
		DPt		X							
	Mapping	Discrete									
		Co-located									
		Embedded	X	X	X	X	X	X	X	X	X
	Correspondence	Symbolic						X	X	X	X
		Indexical									
		Literal	X	X	X	X	X				
		Individual						X			
Social Interaction	*Mode of Play*	Collaborative	X	X	X	X	X		X		X
		Competitive								X	
	Coordination	Other Player	X	X	X	X	X		X		
		NPC									
		None									X
World	*Environment*	Physical	X	X	X			X	X		
		Mixed				X		X		X	X
		Virtual					X			X	X

(Continued)

TABLE 7.1 (Continued)
List Of Categorized Embodied Learning Games and Simulations.

Design			Tangible Tabletops								Tangible Objects				
			Nano Zoom [99]	Mapping Place [29]	LightTable [42, 113, 114]	Flow of Electrons [32, 33]	Youtopia [17, 144]	Touch Wire [123]	Futura [9, 14, 132]	Eco Planner [40]	MoSo Tangibles [19, 20]	Phono Blocks [43]	Paper-Based Urban Planning [129]	Kurio [2]	TUI Heart [130]
	Physicality	Direct	X												
		Embodied													
		Enacted													
		Manipulated	X	X	X	X	X	X	X	X	X	X	X	X	X
		Surrogate													
		Augmented												X	X
Physical Interaction	*Transforms*	PPt													
		PDt	X	X	X	X	X	X	X	X	X	X	X	X	X
		DPt													X
		Discrete		X							X	X	X	X	
	Mapping	Co-located	X		X	X	X	X	X						
		Embedded	X	X						X				X	
		Symbolic	X	X			X		X	X					
	Correspondence	Indexical	X	X				X							
		Literal			X	X					X	X	X	X	X
		Individual									X	X			X
Social Interaction	*Mode of Play*	Collaborative	X	X	X		X	X	X	X			X	X	
		Competitive													
		Other Player	X	X	X		X	X	X	X			X	X	
		NPC				X									
	Coordination	None									X	X		X	X
		Physical									X	X			
World	*Environment*	Mixed									X	X	X	X	X
		Virtual	X	X	X	X	X	X	X	X				X	X

(Continued)

TABLE 7.1 (Continued)
List Of Categorized Embodied Learning Games and Simulations.

Category	Subcategory	Item	Tangible Spaces				Touchless Motion-Based									
			Tangible Programming Space [44]	Tangible Earth [71]	Hunger Games [48]	Snark [115]	Bump Bash [23]	A Mile in My Paws [82, 83]	Target Kick [23]	Kinems [69]	Children Make Terrible Pets [54]	Motion Autism Game [25]	BESIDE [153]	Kinect Recycling Game [59]	TASC [28]	Sorter Game [73]
Design	Physicality	Direct														
		Embodied														
		Enacted														
		Manipulated													X	
		Surrogate	X	X	X											
		Augmented				X	X	X	X	X	X	X	X	X	X	X
Physical Interaction	Transforms	PPt	X	X	X	X	X	X	X	X	X	X	X	X	X	X
		PDt														X
		DPt	X	X	X	X	X	X	X	X	X	X	X	X	X	X
	Mapping	Discrete														
		Co-located														
		Embedded														
		Symbolic	X			X	X	X	X	X	X	X	X	X	X	X
	Correspondence	Indexical														
		Literal		X	X		X	X								
Social Interaction	Mode of Play	Individual								X				X		
		Collaborative	X	X		X					X	X	X	X	X	X
		Competitive			X	X			X					X		
	Coordination	Other Player	X	X	X	X						X		X		X
		NPC									X					
		None				X	X	X	X	X			X		X	
		Physical			X											
World	Environment	Mixed	X												X	
		Virtual		X		X	X	X	X	X	X	X	X	X		X

(Continued)

TABLE 7.1 (Continued)
List Of Categorized Embodied Learning Games and Simulations.

Design			Scratch Direct Embodiment [41]	Wiimote Gravity [6]	EstimateIT™ [18]	Miscellaneous				
						Tangible Landscape [49, 106]	Embodied Puppet [31, 91]	EarthShake [149–151]	ALERT [27, 28]	Human SUGOROKU [5, 100]
	Physicality	Direct								
		Embodied								
		Enacted	X							
		Manipulated		X	X	X				
		Surrogate					X			
		Augmented						X	X	X
		PPt	X			X	X	X	X	X
	Transforms	PDt		X	X		X	X	X	X
		DPt		X	X				X	
Physical Interaction	*Mapping*	Discrete		X	X					
		Co-located								
		Embedded	X			X				
		Symbolic			X		X	X	X	X
	Correspondence	Indexical		X	X	X				
		Literal	X		X					
		Individual	X		X		X			
	Mode of Play	Collaborative		X	X	X		X	X	
		Competitive								X
		Other Player		X		X		X	X	X
Social Interaction	*Coordination*	NPC								
		None	X		X		X			
		Physical	X	X	X					
World	*Environment*	Mixed		X	X	X		X	X	X
		Virtual					X			

REFERENCES

[1] Olivier Oullier, Gonzalo C. De Guzman, Kelly J. Jantzen, Julien Lagarde, and J. A. Scott Kelso Social coordination dynamics: Measuring human bonding. *Social Neuroscience* 3, 2 (2008).

[2] Ron Wakkary, Marek Hatala, Kevin Muise, Karen Tanenbaum, Greg Corness, Bardia Mohabbati, and Jim Budd. 2009. *Kurio: A museum guide for families*. In *Proceedings of the third international conference on Tangible, embedded, and embodied interaction - TEI'09*. 215–222.

[3] Dor Abrahamson. 2014. Building educational activities for understanding: An elaboration on the embodied-design framework and its epistemic grounds. *International Journal of Child-Computer Interaction* 2, 1, 1–16.

[4] Dor Abrahamson and Arthur Bakker. 2016. Making sense of movement in embodied design for mathematics learning. *Cognitive Research: Principles and Implications* 1, 1, 33.

[5] Takayuki Adachi, M Goseki, K Muratsu, Hiroshi Mizoguchi, Miki Namatame, Masanori Sugimoto, Fusako Kusunoki, Etsuji Yamaguchi, Shigenori Inagaki, and Yoshiaki Takeda. 2013. *Human SUGOROKU: Full-body interaction system for students to learn vegetation succession*. In *Interaction Design and Children*. 364–367.

[6] Zeynep Ahmet, Martin Jonsson, Saiful Islam Sumon, and Lars Erik Holmquist. 2011. *Supporting embodied exploration of physical concepts in mixed digital and physical interactive settings*. In *Proceedings of TEI '11*.

[7] Stamatina Anastopoulou, Mike Sharples, and Chris Baber. 2011. An evaluation of multimodal interactions with technology while learning science concepts. *British Journal of Educational Technology* 42, 2, 266–290.

[8] Alissa N Antle. 2007. *The CTI framework: Informing the design of tangible systems for children*. In *Proceedings of the 1st International Conference on Tangible and Embedded Interaction*. ACM, 195–202.

[9] Alissa N Antle, Allen Bevans, Josh Tanenbaum, Katie Seaborn, and Sijie Wang. 2011. *Futura: Design for collaborative learning and game play on a multi-touch digital tabletop*. In *Proceedings of the fifth international conference on Tangible, embedded, and embodied interaction*. ACM, 93–100.

[10] Alissa N Antle, Greg Corness, and Allen Bevans. 2011. *Springboard: Designing image schema based embodied interaction for an abstract domain*. In *Whole Body Interaction*. Springer, 7–18.

[11] Alissa N Antle, Greg Corness, and Allen Bevans. 2013. Balancing justice: Comparing whole body and controller-based interaction for an abstract domain. *International Journal of Arts and Technology* 6, 4, 388–409.

[12] Alissa N Antle, Greg Corness, and Milena Droumeva. 2008. What the body knows: Exploring the benefits of embodied metaphors in hybrid physical digital environments. *Interacting with Computers* 21, 1–2, 66–75.

[13] Alissa N Antle, Milena Droumeva, and Greg Corness. 2008. *Playing with the sound maker: Do embodied metaphors help children learn?*. In *Proceedings of the 7th international conference on Interaction design and children*. ACM, 178–185.

[14] Alissa N Antle, Joshua Tanenbaum, Allen Bevans, Katie Seaborn, and Sijie Wang. 2011. *Balancing act: Enabling public engagement with sustainability issues through a multi-touch tabletop collaborative game*. In *IFIP Conference on Human-Computer Interaction*. Springer, 194–211.

[15] Alissa N Antle and Sijie Wang. 2013. *Comparing motor-cognitive strategies for spatial problem solving with tangible and multi-touch interfaces*. In *Proceedings of the 7th International Conference on Tangible, Embedded and Embodied Interaction*. ACM, 65–72.

[16] Alissa N Antle and Alyssa F Wise. 2013. Getting down to details: Using theories of cognition and learning to inform tangible user interface design. *Interacting with Computers* 25, 1 (2013), 1–20.

[17] Alissa N Antle, Alyssa F Wise, Amanda Hall, Saba Nowroozi, Perry Tan, Jillian Warren, Rachael Eckersley, and Michelle Fan. 2013. *Youtopia: A collaborative, tangible, multi-touch, sustainability learning activity.* In *Proceedings of the 12th International Conference on Interaction Design and Children.* ACM, 565–568.

[18] Ivon Arroyo, Matthew Micciollo, Jonathan Casano, Erin Ottmar, Taylyn Hulse, and Ma Mercedes Rodrigo. 2017. *Wearable learning: multiplayer embodied games for math.* In *Proceedings of the Annual Symposium on Computer-Human Interaction in Play.* ACM, 205–216.

[19] Sasykia Bakker, Alissa N Antle, and Elise Van Den Hoven. 2012. Embodied metaphors in tangible interaction design. *Personal and Ubiquitous Computing* 16, 4, 433–449.

[20] Saskia Bakker, Elise Van Den Hoven, and Alissa N Antle. 2011. *MoSo tangibles: Evaluating embodied learning.* In *Proceedings of the Fifth International Conference On Tangible, Embedded, And Embodied Interaction.* ACM, 85–92.

[21] Wolmet Barendregt and Berner Lindström. 2012. *Development and evaluation of Fingu: A mathematics iPad game using multi-touch interaction.* In *Proceedings of the 11th International Conference on Interaction Design and Children.* 204–207.

[22] Lawrence W Barsalou, Paula M Niedenthal, Aron K Barbey, and Jennifer A Ruppert. 2003. Social embodiment. *Psychology of Learning and Motivation* 43 (2003), 43–92.

[23] Laura Bartoli, Clara Corradi, Politecnico Milano, and Matteo Valoriani. 2013. *Exploring motion-based touchless games for autistic children's learning.* In *Proceedings of the 12th International Conference on Interaction Design and Children.* 102–111.

[24] G E Baykal, I Veryeri Alaca, A E Yantaç, and T Göksun. 2018. A review on complementary natures of tangible user interfaces (TUIs) and early spatial learning. *International Journal of Child-Computer Interaction* (2018).

[25] Arpita Bhattacharya, Mirko Gelsomini, Patricia Pérez-Fuster, Gregory D Abowd, and Agata Rozga. 2015. *Designing motion-based activities to engage students with Autism in classroom settings.* In *IDC* 2015. 69–78.

[26] J. B. Black, A. Segal, J. Vitale, and C. L. Fadjo. 2012. *Embodied cognition and learning environment design.* In *Theoretical Foundations of Learning Environments.* 198–223.

[27] Winslow S Burleson, Danielle B Harlow, Katherine J Nilsen, Ken Perlin, Natalie Freed, Camilla Norgaard Jensen, Byron Lahey, Patrick Lu, and Kasia Muldner. 2018. Active Learning Environments with Robotic Tangibles: Children. *IEEE Transactions on Learning Technologies* 1 (2018), 96–106.

[28] Jack Shen-Kuen Chang. 2017. *The design and evaluation of embodied interfaces for supporting spatial ability.* In *Proceedings of the Eleventh International Conference on Tangible, Embedded, and Embodied Interaction.* ACM. 681–684.

[29] Jean Ho Chu, Paul Clifton, Daniel Harley, Jordanne Pavao, and Ali Mazalek. 2015. *Mapping place: Supporting cultural learning through a lukasa-inspired tangible table-top museum exhibit.* In *Proceedings of the 9th International Conference on Tangible, Embedded, and Embodied Interaction - TEI '15.* 261–268.

[30] Andy Clark. 2008. Supersizing the mind: Embodiment, action, and cognitive extension. *Vol. 20.* 286.

[31] Paul Clifton. 2014. *Designing embodied interfaces to support spatial ability.* In *Proceedings of TEI '14.* 309–312.

[32] Bettina Conradi, Martin Hommer, and Robert Kowalski. 2010. *From digital to physical: Learning physical computing on interactive surfaces.* In *ACM International Conference on Interactive Tabletops and Surfaces.* 249–250.

[33] Bettina Conradi, Verena Lerch, Martin Hommer, Robert Kowalski, Ioanna Vletsou, and Heinrich Hussmann. 2011. *Flow of electrons: An augmented workspace for learning physical computing experientially.* In *Proceedings of the ACM International Conference on Interactive Tabletops and Surfaces - ITS'11.* 182–191.

[34] Mattias Davidsson. 2014. Finger Velocity–A Multimodal Touch Based Tablet Application for Learning the Physics of Motion. In *International Conference on Mobile and Contextual Learning.* Springer, 238–249.

[35] Paul Dourish. 2004. *Where the Action is: The Foundations of Embodied Interaction.* MIT press.

[36] Darren Edge and Alan Blackwell. 2006. Correlates of the cognitive dimensions for tangible user interface. *Journal of Visual Languages & Computing* 17, 4, 366–394.

[37] Darren Edge, Kai-yin Cheng, and Michael Whitney. 2013. *SpatialEase: Learning language through body motion.* In *Proceedings of the SIGCHI Conference on Human Factors in Computing Systems (CHI'13).* 469–472.

[38] Barrett Ens and Juan David Hincapié-ramos. 2014. *Ethereal planes: A design framework for 2D information spaces in 3D mixed reality environments.* In *Proceedings of the 2nd ACM Symposium on Spatial User Interaction.*

[39] Noel Enyedy, Joshua A Danish, Girlie Delacruz, and Melissa Kumar. 2012. Learning physics through play in an augmented reality environment. *International Journal of Computer-Supported Collaborative Learning* 7, 3, 347–378.

[40] Augusto Esteves and Ian Oakley. 2011. *Design for interface consistency or embodied facilitation?.* In *CHI 2011 Embodied Interaction: Theory and Practice in HCI Workshop.* 1–4.

[41] Cameron L. Fadjo and John B. Black. 2012. *You're in the game: Direct embodiment and computational artifact construction.* In *Proceedings of the International Conference of the Learning Sciences: Future of Learning* (Vol. 2: Symposia).

[42] Taciana Pontual Falcão and Sara Price. 2011. Interfering and resolving: How tabletop interaction facilitates co-construction of argumentative knowledge. *International Journal of Computer-Supported Collaborative Learning* 6, 4, 539–559.

[43] Min Fan, Alissa N Antle, Maureen Hoskyn, Carman Neustaedter, and Emily S Cramer. 2017. *Why tangibility matters: A design case study of at-risk children learning to read and spell.* In *Proceedings of the 2017 CHI Conference on Human Factors in Computing Systems.* ACM, 1805–1816.

[44] Ylva Fernaeus and Jakob Tholander. 2006. *Finding design qualities in a Tangible programming space.* In *CHI 2006 Proceedings'06.* 447–456.

[45] Kerstin Fischer, Katrin Lohan, and Kilian Foth. 2012. *Levels of embodiment: Linguistic analyses of factors influencing Hri.* In *7th ACM/IEEE International Conference on Human-Robot Interaction (HRI), 2012.* IEEE, 463–470.

[46] Kenneth P. Fishkin. 2004. A taxonomy for and analysis of tangible interfaces. *Personal and Ubiquitous Computing* 8, 5, 347–358.

[47] Arthur M Glenberg. 2010. Embodiment as a unifying perspective for psychology. *Wiley Interdisciplinary Reviews: Cognitive Science* 1, 4 (2010), 586–596.

[48] Alessandro Gnoli, Anthony Perritano, Paulo Guerra, Brenda Lopez, Joel Brown, and Tom Moher. 2014. *Back to the future: Embodied Classroom Simulations of Animal Foraging.* In *Proceedings of the 8th International Conference on Tangible, Embedded and Embodied Interaction - TEI'14.* 275–282.

[49] Brendan Alexander Harmon. 2016. Embodied spatial thinking in tangible computing. *In Proceedings of the TEI'16: Tenth International Conference on Tangible, Embedded, and Embodied Interaction.* ACM, 693–696.

[50] Steve Harrison, Deborah Tatar, and Phoebe Sengers. 2007. *The three paradigms of HCI.* In *Alt. Chi. Session at the SIGCHI Conference on Human Factors in Computing Systems* San Jose, California, USA. 1–18.

[51] Anja Hashagen, Corinne Büching, and Heidi Schelhowe. 2009. *Learning abstract concepts through bodily engagement.* In *Proceedings of the 8th International Conference on Interaction Design and Children - IDC'09.* 234.

[52] Sarah Hatton, Ellen Campana, Andreea Danielescu, and David Birchfield. 2009. *Stratification: Embodied poetry works by high school students.* In *Proceedings of the 5th ACM Conference on Creativity & Cognition.* 463–464.

[53] Douglas L Holton. 2010. *Constructivism + embodied cognition = enactivism: theoretical and practical implications for conceptual change.* In *AERA 2010 Conference.*

[54] Bruce D Homer, Charles K Kinzer, Jan L Plass, Susan M Letourneau, Dan Hoffman, Meagan Bromley, Elizabeth O Hayward, Selen Turkay, and Yolanta Kornak. 2014. Moved to learn: The effects of interactivity in a Kinect-based literacy game for beginning readers. *Computers & Education* 74 (2014), 37–49.

[55] Eva Hornecker and Jacob Buur. 2006. *Getting a grip on tangible interaction: A framework on physical space and social interaction.* In *Proceedings of the SIGCHI Conference on Human Factors in Computing Systems.* ACM, 437–446.

[56] Mark Howison, Dragan Trninic, Daniel Reinholz, and Dor Abrahamson. 2011. *The mathematical imagery trainer: From Embodied Interaction to Conceptual Learning.* In *Proceedings of the 2011 annual conference on Human factors in computing systems - CHI'11.*

[57] Caroline Hummels and Jelle Van Dijk. 2015. *Seven principles to design for embodied sensemaking.* In *Proceedings of the Ninth International Conference on Tangible, Embedded, and Embodied Interaction.* ACM, 21–28.

[58] Jörn Hurtienne. 2009. Image schemas and design for intuitive use.

[59] José de Jesús, Luis González Ibánez and Alf Inge Wang. 2015. Learning recycling from playing a kinect game. *International Journal of Game-Based Learning (IJGBL)* 5, 3, 25–44.

[60] Thea Ionescu and Dermina Vasc. 2014. Embodied cognition: challenges for psychology and education. *Procedia-Social and Behavioral Sciences* 128 (2014), 275–280.

[61] Hiroshi Ishii. 2008. *Tangible bits: Beyond pixels.* In *Proceedings of the 2nd international conference on Tangible and Embedded Intreaction (TEI'08).*

[62] Mark Johnson. 2013. *The Body in the Mind: The Bodily Basis of Meaning, Imagination, and Reason.* University of Chicago Press.

[63] Mina C Johnson-Glenberg, David A Birchfield, Lisa Tolentino, and Tatyana Koziupa. 2014. Collaborative embodied learning in mixed reality motion-capture environments: Two science studies. *Journal of Educational Psychology* 106, 1 (2014), 86.

[64] E Kain. 2016. Pokémon Go'is the biggest mobile game in US history-And it's about to top snapchat. (2016). https://www.forbes.com/sites/erikkain/2016/07/13/pokemon-go-is-the-biggest-mobile-game-in-us-history-and-its-about-to-top-snapchat/

[65] Fengfeng Ke and Peter Carafano. 2016. Collaborative science learning in an immersive flight simulation. *Computers & Education* 103 (2016), 114–123.

[66] Joseph R. Keebler, Travis J. Wiltshire, Dustin C. Smith, and Stephen M. Fiore. 2013. Picking up STEAM: Educational implications for teaching with an augmented reality guitar learning system. Lecture Notes in Computer Science (including subseries Lecture Notes in Artificial Intelligence and Lecture Notes in Bioinformatics) 8022 LNCS, *PART* 2 (2013), 170–178.

[67] A Kelliher, D Birchfield, E Campana, S Hatton, M Johnson-Glenberg, C Martinez, L Olson, P Savvides, L Tolentino, K Phillips, and S Uysal. 2009. *Smallab: A mixed-reality environment for embodied and mediated learning.* In *MM'09 - Proceedings of the 2009 ACM Multimedia Conference, with Co-located Workshops and Symposiums.* 1029–1031.

[68] Lora Kolodny. 2016. *Osmo raises $24 million from Sesame, Mattel and other big names in toys and education.* (2016). https://techcrunch.com/2016/12/08/osmo-raises-24-million-from-sesame-mattel-and-other-big-names-in-toys-and-education/

[69] Maria Kourakli, Ioannis Altanis, Symeon Retalis, Michail Boloudakis, Dimitrios Zbainos, and Katerina Antonopoulou. 2017. Towards the improvement of the cognitive, motoric and academic skills of students with special educational needs using Kinect learning games. *International Journal of Child-Computer Interaction* 11 (2017), 28–39.

[70] Vishesh Kumar, Tuhina Dargan, Utkarsh Dwivedi, and Poorvi Vijay. 2015. *Note code – A tangible music programming puzzle tool.* In *Proceedings of the 10th International Conference on Tangible, Embedded, and Embodied Interaction - TEI'15.* 625–629.

[71] Hideaki Kuzuoka, Naomi Yamashita, Hiroshi Kato, Hideyuki Suzuki, and Yoshihiko Kubota. 2014. *Tangible earth: Tangible learning environment for astronomy education.* In *Proceedings of the Second International Conference on Human-Agent Interaction.* 23–27.

[72] Sonya S Kwak, Yunkyung Kim, Eunho Kim, Christine Shin, and Kwangsu Cho. 2013. *What makes people empathize with an emotional robot?: The impact of agency and physical embodiment on human empathy for a robot.* In *2013 IEEE RO-MAN.* IEEE, 180–185.

[73] Chronis Kynigos, Zacharoula Smyrnaiou, and Maria Roussou. 2010. *Exploring rules and underlying concepts while engaged with collaborative full-body games.* In *Proceedings of the 9th International Conference on Interaction Design and Children.* 222.

[74] Byron Lahey, Winslow Burleson, Camilla Nørgaard Jensen, Natalie Freed, and Patrick Lu. 2008. *Integrating video games and robotic play in physical environments.* In *Proceedings of the 2008 ACM SIGGRAPH Symposium on Video Games - Sandbox'08,* Vol. 1. 107.

[75] George Lakoff and Mark Johnson. 2008. *Metaphors We Live Bby.* University of Chicago press.

[76] Joanne Leong, Florian Perteneder, Hans-Christian Jetter, and Michael Haller. 2017. What a life!: Building a framework for constructive assemblies. *In Proceedings of the Tenth International Conference on Tangible, Embedded, and Embodied Interaction.* ACM, 57–66.

[77] Qing Li. 2012. Understanding enactivism: a study of affordances and constraints of engaging practicing teachers as digital game designers. *Educational Technology Research and Development* 60, 5, 785–806. http://link.springer.com/10.1007/s11423-012-9255-4

[78] William Lidwell and Gerry Manacsa. 2011. *Deconstructing Product Design: Exploring the Form, Function, Usability, Sustainability, and Commercial Success of 100 Amazing Products.* Rockport Pub.

[79] Robb Lindgren and J Michael Moshell. 2011. *Supporting children's learning with body-based metaphors in a mixed reality environment.* In *Proceedings of the 10th International Conference on Interaction Design and Children - IDC'11,* Vol. Ann Arbor. 177–180.

[80] Robb Lindgren, Michael Tscholl, and J Michael Moshell. 2013. *MEteor: Developing physics concepts through body- based interaction with a mixed reality simulation.* In *Physics Education Research Conference - PERC'13.* 217–220.

[81] Robb Lindgren, Michael Tscholl, Shuai Wang, and Emily Johnson. 2016. Enhancing learning and engagement through embodied interaction within a mixed reality simulation. *Computers & Education* 95 (2016), 174–187.

[82] Leilah Lyons. 2014. *Exhibiting data: Using body-as-interface designs to engage visitors with data visualizations.* In *Learning Technologies and the Body: Integration and Implementation in Formal and Informal Learning Environments.* Taylor & Francis Group

[83] Leilah Lyons, Brenda Lopez Silva, Tom Moher, Priscilla Jimenez Pazmino, and Brian Slattery. 2013. *Feel the burn: Exploring design parameters for effortful interaction for educational games.* In *Proceedings of the 12th International Conference on Interaction Design and Children- IDC'13.* 400–403.

[84] Anna Macaranas, Alissa N Antle, and Bernhard E Riecke. 2015. What is intuitive interaction? balancing users' performance and satisfaction with natural user interfaces. *Interacting with Computers* 27, 3 (2015), 357–370.

[85] Peter Malcolm, Tom Moher, Darshan Bhatt, Brian Uphoff, and Brenda López-Silva. 2008. *Embodying scientific concepts in the physical space of the classroom.* In *Proceedings of the 7th International Conference on Interaction Design and Children.* 234–241.

[86] Laura Malinverni, Julian Maya, Marie-Monique Schaper, and Narcis Pares. 2017. *The World-as-Support: Embodied exploration, understanding and meaning-making of the augmented world.* In *Proceedings of the 2017 CHI Conference on Human Factors in Computing Systems.* ACM, 5132–5144.

[87] Laura Malinverni, Brenda López Silva, and Narcís Parés. 2012. *Impact of embodied interaction on learning processes: design and analysis of an educational application based on physical activity.* In *Proceedings of the 11th International Conference on Interaction Design and Children.* ACM, 60–69.

[88] Paul Marshall. 2007. *Do tangible interfaces enhance learning?.* In *Proceedings Of The 1st International Conference on Tangible and Embedded Interaction.* ACM, 163–170.

[89] Paul Marshall, Alissa Antle, Elise Van Den Hoven, and Yvonne Rogers. 2013. Introduction to the special issue on the theory and practice of embodied interaction in HCI and interaction design. *ACM Transactions on Computer-Human Interaction (TOCHI)* 20, 1, 1.

[90] Paul Marshall, Sara Price, and Yvonne Rogers. 2003. *Conceptualising tangibles to support learning.* In *IDC '03: Proceedings of the 2003 Conference on Interaction Design and Children.* 101–109.

[91] Ali Mazalek, Sanjay Chandrasekharan, Michael Nitsche, Tim Welsh, Paul Clifton, Andrew Quitmeyer, Firaz Peer, Friedrich Kirschner, and Dilip Athreya. 2011. *I'm in the Game : Embodied Puppet Interface Improves Avatar Control.* In *Proceedings of the Fifth International Conference on Tangible, Embedded, and Embodied Interaction - Tei'11.* 129–136.

[92] Edward Melcer and Katherine Isbister. 2016. *Bridging the physical divide: a design framework for embodied learning games and simulations.* In *Proceedings of the 2016 CHI Conference on Human Factors in Computing Systems.* doi:http://dx.doi.org/10.1145/2851581.2892455.

[93] Edward F Melcer, Victoria Hollis, and Katherine Isbister. 2017. *Tangibles vs. mouse in educational programming games: Influences on enjoyment and self-beliefs.* In *CHI'17 Extended Abstracts.* ACM, Denver, CO, USA.

[94] Edward F Melcer and Katherine Isbister. 2016. *Bridging the physical learning divides: A design framework for embodied learning games and simulations.* In *Proceedings of the 1st International Joint Conference of DiGRA and FDG.*

[95] Edward F Melcer and Katherine Isbister. 2018. *Bots & (Main)Frames: Exploring the impact of tangible blocks and collaborative play in an educational programming game.* In *Proceedings of the 2018 CHI Conference on Human Factors in Computing Systems.* ACM, Montreal, QC, Canada.

[96] Jason Mickelson and Wendy Ju. 2011. *Math propulsion: Engaging math learners through embodied performance & visualization.* In *Proceedings of the Fifth International Conference on Tangible, Embedded, and Embodied Interaction - TEI'11.* 101.

[97] Tom Moher, Syeda Hussain, Tim Halter, and Debi Kilb. 2005. *Roomquake: Embedding dynamic phenomena within the physical space of an elementary school classroom.* In *Proceedings of ACM CHI 2005 Conference on Human Factors in Computing Systems,* Vol. 2. 1665–1668.

[98] Joan Mora-Guiard, Ciera Crowell, Narcis Pares, and Pamela Heaton. 2017. Sparking social initiation behaviors in children with Autism through full-body Interaction. *International Journal of Child-Computer Interaction* 11 (2017), 62–71.

[99] J MoraGuiard and Narcis Pares. 2014. *Child as the measure of all things: The body as a referent in designing a museum exhibit to understand the nanoscale.* In *IDC'14.*

[100] Tomohiro Nakayama, Takayuki Adachi, Keita Muratsu, Hiroshi Mizoguchi, Miki Namatame, Masanori Sugimoto, Fusako Kusunoki, Etsuji Yamaguchi, Shigenori Inagaki, and Yoshiaki Takeda. 2014. *Human SUGOROKU: Learning support system of vegetation succession with full-body interaction interface.* In *Proceedings of the SIGCHI Conference on Human Factors in Computing Systems (CHI'14).* 2227–2232.

[101] Luc Nijs and Marc Leman. 2014. Interactive technologies in the instrumental music classroom: A longitudinal study with the Music Paint Machine. *Computers & Education* 73 (2014), 40–59.

[102] Luc Nijs, Bart Moens, Micheline Lesaffre, and Marc Leman. 2012. The Music Paint Machine: stimulating self-monitoring through the generation of creative visual output using a technology-enhanced learning tool. *Journal of New Music Research* 41, 1, 79–101.

[103] Francesco Novellis and Tom Moher. 2011. *How real is 'real enough'? designing artifacts and procedures for embodied simulations of science practices.* In *Proceedings of the 10th International Conference on Interaction Design and Children.* 90–98.

[104] C. O'Malley and S. Fraser. 2004. Literature review in learning with tangible technologies. Technical Report. 1–52 pages.

[105] Felicia Clare Paul, Christabel Goh, and Kelly Yap. 2015. *Get creative with learning: Word out! a full body interactive game.* In *Proceedings of the 33rd Annual ACM Conference Extended Abstracts on Human Factors in Computing Systems - CHI EA'15.*

[106] Anna Petrasova, Brendan Harmon, Vaclav Petras, and Helena Mitasova. 2014. *GIS-based environmental modeling with tangible interaction and dynamic visualization.* In *Proceedings of the 7th International Congress on Environmental Modelling and Software,* San Diego, CA, USA. 15–19.

[107] Catherine Plaisant, David Carr, and Ben Shneiderman. 1995. Image-browser taxonomy and guidelines for designers. *IEEE Software* 12, 2, 21–32. doi:http://dx.doi.org/10.1109/52.368260

[108] Jan L. Plass, Roxana Moreno, and Roland Brünken. 2010. *Cognitive Load Theory.* Cambridge University Press.

[109] Jan L. Plass, Paul A. O'Keefe, Bruce D. Homer, Jennifer Case, Elizabeth O. Hayward, Murphy Stein, and Ken Perlin. 2013. The impact of individual, competitive, and collaborative mathematics game play on learning, performance, and motivation. *Journal of Educational Psychology* 105, 4, 1050–1066.

[110] Wim TJL Pouw, Tamara Van Gog, and Fred Paas. 2014. An embedded and embodied cognition review of instructional manipulatives. *Educational Psychology Review* 26, 1, 51–72.

[111] Blaine A. Price, Ronald M. Baecker, and Ian S. Small. 1993. A principled taxonomy of software visualization. *Journal of Visual Languages & Computing* 4, 3, 211–266. doi:http://dx.doi.org/10.1006/jvlc.1993.1015

[112] Sara Price. 2008. *A representation approach to conceptualizing tangible learning environments.* In *Proceedings of the 2nd international conference on Tangible and embedded interaction TEI 08.* 151. doi:http://dx.doi.org/10.1145/1347390.1347425

[113] Sara Price, Taciana Pontual Falcão, Jennifer G Sheridan, and George Roussos. 2009. *The effect of representation location on interaction in a tangible learning environment.* In *Proceedings of the 3rd International Conference on Tangible and Embedded Interaction.* ACM, 85–92.

[114] Sara Price and Carey Jewitt. 2013. *A multimodal approach to examining 'embodiment' in tangible learning environments.* In *Proceedings of the 7th International Conference on Tangible, Embedded and Embodied Interaction.* ACM, 43–50.

[115] Sara Price, Yvonne Rogers, M. Scaife, D. Stanton, and H. Neale. 2003. Using tangibles to promote novel forms of playful learning. *Interacting with Computers* 15, 2 (2003), 169–185.

[116] Sara Price, Jennifer G Sheridan, Taciana Pontual Falcao, and George Roussos. 2008. Towards a framework for investigating tangible environments for learning. *International Journal of Arts and Technology* 1, 3–4, 351–368.

[117] Mónica Rikić. 2013. *Buildasound.* In *Proceedings of the 7th International Conference on Tangible, Embedded, and Embodied Interaction - TEI '13.* 395–396.

[118] Jessica Roberts and Leilah Lyons. 2017. The value of learning talk: applying a novel dialogue scoring method to inform interaction design in an open-ended, embodied museum exhibit. *International Journal of Computer-Supported Collaborative Learning* 12, 4, 343–376.

[119] Warren Robinett. 1992. Synthetic Experience: A Taxonomy, Survey of Earlier Thought, and Speculations on the Future. Technical Report. 1–30 pages.

[120] Yvonne Rogers and Henk Muller. 2006. A framework for designing sensor-based interactions to promote exploration and reflection in play. *International Journal of Human-Computer Studies* 64, 1, 1–14.

[121] Yvonne Rogers, Mike Scaife, Silvia Gabrielli, Hilary Smith, and Eric Harris. 2002. A conceptual framework for mixed reality environments: Designing novel learning activities for young children. *Presence* 11, 6, 677–686.

[122] Tim Rohrer. 2007. *The body in space: Dimensions of embodiment.* In *Body, Language and Mind.* 339–378.

[123] Michael Saenz, Joshua Strunk, Sharon Lynn Chu, and Jinsil Hwaryoung Seo. 2015. *Touch wire: Interactive tangible electricity game for kids.* In *Proceedings of the 9th International Conference on Tangible, Embedded, and Embodied Interaction-TEI '15.* 655–659.

[124] Paul Schermerhorn and Matthias Scheutz. 2011. *Disentangling the effects of robot affect, embodiment, and autonomy on human team members in a mixed-initiative task.* In *Proceedings from the International Conference on Advances in Computer-Human Interactions.* Citeseer, 236–241.

[125] Eric Schweikardt and Md Gross. 2008. *The robot is the program: interacting with Ro blocks.* In *Proceedings of the Second International Conference on Tangible, Embedded, and Embodied Interaction - Tei '08.* 167–168.

[126] Elena Márquez Segura, Michael Kriegel, Ruth Aylett, Amol Deshmukh, and Henriette Cramer. 2012. *How do you like me in this: user embodiment preferences for companion agents*. In *International Conference on Intelligent Virtual Agents*. Springer, 112–125.

[127] Orit Shaer, Nancy Leland, Eduardo H Calvillo-Gamez, and Robert J K Jacob. 2004. The TAC paradigm: specifying tangible user interfaces. *Personal and Ubiquitous Computing* 8, 5 (2004), 359–369.

[128] Lawrence Shapiro. 2010. *Embodied Cognition*. Routledge.

[129] Tia Shelley, Leilah Lyons, Moira Zellner, and Emily Minor. 2011. *Evaluating the embodiment benefits of a paper-based tui for spatially sensitive simulations*. In *Extended Abstracts of the 2011 Conference on Human Factors in Computing Systems*. 1375.

[130] Alexander Skulmowski, Simon Pradel, Tom Kühnert, Guido Brunnett, and Günter Daniel Rey. 2016. Embodied learning using a tangible user interface: The effects of haptic perception and selective pointing on a spatial learning task. *Computers & Education* 92–93 (2016), 64–75.

[131] Alexander Skulmowski and Günter Daniel Rey. 2018. Embodied learning: introducing a taxonomy based on bodily engagement and task integration. *Cognitive Research: Principles and Implications* 3, 1, 6.

[132] Tess Speelpenning, Alissa N Antle, Tanja Doering, and Elise Van Den Hoven. 2011. *Exploring how tangible tools enable collaboration in a multi-touch tabletop game*. In *IFIP Conference on Human-Computer Interaction*. Springer, 605–621.

[133] Jürgen Streeck, Charles Goodwin, and Curtis LeBaron. 2011. Embodied interaction: Language and body in the material world. *Embodied Interaction Language and Body in the Material World* (2011), 1–28. http://books.google.com/books?id=vJlSewAACAAJ

[134] Lucy A Suchman. 1987. *Plans and Situated Actions: The Problem of Human-Machine Communication*. Cambridge University Press.

[135] Mike Tissenbaum, Matthew Berland, and Leilah Lyons. 2017. DCLM framework: Understanding collaboration in open-ended tabletop learning environments. *International Journal of Computer-Supported Collaborative Learning* 12, 1, 35–64.

[136] Lisa Tolentino, Philippos Savvides, and David Birchfield. 2010. *Applying game design principles to social skills learning for students in special education*. In *Proceedings of FDG '10*.

[137] Joshua Wainer, David J Feil-Seifer, Dylan A Shell, and Maja J Mataric. 2006. *The role of physical embodiment in human-robot interaction*. In *The 15th IEEE International Symposium on Robot and Human Interactive Communication, 2006*. IEEE, 117–122.

[138] Michael L Walters, Kheng Lee Koay, Dag Sverre Syrdal, Kerstin Dautenhahn, and René Te Boekhorst. 2009. *Preferences and perceptions of robot appearance and embodiment in human-robot interaction trials*. In *Proceedings of New Frontiers in Human-Robot Interaction*.

[139] Chun-wang Wei, Hsin-hung Chen, and Nian-shing Chen. 2015. *Effects of embodiment-based learning on perceived cooperation process and social flow*. In *7th World Conference on Educational Sciences*. Elsevier B.V., 608–613.

[140] Michael Wheeler. 2005. *Reconstructing the Cognitive World: The Next Step*. MIT press.

[141] Andrew D Wilson and Sabrina Golonka. 2013. Embodied cognition is not what you think it is. *Frontiers in Psychology* 4 (2013), 58.

[142] Margaret Wilson. 2002. Six views of embodied cognition. *Psychonomic Bulletin & Review* 9, 4, 625–636.

[143] Terry Winograd, Fernando Flores, *and Fernando F Flores*. 1986. *Understanding Computers and Cognition: A New Foundation for Design*. Intellect Books.

[144] Alyssa Friend Wise, Alissa Nicole Antle, Jillian Warren, Aaron May, Min Fan, and Anna Macaranas. 2015. What kind of world do you want to live in? positive interdependence and collaborative processes in the tangible tabletop land-use planning game youtopia. *International Society of the Learning Sciences, Inc.[ISLS]*.

[145] Peta Wyeth. 2008. How young children learn to program with sensor, action, and logic blocks. *Journal of the Learning Sciences* 17, 4, 517–550.

[146] Peta Wyeth and Helen C. Purchase. 2002. *Tangible programming elements for young children*. In *CHI '02 extended abstracts on Human factors in computing systems - CHI '02*. 774.

[147] Xiao Xiao, Paula Aguilera, Jonathan Williams, and Hiroshi Ishii. 2013. *MirrorFugue iii: Conjuring the recorded pianist*. In *Extended Abstracts of the 2013 CHI Conference on Human Factors in Computing Systems*. 2891–2892.

[148] Xiao Xiao and Hiroshi Ishii. 2016. *Inspect, embody, invent: A design framework for music learning and beyond*. In *Proceedings of the 2016 CHI Conference on Human Factors in Computing Systems*. ACM, 5397–5408.

[149] Nesra Yannier, Scott E Hudson, Eliane Stampfer Wiese, and Kenneth R Koedinger. 2016. Adding Physicality to an Interactive Game Improves Learning and Enjoyment : Evidence from Earthshake. *ACM Transactions on Computer-Human Interaction (TOCHI)* 23, 4, 1–31.

[150] Nesra Yannier, Kenneth R. Koedinger, and Scott E. Hudson. 2013. Tangible collaborative learning with a mixed-reality game: Earthshake. *Artificial Intelligence in Education* (2013).

[151] Nesra Yannier, Kenneth R. Koedinger, and Scott E. Hudson. 2015. *Learning from mixed-reality games: Is shaking a tablet as effective as physical observation? CHI'15*.

[152] Kelly Yap, Clement Zheng, Angela Tay, Ching-Chiuan Yen, and Ellen Yi-Luen Do. 2015. *Word out! learning the alphabet through full body interactions*. In *Proceedings of the 6th Augmented Human International Conference on - AH'15*. 101–108.

[153] Ryuichi Yoshida, Hiroshi Mizoguchi, Ryohei Egusa, Machi Saito, Miki Namatame, Masanori Sugimoto, Fusako Kusunoki, Etsuji Yamaguchi, Shigenori Inagaki, and Yoshiaki Takeda. 2015. *BESIDE: Body experience and sense of immersion in digital paleontological environment*. In *Proceedings of CHI'15*. 1283–1288.

[154] Tom Ziemke. 2002. *What's that thing called embodiment?*. In *Proceedings of the 25th Annual Meeting of the Cognitive Science Society*. 1305–1310.

8 Using Ideation Cards for Designing Mixed Reality Games

Richard Wetzel

Lucerne University of Applied Sciences and Arts

Steve Benford and Tom Rodden

University of Nottingham

CONTENTS

8.1 THE CHALLENGE: DESIGNING MIXED REALITY GAMES

Mixed reality games combine the physical reality with virtual elements. This might be done in the form of Augmented Reality as defined by Milgram and Kishino [31] where 3D objects are overlaid onto the environment either with a headset as in ARQuake [44] or a live camera feed like in Pokémon Go [36]. Alternative forms of mixed reality that do not rely on 3D imaging include Geocaching [18] as an example for location-based games and various other forms of games such as technology-supported escape games [37], live-action roleplaying experiences [23], board games [7], and a whole other range of technology-supported games. They all have in common that they use technology and the real world around us to create compelling new gaming experiences that would otherwise not be possible. By tracking player movement in real time, arriving (or leaving) a physical location can be used as a trigger for digitally presented game content. A game might play differently depending on current weather conditions [17]. City-wide performances change how players perceive their surroundings [6]. At the same time, combining technology with the real world introduces a whole new set of challenges. Spectators or bystanders might interfere or influence the game. Technologies like GPS and mobile data connectivity are unreliable and often imprecise or faulty – a flaw that can be mitigated by seamful design [12]. Mixed reality games combine the design space of physical games and digital games and extend it with their own particular opportunities and challenges. Game designers need to understand technical possibilities and restrictions that enable these new forms of gaming. Likewise, if the game is created for a specific location, the history and stories of this place play an important role as well. This is why mixed reality games are often designed in teams with different areas of expertise: game designers, technologists, and domain experts. The diversity of these teams makes it difficult for them to communicate effectively as they do not necessarily share the same understanding of mixed reality games.

What is needed to facilitate collaborative design sessions in a multidisciplinary domain such as mixed reality games? For us, the following requirements seemed to be most crucial if we wanted to develop a successful tool (or method):

1. Provide design knowledge about mixed reality games
2. Make this design knowledge easily and intuitively accessible
3. Allow collaboration between diverse co-designers (different areas of expertise, different levels of expertise)
4. Inspire new and innovative ideas
5. Turn initial ideas into fleshed-out designs

There are certainly various options to fulfill some of these requirements. For example, utilizing a design patterns approach (either prescriptive [1] or descriptive [8]) would certainly satisfy requirements 1) and 5), and also perhaps 4), due to their encyclopedic nature. However, design patterns are problematic to access and difficult to use during a dynamic design session. Therefore, we looked further and ultimately identified ideation cards as the most suitable tool for our purpose.

In this chapter we will discuss how such a challenging design process can be facilitated with ideation cards. We created our Mixed Reality Game Cards (Figure 8.1) to support experts and inexperienced designers alike in collaboratively generating ideas for mixed reality games and then developing them further to fully-fledged ideas. We take a detailed look at the Mixed Reality Game Cards, their content, and the rules. This is followed by an in-depth look at qualities that illustrate why ideation cards work so well as a design process. We explicitly talk about how randomness and restrictions help designers coming up with creative and new ideas, and how this is further supported by domain-extrinsic Theme Cards from the card game Dixit [40]. We also unpack the roles that the three specific types of cards that make up the Mixed Reality Game Cards play: How Opportunity Cards are the building blocks of an idea, how Question Cards streamline and expand an idea, and lastly how Challenge Cards facilitate the grounding of ideas.

8.2   IDEATION CARDS AS DESIGN TOOLS

As the name suggests, ideation cards are playing cards that are used to mediate ideation sessions. The cards in a deck typically convey certain aspects of the design space under investigation and they allow designers to have a tangible representation of their idea. Perhaps the most prominent example are the IDEO Method Cards [22] that are a card-based collection of design methods but do not convey any design knowledge themselves. Instead, they are used to choose a design approach for a session. In that sense they have a very different purpose to the other ideation cards discussed in this section.

Ideation cards are much more dynamic than design patterns as they share the same affordance as playing cards: They can be shuffled, played on a table, arranged in groups, rearranged, discarded. Brandt and Messeter [10] place them in the category of design games which allow users to playfully collaborate in the design process. This way, ideation cards not only actively shape and support the design process, but they are an integral part of it [19]. This is achieved not only by the cards themselves

FIGURE 8.1   The Mixed Reality Game Cards.

but also by prescribing rules that then guide the resulting interaction. Ideation cards enable collaborative design with cards being used as orienting devices, conversation starters, and pace-makers [20].

Ideation cards have been developed for a variety of domains, both in academic and professional contexts. They typically have in common that they are of playing card size and each single card focuses on a specific concept. Often, this concept is conveyed via a short phrase and an evocative image. Some card decks also feature a longer explanation and perhaps one or more examples how the concept could be applied. Quite a few different ideation card decks exist across a multitude of domains. For some further reading, we recommend the work by Wölfel and Merritt [48] who have conducted a survey of 18 card-based design tools. They classified the decks according to five dimensions: purpose and scope, duration, system, customization, and formal qualities. From this they identified three broad categories of ideation cards: general purpose/repository cards, customizable cards, and context specific cards. In the following we will give a brief overview of ideation card decks that were influential for the design of the Mixed Reality Game Cards. One important quality of these ideation decks is whether they are used for rapid idea generation (such as VNA Cards and PLEX Cards) or to fully develop an idea (as is the case with the Deck of Lenses, the Tangible Interaction Framework Cards, and Exertion Cards).

8.2.1   VNA Cards

Kultima et al. have developed the VNA Cards [26]. VNA stands for Verb, Adjective, Noun which directly describes the type of cards found in the deck (Figure 8.2). There are 80 verbs, 80 nouns, and 80 adjectives. Each of the 240 cards contains exactly one of these words and nothing else. The words are derived from an analysis of 40 digital

FIGURE 8.2 VNA Cards examples: Bounce, Match, People, Instrument, Spooky, and Falling.

and non-digital games. Examples for verbs are bounce, dig, confuse, and bluff; nouns contain words like snake, street, furniture, and nation; and adjectives could be tricky, messy, wooden, and homelike. Using the cards is rather straightforward. The first person draws a verb card and describes a game idea that comes into mind. A second person then draws a noun and extends the idea. Finally, a third person reveals an adjective and uses it to finalize the game idea. Then a new round starts with a different initiator. VNA is used to generate short ideas for games and not fully developed designs. The following is an example idea for a game (Fish mania) that was generated by using VNA Cards [27]: *Player controls fish and his task is to collect a shoal of similar fish and exit the area before it gets too polluted by a ship. There are also predators present which are threat to the player and his shoal.*

8.2.2 PLEX CARDS

Lucero and Arrasvuori have designed PLEX Cards [30] based on a framework for playful experiences [25]. The deck consists of 22 cards each referring to a different category of playful experiences such as captivation, discovery, fellowship, humor, or sensation (Figure 8.3). The cards contain a title and a short one-line explanation of the concept as well as two images illustrating it. Lucero and Arrasvuori describe two ways of using the cards: PLEX Brainstorming and PLEX Scenario, both designed for two participants. PLEX Brainstorming follows a similar approach to VNA. However, the second and third cards are not revealed randomly but instead both participants choose these from their hand of three previously drawn cards. In PLEX Scenario,

FIGURE 8.3   PLEX Cards examples: Humor, Nurture, and Fantasy.

three cards are randomly revealed at the same time. Participants then have to place them on a paper template divided into the following three areas:

Card 1: Beginning. Who are the people in the story? How does this category launch the story?
Card 2: Continuation. How does this category cause the story to continue in a new direction?
Card 3: The End. How does this category bring the story to closure?

8.2.3 DECK OF LENSES

The 113 cards of the Deck of Lenses [41] are commercially available to supplement the book "The Art of Game Design: A book of lenses" [42]. The approach of both book and deck is to provide various different perspectives (lenses) on game design and confront the reader with them in the form of questions (Figure 8.4). One example from the deck is "The Lens of Technology" which is presented as follows: *To make sure you are using the right technologies in the right way, ask yourself these questions: What technologies will help deliver the experience I want to create? Am I using these technologies in ways that are foundational or decorational? If I'm not using them foundationally, should I be using them at all? Is this technology as cool as I think? Is there a "disruptive technology" I should consider instead?"* Examples for other lenses are venue, surprise, challenge, cooperation, balance, juiciness, atmosphere, and playtesting. Each of these lenses is also illustrated with an image. The cards support designers who already have an initial idea to focus on it and develop it further, proofing it against the different lenses.

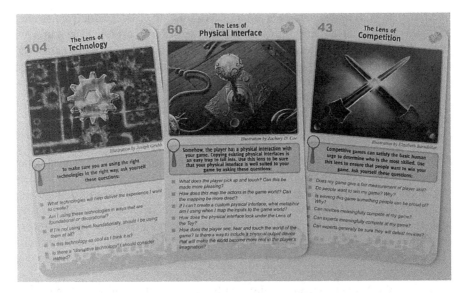

FIGURE 8.4 Deck of lenses examples: The Lens of Technology, The Lens of Physical Interface, and The Lens of Competition.

8.2.4 TANGIBLE INTERACTION FRAMEWORK CARDS

Hornecker [20] has converted a framework for tangible interaction [21] into a deck of ideation cards, the Tangible Interaction Framework Cards. There is a total of 26 cards divided into four categories: tangible manipulation, spatial interaction, embodied facilitation, and expressive representation. Each card features an image, one or two questions, and a subcategory (Figure 8.5). The cards are color-coded and contain an image as well as a reflective question such as *"Can users experience the interaction straight away, from the start?"*, *"Is there a physical focus that draws the group together?"*, or *"Are physical and digital representations of similar strength? Can*

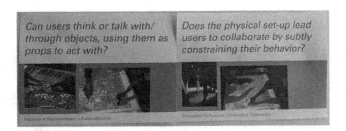

FIGURE 8.5 Tangible Interaction Framework Cards examples: Externalization and Embodied Constraints.

they augment and complement each other?". For using the cards, participants gather having a concrete idea, design, or theme that they want to explore. The cards are shuffled and handed out to participants. They then take turns playing cards and explaining whether and why they deem them as relevant or irrelevant for the design at hand. The group negotiates the final verdict on the card and will often end up clustering them into "very relevant cards", "somewhat related" and "irrelevant ones".

8.2.5 Exertion Cards

Müller et al. have created the Exertion Cards [34] that are also based on an existing framework. The Exertion Framework [33] explores the role of the body and interactive technologies in exertion experiences. The deck consists of 14 cards divided into four categories: *"The Responding Body (how the body's internal state changes over time as a result of exertion, e.g. heart rate);" "The Moving Body (how body parts are muscularly repositioned relative to one another);" "The Sensing Body (how the body is sensing and experiencing the world);"* and *"The Relating Body (how bodies and people relate to one another)."*

Each card consists of a main question, a title, and a "dimension" (Figure 8.6). The dimension allows designers to place their answers within a spectrum. Each end of the spectrum is represented by an image and a brief positive example. The card Exhaustion Management, for example, features the question *"To what extent is managing exhaustion part of the game?"* with the two opposing ends being *"Allows breaks for socializing and tactics negotiation"* and *"Focus on fitness, less on tactics."*

8.2.6 Sound Design in Games Deck

Alves and Roque have developed the Sound Design in Games Deck [3]. It is based on a design pattern language [2] and contains 77 double-sided cards (Figure 8.7). Each card summarizes a different pattern. One side of the card shows the title and three to four screenshots from games as example uses. The other side of the card repeats the title and gives a short explanation. It also puts the card in context within the pattern language noting how other cards relate to it. The card Diegetic Music, for

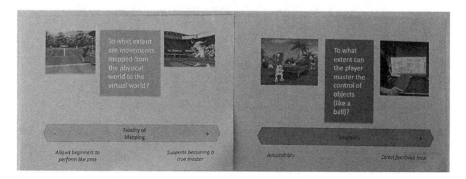

FIGURE 8.6   Exertion Cards examples: Fidelity of Mapping and Tangibility.

FIGURE 8.7   Sound Design in Games Deck examples, front and back: Sound Visualization, In-game Feedback.

example, is explained as *Music happening in the game world* with the following connections to other patterns:

Context: Narrative, Emotional Script

May relate to: Contextual Music and Musical Outcome

May use: Radio

Makes use of: Music and Acoustic Ecology

8.3   MIXED REALITY GAME CARDS

As we have seen in the previous section, ideation cards have been used in a variety of context. Some of them (e.g., VNA Cards) do not directly encapsulate design knowledge but instead provide (hopefully) inspirational stimuli. In our case however it was crucial for the cards to provide such support to the creators. Furthermore, we also wanted to both support the initial idea generation and a more in-depth idea development process. The cards should be inspiring like the VNA Cards and at the same time prompt rich discussion as the Tangible Interaction Framework Cards. Early on in the development process it became clear that this design goal was only achievable by creating different cards for different purposes that together would form the Mixed Reality Game Cards. Namely, we employ the following types of cards: Opportunity Cards, Question Cards, Challenge Cards, and Theme Cards.

Opportunity Cards showcase elements that a game might be built around, such as the sensors that are being used for tracking or the mode of play. These are the building blocks of an idea, and by combining them in different combinations different games can be modeled. We use Opportunity Cards in the first phase of the ideation process to generate an initial idea consisting of just a few cards. Later on, they can also be used to extend an existing idea to add or modify features or change the set-up of the game completely. The chosen Opportunity Cards represent the game idea. These cards are most similar to the cards found in the Sound Design in Games deck.

Question Cards on the other hand are more generic. As the name suggests, they pose questions at the designers which they might not have considered before. Some might require the designers to define the core concept behind the idea, others prompt them to envision the game in a different environment, and how this would change the game experience. Like the Exertion Cards or the Deck of Lenses, these cards are used when an idea already exists and not only ask the designers to further define details but also to create a coherent and strong vision.

Challenge Cards are the last type of cards used toward the end of the design process. These cards confront the designers with common (or less common) problems that can arise in mixed reality games. Examples include adverse weather conditions (including sunshine!) and how the game might cope with them, but also problems like too many players physically at the same location or general safety issues. These cards take on the role of a devil's advocate, again providing pointers for discussing the broad as well as fine details of the design.

Theme Cards are additional cards that are not specific to mixed reality or games. Instead, they are purely there to provide additional inspiration and theme for a group of designers. While we could have created these cards ourselves (and also experimented with this) we ultimately decided to use cards from the card game Dixit which we found to work extremely well for our purposes. These cards show rich surreal paintings and lend themselves to a variety of interpretations.

Throughout the process of creating the individual cards it quickly became obvious that it would be impossible to identify all aspects relevant for the design of these games. Subsequently, we were sure that our deck could never be 100% complete. For this reason, we also added blank cards to the deck. These are cards of each type that contain no information but are instead literally blank. Designers can use these to write down additional Opportunities, Questions, or Challenges that are not covered by the existing cards but are nonetheless seen as crucial for an idea. They can do this not only between sessions but also during a session – whenever they feel that a concept relevant for them is missing from the card deck.

As we developed the card deck iteratively, each iteration consisted of different (amounts of) cards. The final deck of the Mixed Reality Game Cards contains 93 unique cards: 51 Opportunity Cards, 18 Question Cards, and 24 Challenge Cards.

The cards are separated into different categories to both make them visually more appealing and more distinguishable. These categories are audio, gameplay, locations, management, physical, players, sensors, technology, and time.

The concept that each card embodies is represented by an ideally self-explanatory title, a short description, and an image as further illustration and inspiration. The first version of our cards was much more text-heavy. However, this led to interruptions in the sessions as participants had to spend extra time reading the cards – this was especially cumbersome every time a new card was played as then the whole group had to read it that very moment.

The cards printed on professional card stock are 8.9 x 6.4 cm (3.5 x 2.5 inches) in size. Figure 8.8 depicts a selection of cards from the final version of the Mixed Reality Game Cards. Some pictures in this chapter show the previous version with slightly different graphic design being the only notable difference.

FIGURE 8.8 Examples for Opportunity, Question, Challenge Cards, and Theme Cards taken from Dixit Odyssey.

8.3.1 CARD CREATION

In order to create the individual cards, we analyzed academic work about designing mixed reality games, existing mixed reality games, and also drew from our own personal experiences creating these games. This process was in part an intuitive design decision, and in part a systematic look at any concepts that these games and reports surfaced. The overall approach was very similar to how Björk and Holopainen [8] created their collection of design patterns. It is important to note that this activity continued throughout the whole process of developing the Mixed Reality Game Cards. As such we would often revisit games to investigate whether there were additional salient features that might be worth extracting as a card. Likewise, several cards were based on user comments or user-created cards from our studies. In the following, we will take a brief look at some of these games and sources while pointing out which cards are – at least in part – derived from them

Geocaching [35, 38] uses simple Passive Tracking via GPS. Everybody can participate in the Open Authoring and add caches to the game. The Main Mechanic of the game is really simple, and players generally enjoy the Exploration aspect. Because players can prepare by scouting the destination of caches on a map, they can avoid Bland Locations. Geocaching is only successful because it has reached Critical Mass.

Can You See Me Now? [5] combines Online Players with Actors on the street. The latter engage in Exergaming while the former are recruited Worldwide. The game utilizes Passive Tracking and Inaccurate Sensors as well as Unstable Connectivity where two of the most salient features they had to overcome.

Feeding Yoshi [4] and *Insectopia* [39] both make use of the Public Infrastructure and use Collecting as the Main Mechanic. The Duration of the game is infinite and the game can be played Worldwide.

Shhh! [29] and *Blowtooth* [24] play with the Real World Rules and are Subverting Locations by asking players to commit acts usually unacceptable at a library and airport. This contrast is the main source of Fun and Joy for the game.

TimeWarp [9] is an Augmented Reality game that uses Collaboration. Players engage with the Strong Narrative and have to succeed in Mini Games. The two players have Different Roles, and the game utilizes Fitting Locations matching the digital content. The Duration of the game was influenced by considerations concerning the Battery Life of the devices used. Locations were carefully placed to avoid Long Distances, Accidents, and Dynamic Places. A previously Confusing Interface and Unclear Instructions were improved for the final version of the game.

Tidy City [47] deliberately uses a very simple Main Mechanic in order to avoid Phone Zombies. The Core Concept of the game is to solve Riddles as part of a Scavenger Hunt. The game avoids Time Pressure to not turn it into an Unintended Race. Instead, the casual Exploration aspect of the game allows for Collaboration and Open Authoring, let's all players create their own missions. Missions need to take into account the Size of Area to not create Long Distances between game objects, and should be wary of Dynamic Places.

Pervasive Games – Theory and Design [32] was a rich source not only for Opportunity Cards but also for Challenge Cards as the authors give design advice on issues arising while staging a pervasive game.

Example cards include Scavenger Hunt; Roleplaying; Alternate Reality; Exergaming; Performative Play; Public Display; Exploration; Unusual Locations; Set Construction; Technical Artifacts; Worldwide; Beginning; and End, Critical Mass, and Real World Rules.

Game Design Patterns for Mobile Games [13] goes into depth about basic game mechanics that mixed reality games employ. As such, cards derived from this source mainly cover gameplay elements.

Example cards include Augmented Reality, Exergaming, Collecting, Peer-to-Peer, Weather Input, Passive Tracking, Manual Interaction, and Suitable Sensors.

Designing Mobile Augmented Reality Games [46] puts the focus on best practice design and common pitfalls of designing Augmented Reality games and as such was a rich source for Challenge Cards.

Example cards include Augmented Reality, Compelling Audio, Mobile Soundtrack, Useful Props, Different Roles, Actors, Seamful Design, Suitable Sensors, Nothing Digital, Nothing Physical, Gimmicky Tech, Long Distances, Accidents, Dynamic Places, Overcrowding, Confusing Interface, and Inaccurate Sensors.

8.3.2   Rules for Ideation Sessions

The cards come with an intentional brief rule-set that introduces the concept behind the cards and describes the main ways of how to use them in an ideation session. The rule description reads as follows, and a summary of the process can be seen in Table 8.1 as well as Figure 8.9.

Activity 1: Idea generation

You can use the cards for rapidly generating a bunch of ideas. Some of these ideas will be amazing, others weird, and some others not really that exciting. The point of this activity is to create many ideas in the hope that some (or maybe just one) will be useful for later. Therefore, you should not be afraid of proposing something that sounds stupid at first! At this stage, anything goes! There are no "wrong" ideas.

8.3.2.1   Easy Mode

Shuffle the Opportunity Cards and hand out three to everyone. One person goes first by playing a card from their hand and explaining how this creates a rudimentary game. Don't worry too much about implementation or cost at this point, but limit yourself to only a few sentences! Then, someone else plays card and explains how it expands on the previous idea. Continue doing so until everyone has played exactly one card. This is your idea! Note down your game design and which cards you used. Remember, at this point the game description should be really short!

If you have Theme Cards, use one of them as an initial seed before playing any Opportunity Cards.

8.3.2.2   Hard Mode

Again, start by shuffling the Opportunity Cards. Instead of handing everyone a card, just randomly reveal three of them in the middle of the table! If you have any Theme Cards, add one as well. The group now has 3 minutes to come up with an idea that incorporates all three (four) cards.

TABLE 8.1

Overview of the Different Phases of Idea Generation and Idea Development with the Cards. O = Opportunity Card, Q = Question Card, C = Challenge Card, and T = Theme Card

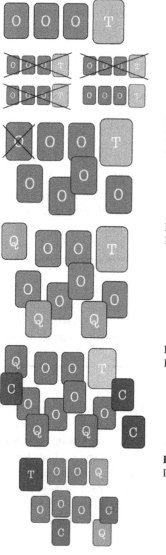

Idea generation

Draw three random Opportunity Cards and one random Dixit card. Discuss a game idea including all four cards.

Repeat process several times.
In the end, choose one idea to develop further.

Idea development
Phase 1: Exploring

Add further Opportunity Cards (from hand) to expand on the idea. Remove cards that are no longer fitting.

Phase 2: Refining

Play Question Cards and discuss how they relate to the idea.

Phase 3: Grounding

Play Challenge Cards and discuss how they relate to the idea.

Phase 4: Finalizing

Discuss the final idea and arrange cards spatially to represent idea. Remove cards that are no longer relevant.

FIGURE 8.9 Idea generation (upper left), idea development phase 3 (upper right), and idea development phase 4 (bottom).

This mode can create quite unique ideas as some of the card combinations will be rather unusual.

Activity 2: Idea development
In this activity we will use all the cards to really explore one idea in more detail. This could be the idea you like best from the previous phase, or maybe you already have something more or less concrete in mind. If that is the case, use post-its to quickly note down all the different elements of your idea. In general, the whole session will probably last 2 hours, but that really depends on the group.

8.3.2.3 Phase 1: Exploring

In this phase you want to expand your idea. Everybody should draw three Opportunity Cards and hold them in their hands. Anybody who has a card that they think could enhance the current design can play it onto the table and explain how it changes the game idea. You should also discard cards that you do not like, and in general everybody should always draw back up to three.

Feel free to also remove cards from the center of the table if they do not fit anymore.

> **Variant**: Instead of a free-for-all play card going around the table to give everyone a chance to participate, you might want to start in this mode and then switch to the other one eventually.
>
> **Troubleshooting**: It is a good idea to use a timer and have a quick check every 7 minutes if ideas are still flowing. If that is not the case, try to play some random Opportunity Cards or throw in another Theme Card.

Sometimes you will notice a lack of concreteness and maybe too many cards are "active." Trim regularly and remove cards that are not essential to the game idea!

8.3.2.4   Phase 2: Refining

Put the Opportunity Cards aside and hand everyone three Question Cards. If you think a card you are holding is relevant for the game and should be discussed, play it on the table. The same should be done for cards that seem irrelevant. Some people might disagree! Use the cards to further define your idea and talk about the important aspects. The goal is to go through all of the cards eventually. It works best if you keep the "important" cards on the table as a reminder, and to use post-its to quickly note down interesting answers to them.

> **Variant**: Instead of going through all Question Cards one by one, take all and sort them in order of importance for your game design.
>
> **Troubleshooting:** If you feel that your idea is still a bit vague after phase 1, start with the red Question Cards.

8.3.2.5   Phase 3: Grounding

This phase is identical to the previous one, but this time you should use the CHALLENGE CARDS. They will help you identify potential problems in your design.

> **Variant**: As above.
>
> **Troubleshooting**: Sometimes it is tempting to instantly disregard a card. Instead try to find other interpretations that might be affecting your game.

8.3.2.6   Phase 4: Finalizing

In this phase you should try to summarize the whole game idea. This usually works best by arranging the cards according to themes or by importance for the overall design. Sticking the cards onto a poster enables you to draw lines and add annotations, as does using a whiteboard.

8.4   DESIGN SESSIONS

We have used the Mixed Reality Game Cards in multiple design sessions. Participants came from very diverse backgrounds and had different levels of expertise. Users included students, researchers, artists, and professionals; some of them with extensive experience of mixed reality games, others with a generic game design or development background, and some with no directly helpful knowledge. In this section we will take a look at two of these sessions to illustrate the design process in more detail and to show the breadth of games that have been conceived.

8.4.1   EXAMPLE SESSION: IDEA GENERATION

We were approached by a British charity Sustrans (https://www.sustrans.org.uk/) that advocates the use of public transport as well as walking or cycling (and in turn reduce the reliance on cars). They wanted to explore the potential of mixed reality games to raise awareness of their cause and engage an audience this way. To this end we organized a design session with three of their employees who were joined by an artist with experience in location-based games. We introduced them to the Mixed Reality Game Cards and facilitated an idea generation session. We used the "hard mode" outlined in the previous section: Three random Opportunity Cards were revealed as well as a Dixit card. The four participants then had 5 minutes to incorporate all four cards into a coherent game design idea which would fit the mission of the charity. Subsequently, the idea was noted down before the whole process started again. Together, they came up with a total of six ideas in just a little more than 30 minutes. While we did not force the group to make the ideas fit with the charity's mission, four of them were directly suitable. After the card session, we spent some time with the group exploring the ideas in more detail during which the unfitting ideas were adjusted. Figures 8.10 to 8.15 show the drawn cards as well as the resulting ideas. However, we invite the reader to spend some time coming up with their own ideas before reading about the session results.

8.4.2   EXAMPLE SESSION: IDEA DEVELOPMENT

FORMAT is the biggest photography festival in the UK (http://www.formatfestival.com/). It takes place in the city of Derby and attracts over 100,000 visitors each year over the course of 1 month. It is organized by QUAD, a local center for art and film (https://www.derbyquad.co.uk/). QUAD wanted to stage a mixed reality game alongside the festival to increase visitor engagement. In order to develop a suitable game concept, we organized a session with the Mixed Reality Game Cards that focused on idea development. The following people participated in the session: a digital participation curator, a digital technical officer, the coordinator of the festival, and a mobile app developer. After a brief warm-up exercise of idea generation with the cards, we began the idea development process. In this case the basic idea was not generated with the help of the cards but instead the participants had already collected some ideas on what interesting and/or important elements for the game could be. We discussed these ideas looking for recurring themes and design constraints that would

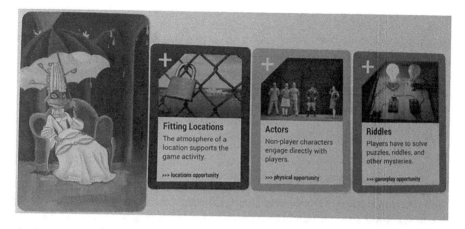

FIGURE 8.10   A game at Bletchley Park where teams are competing to crack codes the fastest and advance through the compound. Actors are there to confuse players, so nobody knows who is an actor, another player or just a normal visitor. Recreating the chaos from Blechley Park. Later modified into: Change setting of the game from Bletchley Park to a street that has to been cleaned up. Two teams are competing against each other.

FIGURE 8.11   A scavenger hunt game where players have to find miniature phone boxes hidden in the environment.

guide the design process. Together, we identified the following topics as most important for the final design: evidence/detective; photo art; 30 venues; 30 days; and data visualization. We decided to leave out the proposed gameplay elements as we preferred to start with a clean slate and not too many preconceived ideas. We transferred the themes onto post-it notes to have an appropriate physical representation that would complement the Mixed Reality Game Cards. Afterwards we went through the complete design process: Opportunity Cards, Question Cards, and Challenge Cards.

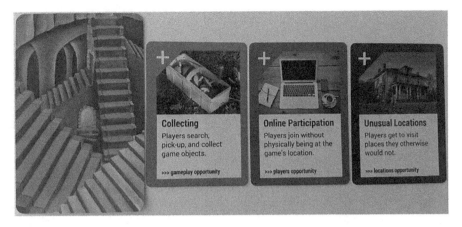

FIGURE 8.12 3D models of famous staircases can be collected by players in VR. Later modified into: In order to collect the staircases, players have to take specific amount of steps that are measured with a pedometer.

FIGURE 8.13 Visitors of a festival need to keep pedaling on exercise bikes to produce enough electricity to keep the music and lights going.

8.4.2.1 Phase 1: Exploring with Opportunity Cards

The participants used the Opportunity Cards together with the aforementioned post-it notes to slowly build and expand their envisioned game design. Therefore, everybody started out with three Opportunity Cards in their hand and was encouraged to redraw cards whenever deemed necessary. There was no formal turn-order. This allowed card players to proceed unrestricted: Participants could react to a new card by playing one of their own. This was usually accompanied with a statement like "I think this fits well with…" or "We can build on this by…" As a guiding structure we set an alarm clock to 7-minute intervals. After each of these intervals we would

FIGURE 8.14   Players explore the city based on locations from a book. When they arrive at a location, they need to find the beauty in it and describe it (and the current conditions) in a positive way.

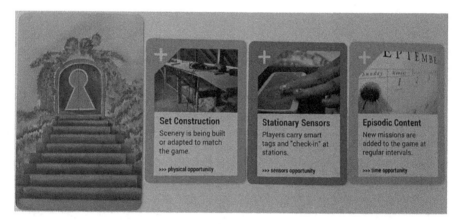

FIGURE 8.15   Players cycle along paths uncovering a narrative that asks them to find a new safe hiding place for the queen.

evaluate the state of the idea to decide whether we should continue or if the idea was sufficiently developed. Overall, it took us six of these intervals (42 minutes in total) before reaching a point where the cards seemed to no longer meaningfully change the idea. The idea was rather elaborate at this point, and we had gone through the whole deck of Opportunity Cards. The core of the experience was captured in cards that came out during the first two intervals (sorted by order of play):

STRONG NARRATIVE: The game is mainly based on a story that needs to be uncovered.

USEFUL PROPS: Simple objects support the players or add to the atmosphere.

STATIONARY SENSORS: Players carry smart tags and "check-in" at stations.

TELEPHONY: Players receive phone calls or text messages (manual or automated).

ROLEPLAYING: Players take on new personalities and act accordingly.

ACTORS: Non-player characters engage directly with players.

PERFORMATIVE PLAY: An audience is invited to watch and perhaps participate.

DIFFERENT ROLES: Players have different abilities and tasks to perform.

COLLABORATION: Players are working together in teams and support each other.

RIDDLES: Players have to solve puzzles, riddles, and other mysteries [played during interval three].

During this initial evolution of the game, the following two aspects emerged as highly desirable for the game: A strong theme and atmosphere (STRONG NARRATIVE, TELEPHONY, ROLEPLAYING, ACTORS) and going beyond a traditional screen-based mobile phone game (USEFUL PROPS, STATIONARY SENSORS, TELEPHONY, ACTORS). Both goals complemented each other as evidenced by the associated cards. Together, they formed the focus of design with cards like PERFORMATIVE PLAY, DIFFERENT ROLES, COLLABORATION, and RIDDLES going more into detail about the flow of the game (i.e., teams competing against each other and having to solve puzzles at the different locations). This is a theme that is also evidenced by the additional cards that were played throughout the following intervals: TIME PRESSURE, PUBLIC DISPLAY, HEADQUARTER, ONLINE PARTICIPATION, WORLDWIDE, EPISODIC CONTENT, AUTOMATED TRACKING, PEER-TO-PEER, EXPLORATION, TIMED EVENTS, and MINI GAMES. Like before, these cards were used to further flesh out the idea without actually changing the original idea in a sweeping way.

The participants were very satisfied with the progress that we made. They came in with a rough idea of game elements and a general theme for the idea and over the course of 42 minutes they turned it into a rather elaborate idea. One participant commented: "This writes part of your elevator pitch." Figure 8.16 shows the chosen cards at the end of this phase.

8.4.2.2   Phase 2: Refining with Question Cards

After engaging with the Opportunity Cards, the Question Cards were introduced to the participants. Again, participants drew three of these each, and then redrew additional cards when necessary or desired. The cards supported reflecting on the evolving idea, and the following ones were most fruitful in this process (including the shorthand answers of the group):

FUN AND JOY: Why is the game fun to play? What is engaging about it? => Narrative

THEME AND STORY: What is the overall content of the game? How is that conveyed? => Investigators

FIGURE 8.16   Game idea after phase 1 (left) and phase 4 (right).

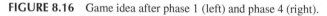

CHALLENGING: What makes the game challenging? How difficult is it? => More cards than needed and more difficult levels

LOCATIONS: What role are the locations playing? How important are they? => Riddles match locations

NOTHING DIGITAL: How could the game be played without tech? Why is tech needed? => Paper version (like a bingo card)

TARGET GROUP: What are the typical players like? How is the game made for them? => Smartphone users: Families! and Kids!

EXPERIENCE FLOW: How do players journey through the game? => No set path; Different days; Drop-in/drop-out; and Facilitated tour

8.4.2.3   Phase 3: Grounding with Challenge Cards

The participants also used the Challenge Cards to think about their game from another perspective. Again, cards were handed out and participants could play and redraw cards whenever they thought it to be suitable. This phase lasted roughly 30 minutes and the participants inspected all available cards.

They deemed the following Challenge Cards most important for their game design idea and discussed them in more depth:

UNCONTROLLABLE PLACES. Is it likely that any locations will "change" before/during the game?

PHONE ZOMBIES. Will players be starting at their screens most of the time?

GIMMICKY TECH. Is technology used in a meaningful way or just for the sake of it?

CONFUSING INTERFACES. Is the interface easy to understand and use for new users?

UNCLEAR INSTRUCTIONS. How easy is it for the players to understand what they have to do?

FEATURE CREEP. Does the game try to include too many different elements?

LIMITED RESOURCES. What happens when too many people play at the same time?

BATTERY LIFE. What elements of the game are draining the battery?

RELOCATION. How difficult is it to move the game to a different location?

GREAT MARKETING. [This was a card created by the participants in which they acknowledged that marketing the game in the right way would be an important factor for its success.]

8.4.2.4 Phase 4: Finalizing

Lastly, we discussed the whole idea again, discarded less relevant cards, and arranged the remaining ones into thematic groups (as also shown in Figure 8.16):

- *Core.* These cards encompass the basic idea of the game. [FITTING LOCATIONS, STRONG NARRATIVE, EXPERIENCE FLOW, LIMITED RESOURCES]
- *Examples.* These cards further flesh out the core game idea and provide ideas how the different tasks at the different locations might be implemented. [MINI GAMES, RIDDLES, TELEPHONY, USEFUL PROPS, ACTORS]
- *Reminders.* Consisting solely of Challenge Cards, the participants agreed that these were not only important design considerations that were crucial for the success but also for the desired style of game. [FEATURE CREEP, PHONE ZOMBIES, GIMMICKY TECH, CONFUSING INTERFACE, UNCLEAR INSTRUCTIONS]
- *Engagement.* A variety of ideas that were aimed at increasing the engagement with the game and reaching a wider audience. [HEADQUARTER, PUBLIC DISPLAY, TEAM PLAY, TAKING PHOTOS, SOCIAL MEDIA ENGAGEMENT]
- *Potential Elements.* Design ideas that seemed interesting but not necessarily crucial to include. [TIMED EVENTS, TIME PRESSURE]
- *Future.* Participants thought that these ideas, while interesting, were too difficult to implement at this point and should therefore be kept in mind for future iterations. [ONLINE PARTICIPATION, WORLDWIDE, PUBLIC VOTING, NOTHING DIGITAL]
- *Authoring for other Events.* These cards describe the core considerations when transporting the game to a different city and festival. [THEME AND STORY, FUN AND JOY, TARGET GROUP, RELOCATION]

8.4.2.5 Outcome: DETECT

The game was developed and staged during FORMAT15 under the name DETECT (http://www.formatfestival.com/detect). It was browser-based to allow any smartphone user to participate. The game consisted of 21 missions spread across seven venues partaking in the festival. The game was rather close to the result of the ideation session with a focus on tangible experiences and tightly integrated riddles with the environment. For example, in one mission players get the clue "We're currently tracing a phone call on the 2nd floor and need you to listen in. Find the silver phone." They then had to locate the phone in question and pick up the receiver in order to

FIGURE 8.17   Impressions from DETECT, courtesy of QUAD.

trigger an automated message providing the next clue. Figure 8.17 shows some impressions from the game.

8.5   USING IDEATION CARDS

We used the Mixed Reality Game Cards in several studies and at other opportunities, with professionals, academics, artists, students, and domain experts. Some of them had extensive knowledge of games or even mixed reality games, others barely had any or none. However, we found that the cards were useful for all of these different users, and likewise when working in homogenous or diverse groups. To explore our ideation card deck in more detail, we are now going to take a closer look at some of the elements that were crucial for its success. From a rules point of view, instructing participants to randomly reveal cards and then incorporate all of them into an idea (called "hard mode" in a previous section) had the most impact on our sessions. While idea development with all of the cards was a much more free-flowing process, rapid idea generation worked best under these constraints. We will then also take a look at how the four different types of cards shaped the design process: Theme Cards encouraging more flavorful ideas, Opportunity Cards as the building blocks, Question Cards to reflect on the idea, and finally Challenge Cards to provide more grounding.

8.5.1   RANDOM DRAW AND RESTRICTING CHOICE

Ideation decks like PLEX and VNA restrict their users by not allowing them to choose cards to build an idea from. Instead, it is left to a random card draw – and then an idea has to be created exactly from this combination of cards. During our studies with the Mixed Reality Game Cards, we have been experimenting with different variations on these rules: a) having participants reveal cards randomly and then having to use all of these for their idea; b) having participants draw a hand of cards and then choosing one (or multiple) cards from their hand as building blocks for their idea. While b) still limits their choice, we noticed a significant difference in both perception as well as behavior. In order to illustrate this, we will take a look at two short vignettes from two studies. Both cases revolve around the card Augmented Reality and how its perceived contradiction with other cards was handled by each group.

In the first instance, we instructed a group to each draw up three Opportunity Cards and then, in turn-order, play one card and explain how it creates or extends a game idea. The first participant played the card DOMINANT AUDIO and the group discussed a few potential setups of a game that relies purely on audio. The next participant then played the aforementioned card AUGMENTED REALITY. Almost immediately, the three other participants started to criticize this choice as it did not "fit" with their current idea. They were unwilling to embrace this new element as they could not see an easy/obvious way on how to include it into the idea. Eventually, they convinced the second participant to withdraw the card and replace it with the more palatable card PEER-TO-PEER.

In the second instance, a different group was tasked to generate ideas by randomly revealing three Opportunity Cards (and a Theme Card) and then making sure to include all of these cards in their idea. As seen in Figure 8.18, the group drew the Opportunity Cards LOW TECH, SEAMFUL DESIGN, and AUGMENTED REALITY as well as a Theme Card (at this point we did not utilize Dixit cards but Theme Cards that featured short phrases). The group immediately identified the incompatibility between AUGMENTED REALITY and LOW TECH. Unlike the other group, however, these participants challenged themselves and worked hard to include all cards into their idea. In the end they created the game idea for Restickulous: You have to sneak a cardboard cut-out of the Eiffel Tower attached to a long stick into selfies that other people take (see Figure 8.18).

In the post-session interview with the second group, they reflect on this design process and attribute the idea directly to the cards: "That game is exactly the three cards that we got." Another participant agrees: "We made those exact three cards into a game. We didn't deviate I guess is the thing." The previous participant explains it further: "So it was literally us thinking about those three things, and we thought it'd be funny and that's where that came from. […] We would have never come up with that otherwise."

The random selection of cards and the fact that they have to be used, creates unusual combinations of, for example, game mechanics and this way leads to unusual (or in other words: creative) designs such as seen with Restickulous. Allowing to choose from cards or discarding them in turn arguably leads to less daring and

FIGURE 8.18   The cards (left) spawning the idea for Restickulous (right).

perhaps more conservative designs. The random element of the card draw is equivalent to what Schön [43] sees as practitioners being "stimulated by surprise" in a beneficial way during the creative process. Dorst and Cross [15] also stress the importance of surprise: "Surprise is what keeps a designer from routine behaviour. The 'surprising' parts of a problem or solution drive the originality streak in a design project." Drawing cards randomly during a session facilitated with ideation cards creates new contexts as well as design constraints that participants have to deal with. Similar to surprise, such constraints are likewise seen as a crucial element for promoting creativity. Finke et al [16] conducted a study where they observed that a random selection (from which to build a design) resulted in more creative solutions than when participants could choose freely. A follow-up study supported these results: they see creativity as something that has more to do with making something out of a situation in which you are placed than with planning something "from the ground up." When operating under constraints, designers cannot follow the "path-of-least-resistance" or POLR [45]. Instead, they have to find unique solutions to their design problems.

However, finding these unique solutions is at the same time also a more challenging design activity. It might not necessarily be surprising to find out that a group of experienced academics created Restickulous, whereas a group of less experienced students decided to discard the contradictory card. This difficulty of idea generation under heavy constraints has also been observed by Lucero and Arrasvuori [30]: "The randomness present in PLEX Brainstorming can lead to the creation of radically new ideas, but occasionally can lead to a creative dead-end which results in discarding the current hand of cards." We made similar observations, perhaps best exemplified with study participants who are less used to creative design exercises. After the Sustrans session, the participants stressed the fact that it was not an easy process for them:

CHARITY 2 But frankly *I found the whole thing really hard.* Simply because I don't think like that. I'm not at all… It made me realize how ingrained I am in my thinking. You know. *It was quite difficult to think differently.*

INTERVIEWER Did you manage to think differently?

CHARITY 2 I'm not entirely sure that I did.

INTERVIEWER Because I had the feeling that you were also equally participating. I didn't notice anybody who didn't.

CHARITY 2 Yeah, but *I found it hard. Really hard.* I think you [the artist] found it easy!

ARTIST Yes, but not necessarily for a good reason. I think I found it easy because I had some reference points to draw on because I participated in or constructed a lot of these things. So I was able to copy to some extent what I already had in my head. Whereas what I was amazed about were the things that the three of you were coming up with. *Which seemed much more original than the reference points I had in my head* quite a lot of the time. So that worked, I thought.

CHARITY 2 I found it hard though, quite hard.

Here, the members of the charity clearly found the process more of a challenge than the participating artist who was more experienced in location-based mixed reality games. However, as the artist states, the fresh look that the charity members brought to the table actually also had a positive impact on the session as their ideas were not as relying on established concepts as in contrast to the artist's ones.

The group also further reflected on the constraint that all cards had to be used:

ARTIST I wonder if it is productive to allow people to just put things aside. Because there is potential to take that as a shortcut, whereas actually trying to incorporate all of the cards in the way you just described actually does do that. But you have to stick at it. Rather than saying: 'Here's three that fit and this one that doesn't'. *Actually the creative bit is making the one that doesn't fit, fit with the three that do.* And that's where the hard work comes in generally. Otherwise there's the danger that what the game becomes is just making connections between three of the four. And jettison the missing one. And that becomes the task then. *Whereas actually the task should be to allow yourself to say anything. To force you almost to say something different.*

INTERVIEWER Yeah, I noticed, I think during the second time, you wanted to skip the Dixit card. But then someone said "Nonono, last time we even used the frog." Which was even a more obscure card. [Referring to the Theme Card shown in Figure 8.10]

CHARITY 3 I must admit, I found myself then in another role where I felt that the card with the stairs was gonna be discarded. *I was kind of quite keen to make sure that they didn't.*

ARTIST And that worked actually for the stairs one, didn't it? ["stairs" referring to a Theme Card; see Figure 8.12]

The group was well aware that they made their own life more difficult by following the rules, but decided that the extra effort was well worth it.

In contrast, some groups partaking in other studies voiced a clear dislike of the random draw and preferred choosing cards themselves (from a randomly drawn hand). This sentiment is perhaps best explored in the following snippet from a post-session interview. The participants are experienced designers of mixed reality experiences.

INTERVIEWER What do you think is the difference between 'draw three cards and make a game out of them' and 'play whatever you like'? Any opinions on the differences between.

P10 I'm a technical background guy and I feel if we can play any card we like *it's much easier* because *I can decide* what we are going to build. If we are just playing some cards that we have been forced upon by the process – *I don't really want to* hypothesize a social media based game with gps and augmented reality and stuff just because the cards told me so. I don't believe in fortune tellers. And *I don't believe in the cards telling me what to do*, because I still have to do it afterwards, so I would like to have the feeling of control. I would like to have the random glimpse of ideas from the cards which I think they give me very nicely. But I also – it's a thing that we want to build afterwards so *we have to be in control.*

P9 I think it probably works better when you've got the degree of choice because you can sort of *guide it in a direction you want.* Whereas when it's, you know, you got the three cards down there and there it's telling you exactly what to do. It's just more down to the *luck of the draw.* Well, in both approaches to some degree. Like it's certainly less so when you've got a number of cards and you are choosing which ones. *But when it's just the cards down there it could turn out really brilliantly because the cards could design something for you, or give you the seeds for something really cool.*

P10 That's a good point.

P9 But there's probably more chance that they're gonna be *random things that don't go very well together* and *it's gonna be hard* to create something out of.

One participant mentioned an interesting phenomenon that we observed regularly when participants were talking about the card session and their ideas. We have already seen this in the snippet talking about Restickulous: Participants attribute the idea itself to the cards instead of claiming ownership over them (and seeing the cards just as a facilitator for their own creativity). We noted this both for ideas that the groups were proud of as well as ideas that the groups thought were weak. The following shows some examples for the language that participants used when talking about the cards and their ideas (in this instance from a study conducted with students and post-session questionnaires):

They helped to generate ideas but with *a bad combination* they were quite limiting.

Often the cars were a great help in coming up with ideas, however if a *poor card or cards game up*, it could be quite limiting to have to include certain design concepts. These we usually gave minimal focus.

For this game the cards we got *didn't have many games that could be made with* the Dixit Card and weren't synergetic overall.

Some ideas were better than others. The ones which were better had a *better selection of cards*, i.e. Physiological Input is hard to use.

The cards that we had *forced us to create a Geocaching game* based on coordinates texted to the player.

While this perception might be seen as just a quirk, it also showcases that the cards provided the participants with an alibi. If an idea turned out to be bad, it was not the participants themselves who were at fault, but instead the (randomly drawn) cards. Furthermore, as participants were required to include all cards into their ideas, they often at times had to voice unconventional ideas that in turn might be seen as unfitting, inappropriate, or plain bad by the rest of the group. Unlike the time when a participant deliberately played the card AUGMENTED REALITY (as described above), the ensuing criticism would not be directed at the card player. In turn, this creates a more encouraging atmosphere that does not punish the proponent of such ideas. This quality was explicitly mentioned when reflecting on the design process during the QUAD session:

QUAD 2   And I think when you are working with other people, like a lot of people who maybe not feel as confident about talking through with a group... Or people who maybe don't normally work in those kind of processes. I think *giving them these prompts is incredible and useful.*
QUAD 4   *The fear of looking stupid.*
QUAD 2   Yes exactly, yeah, you are reading a card, it's the card you played, *it is not your crap idea, it's the card told me to do it.*

A similar observation was made by participants from the Sustrans session:

ARTIST   Saying it out loud as well I think. And almost just talking out loud was a little bit useful. Without worrying too much about what you were saying.
SUSTRANS 2   It's quite inhibiting, sometimes, isn't it, people's perception of daft-ness. You stressed it a lot in beginning "You can't say anything wrong". But I don't think actually we really believed that. [...] I think it's quite difficult to be like that. *Just say daft things.*

In summary, we found that forcing participants to rely on a random draw of cards of which they had to use all was more beneficial to the process despite the added level of difficulty. This certainly led to cases where a group would not be able to come up with a usable idea; however, the overall idea generation process is designed to create a variety of ideas over a short amount of time. As such, unusable ideas can then easily be disregarded after the session, and the following idea development can focus on an idea that the group finds most promising. Randomly drawing the cards however did not only lead to more unique ideas, it also removed agency from the participants. While this was not necessarily appreciated by all participants, we believe that the alibi that this creates for participants is highly desirable for a positive, creativity inspiring overall atmosphere of a design session.

8.5.2   THEME CARDS

After our first iteration of design sessions with the Mixed Reality Game Cards we noticed on reflection that many of the created game ideas where somewhat bland and lacked a certain theme or setting. For example, groups would draw the card Collecting and in turn decide that players have to collect "something.". They would not neces-sarily specify what exactly they need to collect and thus the game ideas often stayed at an abstract level. In order to mitigate this problem and encourage users to come up with more flavorful ideas we decided to add domain-extrinsic Theme Cards. Our first attempt consisted of selecting short phrases and printing these on additional cards. However, feedback by participants of that workshop was mostly negative. While they appreciated the goal behind the introduction of these cards, they felt too restricted by them instead of being inspired. At this point we came across a paper by Kwiatkowska et al. [28] who compared cards from the game Dixit with PLEX Cards as a source of inspiration for designers. Small groups of designers were given personal problems to solve and had to do so without any additional support material and with the two aforementioned card decks. In general, PLEX cards and Dixit cards led to more generated ideas, and participants saw the Dixit cards as most helpful: "They [the Dixit cards] allowed for free interpretation making it easier for designers to find the entry points on the given card and work further with them." Due to their surreal nature, they enable participants to derive several different meanings from them, and they can also focus on small aspects of the card and thus create even more diverse meaning from them. The fact that Dixit cards are very abstract had both positive and negative effects: "Sometimes the level of abstraction of the card was too high and it was difficult to find any association between the picture and the tackled problem." [...] "Such a level of abstraction increased the possibility that a few ideas might be innovative and provide surprising solutions."

To us it seemed that the surreal Dixit cards possessed exactly the qualities that we were looking for in Theme Cards and thus we decided to include them in all future sessions (based on promising early results). The influence of the Theme Cards can easily be seen in the game ideas that the charity members created in the session described earlier in this chapter. The session participants also reflected on this:

SUSTRANS 3   I liked the fact that the three coloured cards with the words on them set some rules around the game. And then *the picture card then kind of takes it off.*

SUSTRANS 2   It's like *a wild card* isn't it.

SUSTRANS 3   So you read the words on the cards, for me I think *the picture card adds some images*, some imagery, that then *takes the idea off in a way* that couldn't be achieved if you just had four of the coloured cards and no strange picture card.

Similar to Kwiatkowska et al. we also observed that Dixit cards sometimes did not work in helping in the design process as their surreal images was blocking the creativity of some participants. In such instances, being forced to include the card nonetheless was seen as limiting and overcomplicating things. At other times, however, the Dixit cards worked beautifully and enabled groups to quickly define and expand on a theme. Dixit cards in general seemed to be "hit-or-miss." It is clear however, that the addition of the Dixit cards had positive effects on the ideas being generated. Participants overall agreed that ideas included in Dixit cards were in general of a different quality. While not necessarily better ideas, participants described them as "more fleshed-out" and "more detailed." Dixit cards helped to move away from abstract ideas and created more colorful and descriptive ones based on a strong theme. Participants from the Sustrans study thought that the Dixit card "takes the idea off" and a QUAD participant remarked that "the Dixit card allowed us to think outside of the box."

An important component toward the success of a Dixit card seemed to be when it was applied in the ideation round. If a game started off based on a Dixit card, the theme would obviously be more integrated than when the Dixit was the last card to be thrown into the mix, often "shoehorning a theme onto an idea" as noted by one participant. When, on the other hand, a theme was integrated from the beginning of the process, the theme could then evolve naturally and in unison with the remaining other (mechanical) aspects from the Opportunity Cards.

When looking at other ideation cards decks the inclusion of Theme Cards is a unique characteristic of the Mixed Reality Game Cards. PLEX Cards, The Deck of Lenses, Exertion Cards – they all focus on the topic itself but provide no additional guidance or source of inspiration for the users. This is fine when using the cards for analyzing an existing design (e.g., Deck of Lenses), however for creating an initial idea the addition of Theme Cards has proven to be a great resource, despite the described flaws. Theme Cards provide an additional trigger for new ideas and offer refreshing new perspective. They help create more fleshed-out ideas, but at the same time can put some people off if they cannot easily make sense of them – something that might just be a matter of experience with the cards. "Good" Theme Cards however need exactly this vagueness to function properly: Rich images that include lots of little detail so that they can be interpreted in multiple ways. It is also important to include Theme Cards already in the beginning of the process – otherwise the game idea will not naturally evolve but the theme will be forced onto the idea. While Dixit cards worked really well for our purposes, other existing card decks are probably equally well suited (e.g., artistic tarot cards); alternatively, one could create their own deck by selecting suitable imagery from online image repositories.

8.5.3 OPPORTUNITY CARDS

By combining different Opportunity Cards at the beginning of the design process, designers map out the important elements of their game and give it shape. As such, Opportunity Cards make up the building blocks of an idea. They cause *inspiration* because they do not restrict participants but instead provide interesting elements to first base an idea on and then later add to it. This way they foster *discussions* between participants because they can use the cards as an alibi while getting just enough knowledge from them to be able to participate even without much previous experience. There is however a certain danger that Opportunity Cards can create very large and complex ideas because they tempt users to add more and more cards – thus potentially needlessly extending an idea unless *restraint* is employed.

8.5.3.1 Inspiration

One of the foremost qualities of the Opportunity Cards is their ability to inspire ideas. During one workshop, a group created an asymmetric VR coffin experience called Taphobos [11]. The trigger for this idea was the card UNUSUAL LOCATIONS. It shows the images of an abandoned and rotting house that inspired the group to create a survival horror game (Figure 8.19). This underlines the importance of the images featured on the cards which – together with the Theme Cards – are a rich source of inspiration. However, it is not the images alone that made the Opportunity Cards inspiring. Instead, as another participant puts it, "the positives [the Opportunity Cards] are inspiring ideas, they are things [...] that we didn't think really think about

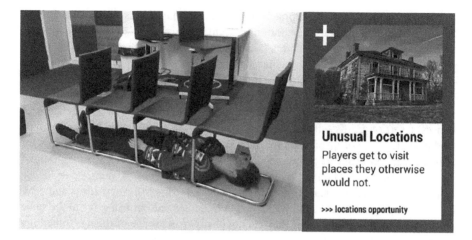

Unusual Locations

Players get to visit
places they otherwise
would not.

>>> locations opportunity

FIGURE 8.19 Low-fidelity prototype of immersive coffin experience Taphobos (left) and
the card that mainly inspired it (right).

before." This can be attributed to the fact that the Opportunity Cards describe design
possibilities of mixed reality games. As such they showcase potential elements that
might be part of a game, each of them being a valid option for a game. The Opportunity
Cards are building blocks of an idea from which the card users can pick and choose
from. Other study participants remarked that the Opportunity Cards made them
"think about other things to add" and that they "suggest more ways to take them [the
ideas] further." Interacting with the Opportunity Card phase was labeled as "blue sky
thinking" by a participant from QUAD. When using these cards, the participants
were not restricted by concerns of realism or feasibility. Instead, they were allowed
to freely brainstorm in a completely positive environment. They could add whatever
cards they liked without having to think of any negative repercussions that it might
have. The importance of allowing this careless free-wheeling before engaging with
the other cards was stressed by QUAD participants as well: "adding the negative and
the plus [cards] together [...] would ruin part of the creativity that the plus cards are
bringing up."

8.5.3.2   Discussions

Participants often remarked how the cards enabled them to "pull in an idea" because
they got "people talking." This is of course rather important for a collaborative design
activity. The cards gave the ideation session structure by providing direct and tangible elements to discuss and use as a jumping off point for generating ideas. Cards
were described as "ice breakers." This was especially useful in the QUAD session as
here the participants had not worked together beforehand. The cards mitigated the
issue as participants were enabled to be "just reading the cards ourselves and then
giving our opinions." The cards gave them "prompts" that were "incredible and useful" thus also enabling people who "maybe not feel as confident" to participate. They
mention the alibi that the cards gave them because the idea that you are proposing

"it's the card you played, it is not your crap idea". This again strengthens less confident participants as it is not them that might get criticized directly but instead the card. The cards remove "the fear of looking stupid." A less experienced participant remarked that the cards provide enough titbits of information: "it's a process that anybody could participate in."

8.5.3.3 Restraint

The described lack of restriction however also caused problems. Some groups could become overwhelmed by the sheer amount of possibilities so that after a certain amount of Opportunity Cards had been used to develop an idea, additional ones were rather detrimental to progress: "Adding more just lead to irrelevant or over-complicated features." Game ideas were saturated so that "the game did not develop much further than the initial concept at this stage." A similar notion surfaced in the QUAD session where the participants ended up with 24(!) Opportunity Cards after the first phase. The cards just seemed too tempting not to put in as they always felt "that could be a great aspect, this could be a great aspect." This way they ended up with a "very sprawling idea" as the participants themselves observed. In another group, the temptation to add more and more Opportunity Cards was so strong that, according to one participant, "people threw in cards a little bit for fun" which created a "bloated idea" that lacked focus and coherence. The lack of limitations also caused a lack of aim for some groups. For one group a very lengthy session with the Opportunity Cards did not yield any results as the group was just "swirling around." The Opportunity Cards allowed them to stay vague and not really work on developing the idea further – or making actual decisions of what should be part of the idea and what should not.

The aforementioned problems can be somewhat mitigated if the groups employ self-monitoring and regularly cull cards that no longer are relevant. However, this requires attention and a certain level of experience both with mixed reality games in general and with the Mixed Reality Game Cards in particular.

8.5.4 QUESTION CARDS

The Question Cards come into play to deepen the understanding of the existing idea. Where Opportunity Cards build the idea, Question Cards look at the idea as a whole and prompt users to fully define it and are a crucial element of the overall design process. They help groups to break deadlocks and to reduce the game idea to the core concept behind it. They support *detailing* and *streamlining the idea*, and foster *focusing on the task* at hand. Crucial for doing so successfully is the *timing* of when these cards are introduced into the design process.

8.5.4.1 Detailing the Idea

The Question Cards push users to provide more specific descriptions of their idea. In case of the QUAD session, the participants realized the role that LOCATIONS had in the game and how this affected the RIDDLES (the riddles should match the location). Likewise, the card EXPERIENCE FLOW helped them understand how the game will be played (i.e., not in a linear fashion but instead with drop-ins and drop-outs throughout its duration). In a larger study with students, the participants reported how the

Question Cards made them think about how to implement the idea, reflecting that by doing so "the main idea didn't change but became more focused" whereas others described how the ideas "could be fine-tuned in order to create a better gaming experience" or they were able to "elaborate on the idea in greater detail."

The students were also able to make these decisions about their idea because the Question Cards made them explore the several options they could take from their idea. One participant from described them as "what-if questions which made us think about the possible scenarios." Another student spoke of "alternate methods to play the game" and that the cards "opened up several possible options the game could use/change." Coming back to the QUAD group, the participants discussed their reliance on smartphones in response to the cards TARGET GROUP and NOTHING DIGITAL. Here, they realized that their tech-heavy focus might restrict their audience and as a response they decided to emphasize physical objects as part of the gameplay reducing the technological requirements drastically.

8.5.4.2   Streamlining the Idea

The Question Cards also are a good way of reducing an idea that might have grown rather big and unwieldy. Whereas the QUAD group had a "sprawling idea" after using the Opportunity Cards, according to them the Question Cards worked to "strip things" and they helped them "weed out a lot." In this instance, for example, they previously planned on having two opposing teams play the game but a discussion triggered by the card THEME AND STORY made them get rid of this additional element.

Other groups reported this effect of the Question Cards as well. On self-reflection they stated that the Question Cards helped them to deal with a "bloated idea" by encouraging them to "eliminate things and to ask ourselves what exactly we are doing," even if the cards ultimately failed to be 100% effective.

Similarly, another participant reported that the cards were a "help for tiding the game idea up." In general, discussing the questions helped participants develop a unified vision of the idea. The Question Cards force users to discuss and decide on the important elements of the game. In case of the QUAD group cards like FUN AND JOY and CORE CONCEPTS led to fruitful discussions about the overall view on the game.

8.5.4.3   Focusing on the Task

The Question Cards also supplied guidance that kept participants on track. Feedback included that the Question Cards provided "some structure that pulls you back" stopping groups from going "too broad and being just crazy." One group also attested that "they helped us focus" because they were "the right questions to think about." The Question Cards stopped them from "swirling around" and instead they got them "to the concrete part quickly."

This effect of the cards was also evident when they were used to overcome deadlocks. When one experienced group "couldn't figure out how to make it [their current idea] a game" they turned to the Question Cards "to see if that could break us." While it did not directly provide them with a solution, the cards did guide them and ultimately allowed them break through their deadlock.

8.5.4.4 Timing

The success of the Question Cards was often reliant on the timing of when they were introduced into the process. One group that went through them rather quickly (and therefore did not perceive them as very helpful) reasoned this was due to them having had already "talked much about the definite idea." The group stressed the importance of having to use them right after you "have a direct idea what you want to do" and that it was important to not "develop the entire idea before you get on to them." A different group likewise regretted not having used the Question Cards earlier – however not because their idea was already far developed but because they made them stop "swirling around" (see above). Timing was a recurring issue across many groups, with others stating that the Question Cards failed to be much helpful because they "already had a good idea of the design" or "had the final idea of what the game should be after the first stage."

8.5.5 CHALLENGE CARDS

The Challenge Cards are the final type of card that is being used in the ideation process. They feature common design issues of mixed reality games and as such prompt the designers to examine their ideas for their occurrence. Feedback indicates a strong similarity to the Question Cards with some of the positives and negatives being very similar between the two types of cards. This is perhaps not surprising as they both fulfill the task of reflection over an idea in opposition to building an idea with the Opportunity Cards. Overall, the Challenge Cards were an important part of the overall design process. They allow *grounding of ideas* and serve as *reminders* of what problems might arise. By providing *no solutions*, Challenge Cards not only motivate further discussion but also run the risk of participants not pushing themselves hard enough and giving up on solving an issue at hand.

8.5.5.1 Grounding Ideas

Unsurprisingly the Challenge Cards gave participants insight into what kind of issues the game might encounter. Participants reported that the cards made them realize "the limitations of the game" and allowed them to look at "some very potential flaws with the game" because the cards "brought multiple issues to the surface of the development discussion." For at least one participant they were "the most important part of the development process" as it made the group revaluate previous design decisions. Mostly, the Challenge Cards did not lead to sweeping changes of the game idea. Instead, the ideas were often just fine-tuned and slightly adjusted. Participants described how the cards made them "change some features to be feasible" allowing them to "fix and improve the game further." Their approach typically included "using the overall old design and components without adding new ideas." The cards forced them to "find alternate ways to achieve the end goal without running into these issues." Challenge Cards also supported narrowing down the idea. They pose "specific problems that will explicitly take out other items" until "you stripped away so much that you have focus" as noted by a QUAD session participant. As a result, the participants felt that their ideas had become more realistic. In contrast to the open brainstorming with the Opportunity Cards, the Challenge Cards helped to "fine tune the ideas and put them into realistic and manageable area." Another participant described this as creating an "interesting grounding perspective to the game that brings it closer to being a reality."

8.5.5.2   Reminders

The Challenge Cards were often kept in the design as reminders informing any future development. In the QUAD session, for example, they kept PHONE ZOMBIES, GIMMICKY TECH, CONFUSING INTERFACE, UNCLEAR INSTRUCTIONS, LIMITED RESOURCES, RELOCATION, and FEATURE CREEP in the design. They did so to make sure that these flaws would not be retroactively added to the design after the session. Instead, they wanted to do their best to prevent these from happening as they would greatly and negatively affect the desired final experience, or, as they put it, "things that we should really be mindful of." Some other groups actively struggled with finding an answer for the posed problems. This was especially evident with less experienced participants such as students from one study. Such groups would often keep Challenge Cards as a part of their design "as limitations to the game" due to them having "no apparent solution."

8.5.5.3   No Solutions

An important element of the Challenge Cards is the fact that they are presented in the form of questions. This way, the cards speak directly to the users which makes it more difficult for them to disregard the card as irrelevant. Instead, the Challenge Cards create a discussion. As one participant puts it: "They simply forced us to find alternate ways to achieve the end goal without running into these issues." Of course, the cards have no built-in means of making sure that users actually force themselves to solve these problems. Some participants reported that several Challenges "proved to be tricky to implement." From their perspective, this created a certain danger that others might "accept it as a potential risk" instead of "planning around it." If participants did not challenge themselves enough, they often just gave up when the cards did not provide an "apparent solution." This then typically either lead to discarding a card out of frustration or accepting certain issues "as limitations of the game" without delving deeper into them (see Reminders above).

8.6   CONCLUSIONS

Ideation cards are being used in many different domains. From our experiences, they are extremely well suited to support collaborative and multidisciplinary design sessions. They enable less-experienced users to work with expert designers, or even completely without them. The facilitate discussion as each card is a prompt that can be used easily and naturally – just by playing it. Furthermore, they inspire the creation of new ideas and are thus very suited to be used in the game design process. In this chapter we have described our Mixed Reality Game Cards: How we created them by looking at existing games, the rules that accompany them, and we have given examples of two design sessions to showcase their suitability for rapid idea generation as well as in-depth idea development.

For idea generation, we believe that forcing participants to combine cards with each other they normally would not have chosen has the biggest potential to create new and inspiring ideas. While this is certainly more demanding of the users (as it requires more out-of-the-box thinking), this is exactly what we want to achieve in an ideation session. Another important factor is the inclusion of domain-extrinsic Theme Cards as these give color and flavor to ideas. They prevent users from staying on an abstract level by just combining mechanics, but instead foster ideas that contain strong themes or interesting settings.

For idea development, we believe that it is important to utilize different types of cards at the right time of the process. Opportunity Cards are well suited to build up an initial idea (e.g., as part of idea generation). However, in order to transform this into a more fleshed-out and detailed idea we find it necessary to supplement these cards with the reflective Question and Challenge Cards. These very specific roles for the cards are similar to the Six Hats method for brainstorming [14]. It is based on six different types of metaphorical hats, that restrict the allowed input to an idea to specific times. We do the same when we first build up an idea with Opportunity Cards, flesh it out with Question Cards, and then lastly ground it by confronting it with Challenge Cards.

While the content of the Mixed Reality Game Cards is domain-specific, we believe that the underlying rules and utilized card types create a framework for designers of ideation cards that can be followed to create a wide variety of new decks for other areas of software development and beyond.

ACKNOWLEDGMENTS

The authors would like to thank all participants of the ideation workshops that we conducted. This research was conducted as part of the PhD studies of the first author as a member of the Mixed Reality Lab at the University of Nottingham. Furthermore, the work was partially funded by EPSRC research project ORCHID (grant EP/I011587/1).

REFERENCES

[1] Christopher Alexander, Sara Ishikawa, Murray Silverstein, Max Jacobsen, Ingrid Fiksdahl-King, and Shlomo Angel. 1977. *A Pattern Language: Towns, Buildings, Construction*. New York: Oxford University Press.

[2] Valter Alves and Licinio Roque. 2010. *A Pattern Language for Sound Design in Games*. In *Proceedings of the 5th Audio Mostly Conference: A Conference on Interaction with Sound (AM '10)*, 12:1–12:8. doi: 10.1145/1859799.1859811

[3] Valter Alves and Licinio Roque. 2011. *An inspection on a deck for sound design in games*. In *Proceedings of the 6th Audio Mostly Conference: A Conference on Interaction with Sound (AM '11)*, 15–22. doi: 10.1145/2095667.2095670

[4] Marek Bell, Matthew Chalmers, Louise Barkhuus, Malcolm Hall, Scott Sherwood, Paul Tennent, Barry Brown, Duncan Rowland, Steve Benford, Mauricio Capra, and Alastair Hampshire. 2006. *Interweaving mobile games with everyday life*. In *Proceedings of the SIGCHI Conference on Human Factors in Computing Systems (CHI '06)*, 417–426. doi: 10.1145/1124772.1124835

[5] Steve Benford, Andy Crabtree, Martin Flintham, Adam Drozd, Rob Anastasi, Mark Paxton, Nick Tandavanitj, Matt Adams, and Ju Row-Farr. 2006. Can you see me now? *ACM Trans. Comput.-Hum. Interact* 13, 1: 100–133. doi: 10.1145/1143518.1143522

[6] Steve Benford, Martin Flintham, Adam Drozd, Rob Anastasi, Duncan Rowland, Nick Tandavanitj, Matt Adams, Ju Row-Farr, Amanda Oldroyd, and Jon Sutton. 2004. *Uncle Roy All Around You: Implicating the city in a location-based performance.* In *Proc. Advances in Computer Entertainment (ACE 2004)* 21: 47.

[7] Karl Bergström and Staffan Björk. 2014. The Case for Computer-Augmented Games. *Transactions of the Digital Games Research Association* 1, 3. Retrieved August 12, 2016 from http://todigra.org/index.php/todigra/article/view/32

[8] Staffan Björk and Jussi Holopainen. 2005. *Patterns In Game Design.* New York: Cengage Learning.

[9] Lisa Blum, Richard Wetzel, Rod McCall, Leif Oppermann, and Wolfgang Broll. 2012. *The final TimeWarp: using form and content to support player experience and presence when designing location-aware mobile augmented reality games.* In *Proceedings of the Designing Interactive Systems Conference (DIS'12)*, 711–720. doi: 10.1145/2317956.2318064

[10] Eva Brandt and Jörn Messeter. 2004. *Facilitating Collaboration Through Design Games.* In *Proceedings of the Eighth Conference on Participatory Design: Artful Integration: Interweaving Media, Materials and Practices - Volume 1 (PDC 04)*, 121–131. doi: 10.1145/1011870.1011885

[11] James Brown, Kathrin Gerling, Patrick Dickinson, and Ben Kirman. 2015. *Dead fun: Uncomfortable interactions in a virtual reality game for coffins.* In *Proceedings of the 2015 Annual Symposium on Computer-Human Interaction in Play*, 475–480.

[12] Matthew Chalmers and Areti Galani. 2004. *Seamful interweaving: heterogeneity in the theory and design of interactive systems.* In *Proceedings of the 5th conference on Designing interactive systems: processes, practices, methods, and techniques (DIS '04)*, 243–252. doi: 10.1145/1013115.1013149

[13] Ola Davidsson, Johan Peitz, and Staffan Björk. 2004. *Game Design Patterns for Mobile Games.*

[14] Edward De Bono. 2000. *Six thinking hats.* London, UK: Penguin Books.

[15] Kees Dorst and Nigel Cross. 2001. Creativity in the design process: Co-evolution of problem–solution. *Design Studies* 22, 5: 425–437. doi: 10.1016/S0142-694X(01)00009-6

[16] Ronald A. Finke, Thomas B. Ward, and Steven M. Smith. 1992. *Creative Cognition: Theory, Research, and Applications.* Cambridge, MA: MIT Press.

[17] Joel Fischer, Irma Lindt, Peter Mambrey, and Uta Pankoke-Babatz. 2007. *Evaluation of Crossmedia Gaming Experiences in Epidemic Menace.* In *Proc. of the PerGames 2007, the 4th international symposium on pervasive games*, Salzburg, Austria.

[18] Inc Groundspeak. Geocaching - The Official Global GPS Cache Hunt Site. *Geocaching - The Official Global GPS Cache Hunt Site.* Retrieved May 20, 2015 from http://www.geocaching.com/

[19] Kim Halskov and Peter Dalsgaard. 2006. *Inspiration Card Workshops.* In *Proceedings of the 6th Conference on Designing Interactive Systems (DIS '06)*, 2–11. doi: 10.1145/1142405.1142409

[20] Eva Hornecker. 2010. *Creative Idea Exploration Within the Structure of a Guiding Framework: The Card Brainstorming Game.* In *Proceedings of the Fourth International Conference on Tangible, Embedded, and Embodied Interaction (TEI'10)*, 101–108. doi: 10.1145/1709886.1709905

[21] Eva Hornecker and Jacob Buur. 2006. *Getting a Grip on Tangible Interaction: A Framework on Physical Space and Social Interaction.* In *Proceedings of the SIGCHI Conference on Human Factors in Computing Systems (CHI'06)*, 437–446. doi: 10.1145/1124772.1124838

[22] IDEO. 2002. *IDEO Method Cards.* San Francisco: IDEO.

[23] Staffan Jonsson, Markus Montola, Annika Waern, and Martin Ericsson. 2006. *Prosopopeia: Experiences from a Pervasive Larp.* In *Proceedings of the 2006 ACM SIGCHI International Conference on Advances in Computer Entertainment Technology (ACE'06).* doi: 10.1145/1178823.1178850

[24] Ben Kirman, Conor Linehan, and Shaun Lawson. 2011. Blowtooth: A provocative pervasive game for smuggling virtual drugs through real airport security. *Personal and Ubiquitous Computing* 16, 6: 767–775. doi: 10.1007/s00779-011-0423-z

[25] Hannu Korhonen, Markus Montola, and Juha Arrasvuori. 2009. *Understanding playful user experience through digital games.* In *International Conference on Designing Pleasurable Products and Interfaces*, 274–285.

[26] Annakaisa Kultima, Johannes Niemelä, Janne Paavilainen, and Hannamari Saarenpää. 2008. *Designing Game Idea Generation Games.* In *Proceedings of the 2008 Conference on Future Play: Research, Play, Share (Future Play'08)*, 137–144. doi: 10.1145/1496984.1497007

[27] Annakaisa Kultima, Janne Paavilainen, Johannes Niemelä, and Hannamari Saarenpää. 2008. *1001 Game Ideas.* Retrieved August 22, 2016 from http:/gameresearchlab.uta.fi/gamespacetool/FILES/Tools/GuideBook_for_GameSpaceIdeaTools.pdf

[28] Joanna Kwiatkowska, Agnieszka Szóstek, and David Lamas. 2014. *(Un)Structured Sources of Inspiration: Comparing the Effects of Game-like Cards and Design Cards on Creativity in Co-design Process.* In *Proceedings of the 13th Participatory Design Conference: Research Papers - Volume 1 (PDC'14)*, 31–39. doi: 10.1145/2661435.2661442

[29] Conor Linehan, Nick Bull, and Ben Kirman. 2013. BOLLOCKS!! Designing Pervasive Games That Play with the Social Rules of Built Environments. In *Advances in Computer Entertainment*, Dennis Reidsma, Haruhiro Katayose and Anton Nijholt (eds.). Springer International Publishing, 123–137. doi: 10.1007/978-3-319-03161-3_9

[30] Andrés Lucero and Juha Arrasvuori. 2010. *PLEX Cards: A Source of Inspiration when Designing for Playfulness.* In *Proceedings of the 3rd International Conference on Fun and Games (Fun and Games'10)*, 28–37. doi: 10.1145/1823818.1823821

[31] P. Milgram and F. Kishino. 1994. A taxonomy of mixed reality visual displays. *IEICE TRANSACTIONS on Information and Systems* 77, 12: 1321–1329.

[32] Markus Montola, Jaakko Stenros, and Annika Waern. 2009. *Pervasive Games: Theory and Design.* CRC Press, USA.

[33] Florian "Floyd"Mueller, Darren Edge, Frank Vetere, Martin R. Gibbs, Stefan Agamanolis, Bert Bongers, and Jennifer G. Sheridan. 2011. *Designing Sports: A Framework for Exertion Games.* In *Proceedings of the SIGCHI Conference on Human Factors in Computing Systems (CHI'11)*, 2651–2660. doi: 10.1145/1978942.1979330

[34] Florian Mueller, Martin R. Gibbs, Frank Vetere, and Darren Edge. 2014. *Supporting the Creative Game Design Process with Exertion Cards.* In *Proceedings of the 32Nd Annua (CHI '14)*, 2211–2220. doi: 10.1145/2556288.2557272

[35] Carman Neustaedter, Anthony Tang, and Tejinder K. Judge. 2011. Creating scalable location-based games: lessons from Geocaching. *Personal and Ubiquitous Computing* 17, 2: 335–349. doi: 10.1007/s00779-011-0497-7

[36] Niantic Labs. 2016. *Pokémon Go.*

[37] Scott Nicholson. *Peeking behind the locked door: A survey of escape room facilities.* Retrieved June 23, 2015 from http://scottnicholson.com/pubs/erfacwhite.pdf

[38] Kenton O'Hara. 2008. *Understanding Geocaching Practices and Motivations.* In *Proceedings of the SIGCHI Conference on Human Factors in Computing Systems (CHI '08)*, 1177–1186. doi: 10.1145/1357054.1357239

[39] Johan Peitz, Hannamari Saarenpää, and Staffan Björk. 2007. *Insectopia: exploring pervasive games through technology already pervasively available.* In *Proceedings of the international conference on Advances in computer entertainment technology (ACE '07)*, 107–114. doi: 10.1145/1255047.1255069

[40] Jean-Louis Roubira. 2008. *Dixit.* Poitiers, France: Libellud.

[41] Jesse Schell. 2008. *The Art of Game Design: A Deck of Lenses.* Pittsburgh, PA, USA: Schell Games.

[42] Jesse Schell. 2008. *The Art of Game Design: A Book of Lenses.* CRC Press, Amsterdam; Boston.

[43] Donald A. Schön. 1983. *The Reflective Practitioner: How Professionals Think in Action.* New York, NY, USA: Basic Books.

[44] Bruce Thomas, Ben Close, John Donoghue, John Squires, Phillip De Bondi, and Wayne Piekarski. 2002. First Person Indoor/Outdoor Augmented Reality Application: ARQuake. *Personal Ubiquitous Comput.* 6, 1: 75–86. doi: 10.1007/s007790200007

[45] Thomas B. Ward, Steven M. Smith, and Ronald A. Finke. 1999. Creative Cognition. *Handbook of Creativity*: 189, 189–212.

[46] Richard Wetzel, Lisa Blum, Wolfgang Broll, and Leif Oppermann. 2011. Designing mobile augmented reality games. In ed. Borko Furht *Handbook of Augmented Reality*. New York, NY, USA: Springer, 513–539.

[47] Richard Wetzel, Lisa Blum, Feng Feng, Leif Oppermann, and Michael Straeubig. 2011. Tidy City: A Location-based Game for City Exploration Based on Usercreated Content. In *Mensch & Computer 2011*, 487–496. Retrieved March 20, 2013 from http://www. oldenbourg-link.com/doi/abs/10.1524/9783486712742.487

[48] Christiane Wölfel and Timothy Merritt. 2013. Method Card Design Dimensions: A Survey of Card-Based Design Tools. In *Human-Computer Interaction – INTERACT 2013*, Paula Kotzé, Gary Marsden, Gitte Lindgaard, Janet Wesson and Marco Winckler (eds.). Springer Berlin Heidelberg, 479–486. Retrieved July 22, 2014 from http://link. springer.com/chapter/10.1007/978-3-642-40483-2_34

9 From Role-Playing Game to Exergame
A Modification for The Elder Scrolls V: Skyrim

Rahul Kumar, Jak Tan
University of Auckland, New Zealand

Paul Ralph
Dalhousie University, Canada

CONTENTS

9.1 INTRODUCTION

Physical exercise is associated with diverse health improvements [1], including helping obese and overweight people lose weight. Obesity is a serious problem—an epidemic. Here in New Zealand, two-thirds of adults and an increasing proportion of children are either obese or overweight [2].

Meanwhile, two-thirds of New Zealanders also play video games [3]. Playing video games is associated with heightened motivation [4], engagement [5], mindfulness [6] and flow [7–9]—a mental state characterised by focus, enjoyment and strong performance [10].

Good games are *immersive* [11]—the player's consciousness is consumed by the game world. Players feel like they are really there, in the game. They are fully present. If a gorilla walked by, they would not notice. Immersion is the degree of a player's mental involvement in a game. Immersive games are the ones that motivate players to keep coming back, and often to work diligently for in-game rewards; for example, mining and smelting ore for armour in *The Elder Scrolls V: Skyrim.*

Good exercise, in contrast, is *intense.* For most people, this means running not walking, lifting heavy weights not "just toning," and playing hard not just showing up. Intensity is the degree of exertion (both muscular and cardiovascular) during exercise. Unfortunately, many largely sedentary people wrongly believe that just going for a walk after dinner some nights is sufficient, but the fact is that health benefits are positively related to exercise intensity [1].

If exercise and video games are on either side of a lever, *motivation* is its fulcrum. Beginning and adhering to a good exercise programme takes substantial motivation [12]. Video games are highly motivating [4]. This raises the following question.

Research Question: *Can an immersive video game motivate high-intensity exercise?*

Next, we describe existing exercise games or "exergames" (Section 2). Then, we present the design and implementation of the proposed exergame (Section 3), followed by some key lessons learned (Section 4). Section 5 concludes the paper with a broad agenda for future research.

9.2   EXERGAMES

As explained in the introduction, it seems plausible that video games could be designed to motivate an active lifestyle. This inspires a growing class of video games called exercise games, or *exergames.* Numerous exergames have been developed, beginning with *Foot Craz* for the Atari and *Family Trainer* for Nintendo in the late 1980s.

Empirical evidence on these games is decidedly mixed. Most exergames "facilitate light- to moderate-intensity physical activity" [13], in the sense that players *can* get light- to moderate-intensity exercise while playing. However, most exergame-based interventions have not significantly increased physical activity among players [14]. Exergaming interventions "may produce small effects in terms of improving BMI among children who are overweight/obese" [15].

To understand why current exergames have limited effectiveness, we have to examine how different kinds of exergames work. Today, most exergames fit into one of the three broad categories:

1) Living-room exergames such as *Dance Dance Revolution* and *Wii Fit* involve performing physical exercise, including dancing, aerobics and yoga, typically while at home in front of one's television.
2) Cardio machine exergames such as the *Fish Game* on the Concept 2 rowing machine [16] are played while using specific training apparatus-some use virtual reality.
3) Mobile exergames use accelerometers, global positioning systems or similar technologies to track player movement and affect gameplay. In Zombies and Run!, for example, the runner/player must speed up when chased by zombies.

Even if a living-room exergame delivers high-immersion gameplay (and most do not), getting an intense, balanced workout in one's living room is extremely difficult. Mobile exergames have the opposite problem—it is extremely difficult to make an immersive game that can be played *safely* while running, swimming, cycling or otherwise moving rapidly outdoors. Activity tracking applications including Fit Bit, Fitocracy and Nike+, which attempt to gamify (cf. [17]) the fitness logging process, similarly lack immersive gameplay. Cardio machine exergames, in contrast, could potentially deliver both intense exercise and immersive gameplay, but we are not aware of any immersive cardio machine exergames. Even if one could be made, require specialised (i.e. expensive) hardware.

It is not difficult to postulate why these games might have limited effectiveness. Either the game is not immersive enough to keep the player engaged, the player is not exercising intensely enough to get substantial benefits, or both. This presents a paradox: when a person plays a game while exercising, high-intensity necessitates low immersion and vice versa.

But what if the person played the game and exercised at different times?

We are aware of only a few attempts at this sort of exergame. Two *Pokémon* games (*HeartGold* and *SoulSilver*) included a pedometer called the Pokéwalker. Walking with the Pokéwalker earned several kinds of in-game resources. Additionally, *NBA 2K17* included Fitbit integration that provided in-game bonuses for meeting walking goals. Neither of these attempts promoted intense exercise.

In summary, motivation is positively related to both game immersion [4] and physical exercise [18]. Meanwhile, health benefits are positively related to exercise intensity [1]. Therefore, immersive, intense exergames should be more effective. However, combining immersion and intensity is difficult when players exercise while playing the game, as in most existing exergames. This suggests developing an exergame that promotes exercise outside of play sessions.

9.3 CONVERTING *SKYRIM* INTO AN EXERGAME

9.3.1 OVERVIEW

The basic idea is to create an immersive game experience in which developing the player character (i.e. levelling up) is central to progress. The player character levels up based on the player's real-world physical activity, rather than in-game activity.

Since developing a good, immersive game from scratch is expensive and time-consuming, we decided to modify an existing one—*The Elder Scrolls V: Skyrim*.

Similarly, since developing our own exercise logging platform is expensive and time-consuming, we simply use an existing one—*Exercise.com*.

Our design was informed by contemporary game design theory, especially Schell's lenses [19] and the Unified Theory of Digital Games [20].

The most recent version of mod, *Skyrim Exergaming Mode*, is available on Nexus Mods.[1]

9.3.2 SKYRIM AND EXERCISE.COM

Skyrim is a single-player western role-playing game developed by Bethesda for the PC, PlayStation 3 and Xbox 360 (Figure 9.1). It was later re-released for the PlayStation 4, Xbox One and Nintendo Switch. It has a medieval fantasy setting including dragons and magic. The player character in *Skyrim* has three main attributes: Health, Stamina and Magicka, along with 18 different skill trees (e.g. Archery, Illusion and Pickpocketing). The player earns experience by using skills. When enough experience is gained, the player levels up, choosing attributes to improve and skills to learn. We chose the role-playing game *The Elder Scrolls V: Skyrim* for the following three reasons.

1) It is well-designed and very popular, having sold over 20 million copies [21].
2) With over 300 hours of content [22] and a strong progression aesthetic [23], it could support several months of physical training.
3) With a built-in modification kit (called Creation Kit) and vibrant modding community, *Skyrim* is easy to modify. Furthermore, its three-character attributes map well into fitness data (see below).

The PC version of *Skyrim* ships with a modification development kit provided, called Creation Kit (Figure 9.2). Creation Kit is a platform that allows players to alter the

FIGURE 9.1   *Skyrim* gameplay.

FIGURE 9.2 Creation Kit.

game, for example, by creating new quests, non-player characters (NPCs) and items. It uses a proprietary scripting language called Papyrus, as well as a creation system with a graphical interface. This has led to many publicly available mods including improved texture packs, new quests and new armour models. The modding community has created many helpful resources and documentation to assist with creating mods for the game. There are also forums and IRC channels available for Creation Kit modding support.

Similarly, after evaluating various fitness tracking applications, we chose Exercise. com (Figure 9.3) for the following three reasons:

1) It allows users to track a wide variety of exercises including strength, cardio and sport training.
2) It has good cross-platform compatibility with free web, Android and iPhone applications.
3) It has a ready-made point system that may be used to convert exercise data into *Skyrim* experience points.

While Exercise.com does not have its own public API it syncs with another platform, Runkeeper, which does provide a public API. We then used the Runkeeper API to retrieve data created on Exercise.com.

9.3.3 PROPOSED EXERGAME MODEL

There are four steps to our exergame model:

(1) A user performs some physical activity, such as any form of cardio, strength training, sports, stretching or fitness classes.

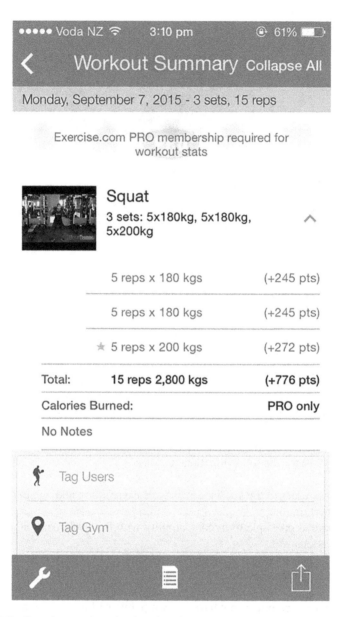

FIGURE 9.3   Exercise.com Logging Interface for iPhone.

(2) The user logs their activity using Exercise.com's logging platform.

(3) When the game is opened, it fetches exercise data using the Runkeeper API.

(4) The user is notified of his or her levelling status and resumes playing the game.

If the user has logged enough activity to level up, they will be notified about how their attribute bonuses have been allocated. Otherwise, they will be notified about how far they are from levelling up (Figure 9.4).

FIGURE 9.4 Exergame model and exercise to attribute mappings.

There are three character attributes in *Skyrim*: health, stamina and magicka. Health is how much damage a character can take before dying; stamina is the energy system used for running and performing special physical attacks; and magicka is the energy system for performing magic. We mapped different types of physical activity into game attributes—weight training increases maximum health, cardio increases maximum stamina and everything else (sports, stretching, martial arts, fitness classes) increases maximum magicka. The inherent progression of game difficulty creates an incentive for players to continue exercising to progress with the game.

9.3.4 ARCHITECTURE

Implementation was split into two key components. The mod was developed using Creation Kit, and a DataSync client was developed using Python that would retrieve data from Runkeeper. The architecture of the mod is shown in Figure 9.5.

The DataSync client first retrieves user data that is logged through Exercise.com using the Runkeeper API. JSON objects are returned in the response from the Runkeeper API and the DataSync client sorts through these objects, extracts the relevant information about activities, translates these values into points and stores these points into an experience points file.

The *Skyrim* mod then reads this experience points file when a player loads their saved game, applies experience in-game and awards a level up if enough experience has been earned and then updates the experience points file. The updates to the experience points file are done to prevent players from being able to reload the game over and over again and have the same experience being reapplied.

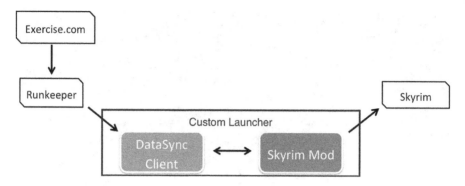

FIGURE 9.5   Mod architecture.

The DataSync client and the *Skyrim* mod are encapsulated within a custom launcher, which simplifies the starting of *Skyrim* for users. The user simply clicks on the custom launcher to log into Runkeeper, sync fitness data and start *Skyrim*.

9.3.5   CREATION KIT MOD IMPLEMENTATION

Using Creation Kit we created our own NPC named Exer of Cise. Players can speak to this NPC in the game's first town to receive a quest to turn on exergame mode in *Skyrim*. This quest manages all exergame mode concerns such as levelling up the player, adjusting the experience requirements depending on the player and updating the exercise experience points file after experience has been applied.

9.3.5.1   Quest Stages

This quest is divided into six stages. Each stage is used to indicate a different state the player is currently in for the exergame mode.

1) Exergame mode is turned off and the player is playing vanilla *Skyrim*.
2) The player first accepts the quest from Exer of Cise. A notification appears on the player's screen showing that they have accepted the exergame quest. Exer of Cise offers exergame mode specific dialogue. The player exits the dialogue.
3) The player receives an immediate level-up for accepting the quest. This communicates that levelling up is not too difficult.
4) Experience points of the player's first workout are received and this triggers a level up regardless of the content of the workout.
5) Stage five begins immediately after the player's first workout is processed and lasts for 1 week. Each time *Skyrim* starts, the DataSync client logs all exercise points earned and saves them into a specific field in the exercise points file used to track how much exercise a player typically does during 1 week. During this first week, all players use receives level-ups based on a default experience curve. This is necessary because insufficient data exists to support the tailored levelling system used in stage six.

6) Stage six comprises the rest of the game. Experience requirements are tailored to the player and increasing exercise magnitude, duration and intensity accelerates levelling (see below for details).

9.3.5.2 On Load Game Level Ups

Creation Kit uses event-driven programming and for the exergame quest, the OnPlayerLoadGame, event is used as a trigger to check if a player has earned a level up. The exercise points file is read in and saves how much total strength, cardio and sport exercise points a player has. If a player has enough points in total to level up, they will be levelled up and a message box is shown congratulating the player and showing how much each attribute has increased by. If they have not levelled up, the player is shown a message box telling them how much more experience is required to level up.

The remaining experience points a player has will then be used to check whether the player has earned any more level ups to put onto the "Level Stack" (see below).

Finally the OnPlayerLoadGame event method overwrites the experience points file so that players cannot load the same data file over and over to receive free level ups.

9.3.5.3 Level Stack

The "Level Stack" is a concept used to encourage players to balance their game playtime in proportion to their exercise time. The stack works by awarding a player the first level when they have enough experience for on load game and then checking if they have enough experience for any subsequent levels. If the player does, they will be given an item called an "Orb of experience" for each level they have on the stack.

After every hour of playtime an update method performs a check to see if the player has an "Orb of experience" in their inventory. If the player has one or more orbs, they will experience a level up similar to an OnPlayerLoadGame level up and one orb will be consumed. The orbs also allow the players to see if they have any pending level ups.

9.3.5.4 Level Ups

All level ups grant ten attribute points distributed between the player's health, stamina and magicka. The distribution of these points will depend on the exercises logged. For instance, if a player has only logged strength training since their last level up, they will receive all ten points to their health attribute. In contrast, if they have 70% of their points through cardio and 30% through sports, they will receive seven points into stamina and three points into magicka.

9.3.6 GAME DESIGN

9.3.6.1 Points System

Exercise.com's point system returns the number of points earned in each logged training session. These number of points received will be in proportion to the quantity and quality of activity that is logged. The calculation of these points will depend on many factors including intensity, duration, difficulty, the type of equipment used and the muscle groups involved. These calculations are very complex and have been developed by a large team of domain experts aided by community feedback. A point system is essential for our exergame model as it provides a metric that allows us to translate physical activity into in-game experience. Unfortunately, Exercise.com's point system is not accessible through the Runkeeper API, and as such we had to develop our own rudimentary point system.

For the fitness activities (cardio and sports) each activity is assigned an intensity modifier between 1.5 and 2.5, depending on the intensity of the activity. This intensity modifier multiplied by the duration of the activity is how we determine the amount of points obtained from each fitness activity:

$$Points = IntensityModifier * Duration \qquad (9.1)$$

where $1.5 < Intensity\ Modifier < 2.5$ in (9.1).

For the purpose of our points and experience system, we required a baseline that all calculations are relative to. This is so that all points obtained across different types of activities and intensities can be scaled and fitted together in the same experience tree. The baseline that was chosen is a fitness activity of intensity two and duration of 90 minutes. An activity of moderate intensity done for 90 minutes is what we have interpreted as an "average" fitness activity session.

For the strength activities, we used tonnage as the base metric for evaluating points obtained from each exercise. Tonnage is defined as (*weight * sets * reps*). Tonnage cannot be directly translated into our point system as the numeric value would be too high, so it is scaled down to fit with other fitness activities. This meant that an average strength training session should give a similar amount of points as an average fitness activity session. To do this we analysed the strength sessions of three trainees with average strength levels. The tonnage of each individual session was analysed and heavy sessions were compared with light sessions. Heuristic analysis was performed and it was found that a balancing constant of 29 would normalise the tonnage values to be able to fit alongside the fitness activities. The formula was then applied to an advanced trainee's sessions in order to see how it would scale appropriately. It was found that the increase in points was reasonable and was relatively proportional to an advanced fitness training session.

$$Points = \frac{Sets * Reps * Weight}{Balancing\ Constant} \qquad (9.2)$$

where *Balancing Constant* = 29 in (9.2).

9.3.6.2 Experience System

Many video games, like physical exercise [24], exhibit decreasing returns. Decreasing one's 10 km run time from 60 minutes to 55 minutes typically takes less effort than decreasing it from 55 minutes to 50 minutes. Similarly, in most video games it takes less effort to get from level 5 to level 6 than to get from level 15 to level 16. This is part of the steadily increasing challenge curve used by games to keep players motivated. We therefore wanted to implement an experience curve with decreasing returns.

However, to reach a larger demographic, an exergame should scale across a wide range of fitness activity levels. The game should still be playable whether the player trains one per week and plays every day, or trains every day and plays once a week. Obviously this is extremely challenging. To proceed, we first work through an example for a typical player and then generalise the example to a broader range of players.

We divided the skeleton of the experience requirements for levelling into different brackets because linear progression in training eventually results in diminishing returns. Instead, piecewise functions were chosen such that the amount of time spent training would closely resemble the amount of time it took to level up in the original game. We used four brackets: 4–9, 10–19, 20–29 and 30+. We made level 30 the lower bound for our last bracket because it was found that this is approximately the point where the player's character is potentially strong enough to complete any part of the game. Once the different experience brackets had been established, we needed to figure out the experience requirements of each bracket. Note that levels 1–4 are free. The player begins on level 1, receives level 2 during the tutorial (before enabling exergaming mode), receives levels 3 upon accepting the exergaming quest and receives level 4 on first sync. The first bracket therefore comprises level 4–9.

To proceed, we make two assumptions:

1) An average training session lasts for 90 minutes. (Since the average intensity modifier for a fitness activity is two, this gives 180 points per session).
2) An average player trains three times per week (giving 540 points per week).

While these numbers are much too high for sedentary or high-risk populations, initial testing is planned for low-risk, physically active young adults.

To scale well with gameplay, we want players to reach approximately level 9 by the end of the first week; therefore, we make the total experience requirements for levels 4–9 approximately 540 points. *Skyrim*'s levelling formula for the experience requirement at a fixed level is:

$$
\begin{aligned}
\text{XP Required For Level}_n = & \left(\text{Level}_n - 1\right) * f\left(\text{XP Level Up Mult}\right) \\
& + f\left(\text{XP Level Up Base}\right)
\end{aligned} \tag{9.3}
$$

where Level_n is the desired level, and $f(\text{XP Level Up Mult})$ and $f(\text{XP Level Up Base})$ can be manipulated programmatically in (9.3). Below, fXPLevel Up Base will be referred to as $v1$ and fXPLevel Up Mult will be referred to as $v2$ for simplicity

- $v1$ and $v2$ are the only variables that can be manipulated for adjusting the experience requirements and so these will be changed for each level bracket. We set $v1 = 16$ and $v2 = 10$ to get 546 points for week 1 (levels 4–9).
- For the second bracket (levels 10–19) we want the player to increase his or her activity level and complete the bracket in about 2 weeks. Assuming four, 90-minute sessions per week (or three, 120-minute sessions), we want

approximately 1440 points in this bracket. Setting $v1 = 65$ and $v2 = 5$ gives 1425 points which is close enough to our desired value.

- The same process is repeated for the third bracket. We want the third bracket to take ten sessions, which takes 2.5 weeks at the rate of four sessions per week or remains at 2 weeks if the player increases activity to five sessions per week. Setting $v1 = 105$ and $v2 = 3$ gives us 1815 points.
- At level 30 and beyond we fix the experience requirements to increase linearly as this is the point where levelling up has lower importance in relation to the rest of the game. We have chosen 14 sessions per bracket of ten levels. We chose $v1 = 158$ and $v2 = 2$ which results in 2520 points per ten levels for levels above 30.

To generalise this to a range of players, we retain the first bracket to acquire initial training data in week 1 and then tailor the levelling curve based on previous data, according to the following formulas.

To reach a larger demographic, an exergame should scale across a wide range of fitness levels. The experience function described above cannot be fixed like the original game and instead we will need to tailor it to the user's fitness levels. The previously designed experience skeleton can be set up entirely with just the initial first week points, i.e. 540 points. This means that if the same proportions of $v1$ and $v2$ are kept relative to the initial skeleton and only the points in the initial week are modified, the experience skeleton can be scaled based on the amount of activity done in week one. The following formulas are generated:

$$Bracket1 : V1 = b1 * \frac{16}{540}, V2 = b1 * \frac{10}{540}$$

$$Bracket2 : V1 = b2 * \frac{16}{540}, V2 = b2 * \frac{10}{540}$$

$$Bracket3 : V1 = b3 * \frac{16}{540}, V2 = b3 * \frac{10}{540}$$

$$Bracket4 : V1 = b4 * \frac{16}{540}, V2 = b4 * \frac{10}{540}$$

where

$$BracketOnePoints : b1 = UserInputFromWeekOne$$

$$BracketTwoPoints : b2 = BracketOnePoints * 2.6667$$

$$BracketThreePoints : b3 = BracketTwoPoints * 1.25$$

$$BracketFourPoints : b4 = BracketThreePoints * 1.40$$

These formulas impose a soft cap of level 9 during the first week; that is, the curve scales such that no one could conceivably train hard enough to reach level 9. Capping progress in the first week is necessary to prevent players from levelling too quickly, which would make the game too easy and therefore boring. However, imposing a soft cap (where the player appears to continue advancing towards level 9) keeps the player motivated.

9.4 LESSONS LEARNED AND FUTURE WORK

We learned several important lessons by developing this prototype exergame:

1) Creation Kit does not fully support object-oriented practices or interactions with web services. Modders have to create their own object-like classes. In-game persistence and available data structures are also limited. We therefore had to save state using a custom inventory item and write a python web client to retrieve the exercise data.

2) Early in the game, it is possible for the player to increase multiple levels from one exercise session. Levelling up too quickly can degrade game balance and feel overwhelming to a new player. To prevent this from happening, we implemented a level stack such that, if a player earns several level ups at once, they receive the first immediately; however, subsequent level ups are stored in inventory as "orbs of experience." Each hour of play, one orb of experience is automatically consumed, triggering a level up.

3) Players may also decide to neglect one or two exercise categories; for example magicka is of little value to a melee oriented character. This issue remains unresolved and we are waiting to see its effect in upcoming user studies.

4) The exercise point system is rudimentary and the intensity modifier only roughly captures trainee effort. While we hard-coded checks for low range-of-motion strength exercises (e.g. calf-raise and shrug), which would generate too many points otherwise, a more comprehensive approach is needed. Fortunately, Exercise.com seem willing to provide us with a way of accessing their point system in the future.

5) Only one save file is supported. This may frustrate some players and should be addressed in future work. This is because all experience points a player has earned are applied to the character when the game is loaded. After points have been applied, they are removed from the experience points file to prevent players from re-importing old data to get free level ups.

9.4.1 THE BIGGER PICTURE

Different fitness tracking applications appeal to different kinds of trainees and different kinds of games appeal to different players. Players, moreover, tire of one game and move on to another. The broader aim of this project is therefore not simply to build a specific exergame but to create tools and technologies to facilitate exergaming modes in many games, which harvest data from many sources.

The prototype suggests that such a system might have a three-tier architecture (Figure 9.6):

1) Fitness data services including wearables (e.g. Fit Bit), manual tracking applications (e.g. Exercise.com) and automatic tracking applications (e.g. Runkeeper).

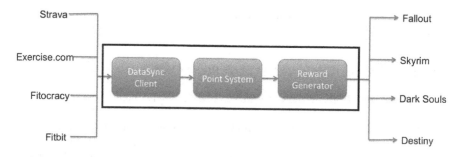

FIGURE 9.6   Future development.

2) A data integration layer, which transforms raw fitness data into information, that makes sense to and is more directly usable by game designers. This would include an exercise point system.
3) Video games with exergaming modes and stand-alone exergames.

9.4.2 Updates and Public Release

This chapter describes our first attempt at a *Skyrim* Exergaming Modification. A later version of the mod, dubbed "Exergaming Mode," was publicly released in September, 2017 through Nexus Mods[1]. This later version is somewhat simpler than our first design. Exergaming mode is enabled through a menu instead of accepting a quest. The mod connects directly to Exercise.com, so Runkeeper and the bespoke points system are no longer necessary. The initial levelling has been simplified, eliminating the need for orbs of experience and free levels.

9.5   CONCLUSION

In summary, this paper argues that exergames' effectiveness depends on both how immersive the game is and how intense the exercise is. To deliver both intense exercise and immersive gameplay, we propose constructing *asynchronous* exergames (where gameplay and training occur separately). We present a prototype implementation to illustrate the approach and demonstrate its feasibility.

Two avenues of future work are evident. Randomised controlled trials are needed to investigate whether the proposed exergame leads to increase physical activity and subsequent health benefits. Furthermore, exergaming modifications of other games are needed to investigate the feasibility and effectiveness of the proposed approach with other game genres.

More generally, commercial game developers implement various modes including online competitive multiplayer, offline co-operative multiplayer ("couch co–op") and variations with enhanced difficulty ("hardcore mode"). The long-term objective of this research is to convince game publishers such as Sony, Microsoft, EA and Nintendo that it will be easy, profitable and ethical to add exergame modes to many of their games, maximising the positive effect on societal health and well-being.

This will create a broad research programme around how to implement exergaming modes in different kinds of games (e.g. puzzle, turn-based strategy and role-playing) and the relationship between numerous game features and effects on player motivation, health and fitness. Only when exergaming modes are as ubiquitous as online multiplayer can the full benefits of exergaming be realised.

NOTE

1 https://www.nexusmods.com/skyrim/mods/86460

REFERENCES

[1] P. O'Rourke K.A. Shaw, H.C. Gennat and K.C. Del Mar 2006. Exercise for Overweight or Obesity. *Cochrane Database for Systematic Reviews* (October 2006).

[2] New Zealand Ministry of Health. 2014. Obesity Data and Stats: 2014. Retrieved April 14, 2014 from http://www.health.govt.nz/nz-health-statistics/health-statistics-and-data-sets/obesity-data-and-stats

[3] J. Brand. 2014. Digital New Zealand 2014. http://www.igea.net/2013/10/digital-new-zealand-2014/

[4] C.S. Rigby A.K. Przybylski and R.M. Ryan 2010. A Motivational Model of Video Game Engagement. *Review of General Psychology* 14, 2, 154–166.

[5] T.M. Connolly, E.A. Boyle, E. MacArthur, T. Hainey, and J.M. Boyle. 2012. A Systematic Literature Review of Empirical Evidence on Computer Games and Serious Games. *Computers & Education* 59, 2, 661–686.

[6] J. Gackenbach and J. Bown. 2011. Mindfulness and Video Game Play: A Preliminary Inquiry. *Mindfulness* 2, 2, 114–122.

[7] D. Choi and J. Kim. 2004. Why People Continue to Play Online Games: In Search of Critical Design Factors to Increase Customer Loyalty to Online Contents. *CyberPsychology & Behavior* 7, 1, 11–24.

[8] T.-J. Chou and C.-C. Ting. 2004. The Role of Flow Experience in Cyber-Game Addiction. *CyberPsychology & Behavior* 6, 6, 663–675.

[9] O.V. Mitina A.E. Voiskounsky and A.A. Avetisova. 2004. Playing Online Games: Flow Experience. *PsychNology Journal* 2, 3, 259–281.

[10] M. Csikszentmihalyi. 2000. *Beyond Boredom and Anxiety*. Jossey-Bass.

[11] J. Madigan. 2010. The Psychology of Immersion in Video Games. Retrieved May 12, 2014 from http://www.psychologyofgames.com/2010/07/the-psychology-of-immersion-in-video-games/

[12] G.C. Roberts. 1992. *Motivation in Sport and Exercise*. Human Kinetics Books.

[13] W. Peng, J.-H. Lin, and J. Crouse. 2011. Is Playing Exergames Really Exercising? A Meta-Analysis of Energy Expenditure in Active Video Games. *Cyberpsychology, Behavior, and Social Networking* 14, 11, 681–688. doi: 10.1089/cyber.2010.0578

[14] W. Peng, J. C. Crouse, and J.-H. Lin. 2013. Using Active Video Games for Physical Activity Promotion: A Systematic Review of the Current State of Research. *Health Education & Behavior* 40, 2, 171–192. doi: 10.1177/1090198112444956.

[15] A. Ahmad, S. Hormoz, S. Mohsen, and G. Koenig Harold. 2018. Impact of Game-Based Health Promotion Programs on Body Mass Index in Overweight/Obese Children and Adolescents: A Systematic Review and Meta-Analysis of Randomized Controlled Trials. *Childhood Obesity* 14, 2, 67–80. doi: 10.1089/chi.2017.0250.

[16] How to Use Your PM5|Fish Game. (2016). Retrieved January 12, 2016 from http://www.concept2.com/service/monitors/pm5/how-to-use/fish-game

[17] H. Cavusoglu A. Kankanhalli, M. Taher and S.H. Kim. 2012. *Gamification: A New Paradigm for Online User Engagement. Proceedings of the International Conference on Information Systems, AIS (2012).*

[18] M. Richard, M. F. Christina, L. S. Deborah, N. Rubio, and M. S. Kennon. 1997. Intrinsic Motivation and Exercise Adherence. *International Journal of Sport Psychology* 28, 4, 334–354.

[19] J. Schell. 2008. *The Art of Game Design: A Book of Lenses.* Morgan Kaufmann.

[20] P. Ralph and K. Monu. 2015. Toward a Unified Theory of Digital Games. *The Computer Game Journal* 4, 1, 81–100.

[21] Bethesda. 2013. E3 2013: ESO Arriving on PlayStation 4, Xbox One!. Retrieved January 27, 2016 from http://www.bethblog.com/2013/06/10/e3-2013-eso-arriving-on-playstation-4-xbox-one/

[22] GameLengths: Average Play Times for *The Elder Scrolls V: Skyrim.* (2016). Retrieved January 12, 2016 from http://www.gamelengths.com/games/playtimes/The+Elder+Scrolls+V%3A+Skyrim/

[23] M . LeBlanc, R . Hunicke and R . Zubek. 2004. *MDA: A formal approach to game design and game research. Proceedings of the AAAI Workshop on Challenges in Game AI 4,* 1 (July 2004), 1–5.

[24] T.R. Baechle and R.W. Earle. 2008. *Essentials of Strength Training and Conditioning.* Human Kinetics.

10 Survey on Software Architecture, Creativity, and Game Technology

Alf Inge Wang and Njål Nordmark

Norwegian University of Science and Technology

CONTENTS

10.1 INTRODUCTION

Game development can be challenging as game engines and game hardware and development platforms changes rapidly, and code modules crafted for specific games offer less than 30% reuse [1]. In the first decade of the video game history, game development was carried out by small teams. The software architectures of these games were typically made out of a few modules such as 2D graphics, simulation, sound, streaming of I/O, and a main module. At this time, the main focus was on how to create an exciting game with the limited hardware resources available rather than a focus on software architecture and software engineering. The growth of the video game industry along with the progress in hardware has resulted in vastly larger and more complex games rendering and simulating huge interactive virtual worlds developed by large multidisciplinary teams. The growth in size and complexity of games have resulted in similar growth in size and complexity of game architectures [2]. The game projects producing a typical AAA game title today are very large, and the game software itself has a complex software architecture with many interconnected modules. Many quality attributes in game development are the same as in traditional software development such as modifiability, reliability, security, and usability, but one aspect that makes software architectures for games challenging is the absolute real-time requirements and the need to support the creative processes in game development [1]. Game development requires often to a larger extent than traditional software development a multitude of computer science skills [3] as well as other disciplines as art, game design, and audio/music [4]. The direct involvement of professions with very different background, knowledge, and skills (e.g., the technical team vs. the creative team) poses challenges for how a game is developed. Based on all the challenges described above, game development is an interesting domain for software engineering research, as well as the fact that game development is a very big, successful, and innovative industry.

So far, most of the software engineering research related to game development has focused on requirement engineering, and there is a lack of empirical work [5]. This chapter presents a study on how game developers think about and manage software architecture, how the creative processes affect the development, and how game development and game technology has changed in the recent years. The study investigates the relationship between creative design and software development, and how the technical and creative teams collaborate. The results presented are based on responses from a survey aimed at game developers. The initial survey was extended with a follow-up survey where in-depth questions were asked. Along with our own experience from game development and with support from research literature, this chapter draws a picture of how game developers work with and manage software architecture, how creative development processes are managed, and how game development and technology has changed in the recent years. To our knowledge, this is the first study of this kind within software engineering. This chapter is based on a master thesis at the Norwegian University of Science and Technology [6], and parts of this study has previously been published in [7].

The rest of the chapter is organized as follows. Section 2 presents related work on software architecture and games and software engineering and games. Section 3 describes the research goal, research questions, and research methods used. Section 4 presents the results from the initial survey addressed to game developers. Section 5 describes the results from the more focused follow-up survey. Section 6 discusses the validity of the research and results presented, and Section 5 concludes the chapter.

10.2   RELATED WORK

As far as we know, there are no similar studies that focus both on software architecture and creative processes in game development. However, there are studies that focus on the software architecture in games and studies focusing on the creative processes. In this section, we will present work in the field of software engineering and game development.

As games over the years have grown into large complex systems, the video game industry is facing several software engineering challenges. Kanode and Haddad have identified the software engineering challenges in game development to be [8]: diverse assets include both code and graphics and audio assets, a large project scope that can be difficult to define, high risk of game publishing, project management with a very tight schedule, and involvement of many professions, inter-disciplinary team organization, development process that includes more than just software, and third-party technology. In this article we will mainly focus on project management, team organization, development process, and cost and complexity related to third-party technology. Similarly, Petrillo et al. found through a survey of game postmortems that game development and traditional software development suffers from similar main problems such as unrealistic scope, over budget, and loss of professionals [9]. A major difference found was that game development had a bigger problem with crunch time. Lewis and Whitehead describes the intersection of software engineering and game development and investigates four main areas: development of games, how games are designed, how middleware supports creative processes, and how games are tested [10]. This research focuses on two topics in our chapter: the difference between traditional and game development and tool support for creative processes. As in traditional software development, a major challenge of game development is testing and dealing with bugs. Lewis, Whitehead, and Wardrip-Fruin have established a taxonomy of video game bugs extracted from online user documentation [11]. The taxonomy covers bug areas like timing, position, graphical representation, change of value, artificial behavior, information, and action. There have also been several proposals from the research community to game developers to adopt software engineering practices, such as the use of ISO/IEC 29110 (life cycle profiles for very small entities) in game development [12]. So far, the impact of introducing new software engineering practices on the gaming industry has been limited.

To our knowledge, only one systematic literature review related to software engineering and game development has been conducted [5]. The goal of this review was to establish the state of the art on research concerning software engineering in the video games domain. The result of this literature review showed that the main emphasis in this research domain is on requirement engineering, as well as coding tools and techniques. Research related requirement engineering in games focuses on the problem of going from a game concept that should be fun and engaging to functional requirements, and software architectures and software designs that can produce game software realizing the game concept [13]. The initial requirements for a game can be labeled emotional requirements containing the game designer's intent and the means which the game designer expects the production team to induce that emotional state in the player [4]. Another area within software engineering and game development is research on coding tools and techniques including development of game engines [14–16], component-based game development [17], the use of game engines and tools [18–21], development of serious games [1, 22, 23], and challenges and solutions for networked multiplayer games [24–28]. Further, there are articles focusing on software architectures [29–36] and design patterns [37–39] for games. Such articles propose software architectures and/or design patterns to solve particular problems in game development. However, unlike our chapter, these articles say very little about the processes in which the architectures and patterns are used, and how the game development process is affected by various roles.

There are articles discussing the game development process and the involved roles. In [40], Scacchi presents how the free and open source development practices in the game community differs from traditional software engineering practices in that the process does not fit into a traditional lifecycle model or partially ordered as a spiral process. Also, the requirements are not found in requirement specification documents, but they are extracted from threaded messages or discussions on web sites. In [41], a survey of problems in game development is presented based on an analysis of postmortems (summaries of what went right and what went wrong in completed projects) written by various game developers. According to Flood, all game development postmortems say the same things: the project was delivered behind schedule; it contained many defects; the functionalities were not the ones that had originally been projected; and it took a lot of pressure and an immense number of development hours to complete the project [42]. This description also fits well with typical problems within conventional software engineering. Petrillo et al. further details the specific problems found in game development postmortems to be unrealistic: scope, feature, cutting features during development, problems in the design phase, delays, technological problems, crunch time, lack of documentation, communication problems, tool problems, test problems, team building, number of defects, loss of professionals, and over budget [41]. The problems that clearly differentiate game development from conventional software development are more issues related to unrealistic scope, feature creep, lack of documentation, and crunch time.

Several studies have examined the tension between being creative and working structured and goal-oriented in game development [43]. In their study, Tschang and Szczypula found that game design results from individuals' creative actions, idea creation, constructivism, and evolution [44]. Another study of 65 project reports by Tschang showed that the same processes are used in game development as those used in the creation of other creative products [45]. A case study of how game studios produce games by Stacey and Nandhakumar, revealed that the game development process was an alternation of routine and improvisation [46]. The need for improvisation in game development is routed in the fact that game development is all about innovation and about producing a product the user will first of all enjoy and have a great experience with. The unique and close relationship between the product and the user in game development, produce a strong dependency between the game developer and the player community, which is very different from traditional software development [47]. Although game development always has been strongly influenced by creativity and artistic freedom, a study based on interviews with the game industry by Kultima and Alha indicate a rise of instrumentalist views within game industry opposed to more artistic and personal view [48].

A study by Petrillo and Pimenta investigates if (and how) principles and practices from agile methods have been adopted in game development by analyzing postmortems of game development projects [49]. The conclusion of this study was that game developers are adopting a set of agile practices, although informally. This means that game developers can easily start using agile methods, like Scrum and XP, since they have already several agile practices in place. One aspect of agile methods that is very relevant to our research is the emphasis on frequently gathering relevant stakeholders to bridge the gap between all involved in the project [50]. This is related to our study where we investigated how the creative team, the technical team, and the management collaborate and coordinate.

10.3 RESEARCH GOAL, QUESTIONS, AND METHODS

The research method used in case study is based on the Goal, Question, and Metrics (GQM) approach where we first define a research goal (conceptual level), then define a set of research questions (operational level), and finally describe a set of metrics to answer the defined research questions (quantitative level) [51]. The metrics used in our study is a mixture of qualitative and quantitative data [52].

The research goal of this study was defined as the following using the GQL template:

> The purpose of this study is to *examine how software architecture is used and how creative processed are managed* from the point of view of a *game developer* in the context of *video game development*.

The following research questions were defined by decomposing the research goal:

RQ1: What role does software architecture play in game development?
RQ2: How do game developers manage changes to the software architecture?
RQ3: How are the creative processes managed and supported in game development?
RQ4: How has game development evolved in the last couple of years?

To find answers to the research questions, we used a combined approach that included a questionnaire, a follow-up survey, and a literature study to support the findings. The questionnaire consisted of 20 statements where the respondents state whether they agree or not, using the Likert's scale [53]. In addition, the questionnaire provided a free text comment for every statement. The statements in the questionnaire were constructed from the research goal and the research questions presented above. The subjects of the study were recruited from the Nordic booth at the Game Developer Conference in San Francisco, as well as direct emails sent to game developers. The questionnaire was answered both on paper and using web-forms created using surveymonkey.com.

After receiving questionnaire responses, a follow-up survey with eight open-ended questions were sent out to the respondents from the questionnaire willing to give more detailed answers. The survey was conducted on the web only using surveymonkey.com.

10.4 RESULTS FROM QUESTIONNAIRE

This section presents the quantitative results from the questionnaire, comments from the respondents, as well as reflections from the research literature. Responses from 13 game companies were received. Figure 10.1 shows the distribution of number of

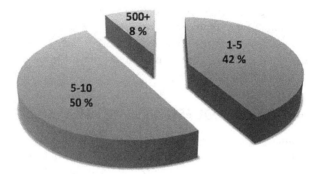

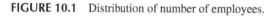

FIGURE 10.1   Distribution of number of employees.

employees of the 13 companies. Only one big game developer responded (with 500+ employees), half of them (50%) had 5–10 employees, and the rest (42%) had between one and five employees. None of the game companies wanted their name to be public. The complete results from the questionnaire and the follow-up survey presented in next section can be found in [6].

10.4.1   Design of Software Architecture (RQ1)

The first part of the questionnaire focused on the design of software architecture in game development, and the responses from the first six statements are shown in the Tables 10.1–10.6.

This statement assessed the importance of software architecture among game developers. The result shows that most of the game developers in our study considered software architecture to be an important part of game development. One comment from the respondents clearly illustrates the importance of software architecture in games (the given response on Likert's scale is shown in parenthesis):

- *Oversight in the game software architecture may lead to serious dead ends, leading to a need to rewrite the entire system.* (Agree)

In the early years of the video game industry, simple game software architectures were made by small teams of one to three persons. As game technology, user demands, and the game industry have grown, careful designing and planning of software architectures have become necessary to manage the complexity and size and the

TABLE 10.1

"Design of Software Architecture is an Important Part of our Game Development Process"

Agree	Neutral	Disagree
75%	16%	9%

TABLE 10.2

"The Main Goal of our Software Architecture is Performance"

Agree	Neutral	Disagree
59%	16%	25%

TABLE 10.3

"Our Game Concept Heavily Influences the Software Architecture"

Agree	Neutral	Disagree
75%	9%	16%

TABLE 10.4

"The Creative Team is Included in the Design of the Software Architecture"

Agree	Neutral	Disagree
75%	16%	9%

TABLE 10.5

"Our Existing Software Suite Provides Features Aimed at Helping the Creative Team Do Their Job"

Agree	Neutral	Disagree
92%	8%	0%

TABLE 10.6

"Our Existing Software Architecture Dictates the Future Game Concepts We Can Develop"

Agree	Neutral	Disagree
15%	47%	38%

involvement of many involved developers [2]. Although the majority of respondents represent smaller game developers, the complexity of game engines and use of other libraries and APIs demands a focus on software architectures to create platforms that can cope with changing requirements during the project [17]. Another reason software architecture has become very important in game development is the fact that the quality attributes are so important. It is impossible to have success with a game that suffers from bad performance (low and/or unstable framerates), bad usability, poor portability, poor testability (resulting in many bugs), and limited modifiability (hard to extend after release) [29]. In addition, for massive multiplayer online games (MMOGs), quality attributes such as security (to avoid cheating) and availability are crucial for success [54]. Careful design and evaluation of the software architecture is the main approach to achieve predictable and acceptable quality attributes in software development [55].

The second statement in the questionnaire addressed the purpose of software architecture in game development (see Table 10.2).

The majority of the companies in the survey agreed that the main goal of the software architecture for them was to ensure sufficient performance. However, the respondents clarified that there are quality attributes other than performance that must be taken into account. Here are some comments regarding this statement:

- *Performance plus functionality.* (Agree)
- *Also, future change, ability to be data-driven, optimized deployment processes, ease [of] automation/script-ability, and testability.* (Agree)
- *Main goals are: Performance, Memory consumption and Actual purpose of the software. Real time software as games must perform according to the platform requirements in order to see the light of the day regardless of the content.* (Agree)

The next statement in the questionnaire investigated the relationship between the game concept and the software architecture (see Table 10.3).

Three out of four game developers agreed that the game concept heavily influences the software architecture. This result was a bit surprising, as usage of game engines should ideally make the software architecture less dependent on game concept and game design. One respondent provided the following comment:

- *Entirely depends on the game concept requirements, but in general: more generic – within boundaries – the better. This highlights that the importance of separating generic modules (core) with modules specific for a game (gameplay). Such an approach will allow reuse of core components, and at the same time provide sufficient freedom in development of game concept.* (Agree)

How much the game concept will influence the game software architecture is really a question about where to draw the line between the game and the game engine. Currently, most game engines target one or few game genres, such as real-time strategy (RTS) games or first-person shooters (FPSs). As there is yet no taxonomy that can be used to specify all types of games, there exist few game engines that are independent of genres [29]. Plummer tries to overcome this problem by proposing a flexible and expandable architecture for video games not specific to a genre [31]. However, too general game engines will most likely have poor performance and heavy usage of memory due to overhead in the code. This means that the design of game engines must balance performance and use of resources vs. modifiability. Thus, games that stretch game genres will result in software architectures that deviate from the architecture of the game engine [29].

Statement four in the questionnaire asked whether the creative team is included in the design of the software architecture (see Table 10.4).

The large majority of the respondents agreed that the creative team is included in the design of the software architecture. It should be noted that the majority of the game developers in this survey were small companies, which makes it easier for the whole team to be involved in the whole development process. In smaller companies, many employees play several roles and work both with software development as well as creative design. A comment from one company with 5–10 employees highlights how the creative team can be involved in the software architecture:

- *Only because I am a programmer and also the lead designer. Other creative people don't know enough to be productively included.* (Agree)

It is interesting to note that the only large developer with 500+ employees said that they were neutral to this statement. We have seen at least three ways the creative team can contribute to the software architecture:

Which game to make: The decision of the game to make will give the foundation for the main constraints of the software architecture.

New in-game functionality: The creative team might request new in-game functionality that changes the software architecture.

New development features: Request for new development features (e.g., tool support and/or tool integration) might lead to changes in the software architecture.

Another comment related to this statement was:

- *This is mostly true when working on the tools the creative team will be using. It rarely applies to in-game specific features.* (Agree)

Experiences from postmortems of game development projects show the importance of making the technical and creative team overlap going from game concept into developing the actual game software [41].

The next statement in the questionnaire is related to how well the creative team is supported by the tools provided for development (see Table 10.5).

The response concludes that the game engine and the supporting tools provide features helping the creative team in their work. This is further supported and refined in the comments:

- *Our third-party tools do not do this, but we've developed in-house extensions that do.* (Agree)

- *Use two software tiers that aims at very different levels of artist integration: Visual Studio and Unity3D.* (Agree)

The latter comment describes the situation that it is not always the ideal tools the creative teams have to use. Ideally, the creative team should be supported by various GUI editors and high-level scripting. However, in practice, it might be necessary to dive into the source code to get the game where the creative team wants it to go. This process is normally carried out in collaboration with the technical team.

Table 10.6 shows the response to statement six regarding whether existing software architectures put restrictions on future game concepts.

A strong drive for game development is creativity coming up with innovative fresh game concepts. The response shown in Table 10.6 shows that this is for the most part true. This topic relates to the core of how game companies see themselves, if they are constrained by existing technology, or can they create whatever the creative team comes up with. Half of the respondents are neutral to this statement, which shows that in practice they have to go for the middle ground. Here are some comments to this statement:

- *We have engines that gives us a great benefit when building new games and we would prefer to continue on the same engines. However, it doesn't fully dictate the games we will make in the future. This is primarily market-driven.* (Neutral)
- *It may influence, but not dictate whenever possible.* (Neutral)
- *It makes it a bit more expensive to go to certain genres, but that's it.* (Disagree)

The first two comments show that game developers want to be free to create whatever they want, but at the same time they are constrained by market, convenience, and budget. The third comment (disagree) indicates that the influence exerted by the existing software architecture is a direct result of a cost-benefit trade-off. The higher the cost of change, the more influence the existing software architecture exerts on the game concepts.

10.4.2 CHANGES TO THE SOFTWARE ARCHITECTURE (RQ2)

This section presents results from the questionnaire on statements on how game developers cope with changes to the software architecture shown in the Tables 10.7–10.12. Table 10.7 shows the response to a statement on whether the creative team's ideas are restricted by existing game engine.

No clear conclusion could be drawn based on how the game companies responded. However, here are some comments that might explain the divergence in the responses:

- *Technical realities are always something the creative side has to work around.* (Agree)
- *Depending on structure. For assets handling, yes, but creatively, not so much. In latter case, the challenge is put to programmers to extend usage.* (Neutral)

TABLE 10.7

"The Creative Team Has to Adapt Their Ideas to the Existing Game Engine"

Agree	Neutral	Disagree
31%	46%	23%

- *Most of the time, the creative team is not fully aware of the game engine limitation's, so it is not their job to make it work by locking the creativity to things known to have been done with the engine before, the people who implements just need to make the ideas work one way or another.* (Disagree)
- *That is not the way we do it here. The game design comes first, then we build what is necessary to make it happen.* (Disagree)

These comments indicate a trade-off between creative freedom and the technical limitations. It is axiomatic that if an idea not supported in the current technology should be implemented, either the idea has to be adapted to the existing technology, the technology adapted to the idea, or something in between. Which one to be chosen depends on a cost-benefit analysis.

The next statement asked if changes of the software architecture can be demanded by the creative team (see Table 10.8).

The majority of the respondents agree that the creative team can demand changes to the software architecture and none disagreed to this statement. There were two comments to this statement:

- *Depends how far in development and how big of a change, the odds of re-factoring an entire system late in production are close to nil, but the development team keeps an open mind at all times.* (Neutral)
- *But again, only because the head of the creative team is president of the company and also wrote the original version of the game engine. If someone who doesn't know how to program were to come to me and demand changes to the software architecture, I would probably not listen very seriously.* (Agree)

Based on the comments of two statements in Table 10.8, game developers are inclined to prioritize the wants and needs of the creative team, given that the cost-benefit

TABLE 10.8

"During Development, the Creative Team Can Demand Changes to the Software Architecture"

Agree	Neutral	Disagree
69%	31%	0%

TABLE 10.9

"Who Decides if Change-Requests from the Creative Team Are Implemented?"

Technical team	Management	Creative team
10%	40%	50%

trade-off is favorable. Another important issue is the phase the project is in. Later in the project (production), less changes and request from the creative team is possible. Boehm and Basili estimate that requirements error can cost up to 100 times more after delivery if caught at the start of the project [56]. A possible solution to this problem is to spend more time in the preproduction phases (25%–40% of the project time) before moving to production, as it would leave relatively few surprises in the production phase [57]. In practice, this might be very difficult as the majority of playtesting of the game happens in the production phase, which might reveal major problems with the core gameplay.

Table 10.9 shows the response to decide if change-request from creative team should be implemented.

The responses to this question were mainly divided between management and the creative team. Here are the respondents' comments to this statement:

- *Ultimately, the management can overrule everybody, but I would like to check the 3 options here, the creative team judges how important the change is, the technical team decides if it is realistic, and the management makes sure it can be afforded. So mostly, it is a team decision.* (Management)
- *Actually, it is all of the above, but the question would not let me put that as an answer.* (Management)
- *Sort of. The technical team advices what is possible, and as such has the final word. If it is possible, the decision falls on management, as it is usually related to economic costs.* (Technical team)
- *Depends very much on the scale of change, we try as much as possible to keep this within and as a dialogue between the tech/creative teams, but if it means major change it goes to management. We also aim to be as much product/feature driven as possible, as the primary owner is in the creative team.* (Creative team)

The responses from the developers indicate that all three branches (administration, technical, and creative) are involved in change decisions. More game developers have also started to adopt agile development practices, where it is more common to have frequent planning and decision meetings where various professions are involved [58].

The next statement asks whether the technical team implements all features required by the creative team (see Table 10.10).

TABLE 10.10

"The Technical Team Implements All Features Requested by the Creative Team"

Agree	Neutral	Disagree
75%	15%	8%

The majority of the game companies agreed that the technical team implements all features requested by the creative team. There were several comments to this statement that provide more details:

- *It can happen that the creative team contributes on technical aspects during prototyping phase. Production quality code is however left to the technical people.* (Agree)
- *Of course, if the requests are decided to be implemented in the first place.* (Agree)
- *It's very much a dialogue, we try not to have too formal split between tech and creative team when thinking about this but prioritize what the user experience should be and when we can ship at target quality.* (Agree)
- *Some requested features are not tech. feasible.* (Disagree)

Table 10.11 shows the results from the statement regarding adding features to a near complete game engine.

The majority of the respondents agree that it is easy to add new gameplay elements after the core game engine has been completed. However, the comments related to this statement suggest that adding new gameplay elements after completing the core game engine is often not possible, recommended, or wanted:

- *It is simple during prototyping phase, technology-wise. However, from a game concept point of view, it is highly dis-recommended and the fact it is simple does not motivate the team to stack up features because the existing one are just not convincing enough.* (Agree)
- *This really depends a lot and can only be answered on a case to case effect.* (Neutral)

TABLE 10.11

"It Is Easy to Add New Gameplay Elements after the Core of Our Game Engine Has Been Completed"

Agree	Neutral	Disagree
82%	18%	0%

- *Depends on the type of element – some may require significant underlying engine changes.* (Neutral)

One of the most common motivations for designing of software architecture is to provide a system that is easier to modify and maintain. In game development, modifiability must be balanced with performance. There are mainly two contrasting approaches to design modifiable game environments [59]: 1) *Scripting* that requires developers to anticipate, handcraft, and script specific game events; and 2) *Emergence* that involves defining game objects that interact according to rules to give rise to emergent gameplay. The most common approach is to create or acquire a game engine that provides a scripting language to create a game with predefined behavior. The emergence approach involves creation of a simulation of a virtual world with objects that reacts to their surroundings. The use of scripting makes it complex to add new gameplay elements, as everything is hardwired. The emergence approach makes it much easier to add new gameplay elements later in the project, with the price of being harder to test (large number of possible game object interactions).

The next statement focused on the creative team's use of existing tools and features during development (see Table 10.12).

It is not possible to draw a conclusion based on the results from the statement above. The comments from the respondents give more insights:

- *The ones already available and the ones they request along the way.* (Agree)
- *New tools can be made. However, it is certainly best to keep within the suite offered.* (Disagree)
- *Our current engine (Unity) is easily extensible.* (Disagree)

This statement is really about cost. Adding new tools and features during development is costly and might also add risk to the project. However, in some cases new tools and features must be added to get the wanted results. The only large company with 500+ employees responded neutral to this statement to indicate that it depends on the circumstances.

10.4.3 Supporting the Creative Processes (RQ3)

The responses on statements presented in Table 10.13–10.16 relate to how creative processes are supported through technology and processes. Table 10.13 shows the

---

TABLE 10.12

"During Development, the Creative Team Has to Use the Tools and Features Already Available"

Agree	Neutral	Disagree
47%	15%	38%

TABLE 10.13

"Our Game Engine Supports Dynamic Loading of New Content"

Agree	Neutral	Disagree
92%	8%	0%

TABLE 10.14

"Our Game Engine Has a Scripting System the Creative Team can Use to Try Out and Implement New Ideas"

Agree	Neutral	Disagree
70%	15%	15%

TABLE 10.15

"The Creative Team Is Included in Our Development Feedback Loop (e.g., Scrum Meetings)"

Agree	Neutral	Disagree
91%	9%	0%

TABLE 10.16

"Our Game Engine Allows Rapid Prototyping of New Levels, Scenarios, and NPCs/Behavior"

Agree	Neutral	Disagree
91%	9%	0%

responses to a statement whether the game engines used by the game companies support dynamics loading of new content (not require recompiling or building).

The response from the game developers shows that current game engines allow dynamic loading of new content. However, the comments to this statement show that there are some restrictions in terms of when and how it can be done:

- *At some extent, in editor mode yes, at run-time only a subset of it.* (Agree)
- *With some constraints, content must be properly prepped of course.* (Agree)

Different game engines provide different flexibility regarding changes that can be carried out at run-time. Most game engines support changes to the graphic as long as the affected graphical structures are similar. Similarly, many game engines allow run-time changes using a scripting language that can change the behavior of the game. However, substantial changes to the gameplay and changes of the game engine itself usually cannot be changed in run-time.

The next statement asked if the game engine used had a scripting system than can be used by the creative team (see Table 10.14).

Most of the respondents say they have a scripting system that can be used by the creative team. However, there are also game developers in the survey that use own game engines without scripting capabilities. Especially for small game developers, it can be too expensive and too much work to create support for scripting in their own game engine. In addition, small game developers do not necessarily have the competence to develop such flexible game engines. The comments related to this statement were:

- *Yes, but could be better and more flexible (as always...)* (Agree)
- *Our 'scripting system' is typing in C++ code and recompiling the game.* (Disagree)

A recognized problem of letting the creative team script the game engine, is that they usually do not understand the underlying low-level mechanisms related to performance [60]. Until the game engines can optimize the scripts automatically, the technical team often must assist the creative team with scripting.

Table 10.15 shows the results to a statement that asked whether the creative team was included in the company's development feedback loop or not.

As the majority of the game developers in this survey are rather small organizations, it is natural that the creative team is included in the development feedback loop. However, even the large game developer in the survey (500+ employees) said that the creative team was included in development feedback loops. This is in alignment with what has been found in other studies [40, 49, 58]. The only comment related to this statement was:

- *Depends on the phase of the project.* (Neutral)

The next statement focused on rapid prototyping using game engines (see Table 10.16).

This statement is related to the statement in Table 10.14, and the response was also the same. Game engines supporting scripting normally provide rapid prototyping. There was only one comment related to this statement:

- *While most of the systems are designed with simplicity and fast iteration time in mind, certain things still require time consuming tweaking tasks.* (Agree)

10.4.4   Changes over Time (RQ4)

Tables 10.17–10.20 show the response to statements that investigate how game development has changed in the last couple of years. Table 10.17 shows the results from statement on the change of usage of third-party modules.

The response to this statement seemed to be that the majority uses more third-party modules than 3 years ago. This confirms the predictions that buying a good

TABLE 10.17

"Today Our Company Uses More Third-Party Modules than 3 Years Ago"

Agree	Neutral	Disagree
67%	22%	12%

TABLE 10.18

"It is Easier to Develop Games Today than It Was 5 Years Ago"

Agree	Neutral	Disagree
77%	8%	15%

TABLE 10.19

"Middleware Is More Important to Our Company Today than 3 Years Ago"

Agree	Neutral	Disagree
65%	18%	18%

TABLE 10.20

"Game Development Is More Like Ordinary Software Development Today than 5 Years Ago"

Agree	Neutral	Disagree
38%	24%	38%

middleware will provide a better result than what an organization can produce at the same prize [61]. The only comment to this statement was "It is about time ... " for more usage of third-party modules.

Table 10.18 shows the results from statement on whether game development has become easier in recent years.

The vast majority in the survey agrees that it is easier to develop games today than it was 5 years ago. The complexity of games and the players' expectations have increased over the years [2], but the tools and the engines have also made it easier to manage complexity as well as achieving higher fidelity. The comments from the respondents highlight that the technical part has probably become easier, but the overall challenge of game development probably not:

- *The challenges have changed, and the quality bar has risen, it is more accessible to people less interested in nerdy things nowadays (engines like Unity reduced/removed the low-level aspect of the development), but developing a*

great game is still as challenging as before, the problems to solve just have evolved. (Disagree)
- *Technically and graphically, yes. Conceptually, no.* (Agree)

The next statement investigates how the importance of middleware has changed over time (see Table 10.19).

The majority of respondents agreed that middleware is more important to the company today than 3 years ago. Table 10.20 shows the results from a statement comparing how game development and software development has changed over time.

The feedback on this statement was mainly divided into two camps. It is interesting to note that the large game developer with 500+ employees answered neutral to this statement. The only comments to this statement came from those disagreeing that game development is becoming more like ordinary software development:

- *Game development requires a more eccentric creative problem solving than development in most of other industries and this will probably remain true forever* (Disagree)
- *Nope. It was software development then, and still is now.* (Disagree)
- *I think the tools available today moves game development further away from 'ordinary software development'.* (Disagree)

Several differences between game development and conventional software development have been identified in the literature. One example is that games usually have more limited life cycle than conventional software products and that the maintenance of games mainly only focuses on bug fixing without charging the end-user [62]. Another example is that game development does not include functional requirements from the end-users. Typical end-user requirements to a game are that the game must be fun and engaging [13]. The latter poses a challenge of going from preproduction phase that produces a game design document (and maybe a prototype), to the production phase where all the software, game design, art, audio, and music will be produced [13]. From a software engineering point of view, a challenge in game development is to create functional requirements from a game design document that describes the game concept. Another difference between conventional software systems and games is the importance of usability. A software system might be used if it provides much needed functionality even if the usability is not the best. However, a game with low usability is very unlikely to survive [63]. Usability tests and frameworks are also used within game development, but they are tailored specifically for the game domain [64, 65].

10.5   RESULTS FROM FOLLOW-UP SURVEY

In this section you can find a summary of the results from a more in-depth survey with free text questions targeting six of the 13 game developers who responded to the questionnaire in previous section.

10.5.1 Game Engines and Middleware

Four out of the six respondents said they use external game engines where two use custom-made or their own. External game engines used by the respondents were Away3D (3D engine for Flash/ActionScript), Unity 3D, and Unreal Engine 3. In addition to these game engines, a variety of external tools are being used such as Autodesk Beast (lightning), Autodesk Scaleform (user interfaces), Bink (video codec for games), Box2D (physics), DirectX (multimedia API), FMOD (audio), libvorbis (audio codec), NVIDIA PhysX (phystics), SpeedTree (plugin/tools for tree and plants), Substance (texture designer), Flash (Web-platform), and Umbra (rendering optimization).

In the survey we asked about where game engines are heading in the future, and the following key points summarize their responses:

Multiplatform: The ability to create a game once and build it to run on different platforms allows game developers to reach a much larger audience, and at the same time being able to focus on the work of creating the game without always considering porting.

Quality of features: While most game engines today frequently present new features, the quality of the feature is more important than the quantity. Even if a really impressive, bleeding-edge feature is included in the game engine, most game developers will not use it until it works properly and is simple to integrate in the game.

Simplicity: The usability of a game engine has improved rapidly since the earliest game engines to those who dominate the market today. The replies indicate that this trend will only continue, and that game engines, which are difficult to use, will fall behind in the competition. However, ease of use must not be at the expense of freedom. As there are limits to how much freedom a point-and-click interface can provide, the companies should still be able to edit the source code, allowing them to develop new and novel features.

Completeness: A game engine today must present more than "just" a rendering engine, which accepts input data, and produces a game. The game engine needs to have a host of supporting features and tools, relieving the individual organizations from tasks like taking models from modeling tools and converting them to game engine-compatible data formats, or handling save games.

10.5.2 Software Architecture and Creative Team

Two recurring themes were recognized in how the creative team contributes to the design of the software architecture. *Firstly*, the creative team affects the software architecture indirectly through working with the technical team. *Secondly*, the main areas they affect relate to how tools interact with the game. This can be a result of discussions regarding workflow issues or based on the functional needs of the creative teams. Thus, the creative team does not affect the software architecture directly, but through requests made to the technical team.

To specify more in detail how the creative team affects the software architecture, we asked about which features are needed to help the creative team do their job. The responses showed that all companies desire functionality letting the creative team import new assets and try them out in-game. This allows rapid prototyping of new ideas, which again demands a software architecture that can provide such run-time flexibility. The goal for many is to achieve a more data- and tool-driven development that empowers the creative team. A part of this process is to achieve automatic transition from tools to the game. In practice, this means that the creative team can test out new ideas faster and more frequently, and thus produce better and more original games. Additionally, if the creative team possesses some programming skills, they could alter the source code on their own copy of the game project. This allows for a more fundamental approach to implement new features. Alternatively, "featured-oriented teams" can be used in game development, as suggested by one of the respondents. Such a team consists of at least one coder, one artist, and one designer. The composition of roles allows them to focus on particular features represented as a single unit, allowing work to progress quickly without having to wait for any external resources. The use of feature-oriented teams is also a way of reducing the problems related to the transition from preproduction to production in game development [13]. An overlap in roles of technical and creative teams is also recommended to bridge the code/art divide that many game development projects suffer from [66].

10.5.3 IMPLEMENTING CHANGES

From the feedback of the respondents we recognized a pattern for the decision process on how companies are reasoning about implementing changes. *Firstly*, the importance of the feature from a user experience perspective must be assessed through asking how much better will the game be with this feature or how much will be lost if it is not implemented? *Secondly*, it must be asked how much it will cost in terms of time and resources to implement this feature, and can the added workload and extra use of resources be justified? If both parts evaluate positively, the organization will start considering how the features should be implemented. This process starts in a discussion involving both the creative and technical team. Here the initial goal as seen from the creative team is subjected to technical considerations. Based on this feedback and feed-forward, the creative team ends up with a specification of the features. The technical team will produce a prototype based on this specification. When both teams are happy with the prototype, it is fixed into production quality code.

The last topic we touched upon in this survey was about who are involved in the decision process and how important are the opinions of the creative team, the technical team, and the management. The responses from the survey gave some indications for how these decisions take place in game development companies. *Firstly*, management has the final say if the change significantly alters budget or time estimates. This is not to say that it is not done without involvement from either the creative team or the technical team, but in the end, management decides. *Secondly*, for the companies that replied in our survey, all three groups (management, creative, and technical) seem to be treated equally in the decision process. This makes sense as these three groups have three different responsibilities. Management should get the game launched on time and budget, the creative team should produce a game which is fun and involving, and the technical team should enable the technology to drive the creative team's content through in a reliable way.

10.6   THREATS TO VALIDITY

This section addressed the most important threats to the validity. There are mainly three validities that must be discussed: intern, construct, and external.

The *intern validity* of an experiment concerns "the validity of inferences about whether observed covariation between A (the presumed treatment) and B (the presumed outcome) reflects a causal relationship from A to B as those variables were manipulated or measured" [67]. If changes in B have causes other than the manipulation of A, there is a threat to the internal validity. The main internal threat in our study is that the sample of subjects in the experiment was not randomized. The respondents to the questionnaire were recruited in two ways. The first group was game developers that visited the Nordic booth at the Game Developer Conference that volunteered to fill out a paper questionnaire at the booth. The second group consisted of game developers that responded to emails we sent to many game developers. We would have preferred more respondents and especially more larger game developers. However, we have learned that it is very difficult to get game developers to respond to questionnaires as they are always behind schedule and overworked, so we were pleased getting 13 responses in the end.

Construct validity concerns the degree to which inferences are warranted, from (1) the observed persons, settings, and cause and effect operations included in a study to (2) the constructs that these instances might represent. The question, therefore, is whether the sampling particulars of a study can be defended as measures of general constructs [67]. Our approach was to first create a questionnaire with the goal of answering our research questions that were decomposed from our research goal. The goal of our research was to obtain the participants' quantitative responses in addition to the contexts for the responses. To achieve this, we encouraged the respondents to comment on how they answered the 20 statements. Further to get more qualitative data, we conducted a survey for those game companies who were willing to go more into details.

The issue of *external validity* concerns whether a causal relationship holds (1) for variations in persons, settings, treatments, and outcomes that were in the experiment and (2) for persons, settings, treatments, and outcomes that were not in the experiment [67]. The results found in this study can mainly be generalized for smaller game companies (from one to ten employees), since we only had one large game developer among the respondents. Also, since we only received 13 responses to the questionnaire, the quantitative results must only be seen as indicators on how game developers think about the various statements. The qualitative data in the questionnaire and survey along with support from research literature strengthen the results and its validity.

10.7   CONCLUSIONS

This chapter presents the findings from a questionnaire and the follow-up survey on how game developers use and manage software architecture and how creative development processes are managed. The results presented are a combination of the response from 13 game companies and findings in research literature.

The *first* research question (RQ1) addressed the role software architecture plays in game development. The game developers in our survey stated that software architecture is important in game development, especially to manage complexity and achieve quality attributes such as modifiability and performance. Another finding was that the game concept heavily influences the software architecture mainly because it dictates the choice of game engine. Further, the ways the creative team can affect the software architecture is through the creation of the game concept, by adding in-game functionality, and by adding new development tools. Finally, a cost/benefit analysis will decide whether an existing software architecture may dictate future game concepts or not. Whenever it is possible, reuse of the software architecture is wanted.

The *second* research question (RQ2) investigated how game developers manage changes to the software architecture. We found that the creative team has to adjust some extent their game ideas to existing software architecture based on a cost/benefit analysis. The creative team can demand changes to the software architecture during development, but this decision depends on how far the project has progressed and the cost and benefit of making the change. Decisions on change-requests are usually made by personnel from technical team, creative team, and management, but the management has the final word due to economical justifications. Further, the technical teams to a large extent implement all features and tools requested by the creative team (within reasonable limits), and that most developers said it was easy to add new gameplay elements after the core game engine was complete (although not recommended late in the project). The literature highlighted two approaches to deal with adding gameplay elements to a game: Scripting – where the behavior of the game is predeterministic and acting according to a script, and Emergence – where the behavior is non-deterministic, and a virtual world is created by game objects that reacts to the environment around them. The former has the advantage of being easier to test, and the latter has the advantage of being easier to extend gameplay.

The *third* research question (RQ3) addressed how the creative processes are managed and supported in game development. Most of the game developers in this study said they used game engines that support dynamic loading of new game elements (although not everything in run-time). The majority of the respondents use game engines that support scripting. Only game developers with own developed game engines did not support scripting. Finally, the majority of the developers said they used game engines that enable rapid prototyping of new ideas. The conclusion of this research question is that current game engines enable creative processes through support of GUI tools, scripting, and dynamic loading of elements.

The *fourth* research question (RQ4) asked how game development has evolved in the last couple of years. This question can be summarized as follows: there has been an increased use of third-party software, middleware has become more important, and it is technically easier to develop games. Although the majority of respondents said that the technical aspects of game development have become easier, game development in itself has not become easier due to higher player expectations and higher game complexity. Similarly, there was no clear conclusion whether game development has become more like conventional software development. The main differences were identified to be that in game development there are no real functional requirements, the quality attributes performance and usability are more important, and game development has its own set of tools and engines.

ACKNOWLEDGMENTS

We would like to thank Richard Taylor and Walt Scacchi at the Institute for Software Research (ISR) at the University of California, Irvine (UCI) for providing a stimulating research environment and for hosting a visiting researcher from Norway.

REFERENCES

[1] M. Zyda, "From visual simulation to virtual reality to games," *Computer*, vol. 38, no. 9, pp. 25–32, 2005.

[2] J. Blow, "Game development: Harder than you think," *Queue*, vol. 1, no. 10, pp. 28–37, 2004.

[3] C. E. Crooks, *Awesome 3D Game Development: No Programming Required: Cengage Learning*, Charles River Media, 2004.

[4] D. Callele, E. Neufeld, and K. Schneider, "Emotional requirements," *IEEE Software*, vol. 25, no. 1, pp. 43–45, 2008.

[5] A. Ampatzoglou, and I. Stamelos, "Software engineering research for computer games: A systematic review," *Information and Software Technology*, vol. 52, no. 9, pp. 888–901, 2010.

[6] N. Nordmark, Software Architecture and the Creative Process in Game Development, Master Thesis, Norwegian University of Science and Technology, 2012.

[7] A. I. Wang and N. Nordmark, *"Software architectures and the creative processes in game development."* International Conference on Entertainment Computing (ICEC 2015). Springer International Publishing, Trondheim Norway, September 30–October 2, pp. 272–285, 2015.

[8] C. M. Kanode, M. Christopher, and H. M. Haddad. *"Software engineering challenges in game development."* 2009 Sixth International Conference on Information Technology: New Generations. IEEE, pp. 260–265, 2009.

[9] F. Petrillo, M. Pimenta, F. Trindade, and C. Dietrich. *"Houston, we have a problem... a survey of actual problems in computer games development."* In *Proceedings of the 2008 ACM Symposium on Applied Computing*, pp. 707–711, 2008.

[10] C. Lewis and J. Whitehead. *"The whats and the whys of games and software engineering."* In *Proceedings of the 1st International Workshop on Games and Software Engineering*, pp. 1–4, 2011.

[11] C. Lewis, J. Whitehead, and N. Wardrip-Fruin. *"What went wrong: A taxonomy of video game bugs."* In *Proceedings of the Fifth International Conference on the Foundations of Digital Games*, pp. 108–115, 2010.

[12] J. Kasurinen, R. Laine, and K. Smolander. *"How applicable is ISO/IEC 29110 in game software development?"* In *International Conference on Product Focused Software Process Improvement*, pp. 5-19. Springer, Berlin, Heidelberg, 2013.

[13] D. Callele, E. Neufeld, and K. Schneider. *"Requirements engineering and the creative process in the video game industry."* In *13th IEEE International Conference on Requirements Engineering (RE'05)*, pp. 240–250. IEEE, 2005.

[14] L. Bishop, D. Eberly, T. Whitted, M. Finch, and M. Shantz. "Designing a PC game engine." *IEEE Computer Graphics and Applications*, vol. 18, no. 1, 46–53, 1998.

[15] T. C. Cheah and K-W. Ng. *"A practical implementation of a 3D game engine."* In *International Conference on Computer Graphics, Imaging and Visualization (CGIV'05)*, pp. 351–358. IEEE, 2005.

[16] R. Darken, P. McDowell, and E. Johnson, "The Delta3D open source game engine," *IEEE Computer Graphics and Applications*, vol. 25, no. 3, pp. 10–12, 2005.

[17] E. Folmer, "Component based game development: A solution to escalating costs and expanding deadlines?," *Component-Based Software Engineering*, pp. 66–73: Springer, 2007.

[18] C. A. M. Antonio, C. A. F. Jorge, and P. M. Couto, "Using a game engine for VR simulations in evacuation lanning," *IEEE Computer Graphics and Applications*, vol. 28, no. 3, pp. 6–12, 2008.

[19] J. Kasurinen, J.-P. Strandén, and K. Smolander, *"What do game developers expect from development and design tools?"* In *Proceedings of the 17th International Conference on Evaluation and Assessment in Software Engineering*, pp. 36–41, April 14, 2013.

[20] M. Zhu, and A. I. Wang, *"RAIL: A domain-specific language for generating NPC behaviors in action/adventure games."* In *14th International Conference on Advances in Computer Entertainment Technology* (ACE), London, UK, 2017.

[21] M. Zhu, A. I. Wang, and H. Trætteberg. *"Engine-cooperative game modeling (ECGM) bridge model-driven game development and game engine tool-chains."* In *Proceedings of the 13th International Conference on Advances in Computer Entertainment Technology*, pp. 1–10, 2016.

[22] A. I. Wang, "The wear out effect of a game-based student response system," *Computers & Education*, vol. 82, pp. 217–227, 2015.

[23] A. I. Wang, and J. d. J. L. G. Ibánez, "Learning recycling from playing a kinect game," *International Journal of Game-Based Learning (IJGBL)*, vol. 5, no. 3, pp. 25–44, 2015.

[24] C. Bouras, V. Poulopoulos, I. Sengounis, and V. Tsogkas, *"Networking aspects for gaming systems."* In *Proceedings of the 2008 Third International Conference on Internet and Web Applications and Services*, 2008.

[25] J. Smed, T. Kaukoranta, and H. Hakonen, *A Review of Networking and Multiplayer Computer Games,* TUCS Technical Report 454, Turku Centre for Computer Science, 2002.

[26] T. Hampel, T. Bopp, and R. Hinn, *"A peer-to-peer architecture for massive multiplayer online games."* In *Proceedings of 5th ACM SIGCOMM workshop on Network and system support for games*, Singapore, 2006.

[27] T. Triebel, B. Guthier, R. Süselbeck, G. Schiele, and W. Effelsberg, "Peer-to-peer infrastructures for games," in *Proceedings of the 18th International Workshop on Network and Operating Systems Support for Digital Audio and Video*, Braunschweig, Germany, 2008.

[28] W. Cai, P. Xavier, S. J. Turner, and B.-S. Lee. *"A scalable architecture for supporting interactive games on the internet."* In *Proceedings of the Sixteenth Workshop on Parallel and Distributed Simulation*, pp. 60–67, 2002.

[29] E. F. Anderson, S. Engel, P. Comninos, and L. McLoughlin, *"The case for research in game engine architecture,"* in *Proceedings of the 2008 Conference on Future Play: Research, Play, Share*, Toronto, Ontario, Canada, 2008.

[30] S. Caltagirone, M. Keys, B. Schlief, and M. J. Willshire, "Architecture for a massively multiplayer online role playing game engine," *J. Comput. Small Coll.*, vol. 18, no. 2, pp. 105–116, 2002.

[31] J. Plummer. "A flexible and expandable architecture for computer games." PhD diss., Arizona State University, 2004.

[32] W. Piekarski, and B. H. Thomas. *"An object-oriented software architecture for 3D mixed reality applications."* In *The Second IEEE and ACM International Symposium on Mixed and Augmented Reality, 2003. Proceedings*, pp. 247–256. IEEE, 2003.

[33] A. I. Wang, "Extensive evaluation of using a game project in a software architecture course," *Transactions on Computing Education*, vol. 11, no. 1, pp. 1-28, 2011.

[34] W. Cai, M. Chen, and V. C. Leung, "Toward gaming as a service," *IEEE Internet Computing*, vol. 18, no. 3, pp. 12–18, 2014.

[35] M. Zhu, A. Wang, H. Guo, and H. Trætteberg, "Graph of game worlds: New perspectives on video game architectures." *Computers in Entertainment (CIE)*, vol. 11, no. 2, pp. 1–21, 2015.

[36] M. Zhu, A. I. Wang, and H. Guo, "From 101 to nnn: A review and a classification of computer game architectures," *Multimedia Systems*, vol. 19, no. 3, pp. 183–197, 2013.

[37] P. V. Gestwicki, "Computer games as motivation for design patterns," *SIGCSE Bulletin*, vol. 39, no. 1, pp. 233–237, 2007.

[38] A. Ampatzoglou, and A. Chatzigeorgiou, "Evaluation of object-oriented design patterns in game development," *Information and Software Technology*, vol. 49, no. 5, pp. 445–454, 2007.

[39] D. Nguyen, and S. B. Wong, *"Design patterns for games,"* in *Proceedings of the 33rd SIGCSE technical symposium on Computer science education*, Cincinnati, Kentucky, 2002.

[40] W. Scacchi, "Free and open source development practices in the game community," *IEEE Software*, vol. 21, no. 1, pp. 59–66, 2004.

[41] F. Petrillo, M. Pimenta, F. Trindade, and C. Dietrich, "What went wrong? A survey of problems in game development," *Computer Entertainment (CIE)*, vol. 7, no. 1, pp. 1-22, 2009.

[42] K. Flood, "Game unified process," *GameDev. Net*, 2003.

[43] F. T. Tschang, "Balancing the tensions between rationalization and creativity in the video games industry," *Organization science*, vol. 18, no. 6, pp. 989–1005, 2007.

[44] F. T. Tschang, and J. Szczypula, "Idea creation, constructivism and evolution as key characteristics in the videogame artifact design process," *European management journal*, vol. 24, no. 4, pp. 270–287, 2006.

[45] F. T. Tschang, "Videogames as interactive experiential products and their manner of development," *International Journal of Innovation Management*, vol. 9, no. 01, pp. 103–131, 2005.

[46] P. Stacey, and J. Nandhakumar, "A temporal perspective of the computer game development process," *Information Systems Journal*, vol. 19, no. 5, pp. 479–497, 2009.

[47] T. Burger-Helmchen, and P. Cohendet, "User communities and social software in the video game industry," *Long Range Planning*, vol. 44, no. 5-6, pp. 317–343, 2011.

[48] A. Kultima, and K. Alha. *""Hopefully everything I'm doing has to do with innovation": Games industry professionals on innovation in 2009."* In *2010 2nd International IEEE Consumer Electronics Society's Games Innovations Conference*, pp. 1–8. IEEE, 2010.

[49] F. Petrillo and M. Pimenta. *"Is agility out there? Agile practices in game development."* In *Proceedings of the 28th ACM International Conference on Design of Communication*, pp. 9–15. 2010.

[50] K. Schwaber, and M. Beedle, *Agile Software Development with Scrum*, Prentice Hall PTR, 2002.

[51] V. Basili. "Software modeling and measurement: The goal/question/metric paradigm," University of Maryland, CS-TR-2956, UMIACS-TR-92-96, September 1992.

[52] C. Wohlin, P. Runeson, M. Höst, M. C. Ohlsson, B. Regnell, and A. Wesslén. *Experimentation in software engineering*. Springer-Verlag, Berlin, Heidelberg, 2012.

[53] R. Likert, "A technique for the measurement of attitudes," *Archives of Psychology*, 1932.

[54] T.-Y. Hsiao, and S.-M. Yuan, "Practical middleware for massively multiplayer online games," *IEEE Internet Computing*, vol. 9, no. 5, pp. 47–54, 2005.

[55] L. Bass, P. Clements, and R. Kazman, *Software Architecture in Practice*, 3rd ed.: Addison-Wesley, 2012.

[56] B. Boehm, and V. R. Basili, "Software defect reduction top 10 list," *Foundations of empirical software engineering: the legacy of Victor R. Basili*, vol. 426, no. 37, pp. 426–431, 2005.

[57] E. Bethke, *Game Developer's Guide to Design and Production*. Wordware Publishing Inc., Plano Texas, 2003.

[58] P. Stacey, and J. Nandhakumar, "Opening up to agile games development," *Communications of the ACM*, vol. 51, no. 12, pp. 143–146, 2008.

[59] P. Sweetser, and J. Wiles, "Scripting versus emergence: Issues for game developers and players in game environment design," *International Journal of Intelligent Games and Simulations*, vol. 4, no. 1, pp. 1-9, 2005.

[60] W. White, C. Koch, J. Gehrke, and A. Demers, "Better scripts, better games," *Communications of the ACM*, vol. 52, no. 3, pp. 42–47, 2009.

[61] A. Rollings, and D. Morris, *Game Architecture and Design - A New Edition*. New Riders Publishing, Indianapolis, Indiana, USA, 2004.

[62] M. McShaffry, and D. Graham, *Game Coding Complete*, 4th edition. Course Technology PTR, 2013.

[63] J. L. G. Sánchez, N. P. Zea, and F. L. Gutiérrez, "From usability to playability: Introduction to player-centred video game development process," *Human Centered Design*, pp. 65–74, 2009.

[64] H. Desurvire, and C. Wiberg, "Game usability heuristics (PLAY) for evaluating and designing better games: The next iteration," *Online Communities and Social Computing*, pp. 557–566, 2009.

[65] S. Laitinen, "Better games through usability evaluation and testing," *Gamasutra*. URL: http//www.gamasutra.com/features/20050623/laitinen_01.shtml, 2005.

[66] J. Hayes, "The code/art divide: How technical artists bridge the gap," *Game Developer Magazine*, vol. 14, no. 7, pp. 17, 2007.

[67] W. R. Shadish, T. D. Cook, and D. T. Campbell, *Experimental and Quasi-Experimental Designs for Generalized Causal Inference*. Wadsworth Cengage learning, 2002.

11 Games and Software Engineering Topics
Recent Results and Future Research Opportunities

Kendra M. L. Cooper

Independent Scholar, Canada

CONTENTS

The games and software engineering community addresses numerous and evolving development issues of today's large scale, complex games and software engineering educational environments. Literature surveys have been reported (e.g., [5, 7, 20, 35, 38]) that capture the evolution of topics over time. In 2015, an edited book on computer games and software engineering provides a snapshot of the state-of-the research [28]; it spans software engineering for games and serious educational games for software engineering education. Here, the focus is on the recent body of research (i.e., from 2015 to 2020) to identify currently pursued topics and future research opportunities. This chapter begins with a brief summary of the preceding chapters in Section 11.1. An overview of recent results in the domain is presented in Section 11.1. Research opportunities in game development are considered in Section 11.2. In Section 11.3, concluding remarks are provided.

11.1 SYNOPSIS OF CHAPTERS

The research contributions presented in the preceding chapters of this edited book are organized into two categories: serious games for software engineering education and software engineering for games. Here, the chapters are briefly characterized with respect to their research question, proposed solution, and validation approach.

11.1.1 SERIOUS GAMES FOR SOFTWARE ENGINEERING EDUCATION

In Chapter 2, an exploration of organizational features that characterize game competitions and related game development environments is presented by Walt Scacchi, followed by a qualitative analysis of five events the University of California, Irvine has been involved with. The organizational features focus on the setting of the event, which include academic settings (intra-mural, inter-mural, capstone projects), workshops, festivals, and additional variations; these events involve teams that typically work in parallel to make games. Each event is described and comparatively analyzed to present observations, lessons learned, and opportunities for how to organize and design game jams. The lessons learned and opportunities identified are summarized for the reader in this exploratory study.

In Chapter 3, digital-based learning games for software engineering education are the focus of the results presented by Jöran Pieper. Based on an analysis of 11 games in the literature using nine characteristics, the author proposes an approach to develop transferrable, flexible software engineering competencies. It consists of two separate and complementary learning games, the Essence Kernel Puzzler and the Essence Simulation Game. In addition, a recommendation tool is also presented called the Essence Navigator to monitor and assist in the game progression. The games are established on social constructivist learning theory to provide a rigorous pedagogical foundation and the Revised Bloom's taxonomy is used to characterize the learning objectives. The proposed game-based learning approach is validated with a case study conducted with students.

In Chapter 4, a collection of serious educational games targeting introductory programming concepts under development by Brian Chau et al. is presented. The games within the collection are small and independent. Each game focusses on one or two specific programming concepts (e.g., conditionals and arrays), which allows instructors to flexibly choose an ensemble of games to meet their needs. Each game is designed, built, and extensively play tested almost entirely by undergraduate students, ensuring they are fun and engaging. For each game, an API is extracted which allows instructors and students to modify the game. The collection of games is currently being field tested in CS1/2 classrooms.

In Chapter 5, an enhanced model is proposed for systematically evaluating the quality of games for software engineering education is presented by Giani Petri et al. Based on an analysis of the existing model for the evaluation of educational games (MEEGA), limitations are identified that stem from the presence of overlapping theoretical concepts (motivation and user experience) and some ambiguous phrasing in the questionnaire. To improve the reliability and validity of the model, MEEGA+ is systematically designed and analyzed in a four-step process. An extensive case study evaluation is reported on the evaluation of MEEGA+. It consists of 29 case studies, spanning 13 games (four digital, nine non-digital), responses from 589 students, and six different educational institutions.

In Chapter 6, an assemblage of applied game design methods for educators is presented by Micah Hrehovcsik to help address the current lack of a comprehensive design theory, best practices, and didactic approaches. The assemblage has been used to educate game designers at the HKU University of the Arts Utrecht on the design of applied games. The assemblage addresses three instructional goals: provide students with a means to critique serious games; provide a means to categorize games according to their design, rather than their domain or genre; and provide a tool which guides design choices, spurs design research, and supports capturing the rationale for design choices. Lastly, a game jam format is used to provide an intensive practice-based learning experience concerning applied game design theories, co-design, best practices, and studio operations related to development.

11.1.2 SOFTWARE ENGINEERING FOR GAMES

In Chapter 7, a novel design framework for embodiment is presented by Edward Melcer and Katherine Isbiter. The concept of embodiment recognizes cognition is emergent and multifaceted; it involves the mind, physical interactions, and social interactions in the environment. The framework is based on a careful selection and analysis of 90 articles that involve 66 distinct games and simulations. The analysis results are used to establish the design framework taxonomy. The taxonomy is intended to make designers aware of design choices, rather than prescribing strict mappings of design choices into values. The taxonomy has three levels: groups, dimensions, and possible values (i.e., design choices). The proposed taxonomy is evaluated using three example studies. The first study examines the ability to describe and categorize embodied games and simulations using the framework. The second and third studies apply the framework to identify problematic design spaces and design gaps, respectively.

In Chapter 8, the design of mixed reality games including pervasive games, location-based games, and augmented reality games is explored by Richard Wetzel et al. These games enrich the physical world with technology to create new and exciting gameplay possibilities. The new approach is based on ideation cards, which are an established design technique. The card deck consists of four kinds of cards: opportunity, question, challenge, and theme. A lightweight design process is also introduced that consists of two activities. The first activity is idea generation, in which the goal is to use the cards to rapidly generate numerous ideas over several iterations. In the second activity, designers explore, refine, ground, and organize the cards for the game. The authors report their experiences using the process and the card deck to develop a game for a non-profit organization.

In Chapter 9, a novel design for an exergame is presented by Rahul Kumjar et al. The purpose of exergames is to motivate players to participate in physical exercise by providing enjoyable, immersive environments. The design of an exergame that promotes exercise outside of play sessions is accomplished by re-designing a popular role-playing game *The Elder Scrolls V: Skyrim*. The modified game is called the Skyrim Exergaming Mode, in which the player character levels up based on their real-world physical activity, rather than in-game activity. The exergame design model weaves together physical exercise, quests, points, and a levelling system. Overall, there are four main steps in the exergame. Firstly, the player accepts a quest while playing the game. Secondly, the player engages in physical activities outside the game (e.g., fitness classes, stretching, and sport) and log their activity. Thirdly, the player opens the game; the game acquires the logged exercise data to update the player's points and levelling status. Fourthly, the player is notified of their updated status and resumes playing.

In Chapter 10, a two-part survey that explores a variety of perspectives on software engineering and game development is designed, run, and analyzed by Alf-Inge Wang and Njål Nordmark. The research goals delve into: how game developers think about and use software architecture; how creative development processes are managed and supported; and how the game technology is used. The 13 subjects for the study are a mix of attendees at the Nordic booth at the Game Developer Conference in San Francisco and game developers contacted by email. In the first part of the study, a questionnaire consisting of 20 statements is prepared which are derived from the research questions. The results show that software architectures play a central role in game development. The creative processes are supported using a wide variety of tools such as game engines, middleware, scripting languages, and dynamically loading assets. In the second part of the study, a follow-up survey to acquire additional information from six subjects focusses on: the future of game engines; how the creative team affects the software architecture; and how companies are reasoning and making decisions on implementing changes.

11.2   RECENT RESULTS AND FUTURE OPPORTUNITIES

Today's large scale, complex games present distinct, challenging development challenges. There is an interdisciplinary research community investigating topics at the intersection of software engineering and games. Recently, this community has been pursuing a subset of topics in two broad categories: serious educational games for software engineering and software engineering methods for games. The results have appeared in a wide variety of computer science, education, game, and software engineering publications. Here, the focus is on recently published (i.e., 2015–2020) peer-reviewed work to provide a current, high level snapshot for the reader. The work has appeared at multiple levels of maturity: workshops, conferences, and journals. The articles have been identified using searches in ACM Digital Library, IEEE Xplore, and Scopus databases.

In the first category, serious games for software engineering education, results have been presented that cover engineering and umbrella activities. The engineering activities addressed include requirements engineering, architecture and design, modelling languages, and code quality (e.g., testing and refactoring). Games for umbrella activities embody lifecycle processes and project management topics. In the second category, software engineering methods for games, five groups of topics of topics are identified: analytics and metrics, automation, models, re-use, and user experience.

More generally, it's clear that the two categories investigate possible game development research topics from distinct perspectives (refer to Figure 11.1). For example, one research group may be interested in investigating novel requirements

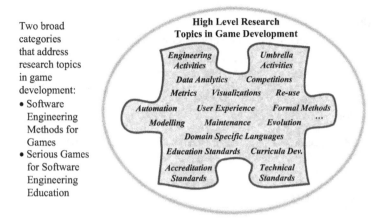

Two broad categories that address research topics in game development:
- Software Engineering Methods for Games
- Serious Games for Software Engineering Education

High Level Research Topics in Game Development

Engineering Activities Umbrella Activities
Data Analytics Competitions
Metrics Visualizations Re-use
Automation User Experience Formal Methods
Modelling Maintenance Evolution ...
Domain Specific Languages
Education Standards Curricula Dev.
Accreditation Standards Technical Standards

FIGURE 11.1 Two broad categories of research for addressing a wide variety of topics in game development.

engineering methods for game development, while another may be interested in creating games for learning about requirements engineering. In the future, both categories of research may benefit from exploring the following question: How can a comprehensive map of possible topics leveraging accreditation, educational, and technical standards (e.g., [3, 19, 47, 48, 49]) in addition to on-going contributions in the research literature be established, maintained, and utilized by the game development community to support systematic progress?

11.2.1 SERIOUS GAMES FOR SOFTWARE ENGINEERING EDUCATION

In the recent literature, 18 articles have been identified that cover topics in software engineering education and training (refer to Table 11.1). They include individual, one-of games with promising validation results that address a subset of engineering activities and umbrella activities. The engineering activities include classic topics such as requirements engineering, architecture, design, code quality (debugging, refactoring, testing), and modelling with a formal specification notation. The requirements engineering games cover the comprehension and application of a notation (user stories) and a standardized process (ISO/IEC/IEEE 29148). The architecture and design games introduce the architecture analysis trade-off method and the use of design patterns. The games focussing on code quality topics include metrics, testing, debugging, and refactoring. The formal specification game covers a state-of-the-art theorem prover, Z3. The umbrella activities include classic topics on lifecycle processes and project management. In the lifecycle process games presented, there are three on agile methods and one for an international standard (ISO/IEC 12207) on the software lifecycle process; four games on project management are available.

Out of necessity, the games developed narrowly focus on specific topics at targeted levels of difficulty. The games reflect the research interests and expertise of the researchers; their development is limited by resource constraints. Developing,

TABLE 11.1

Examples of Recent Results: Serious Games for Software Engineering

Serious Games for Software Engineering	
Topics	**Articles**
Engineering Activities	
• Requirements	[33, 40]
• Architecture and design	[15, 68]
• Modelling langluages (formal specification)	[78]
• Code quality	[12, 27, 36, 41, 64]
Umbrella activities	
• Lifecycle processes	[9, 11, 16, 62]
• Project management	[21, 57, 67, 90]

validating, and publishing the results for a single game, even a prototype, remains challenging. Currently, collections of related games have been reported; however, methods for developing franchises, series, or improved versions remains open. Some umbrella activities have not received attention, yet (e.g., build management, configuration management, and traceability).

In terms of open research problems, numerous opportunities are available to develop serious games for software engineering education and training topics at multiple levels of difficulty. Examples of high-level questions include:

- How can serious educational game franchises, series, and improved versions be developed to cover software engineering topics and their advances over time?
- How can games on build management, configuration management, and traceability topics be effectively developed?
- How can games on more recent lifecycle process models (e.g., DevOps) be effectively developed?
- How can games on evolution and maintenance topics be effectively developed (e.g., crowd source, open source, refactoring, and technical debt)?
- How can games on engineering with newer component paradigms (e.g., microservices and Internet of Things) and interaction devices (e.g., glasses for virtual/augmented reality) be effectively developed?

11.2.2 Software Engineering for Games

There are 65 recently reported results identified in the recent literature on software engineering for games. They span five high level topics: analytics and metrics, automation, models, re-use, and user experience (refer to Table 11.2). The first four topics are classic software engineering topics that focus to support the timely, cost effective development of high-quality games. The fifth topic, user experience, is more specific to games. It considers the intentional invocation of emotional responses to attract and retain players.

Within the categories of topics, analytics for games, methods for their manual and automated analyses have been presented. A comparison of similarity measures for user actions and their application for creating profiles is available. A literature survey on analytics for games has also been presented. For game metrics, multiple proposals for definitions are available, and a literature review have been presented. Methods in the category of automated approaches have received substantial attention. Procedural content generation is an active research area that includes semi-automated and auto-mated methods. Methods using agents, artificial intelligence techniques, graphs, pat-terns, and rule-based approaches have recently been proposed. Automated testing methods at multiple levels (system, beta, acceptance) and playtesting are available. In addition, an alternative approach that proposes a runtime monitoring method is presented, which identifies violations of formally defined properties. In the high-level category for development models and methodologies for games, only one soft-ware development methodology has been recently presented. For development processes, an exploratory study, investigation of success factors for improvement, the use of Scrum, and a literature review are available. Several model driven develop-ment approaches for entertainment and serious games have been considered; one specifically addresses the integration of game engines. Semi-formal (UML), formal (timed automata, XML), and tailored languages (modelling, programming) have been utilized, including a small functional language. In the category of re-use, recent results address a variety of traditional methods, including frameworks, patterns, product lines, and reference architectures that are tailored for games. In the user experience category, results have been reported that span requirements engineering, design, assessment and testing activities.

In terms of research opportunities, addressing the user experience as core quality of service requirements can be explored in a cross-cutting manner across topics in software engineering for games. The topics can be based on established standards (accreditation, education, technical) and the evolving research literature. Examples of high-level questions include:

- How to engineer the user experience with respect to analytics and metrics, automation, models, and re-use methods?
- How to engineer the user experience with respect to traditional engineering activities (e.g., requirements engineering, architecture, design, construction, and testing)?
- How to engineer the user experience with respect to umbrella activities (e.g., build management, configuration management, and traceability)?
- How to engineer the user experiences with respect to software evolution and maintenance topics (e.g., technical debt and refactoring)?
- How to engineer the user experience via lifecycle process models that synthe-size the concepts used in the game and software engineering communities?
- How to engineer the user experience with more recent types of components (e.g., microservices and Internet of Things)?

TABLE 11.2

Examples of Recent Results: Software Engineering for Games

Software Engineering for Games

Topics	Articles
Analytics and Metrics for Games	
• Analytics	[29, 51, 59, 69, 87]
• Metrics	[18, 26, 50, 74, 89]
Automation for Games	
• Procedural content generation	[2, 13, 23, 25, 58, 73, 81, 83, 88]
• Testing	[43, 44, 54, 82, 86, 92, 97]
Development Models and Methodologies for Games	
• Lifecycle process models	[6, 7, 53, 55]
• Model-based development	[34, 60, 98]
• Modelling, domain specific languages	[1, 10, 31, 80, 96]
• Methodologies	[14]
Re-use for Games	
• Frameworks	[42, 72, 93, 94, 95]
• Patterns	[8, 37, 52, 56]
• Product lines	[4, 32, 63, 84]
• Reference architectures	[61, 66, 75, 85]
User Experience for Games	
• Assessment and testing	[17, 77, 79]
• Design	[24, 71, 76]
• Requirements engineering	[22, 30, 91]

11.3   CONCLUSIONS

The interdisciplinary community investigating topics in game development continues to grow and make valuable contributions. This chapter explores recent results in game development from a software engineering perspective and possible opportunities for future research. This chapter begins with a brief synopsis of the nine core chapters of the book. The summaries are organized into two categories: serious games for software engineering education and software engineering methods for game development. This is followed by high-level summary of recent results over the last 5 years. The work includes 18 articles on topics in serious games for software engineering education and 65 articles on software engineering methods for game development. The results appear across a wide variety of publications: computer science, education, gaming, and software engineering. They are peer-reviewed articles at multiple levels of maturity: workshop, conference, and journal. In addition, possible future opportunities are identified in terms of high-level research questions. Given the breadth of the discipline, researchers have ample opportunity to identify topics of interest.

Beyond software engineering, exploring, tailoring, and adopting methods from systems engineering and industrial design (e.g., Kansei engineering) may also yield valuable results. Systems engineering emerged in the late 1940s by the US Department of Defense to develop large-scale, complex projects such as missile-defense systems. Today, established resources are available that address the issues in developing systems (e.g., [45]). They provide guidance for specifying, designing, constructing, and validating/verifying systems (or systems of systems) that involve comprehensive technology stacks (e.g., communication networks, data storage, hardware, operating systems, and software). Many of these development issues are encountered in today's large-scale games: they include distributed, real-time, multiplayer, multiplatform game systems that dynamically collect and analyze game play data. However, systems engineering contributions receive little attention in the game development community. Established industrial design methodologies are also available that explicitly address users' emotional or affective responses to products. For example, Kansei engineering, originally introduced in 1974, relates customers' emotional responses (i.e., physical and psychological) to the properties and characteristics of products or services [70]. In other words, they are designed to intentionally induce specific feelings. Kansei engineering continues to receive attention in a variety of communities (e.g., [46, 65], but not in game development, yet.

REFERENCES

[1] Abbadi, M. et al. (2015) *Casanova: A Simple, High-Performance Language for Game Development.* Vol. 9090. [Online]. Cham: Springer International Publishing.

[2] Abuzuraiq, A. M. et al. (2019) '*Taksim: A Constrained Graph Partitioning Framework for Procedural Content Generation*', In *2019 IEEE Conference on Games (CoG)*. [Online]. August 2019 IEEE. pp. 1–8.

[3] Accreditation Board for Engineering and Technology (ABET), available at https://www.abet.org.

[4] Åkesson, J., Nilsson, S., Krüger, J., and Berger, T. (2019). Migrating the Android Apo-Games into an Annotation-Based Software Product Line. In *Proceedings of the 23rd International Systems and Software Product Line Conference - Volume A (SPLC'19)*. Association for Computing Machinery, New York, NY, USA, 103–107. doi:10.1145/3336294.3342362

[5] Aktaş, A. Z., & Orcun, E. (2016). A survey of computer game development. *The Journal of Defense Modeling and Simulation, 13*(2), 239–251.

[6] Aleem, S., Capretz, L. F., & Ahmed, F. (2016). Critical success factors to improve the game development process from a developer's perspective. *Journal of Computer Science and Technology, 31*(5), 925–950.

[7] Aleem, S., Capretz, L. F., & Ahmed, F. (2016). Game development software engineering process life cycle: A systematic review. *Journal of Software Engineering Research and Development, 4*(1), 6.

[8] Allison, F., Carter, M., Gibbs, M., and Smith, W. (2018). *Design Patterns for Voice Interaction in Games.* In *Proceedings of the 2018 Annual Symposium on Computer-Human Interaction in Play (CHI PLAY'18)*. Association for Computing Machinery, New York, NY, USA, 5–17. doi:10.1145/3242671.3242712

[9] Ammons, B., & Bansal, S. K. (2017). Scrumify: A software game to introduce agile software development methods. *Journal of Engineering Education Transformations*.

[10] Arias J., Marczak R., Desainte-Catherine M. (2019) Timed Automata for Video Games and Interaction. In: Lee N. (eds) *Encyclopedia of Computer Graphics and Games*. Springer, Cham. doi:10.1007/978-3-319-08234-9_298-1

[11] Aydan, U., Yilmaz, M., Clarke, P. M., & O'Connor, R. V. (2017). Teaching ISO/IEC 12207 software lifecycle processes: A serious game approach. *Computer Standards & Interfaces, 54*, 129–138.

[12] Baars, S., & Meester, S. (2019, May). *CodeArena: Inspecting and improving code quality metrics using minecraft.* In *2019 IEEE/ACM International Conference on Technical Debt (TechDebt)* (pp. 68–70). IEEE.

[13] Baldwin, A., Dahlskog, S., Font, J.M., and Holmberg, J. (2017). *Towards pattern-based mixed-initiative dungeon generation.* In *Proceedings of the 12th International Conference on the Foundations of Digital Games (FDG '17).* Association for Computing Machinery, New York, NY, USA, Article 74, 1–10. doi:10.1145/3102071.3110572

[14] Barnard, J., Huisman, M. and Drevin, G. R. (2018). The Development of a Systems Development Methodology for Location-Based Games. *Computers in Entertainments.* 16, 3, Article 1 (September 2018), 47. doi:10.1145/3236492

[15] Bartel, A. and Hagel, G. (2016, April). *Gamifying the learning of design patterns in software engineering education.* In *2016 IEEE Global Engineering Education Conference (EDUCON)* (pp. 74–79). IEEE.

[16] Baumann, A. (2020). *Teaching Software Engineering Methods with Agile Games.* In *Proceedings of the 2020 IEEE Global Engineering Education Conference (EDUCON),* Porto, Portugal, pp. 1550–1553. doi:10.1109/EDUCON45650.2020.9125129.

[17] Bernhaupt, R. (2015). *User experience evaluation methods in the games development life cycle.* In *Game User Experience Evaluation* (pp. 1–8). Springer, Cham.

[18] Birk, M.V., Lürig, C., & Mandryk, R.L. (2015). *A metric for automatically flagging problem levels in games from prototype walkthrough data ACADEMICMINDTREK 2015.* In *Proceedings of the 19th International Academic Mindtrek Conference,* pp. 33–40.

[19] Bourque, P. & Fairley, R. E. (eds.) (2014). *SWEBOK: Guide to the Software Engineering Body of Knowledge.* IEEE Computer Society, Los Alamitos, CA. ISBN: 978-0-7695-5166-1.

[20] Boyle, E.A., Hainey, T., Connolly, T.M., Gray, G., Earp, J., Ott, M., Lim, T., Ninaus, M., Ribeiro, C., and Pereira, J. (2016). An update to the systematic literature review of empirical evidence of the impacts and outcomes of computer games and serious games. *Computers and Educations* 94, C (March 2016), 178–192. doi:10.1016/j.compedu.2015.11.003.

[21] Calderón, A., Ruiz, M., and O'Connor, R. V. (2017, September). *ProDecAdmin: a game scenario design tool for software project management training.* In *European Conference on Software Process Improvement.* pp. 241–248. Springer, Cham.

[22] Callele, D., Dueck, P., Wnuk, K., and Hynninen, P. (2015). *Experience requirements in video games definition and testability.* In *IEEE 23rd International Requirements Engineering Conference (RE),* Ottawa, ON, pp. 324–333, doi:10.1109/RE.2015.7320449.

[23] Campos, J. and Rieder, R. (2019). *Procedural content generation using artificial intelligence for unique virtual reality game experiences.* In *2019 21st Symposium on Virtual and Augmented Reality (SVR).* pp. 147–151.

[24] Canossa, A., Badler, J. B., El-Nasr, M. S., and Anderson, E. (2016). *Eliciting emotions in design of games-a theory driven approach.* In *EMPIRE@ RecSys.* pp. 34–42.

[25] Capasso-Ballesteros, I. and De la Rosa-Rosero, F. (2020). Semi-automatic Construction of Video Game Design Prototypes with MaruGen. *Revista Facultad de Ingeniería Universidad de Antioquia* 9–20.

[26] Charleer, S., Verbert, K., Gutiérrez, F., and Gerling, K. (2018). *Towards an open standard for gameplay metrics.* In *CHI PLAY 2018 - Proceedings of the 2018 Annual Symposium on Computer-Human Interaction in Play Companion Extended Abstracts,* pp. 399–406.

[27] Clegg, B. S., Rojas, J. M., and Fraser, G. (2017, May). *Teaching software testing concepts using a mutation testing game.* In *2017 IEEE/ACM 39th International Conference on Software Engineering: Software Engineering Education and Training Track (ICSE-SEET).* pp. 33–36.

[28] Cooper, K. and Scacchi, W. (Eds.), (2015). *Computer Games and Software Engineering,* Boca Raton, Florida, USA: CRC Press, Taylor & Francis Group.

[29] Dalpiaz, F. and Cooper, K. (2020). Games for requirements engineers: analysis and directions. *IEEE Software,* 37, 1, 50–59, Jan.-Feb. 2020, doi:10.1109/MS.2018. 227105450.

[30] Daneva, M. (2017) Striving for balance: A look at gameplay requirements of massively multiplayer online role-playing games. *The Journal of Systems and Software,* 134, pp. 13454–13475.

[31] De Lope, R. P., & Medina-Medina, N. (2016, September). *Using UML to model educational games.* In *2016 8th International Conference on Games and Virtual Worlds for Serious Applications (VS-GAMES).* pp. 1–4.

[32] Debbiche, J., Lignell, O., Krüger, J., and Berger, T. (2019). *Migrating java-based apogames into a composition-based software product line.* In *Proceedings of the 23rd International Systems and Software Product Line Conference - Volume A (SPLC '19).* Association for Computing Machinery, New York, NY, USA, 98–102. doi:10.1145/3336294.3342361

[33] Delen, M., Dalpiaz, F., and Cooper, K. (2019, September). *Bakere: A serious educational game on the specification and analysis of user stories.* In *2019 IEEE 27th International Requirements Engineering Conference (RE).* pp. 369–374.

[34] do Prado, E. and Lucredio, D. (2015), *A flexible model-driven game development approach.* In *2015 IX Brazilian Symposium on Components, Architectures and Reuse Software,* Belo Horizonte, 2015, pp. 130–139, doi:10.1109/SBCARS.2015.24.

[35] Dondlinger, M. J. (2007). Educational video game design: A review of the literature. *Journal of applied educational technology,* 4(1), 21–31.

[36] dos Santos, H. M., Durelli, V. H., Souza, M., Figueiredo, E., da Silva, L. T., & Durelli, R. S. (2019). *Cleangame: Gamifying the identification of code smells.* In *Proceedings of the XXXIII Brazilian Symposium on Software Engineering.* pp. 437–446.

[37] Emmerich, K. and Masuch, M. (2017). *The impact of game patterns on player experience and social interaction in co-located multiplayer games.* In *Proceedings of the Annual Symposium on Computer-Human Interaction in Play (CHI PLAY'17).* Association for Computing Machinery, New York, NY, USA, pp. 411–422. doi:10.1145/3116595.3116606.

[38] Engström, H., Marklund, B. B., Backlund, P., & Toftedahl, M. (2018). Game development from a software and creative product perspective: A quantitative literature review approach. *Entertainment Computing,* 27, 10–22.

[39] Erdogmus, H., Medvidović, N., and Paulisch, F. (2018), 50 Years of Software Engineering. *IEEE Software,* 35, 5, 20–24, September/October 2018. doi: 10.1109/MS.2018.3571240.

[40] García, I., Pacheco, C., León, A., & Calvo-Manzano, J. A. (2020). A serious game for teaching the fundamentals of ISO/IEC/IEEE 29148 systems and software engineering–Lifecycle processes–Requirements engineering at undergraduate level. *Computer Standards & Interfaces,* 67, 103377.

[41] Haendler, T., & Neumann, G. (2019). *Serious refactoring games.* In *Proceedings of the 52nd Hawaii International Conference on System Sciences.*

[42] Henry, J/, Tang, S., Hanneghan, M., and Carter, C. (2018). *A framework for the integration of serious games and the Internet of Things (IoT)*. In *2018 IEEE 6th International Conference on Serious Games and Applications for Health (SeGAH)*, Vienna, pp. 1–8, doi:10.1109/SeGAH.2018.8401378.

[43] Hernández Bécares, J. et al. (2017) An approach to automated videogame beta testing. *Entertainment Computing*. pp. 1879–1892.

[44] Iftikhar, S. et al. (2015) '*An automated model based testing approach for platform games.*' In *2015 ACM/IEEE 18th International Conference on Model Driven Engineering Languages and Systems (MODELS)*. September 2015 IEEE. pp. 426–435.

[45] INCOSE Systems Engineering Handbook A Guide for System Life Cycle Processes and Activities (2015), 4th Edition, Hoboken, New Jersey, USA: John Wiley & Sons.

[46] Ismail, N. and Lokman, A. (2020). *Kansei engineering implementation in web-based systems: a review study*. In *International Conference on Kansei Engineering & Emotion Researc*, pp. 6676.

[47] ISO/IEC/IEEE International Standard. (2015). *Systems and software engineering -- System life cycle processes*. In *ISO/IEC/IEEE 15288* 1st edition, pp. 1–118, 15 May 2015, doi:10.1109/IEEESTD.2015.7106435.

[48] ISO/IEC/IEEE International Standard. (2015). *Software and systems engineering--Software testing--Part 4: Test techniques*. In *ISO/IEC/IEEE 29119-4:2015*, pp. 1–149, 8 Dec. 2015, doi:10.1109/IEEESTD.2015.7346375.

[49] ISO/IEC/IEEE International Standard. (2011). *Systems and software engineering -- Life cycle processes --Requirements engineering*. In *ISO/IEC/IEEE 29148:2011(E)*, pp. 1–94, 1 Dec. 2011, doi:10.1109/IEEESTD.2011.6146379.

[50] Junaidi, J., Anwar, N., Safrizal, Warnars, H.L.H.S., and Hashimoto, K. Perfecting a video game with game metrics (2018) *Telkomnika (Telecommunication Computing Electronics and Control)*, 16 (3), 1324–1331.

[51] Kang, S. J., & Kim, S. K. (2015). Automated spatio-temporal analysis techniques for game environment. *Multimedia Tools and Applications*, 74(16), 6323–6329.

[52] Karavolos, D., Liapis, A., and Yannakakis, G. (2017). *Learning the patterns of balance in a multi-player shooter game*. In *Proceedings of the 12th International Conference on the Foundations of Digital Games (FDG'17)*. Association for Computing Machinery, New York, NY, USA, Article 70, pp. 1–10. doi:10.1145/3102071.3110568

[53] Kasurinen, J., Palacin-Silva, M., and Vanhala, E. (2017). *What concerns game developers? a study on game development processes, sustainability and metrics*. In *Proceedings of the 8th Workshop on Emerging Trends in Software Metrics (WETSoM'17)*. IEEE Press, pp. 15–21.

[54] Kim, W.H. (2016). Efficient acceptance testing framework for interactive computer game applications. *International Journal of Applied Engineering Research (IJAER)*, 11 (3), 1815–1819.

[55] Kristiadi, D. P., Sudarto, F., Sugiarto, D., Sambera, R., Warnars, H. L. H. S., & Hashimoto, K. (2019). *Game Development with Scrum methodology*. In *2019 International Congress on Applied Information Technology (AIT)*. pp. 1–6.

[56] Liszio, S. and Masuch, M. (2016). *Lost in open worlds: design patterns for player navigation in virtual reality games*. In *Proceedings of the 13th International Conference on Advances in Computer Entertainment Technology (ACE'16)*. Association for Computing Machinery, New York, NY, USA, Article 7, pp. 1–7. doi:10.1145/3001773.3001794.

[57] Lui, R. W. C., Geng, S. and Law, K. M. Y. (2017), *Project management SPOC with animation*. In *Proceedings on 2017 IEEE 6th International Conference on Teaching, Assessment, and Learning for Engineering (TALE)*, Hong Kong, 2017, pp. 29–34. doi: 10.1109/TALE.2017.8252299.

[58] Liu, S. et al. (2019) *'Automatic generation of tower defense levels using PCG.'* In *Proceedings of the 14th International Conference on the Foundations of Digital Games.* [Online]. 2019 ACM. pp. 1–9.

[59] Loh, C.S., Li, I.-H., Sheng, Y. (2016). Comparison of similarity measures to differentiate players' actions and decision-making profiles in serious games analytics. *Computers in Human Behavior*, 64, 562–574.

[60] Matallaoui, A., Herzig, P., & Zarnekow, R. (2015, January). *Model-driven serious game development integration of the gamification modeling language gaml with unity.* In *2015 48th Hawaii International Conference on System Sciences* pp. 643–651.

[61] Marin, C., Chover, M., Sotoca, J.M. (2019). *Prototyping a game engine architecture as a multi-agent system.* In *2019 International Conference in Central Europe on Computer Graphics, Visualization and Computer Vision*, pp. 27–34.

[62] Maxim, B. R., Kaur, R., Apzynski, C., Edwards, D., & Evans, E. (2016, October). *An agile software engineering process improvement game.* In *2016 IEEE Frontiers in education Conference (FIE).* pp. 1–4.

[63] Meftah, C. et al. (2019) Mobile serious game design using user experience: modeling of software product line variability. *International Journal of Emerging Technologies in Learning.* [Online] 14 (23), 55–66.

[64] Miljanovic, M. A., and Bradbury, J. S. (2017, August). *Robobug: A serious game for learning debugging techniques.* In *Proceedings of the 2017 ACM Conference on International Computing Education Research.* pp. 93–100.

[65] Mimura, Y., Tsuchiya, T., Moriyama, K., Murata, K., and Takasuka, S. (2020, July). *UX design for mobile application of e-commerce site by using kansei interface.* In *International Conference on Applied Human Factors and Ergonomics.* pp. 641–647.

[66] Mizutani, W. and Kon, F. (2020) *'Unlimited rulebook: A reference architecture for economy mechanics in digital games.'* In *2020 IEEE International Conference on Software Architecture (ICSA).* [Online]. March 2020 IEEE. pp. 58–68.

[67] Molléri, J. S., Gonzalez-Huerta, J., and Henningsson, K. (2018). *A legacy game for project management in software engineering courses.* In *Proceedings of the 3rd European Conference of Software Engineering Education.* pp. 72–76.

[68] Montenegro, C. H., Astudillo, H., and Álvarez, M. C. G. (2017, September). *ATAM-RPG: A role-playing game to teach architecture trade-off analysis method (ATAM).* In *2017 XLIII Latin American Computer Conference (CLEI).* pp. 1–9.

[69] Morisaki, S., Kasai, N., Kanamori, K., and Yamamoto, S. (2019) *Detecting source code hotspot in games software using call flow analysis.* In *20th IEEE/ACIS International Conference on Software Engineering, Artificial Intelligence, Networking and Parallel/Distributed Computing (SNPD)*, Toyama, Japan, pp. 484–489, doi:10.1109/SNPD.2019.8935822.

[70] Nagamachi, M. (Editor). 2017. *Kansei/Affective Engineering*, Boca Raton, Florida, USA: CRC Press.

[71] Nalepa, G. J., Gizycka, B., Kutt, K., and Argasinski, J. K. (2017). *Affective design patterns in computer games. scrollrunner case study.* In *FedCSIS (Communication Papers).* pp. 345–352.

[72] O'Shea, Z. and Freeman, J. (2019). *Game design frameworks: Where do we start?* In *Proceedings of the 14th International Conference on the Foundations of Digital Games (FDG '19).* Association for Computing Machinery, New York, NY, USA, Article 25, pp. 1–10. doi:10.1145/3337722.3337753

[73] Paduraru, C. and Paduraru, M. (2019) *'Automatic difficulty management and testing in games using a framework based on behavior trees and genetic algorithms.'* In *24th International Conference on Engineering of Complex Computer Systems (ICECCS).* pp. 170–179.

[74] Paschali, E., Ampatzoglou, A., Escourrou, R., Chatzigeorgiou, A., and Stamelos, I. (2020). *A metric suite for evaluating interactive scenarios in video games: An empirical validation.* In *Proceedings of the 35th Annual ACM Symposium on Applied Computing (SAC'20).* Association for Computing Machinery, New York, NY, USA, pp. 1614–1623. doi:10.1145/3341105.3373985

[75] Perez-Medina, J.-L. et al. (2019) ePHoRt: Towards a reference architecture for tele-rehabilitation systems. *IEEE Access: Practical Innovations, Open Solutions.*797159–797176.

[76] Peters, D., Calvo, R. A., and Ryan, R. M. (2018). Designing for motivation, engagement and wellbeing in digital experience. *Frontiers in Psychology*, 9, 797.

[77] Politowski, C., Petrillo, F., and Guéhéneuc, Y. G. (2020, June). *Improving engagement assessment in gameplay testing sessions using IoT sensors.* In *Proceedings of the IEEE/ACM 42nd International Conference on Software Engineering Workshops.* pp. 655–659.

[78] Prasetya, W., Leek, C., Melkonian, O., ten Tusscher, J., van Bergen, et al. (2019, May). *Having fun in learning formal specifications.* In *2019 IEEE/ACM 41st International Conference on Software Engineering: Software Engineering Education and Training (ICSE-SEET).* pp. 192–196.

[79] Pyae, A., and Potter, L. E. (2016). *A player engagement model for an augmented reality game: A case of Pokémon go.* In *Proceedings of the 28th Australian Conference on Computer-Human Interaction.* pp. 11–15.

[80] Quinones, J. and Fernandez-Leiva, A. (2020) XML-Based video game description language. *IEEE Access: Practical innovations, Open Solutions*, 8, pp. 4679–4692.

[81] Sandhu, A. and McCoy, J. (2019). *A framework for integrating architectural design patterns into PCG.* In *Proceedings of the 14th International Conference on the Foundations of Digital Games (FDG'19).* Association for Computing Machinery, New York, NY, USA, Article 49, pp. 1–5. doi:10.1145/3337722.3341839

[82] Schatten, M. et al. (2017). *Towards an agent-based automated testing environment for massively multi-player role playing games.* In *2017 40th International Convention on Information and Communication Technology, Electronics and Microelectronics (MIPRO).* pp. 1149–1154.

[83] Shi, W., Kaneko, K., Ma, C., & Okada, Y. (2019). A framework for automatically generating quiz-type serious games based on linked data. *International Journal of Information and Education Technology*, 9(4), 250–256.

[84] Sierra, M., Pabón, M., Rincón, L., Navarro-Newball, A., and Linares, D. (2019). *A comparative analysis of game engines to develop core assets for a software product line of mini-games.* In *International Conference on Software and Systems Reuse.* pp. 64–74.

[85] Söbke H. and Streicher A. (2016) Serious games architectures and engines. In Dörner R., Göbel S., Kickmeier-Rust M., Masuch M., Zweig K. (eds) *Entertainment Computing and Serious Games. Lecture Notes in Computer Science*, vol 9970. Springer, Cham. doi:10.1007/978-3-319-46152-6_7

[86] Stahlke, S. et al. (2019) 'Artificial Playfulness.' In *Extended Abstracts of the 2019 CHI Conference on Human Factors in Computing Systems.* pp. 6984–6986.

[87] Su, Y., Game Analytics Research: Status and Trends (2020) Lecture Notes on Data Engineering and Communications Technologies, 41, pp. 572–589.

[88] Summerville, A., Snodgrass, S., Guzdial, M., Holmgård, C., Hoover, A. K., Isaksen, A., and Togelius, J. (2018). Procedural content generation via machine learning (PCGML). *IEEE Transactions on Games*, 10(3), pp. 257–270.

[89] Taborda, J., Arango-LĀpez, J., Collazos, C., Vela, F., and Moreira, F. (2019) Effectiveness and fun metrics in a pervasive game experience: A systematic literature review. *Advances in Intelligent Systems and Computing*, 932, pp. 184–194.

[90] Vakaliuk, T., Kontsedailo, V. V., Antoniuk, D. S., Korotun, O. V., Mintii, I. S., & Pikilnyak, A. V. (2019). *Using game simulator Software Inc in the Software Engineering education.* In *Proceedings of the 2nd International Workshop on Augmented Reality in Education*, Kryvyi Rih, Ukraine, March 22, 2019, no. 2547, pp. 66–80.

[91] Valente, L. et al. (2017) Mapping quality requirements for pervasive mobile games. *Requirements Engineering.* 22 (1), 137–165.

[92] Varvaressos, S. et al. (2017) Automated Bug Finding in Video Games. *Computers in Entertainment: CIE.* 15 (1), 1–28.

[93] Vegt, W., Bahreini, K., Nyamsuren, E., and Westera, W. (2019). Toward reusable game technologies: Assessing the usability of the RAGE component-based architecture framework. *EAI Endorsed Transactions on Serious Games*, 5(17), 1–8.

[94] Walk, W., Görlich, D., and Barrett, M. (2017). *Design, dynamics, experience (DDE): an advancement of the MDA framework for game design.* In *Game Dynamics.* pp. 27–45.

[95] Wang, Y., Ijaz, K., Yuan, D., and Calvo, R. (2020). VR-Rides: An object-oriented application framework for immersive virtual reality exergames. *Software - Practice and Experience*, 50 (7), pp. 1305–1324.

[96] Zahari, A. S., Ab Rahim, L., Nurhadi, N. A., & Aslam, M. A. (2020). Domain-specific modelling language for adventure educational games and flow theory. *International Journal onn Advanced Science Engineering Information Technology*, 10, 3, 999–1007.

[97] Zheng, Y. et al. (2019) '*Wuji: Automatic online combat game testing using evolutionary deep reinforcement learning.*' In *2019 34th IEEE/ACM International Conference on Automated Software Engineering (ASE).* [Online]. November 2019 IEEE. pp. 772–784.

[98] Zhu, M., Wang, A. I., & Trætteberg, H. (2016, November). *Engine-cooperative game modeling (ecgm) bridge model-driven game development and game engine tool-chains.* In *Proceedings of the 13th International Conference on Advances in Computer Entertainment Technology.* pp. 1–10.

Index

Page numbers in *italics* refer to figures and those in **bold** refer to tables.
Page numbers followed by "n" refer to notes numbers.